Civil War and the Rule of Law

A project of the International Peace Academy

Civil War
and the
Rule of Law

Security, Development, Human Rights

edited by
Agnès Hurwitz
with Reyko Huang

LYNNE
RIENNER
PUBLISHERS

BOULDER
LONDON

Published in the United States of America in 2008 by
Lynne Rienner Publishers, Inc.
1800 30th Street, Boulder, Colorado 80301
www.rienner.com

and in the United Kingdom by
Lynne Rienner Publishers, Inc.
3 Henrietta Street, Covent Garden, London WC2E 8LU

Library of Congress Cataloging-in-Publication Data
Civil war and the rule of law : security, development, human rights / edited
by Agnès Hurwitz with Reyko Huang.
    p. cm.
    Includes bibliographical references and index.
    ISBN 978-1-58826-531-9 (hardcover : alk. paper) — ISBN 978-1-58826-507-4
(pbk. : alk. paper)
    1. War (International law).   2. Rule of law.   3. Civil war—Protection of
civilians.   4. War victims—Legal status, laws, etc.   5. Human rights.
6. Security, international.   7. Conflict management.   I. Hurwitz, Agnès G.
II. Huang, Reyko.
    KZ6355.C58 2008
    341.6—dc22

                                                        2007037868

British Cataloguing in Publication Data
A Cataloguing in Publication record for this book
is available from the British Library.

Printed and bound in the United States of America

 The paper used in this publication meets the requirements
of the American National Standard for Permanence of
Paper for Printed Library Materials Z39.48-1992.

5 4 3 2 1

Contents

Foreword

Terje Rød-Larsen,
President, International Peace Academy

This volume is the final product of the Rule of Law Project, undertaken as part of the Security-Development Nexus Program of the International Peace Academy. The timing of the project was particularly well chosen as the United Nations sought to bring greater coherence and coordination to its manifold rule of law activities. Even more important, the project also coincided with the launch of the wider reform process endorsed by heads of state at the 2005 World Summit, in which the rule of law was recognized as a core principle of the UN mission to provide security, foster development, and protect human rights.

In recent years, international programs to support the rule of law have garnered increased interest among academics and policymakers. This book presents a critical analysis of the growing emphasis on the rule of law as part of peacebuilding strategies and offers new perspectives on some of the key challenges for the design and implementation of rule of law programs. Its core findings, while providing specific recommendations on issues such as reparations, transitional model codes, and counterterrorism, also question some of the fundamental assumptions that are made by international actors about the rule of law and highlight some of the intractable tensions that exist in assigning multiple objectives to rule of law work.

The book includes contributions from field practitioners, policy experts, social scientists, and legal scholars, presenting a much needed interdisciplinary perspective on the subject. It also benefited tremendously from brainstorming sessions held in New York with policymakers, the authors' meeting convened in Pocantico, and input provided by the policy community throughout the entire Rule of Law Project during policy forums, workshops, and roundtables on criminal justice, transitional model codes, and housing, land, and property issues.

As ever, this project would not have been possible without the generous support provided by the Rockefeller Foundation and the governments of Australia, Belgium, Canada, Germany, Luxembourg, Norway, and the United Kingdom (the latter through the Department for International Development). We are also extremely grateful to the governments of Denmark, Sweden, and Switzerland, as well as to the Ford Foundation and the William and Flora Hewlett Foundation, which have provided core support to the International Peace Academy during the lifetime of this project.

The International Peace Academy feels privileged to have hosted this exciting project. We hope that this publication will allow the project's findings to reach a wider audience, which will be able to draw on its insights for many years to come.

Acknowledgments

This volume was made possible by the invaluable support of many colleagues and friends. At the International Peace Academy (IPA), the Rule of Law Project was housed within a broader research program, the Security-Development Nexus. We are deeply indebted to Neclâ Tschirgi, who directed the program, and to Gordon Peake, Francesco Mancini, and Kaysie Brown for their intellectual guidance and helpful critiques over the course of the project. We are also grateful for the encouragement of former IPA vice president Elizabeth Cousens and president Terje Rød-Larsen. Indeed, all of our former colleagues at the IPA supported this project in one way or another.

We also gratefully acknowledge the chapter authors for their hard work, good humor, and patience. They contributed not only their own chapters, but also critical advice and comments on other chapters and on the volume overall. We are extremely fortunate to have worked with them.

During early discussion of the project, we were able to draw from the invaluable expertise of Andrea Goodman, Jo Moir, Craig Mokhiber, Bill O'Neill, and Fatemeh Ziai. An international conference on the rule of law and peace operations, organized by the IPA and held in October 2004, helped to further highlight the research gaps for the volume to address, and we thank all of the participants of the conference for their contributions. At a meeting of this volume's authors in February 2005, we benefited tremendously from the insights and active participation of Louis Aucoin, Stephen Jackson, and Michael Pugh. Along the way, Neil Cooper and Lone Lindholt also provided valuable contributions.

We also extend our appreciation to our anonymous reviewers for their critical yet constructive comments, to Samar Al-Bulushi and Jeremy Dell for their careful copyediting of the entire volume, and, of course, to the staff at Lynne Rienner Publishers for their expert work on the manuscript. IPA publications officers Clara Lee and, later, Adam Lupel reliably handled the publication process.

Last but certainly not least, this project would not have been possible without the generous support of our donors, identified in the Foreword. They not only supported us financially, but also were actively involved in many aspects of this project from the start, and for this we are very grateful.

1

Civil War and the Rule of Law: Toward Security, Development, and Human Rights

Agnès Hurwitz

In the past decade, the rule of law—a concept whose use and relevance used to be confined to the realm of legal scholarship and judicial rulings—has become a favorite notion among international policymakers and practitioners engaged in peacebuilding. A wide array of international actors, including the World Bank, the Organization for Economic Cooperation and Development (OECD), the US Agency for International Development (USAID), the United Kingdom's Department for International Development (DfID), the Organization for Security and Cooperation in Europe (OSCE), the United Kingdom's Foreign and Commonwealth Office, the US Department of State, the Open Society Institute, and the American Bar Association, have supported or implemented programs to (re)build rule of law institutions. The scope of these programs seems to know no boundaries, encompassing legislative, judicial, and police reforms, as well as support to nongovernmental organizations (NGOs), ombudspersons' offices, and land and property administrations. The objectives assigned to such programs are equally broad. To quote one commentator, "The rule of law is touted as able to accomplish everything from improving human rights to enabling economic growth to helping to win the war on terror. The rule of law is deemed an essential component of democracy and free markets."[1]

The United Nations has not been spared by this unprecedented enthusiasm for the rule of law. The Secretary-General opened the fifty-ninth session of the UN General Assembly in 2004 with these words: "It is by reintroducing the rule of law, and confidence in its impartial application, that we can hope to resuscitate societies shattered by conflict."[2] Since 2004, the number of statements by UN officials and member states about the fundamental importance of the rule of law as part of peacebuilding strategies has grown steadily. The Secretary-General's report on the rule of law and transitional justice in conflict and postconflict societies, released in August 2004 at the request of the Security Council,[3] was a milestone in the recognition of the rule of law as a concept of normative and operational significance in the work of the United Nations. The fact that the report was then discussed by the Security Council in an open debate organized in October 2004 added further prominence to an area of work in which the United Nations has only recently developed explicit capacity.

The question of the UN's role in the promotion of the rule of law was subsequently addressed in a landmark report presented by the Secretary-General in March 2005, which constituted the springboard for the reform process leading up to the sixtieth anniversary of the United Nations.[4] This document, which sought to improve the world organization's ability to tackle a wide range of global challenges, such as terrorism, biosecurity, and underdevelopment, specifically called for the establishment of a rule of law assistance unit within the Secretariat. The 2005 World Summit's outcome document, while weaker in its formulation, still referred to the possible establishment of a rule of law assistance unit "subject to a report by the Secretary-General to the General Assembly."[5] This proposal led, at the end of 2006, to the establishment by the Secretary-General of the Rule of Law Coordination and Resource Group within the Secretariat, mandated to strengthen capacity, enhance institutional memory, and coordinate within the United Nations and with outside actors.[6]

Despite this high-level interest and the large sums invested by international donors—leading to the emergence of a "rule of law industry"[7]—many experts agree that programs seeking to strengthen or reestablish the rule of law in peacebuilding contexts have rarely achieved their nominal objectives of delivering human rights, security, or development. The question that immediately springs to mind is whether this consensus among policymakers about the mutually reinforcing imperatives of "justice, security, and democracy," to quote the rule of law report,[8] is reflected in the programmatic approaches that are implemented in the field and tested in many of these countries. Anecdotal evidence suggests that most rule of law programs tend to reproduce technical solutions and rely on "template" strategies that fail to integrate adequate conflict analysis in their design, in that they are not based on a thorough understanding of the political situation in a given country. The second problem is sustainability, as many programs fail the test of time, with the predictable waste of financial and human resources and the diminished credibility of the international community that ensues. While these diagnoses are well known, innovative approaches to overcome these flaws are still in their infancy. There is in other words a need to reassess current rule of law programming and to develop more systematic and in-depth knowledge of how international actors can strengthen the rule of law. This state of affairs cannot be remedied with technical fixes alone; more fundamental questions must be raised regarding the multiple objectives assigned to rule of law work and the strategies followed by international actors to promote the rule of law.

The first fundamental question that must be addressed is: What is the rule of law? This is far from a rhetorical question. As explained below, the debate about what the rule of law entails is still raging, not only among international policymakers but also among legal theorists. In a recent lecture on the rule of law, Lord Bingham of Cornhill of the House of Lords dryly observed that while judges routinely invoke the rule of law in their judgments, "they have not explained what they meant by the expression and well-respected authors have thrown doubt on its meaning and value."[9] The most noticeable accomplishment of the UN's rule of law report was that it presented a common definition for all UN agencies and departments involved in rule of law programming in peacebuilding contexts:

> The "rule of law" is a concept at the very heart of the Organization's mission. It refers to a principle of governance in which all persons, institutions and entities, public and private, including the State itself, are accountable to laws that are publicly promulgated, equally enforced and independently adjudicated, and which are consistent with international human rights norms and standards. It requires, as well, measures to ensure adherence to the principles of supremacy of law, equality before the law, accountability to the law, fairness in the application of the law, separation of powers, participation in decision-making, legal certainty, avoidance of arbitrariness and procedural and legal transparency.[10]

While slightly redundant in formulation, this definition not only has the advantage of being recent, an important quality in light of the evolutionary nature of the concept, but is also expansive in its embrace of human rights principles as a key ingredient of a society governed by the rule of law. It conforms to the most progressive interpretations of the rule of law adopted in domestic legal systems[11] and endorses the approaches followed by other international organizations such as the OSCE and the European Union, which have expressly emphasized the organic relationship between the rule of law and human rights.[12]

The notion of "rule of law institutions" is afflicted with similar terminological uncertainty. The problem here is a tendency to confuse the institutions that will be the object of reform with the institutions with which one needs to engage and consult to ensure the success of these reforms; the latter, of course, constitute a much broader category. A document published recently by the Office of the High Commissioner for Human Rights on "mapping the justice sector" indicates that no less than "42 different institutions were identified as part of the post-conflict rule-of-law sector"—even if it recognizes that the key institutions of this sector are the judiciary, the police, and the prison system.[13] The paper also emphasizes—rightly—that the identity of all but the core institutions may differ in each specific country setting, hence the importance of a mapping exercise as a key starting point of rule of law programming.[14]

To sum, one may identify in a first circle the "core" institutions of the "bench and the bar": the judiciary, including customary justice mechanisms, prosecutors' offices, correctional institutions, and bar associations.[15] The second circle may include the legislature; relevant ministries (e.g., the Ministry of Justice, the Ministry of Interior); local authorities (e.g., housing and land administrations); law reform commissions; national human rights institutions; human rights NGOs, including victim's associations; academic and training institutions (e.g., law faculties, judicial training centers, research centers and think tanks, police academies); the police[16] and other law enforcement bodies; and forensic institutions. Finally, the widest circle would include institutions whose engagement might prove crucial in the reform process but that are not as such the object of reform, such as the media, the military (unless it has a policing, or even a judicial role, in which case it might be included in the first or second circle), and insurgent groups.[17]

Objectives of the Volume

This book is part of the growing body of literature produced by think tanks working on peace and conflict issues. In past years, research institutes such as the US Institute for Peace, the Clingendael Institute for International Relations, the Carnegie Endowment for International Peace, and the Centre for Humanitarian Dialogue have all had programs devoted to the rule of law.[18] As part of the International Peace Academy's Security-Development Nexus Program, the Rule of Law Project has made significant contributions to policy research and issued reports on key areas of rule of law work undertaken as part of peacebuilding, such as criminal justice and housing, land, and property.[19]

This volume fills a major gap in the literature by offering an innovative thematic analysis of rule of law policies adopted by international actors engaged in peacebuilding. While the themes of certain chapters, such as local ownership and corruption, go arguably beyond the rule of law ambit, these are nonetheless critical in that they provide an enhanced understanding of the specific nature of peacebuilding work and of the specific contribution of the rule of law to it. The volume does not seek to present a unified argument on the substance and outcomes of international policies to support the rule of law; rather, it examines various areas of rule of law work through a common approach and common themes, with a view to

1. assess the relevance and use of rule of law programs as a means to help provide stability in postconflict contexts and prevent the recurrence of conflict;
2. highlight some of the underlying tensions in the all-embracing claims that are commonly made about what the rule of law is expected to achieve in peacebuilding contexts; and
3. identify policy-relevant recommendations in different areas of rule of law programming, as a way to either consolidate existing practice, or

highlight important policy gaps and tensions in rule of law policies undertaken as part of peacebuilding.

Security, Development, and Human Rights:
International Discourses and Policies on the Rule of Law

International programs to support the rule of law are now regarded as important components of the security, development, and human rights agendas. From a security perspective, rule of law institutions are regarded as indispensable for internal security and law enforcement purposes, and for ensuring the transparency, accountability, and control of security forces such as the police and the military. Development agencies also maintain that (re)establishing the rule of law is a prerequisite for the emergence of stable and peaceful societies and economic development. Under the human rights agenda, rule of law programs seek to promote the implementation of and enhance compliance with international human rights instruments at the national level. In other words, the rule of law agenda has now become a critical component of current peacebuilding strategies. It is primarily in its role as a "full service provider for broken societies"[20] that the United Nations has progressively integrated rule of law programs into its operations.[21]

The Rule of Law and Security

Policy developments in UN peacekeeping provide a telling illustration of the growing significance of the rule of law in the security realm. The integration of rule of law assistance in conflict management policy appeared in the two seminal documents of the early 1990s that drove policy development in this area, the *Agenda for Peace* and its *Supplement*. The *Agenda for Peace* mentioned efforts to protect human rights and the restoration of order among the manifold activities of postconflict peacebuilding,[22] while the rule of law was mentioned as part of democratic practices.[23] The *Supplement to An Agenda for Peace* made specific reference to the collapse of state institutions, especially the police and judiciary, that characterized many of the intrastate conflicts in which the United Nations had been asked to intervene. While expressing reluctance regarding the involvement of the United Nations in these matters, it recognized that "international intervention must extend beyond military and humanitarian tasks and must include the promotion of national reconciliation and the re-establishment of effective government."[24]

The progressive integration of rule of law activities into peace missions started with the deployment of field operations that were mandated to monitor the implementation of the peace agreements in El Salvador, Haiti, and Guatemala.[25] Almost a decade later, peace operations in Kosovo and East Timor were characterized by the central role of institution building and institutional reform in the missions' mandates and the executive authority granted to them, particularly in the rule of law area.[26]

The UN's 2000 panel report on peace operations, known as the Brahimi Report, after the Algerian diplomat who headed the panel, helped emphasize the importance of re-establishing the rule of law for postconflict recover and opened the way for formal inclusion of rule of law components in multidimensional peacekeeping operation mandates adopted by the Security Council:

> 39. Where peace missions require it, international judicial experts, penal experts and human rights specialists, as well as civilian police, must be available in sufficient numbers to strengthen the rule of law institutions.
> . . .
> 40. In short, a doctrinal shift is required in how the Organization conceives of and utilizes civilian police in peace operations, as well as the need for an adequately resourced team approach to upholding the rule of law and respect for human rights, through judicial, penal, human rights and policing experts working together in a coordinated and collegial manner.[27]

These policy and institutional developments have now been almost fully digested. At headquarters, they eventually led to the establishment in 2003 of a criminal law and judicial advisory unit within the UN's Department for Peacekeeping Operations, in accordance with the recommendations of the UN's Task Force for Development of Comprehensive Rule of Law Strategies for Peace Operations, established as a subsidiary of the Executive Committee on Peace and Security (ECPS).[28] Recent peacekeeping mandates equally reflect these policy changes. In Liberia, for instance, the UN mission, under the rule of law component, has integrated civil affairs, civilian police, human rights, legal and judicial issues, corrections, and even the gender office,[29] providing a good example of the tendency to "overreach" the boundaries of the rule of law. Another case is Security Council Resolution 1542 of April 30, 2004, on the latest Haiti mission—the UN Stabilization Mission in Haiti (MINUSTAH)—which details the task of MINUSTAH in supporting rule of law institutions, including the police, the judiciary, and the prisons.[30]

The Rule of Law and Development

Support for rule of law institutions has been part of development policy for much longer than is usually acknowledged, under the guise of public sector reforms or good governance and democratization projects.[31] Erik Jensen identifies three waves of rule of law reforms that emerged between the end of World War II and the end of the Cold War.[32] The first wave, rising after World War II and lasting until the mid-1960s, focused on the reform of bureaucratic machineries, with marginal support for the judiciary. The second wave, which became known as the "law and development" movement and lasted from the mid-1960s through the 1970s, promoted both economic and democratic development by, inter alia, emphasizing legal education for lawyers in the civil service. The third wave, in the 1980s, was the first to reach postconflict countries and limited its scope to legal institutions per se.

At the United Nations, the end of the 1960s saw the progressive integration of the human rights and the development discourses, as reflected in the methodology of the UN Development Programme (UNDP); the adoption of the 1968 Proclamation of Tehran, which declared that underdevelopment impeded the full realization of human rights around the world; the 1986 General Assembly resolution on the right to development; and culminating with the mainstreaming of rights-based approaches into development policies.[33]

It was after the end of the Cold War that the rule of law "became the big tent for social, economic, and political change generally—the perceived answer to competing pressures for democratization, globalization, privatization, urbanization, and decentralization."[34] This evolution was formally acknowledged in the UN Secretary-General's *Agenda for Development,* which listed a series of "typical" rule of law activities as part of UN work on good governance, such as constitution drafting, support to domestic human rights laws, enhancing judicial structures, and training human rights officials.[35] By 2003, 60 percent of UNDP funds were being used for democratic governance, which included "justice and human rights" programs.[36]

Donor governments and agencies were also quick to ride on this latest wave. The rule of law focus was particularly evident in the work of USAID, one of the most active development agencies in this field. Its involvement in this area started in the 1980s in Latin America, including countries in the wake of the peace settlements brokered with the support of the international community, such as El Salvador and Guatemala.[37] USAID programs focused on criminal justice and judicial reform, and were implemented by subcontracted consulting firms.[38] One of the most distinctive characteristics of USAID's approach was its early emphasis on democracy—also promoted by prominent US think tanks and academics—as one of the primary rationales of its work,[39] together with free-market reforms. This set it apart from multilateral agencies such as the World Bank and the United Nations, the former being constrained by its mandate, the latter by the highly volatile nature of the democracy debate among its membership. The Secretary-General's 2005 report on UN reforms was a watershed in this respect, in that it proclaimed democracy to be a central objective of the United Nations, asserting that the world body "does more than any other single organization to promote and strengthen democratic institutions and practices around the world, but this fact is little known,"[40] a statement that is indeed borne out by the work of the UN Electoral Assistance Division and UNDP.[41] The report also led to the establishment of a fund to assist countries in their democratization efforts.[42]

The Rule of Law and Human Rights

While various international agencies have emphasized the organic relationship between the rule of law and human rights, this relation is perhaps most evident in the UN context. At the normative level, the connection between human rights and the rule of law was formally acknowledged in the very first human rights instrument adopted by the United Nations, the 1948 Universal Declaration of Human Rights, which proclaimed that "it is essential, if man is not to be compelled to have recourse, as a last resort, to rebellion against tyranny and oppression, that human rights should be protected by the rule of law."[43] Since then, the United Nations has supported the conclusion and implementation of a flurry of international human rights instruments,[44] which demand compliance with due process and fair trial standards considered to be defining characteristics of the rule of law.[45] In 1993 the General Assembly declared that "the rule of law is an essential factor in the protection of human rights" and supported the role of what was then called the Center for Human Rights, now known as the Office of the High Commissioner for Human Rights (OHCHR), in strengthening rule of law institutions at the national level.[46] This original resolution was followed by seven others in the next ten years, which reiterated mutatis mutandis this statement of support and further emphasized the high priority granted to rule of law activities.[47]

The role of UN human rights institutions has also been crucial at the operational level. As is explained in further detail in this volume, rule of law components in peacekeeping missions find their origins in human rights monitoring missions, which compiled information and drew up reports on country human rights situations in order to provide recommendations toward enhanced protection and promotion. This approach, mostly reactive in nature, eventually moved toward more proactive assistance on human rights and institutional reforms.

The UN's role in supporting transitional justice mechanisms, defined by the Secretary-General as the "full range of processes and mechanisms associated with a society's attempts to come to terms with a legacy of large-scale past abuses, in order to ensure accountability, serve justice and achieve reconciliation,"[48] has been another area where the UN has been able to implement the very principles it has promoted since 1948. The establishment of the ad hoc tribunals for the former Yugoslavia and Rwanda in 1993 and 1994[49] reflected the international community's recognition of its responsibility in holding accountable those responsible for the most serious international crimes— and eventually led to the adoption of the Statute of the International Criminal Court, which entered into force in 2002. In addition to its backing of international criminal justice, the United Nations has also been involved through its various agencies and programs in supporting transitional justice mechanisms and rule of law institutions established at the national level, which may be regarded as more effective in addressing human rights violations, seeking reconciliation, and preventing further abuses in the long term.[50]

The apparently harmonious bond between the rule of law and human rights is slightly deceptive, however, and divergences between human rights objectives and rule of law programs surface in several of the thematic chapters of this book, above all where overriding security objectives, such as the fight against terrorism, dominate the policy agenda. These tensions can be explained by the ill-defined nature of the rule of law highlighted earlier. As noted by Thomas Carothers:

> The rule of law appeals broadly across political and intellectual lines. The right, left and centre can all find what they want in the concept, or interpret it in a manner favourable to their interests. Scholars, civic activists, law practitioners and government officials can all find reasons to embrace the concept and assign part of the task to themselves. Like the equally ubiquitous concept of civil society, it is a mellifluous ideal whose pan-ideological or post-ideological quality is unusually well-suited to the post-cold war era.[51]

Given this all-encompassing, mass-appeal nature of the rule of law, the existence of tensions between various aspects of the concept and with regard to its operationalization, while problematic, is unsurprising.

The Rule of Law: An Overview of Academic and Policy-Relevant Literature

It is fair to say that research on international rule of law programs is still in its infancy. A preliminary review of existing literature reveals the relative dearth of academic work on the conception, underpinning principles, implementation, and outcomes of rule of law programs in peacebuilding contexts. Many available sources on the subject tend to consist of unpublished consultancy reports and lessons-learned studies, based on narrow terms of reference and therefore of limited relevance for gaining a better understanding of the broader issues at stake. This being said, it would not be accurate to infer that academic scholarship and rigorous applied research on the rule of law is nonexistent. At least four subareas have received extensive treatment over the past decades.

Any inquiry into the meaning and conceptual relevance of the rule of law must begin with legal theory, or jurisprudence. Also known in the civil law tradition, the rule of law is primarily a normative principle of the common law system formulated by Albert Venn Dicey in 1885.[52] While acknowledged to be "exceedingly elusive,"[53] the rule of law has remained a constant subject of inquiry by such philosophers as Ronald Dworkin, and has received renewed—albeit critical—interest in recent political and legal theory scholarship.[54] As will be explained in further detail in this volume, the theoretical arena is basically dominated by the long-standing tension between a minimalist or "rule-book" approach of the rule of law, which demands that state authority be exercised in accordance with clear, publicly available rules, and a maximalist or "rights"-based conception of the rule of law, as "the ideal of rule by an accurate public conception of individual rights."[55]

Several parts of this collective work highlight the relevance of theoretical considerations for policymakers and practitioners. First, the understanding and contours of the rule of law as a principle of some significance in international affairs and particularly in peacebuilding is still affected by the uncertainties revolving around the notion and its programmatic reach. While the expansive definition adopted by the aforementioned UN rule of law report seems to embrace the "rights" conception of the rule of law,[56] some experts in the development and security realms are still wary of such a rights-based approach, perhaps because success becomes far more difficult to achieve and to measure. Further, philosophical analyses of the rule of law as a mechanism of power distribution between political forces and state institutions may provide important insights for wider peacebuilding goals. Thus in the words of José María Maravall and Adam Przeworski: "The rule of law emerges when, following Machiavelli's advice, self-interested rulers willingly restrain themselves and make their behaviour predictable in order to obtain a sustained, voluntary cooperation of well-organized groups commanding valuable resources. In exchange for such cooperation, rulers will protect the interest of these groups by legal means."[57]

Theory aside, a second category in the existing literature focuses on efforts to promote the rule of law as part of development policies. In most cases, the focus is on countries that have experienced transitions to liberal democracy and free-market economy, such as Eastern Europe, Latin America, and, in the latter sense, China.[58] This largely reflects the regional focus of bilateral rule of law assistance, provided most prominently by USAID. While integrated within the broader category of democratization or governance policies, the judicial and legal reform programs of the 1990s reflected to some extent a revival of the "law and development" movement sparked by US academics in the 1960s,[59] with added components inspired by the human rights movement. The two approaches are indeed remarkably similar insofar as these reforms were primarily conceived with a view to replicate the liberal democracies' institutional frameworks. While much of the regionally focused literature concentrates on US programs, the nature and objectives of programs implemented by other bilateral actors are comparable.[60]

Compared to the theoretical realm, this category of the rule of law literature is marked by a relative absence of controversy. Two recent collective publications are nonetheless worth particular attention, as they seek to question some of the fundamental assumptions about a field where technical approaches have too often prevailed at the expense of more in-depth analyses. In *Beyond Common Knowledge,* Erik Jensen and Thomas Heller offer a stringent critique of the approaches of development actors, noting that "basic questions about what legal systems across diverse countries actually do, why they do it, and to what effect are either inadequately explored or totally ignored. In developed and developing countries, larger questions about the relationship of the rule of law to human rights, democracy, civil society, economic development, and governance often are reduced to arid doctrinalism in the legal fraternity."[61] Jensen and Heller notably question the importance of the role of courts in economic growth and democratic politics, and advocate more rigorous methodologies to measure performance.

A recent compilation by Thomas Carothers of papers published by the Carnegie Endowment for International Peace as part of the Democracy and Rule of Law Project, while slightly different in focus, is also notable for its critical appraisal of international efforts to strengthen the rule of law and related academic endeavors.[62] Thus, Frank Upham challenges some of the main rule of law "orthodoxies" and the assumptions that Western countries have legal systems that are devoid of political influence.[63] New propoor approaches are also advocated by Stephen Golub in his piece on legal empowerment.[64] Most relevant for this volume, Rachel Kleinfeld Belton's contribution stresses the discrepancy between definitions that emphasize the ends of the rule of law and those that focus on the institutional features that are necessary "to actuate the rule of law (such as comprehensive laws, well-functioning courts, and trained law enforcement agencies)." In her analysis, Kleinfeld Belton rightly points at the conceptual confusion of policymakers and practitioners with respect to the multiple and even divergent objectives of rule of law programs and suggests that as a result of this confusion, outcomes tend to be measured on the basis of institutional attributes, which lead to technocratic reform strategies.[65]

Third, the area that has undoubtedly attracted the greatest attention is transitional justice. This might arguably be the domain where the international community has been able to achieve the most tangible results thus far, starting with the establishment of international ad hoc tribunals for the former Yugoslavia and Rwanda, followed more recently by truth and reconciliation mechanisms such as in Sierra Leone and Burundi, "hybrid" tribunals created through an agreement between the United Nations and the national government (e.g., Sierra Leone and Cambodia), and the International Criminal Court. Transitional justice literature has proliferated to such an extent that it would be impossible to cover it adequately here. What is perhaps most striking is the multidisciplinary nature of this relatively new field of inquiry, which goes well beyond legal scholarship to encompass politics, international relations, anthropology, and psychosocial studies. The question of how to address past abuses and how to find redress for victims continues to generate a fierce yet healthy debate within and between these different disciplines.[66]

Finally, a fourth category of the literature focuses on international policies to strengthen the rule of law, focusing generally on postconflict contexts, criminal justice, and specific institutions, primarily the judiciary and the police. Many of the earlier studies in this category were policy- and practitioner-driven in terms of both authorship and targeted readership,[67] and sought to synthesize lessons learned and provide advice on programmatic design and implementation. Academic interest in these questions is in fact quite recent, such as Charles Call's edited volume that examines, on the basis of case studies of the most prominent peacekeeping operations, whether societies emerging from armed conflict can create "systems of justice and security that ensure basic rights, apply the law effectively and impartially, and enjoy popular support."[68] Another recent academic monograph, by Jane Stromseth, David Wippman, and Rosa Brooks, looks at the plight of the so-called new imperialists, and their attempts at (re)-building the rule of law after a military intervention, with a focus on a number of broad themes, including the legality and legitimacy of intervention, the security imperative, judicial reform, transitional justice, "rule of law culture," and local ownership.[69]

Structure and Overview of the Volume

This book is divided into four parts. Part 1 is devoted to a conceptual analysis of international efforts to support the rule of law, opening with Rama Mani's examination, in Chapter 2, of some of the theoretical underpinnings of rule of law programs and their current state. In Chapter 3, Balakrishnan Rajagopal reflects on the increasing prominence of the rule of law as a policy-relevant concept in international affairs through a thought-provoking analysis of the development, security, and human rights discourses.

Part 2 addresses the question of the contribution of rule of law programs to peacebuilding. While there is wide agreement on the existence of specific needs and the relevance of specific strategies in the immediate aftermath of conflict, there is still considerable debate revolving around the longer-term objectives of peacebuilding, a concept that has undergone major conceptual transformations since its original formulation in the UN's 1992 *Agenda for Peace,* which has recently been institutionalized through the establishment of the UN Peacebuilding Commission.[70] In Chapter 4, Chandra Sriram reviews the evolution of the conflict prevention discourse and examines whether and how the rule of law has featured in these new policies. In Chapter 5, William O'Neill reflects on the origins and development of rule of law components in peacekeeping operations and on the many challenges still faced by practitioners in reestablishing law and order in the immediate aftermath of conflict. In Chapter 6, Colette Rausch and Vivienne O'Connor illustrate how rule of law programs can address the key challenges faced by practitioners in peacebuilding contexts, namely the identification of applicable law, by developing rigorous methodologies that are conflict sensitive and adjustable to changing circumstances.

The next two chapters deal with two of the fundamental objectives of international actors involved in peacebuilding: reconciliation and effective sovereignty. In Chapter 7, Simon Chesterman examines the work of transitional administrations on rule of law reforms, casts a critical eye on the discourse of "ownership," and proposes more precise criteria to assess progress in handing over power to domestic actors with a view to achieving full sovereignty. In Chapter 8, Pablo de Greiff, rather than attempting a general treatment of the whole ambit of transitional justice, focuses on reparation programs. Such programs may provide an important and enduring contribution to reconciliation processes, and are a less well known and appreciated mechanism than prosecutions or truth and reconciliation commissions.

Part 3 addresses a series of more specific topics that have acquired heightened relevance for rule of law experts working in countries affected by conflict. In Chapter 9, I advocate a more proactive approach to housing, land, and property disputes by UN policymakers and practitioners through the use of a variety of rule of law tools. In Chapter 10, Madalene O'Donnell examines the advances made by international actors to combat corruption, which is essential to enhance both access to justice and equality before the law. In Chapter 11, Reyko Huang provides an analysis of international efforts to combat terrorism in the wake of the events of September 11, 2001, and the implications of these policy choices for rule of law programs.

Finally, I highlight in the conclusion the key findings that emerge throughout the chapters of the volume with respect to the relevance and use of rule of law programs, the underlying tensions in the all-embracing claims commonly made about their expected achievements, and the identification of policy-relevant recommendations for rule of law programs undertaken as part of peacebuilding strategies.

Notes

I thank Reyko Huang, Adam Lupel, and James Cockayne for their comments on earlier versions of this chapter. All errors are my sole responsibility. The views expressed herein are those of the author and do not necessarily represent the views of the United Nations or of the International Criminal Tribunal for the former Yugoslavia.

1. Rachel Kleinfeld Belton, "Competing Definitions of the Rule of Law: Implications for Practitioners," in *Promoting the Rule of Law Abroad: In Search of Knowledge,* edited by Thomas Carothers (Washington, D.C.: Carnegie Endowment for International Peace, 2006), p. 31; see also Charles T. Call, Introduction to *Constructing Justice and Security After War* (Washington, D.C.: US Institute of Peace, 2006), p. 4.

2. United Nations, *Report of the Secretary-General on the Work of the Organization,* UN Doc. A/59/PV.3 (September 21, 2004).

3. United Nations, *The Rule of Law and Transitional Justice in Conflict and Post-Conflict Societies,* UN Doc. S/2004/616 (August 23, 2004), para. 1.

4. United Nations, *In Larger Freedom: Towards Development, Security, and Human Rights for All—Report of the Secretary General,* UN Doc. A/59/2005 (March 21, 2005).

5. United Nations, *2005 World Summit Outcome Document,* UN Doc. A/RES/ 60/1 (October 24, 2005), para. 134(e). See also UN General Assembly Resolution 61/39 (2006), para. 4, on the rule of law at the national and international levels, which urges the Secretary-General to submit a report on the establishment of a rule of law assistance unit within the Secretariat.

6. United Nations, *Uniting Our Strengths: Enhancing United Nations Support for the Rule of Law,* UN Doc. A/61/636-S/2006/980 (December 14, 2006), paras. 48–50. The report also identifies (para. 38) three main baskets of rule of law activities for purposes of coherence and coordination: rule of law at the international level, rule of law in the context of conflict and postconflict situations, and rule of law in the context of long-term development.

7. To my knowledge, there are no comprehensive reports on the sums invested in rule of law programming that detail expenditures of both bilateral and international agencies. There is tremendous difficulty in calculating a reliable figure because agencies tend to define differently what is included in "rule of law programs." Rachel Kleinfeld Belton, relying herself on Thomas Carothers, notes that "developed countries and international organizations have spent more than a billion dollars over the last twenty years trying to build the rule of law in countries transitioning to democracy or attempting to escape underdevelopment." Kleinfeld Belton, "Competing Definitions of the Rule of Law," p. 5. However, this figure may not be that large, since it spans a period of twenty years.

8. United Nations, *The Rule of Law and Transitional Justice,* p. 1.

9. Lord Bingham of Cornhill, "The Rule of Law," Sixth Sir David Williams Lecture, University of Cambridge, November 16, 2006, http://cpl.law.cam.ac.uk/media /the%20rule%20of%20law%202006.pdf.

10. United Nations, *The Rule of Law and Transitional Justice,* para. 6.

11. Lord Bingham of Cornhill, "The Rule of Law," p. 2.

12. European Union, "Communication from the Commission to the Council and the European Parliament: The EU's Role in Promoting Human Rights and Democratisation in Third Countries," COM (2001) 252, May 8, 2001, http://ec.europa.eu/ external_relations/human_rights/doc/com01_252_en.pdf. In this communication, the Commission identifies democracy, good governance, and the rule of law as some of the priorities of the European Union. In 1990 the OSCE adopted the following statement: "The rule of law does not mean merely a formal legality which assures regularity and consistency in the achievement and enforcement of democratic order, but justice based on the recognition and full acceptance of the supreme value of the human personality and guaranteed by institutions providing a framework for their full expression." "Document of the 1990 Copenhagen Meeting of the Conference on the Human Dimension of the CSCE," p. 3, see also p. 2, point 30, p. 18.

13. UN Office of the High Commissioner for Human Rights (OHCHR), *Rule-of-Law Tools for Post-Conflict States: Mapping the Justice Sector* (Geneva, 2006), p. 5.

14. Ibid.

15. David Tolbert and Andrew Solomon, "United Nations Reform and Supporting the Rule of Law in Post-Conflict Societies," *Harvard Human Rights Journal* 19 (2006): 29–30, 45.

16. Note that the OHCHR's *Mapping the Justice Sector* report includes the police among the key institutions of the justice sector. See also Call, *Constructing Justice and Security After War,* pp. 6–7.

17. The list of rule of law institutions—but not the three "circles"—presented here is loosely based on the OHCHR's *Mapping the Justice Sector* report. See Chapter 5 of this volume, which also adopts an expansive approach of "rule of law institutions."

18. See http://www.isip.org, http://www.clingendael.nl, http://www.ceip.org, and http://www.hdcentre.org. On rule of law and peace operations, see also Jessica Howard and Bruce Oswald, eds., *The Rule of Law on Peace Operations* (Melbourne: Asia Pacific Centre for Military Law, 2002).

19. Project reports include Agnès Hurwitz and Kaysie Studdard, "Rule of Law Programs in Peace Operations" (New York: International Peace Academy, August 2005); Agnès Hurwitz, Kaysie Studdard, and Rhodri Williams, "Housing, Land, Property, and Conflict Management: Identifying Policy Options for Rule of Law Programming" (New York: International Peace Academy, October 2005); Reyko Huang, "Securing the Rule of Law: Assessing International Strategies for Post-Conflict Criminal Justice" (New York: International Peace Academy, November 2005). All project publications are available at http://www.ipacademy.org/publications/publications.htm.

20. Ruth Wedgwood, "United Nations Peacekeeping Operations and the Use of Force," *Washington University Journal of Law and Policy* 5 (2001): 69, 73.

21. Agnès Hurwitz and Gordon Peake, "Strengthening the Security-Development Nexus: Assessing Policy and Practice in the 1990s" (New York: International Peace Academy, April 2004), p. 13, http://www.ipacademy.org/publications/publications.htm.

22. United Nations, *An Agenda for Peace: Preventive Diplomacy, Peacemaking, and Peacekeeping: Report of the Secretary-General,* UN Doc. A/47/277-S/24111 (June 17, 1992), para. 55; see also United Nations, *Supplement to An Agenda for Peace: Position Paper of the Secretary-General on the Occasion of the Fiftieth Anniversary of the United Nations,* UN Doc. A/50/60-S/1995/1 (January 3, 1995), para. 47.

23. United Nations, *An Agenda for Peace,* para. 59.

24. United Nations, *Supplement to An Agenda for Peace,* paras. 13–14.

25. The UN Observer Mission in El Salvador (ONUSAL) (July 1991–April 1995) was established under UN Security Resolution 693 (1991). The UN Mission in Haiti (UNMIH) (1993–1996) was established under UN Security Council Resolution 867 (1993). It was followed by the UN Support Mission in Haiti (UNSMIH) (1996–1997), established under UN Security Council Resolution 1063 (1996); the UN Transitional Mission in Haiti (UNTMIH) (1997), established under UN Security Council Resolution 1123 (1997); and the UN Civilian Police in Haiti (MINOPUH) (1997–2000), established under UN Security Council Resolution 1147 (1997). Finally, the UN Verification Mission in Guatemala (MINUGUA) (1994–2004) was established under UN General Assembly Resolution 48/267 (1994).

26. See Chapter 5 in this volume; UN Transitional Authority in Cambodia (1992–1993); UN Security Council Resolution 74 (1992); Simon Chesterman, *You, the People: The United Nations, Transitional Administration, and State-Building* (Oxford: Oxford University Press, 2004), 74.

27. United Nations, *Report of the Panel on UN Peace Operations,* UN Doc. A/55/305-S/2000/809 (August 21, 2000).

28. United Nations, Peacekeeping Best Practices Unit, Department of Peacekeeping Operations, *Handbook on United Nations Multidimensional Peacekeeping Operations* (December 2003), p. 97; *Final Report of the ECPS Task Force for Development of Comprehensive Rule of Law Strategies for Peace Operations* (August 2002) (on file with author).

29. The UN Mission in Liberia (UNMIL), established under UN Security Council Resolution 1509 (2003). For further information, see http://www.unmil.org.

30. UN Stabilization Mission in Haiti (MINUSTAH), UN Security Council Resolution 1542 (2004); see also UN Assistance Mission in Afghanistan (UNAMA), UN Security Council Resolution 1401 (2002); UN Organization Mission in the Democratic

Republic of Congo (MONUC), UN Security Council Resolution 1291 (2000); UN Security Council Resolution 1493 (2003); UN Security Council Resolution 1565 (2004); UN Operation in Burundi (ONUB), UN Security Council Resolution 1545 (2004).

31. Erik Jensen, "The Rule of Law and Judicial Reform: The Political Economy of Diverse Institutional Patterns and Reformers' Responses," in *Beyond Common Knowledge: Empirical Approaches to the Rule of Law,* edited by Erik Jensen and Thomas Heller (Palo Alto: Stanford University Press, 2003), pp. 336, 345–346.

32. Ibid.

33. *Proclamation of Tehran* (1968), para. 13, http://www.unhchr.ch/html/menu3/b/b_tehern.htm; *UN Declaration on the Right to Development,* UN General Assembly Resolution 41/128 (1986). See Chapter 3.

34. Jensen, "The Rule of Law and Judicial Reform," p. 347.

35. United Nations, *An Agenda for Development: Report of the Secretary-General,* UN Doc. A/48/935 (May 6, 1994), para. 124.

36. Call, *Constructing Justice and Security After War,* p. 4. See also http://www.undp.org/governance/sl-justice.htm. See Chapter 4.

37. USAID, *Achievements in Building and Maintaining the Rule of Law* (Washington, D.C., 2002), pp. 64–74.

38. Funding for USAID's Latin American programs totaled roughly US$200 million between 1983 and 1993. Between 1994 and 1998, another US$196 million was provided in the region. Lynn Hammergren, "International Assistance to Latin American Justice Programs: Toward an Agenda for Reforming the Reformers," in *Beyond Common Knowledge,* edited by Jensen and Heller, pp. 295–296; Charles T. Call, "Democratization, War, and State-Building: Constructing the Rule of Law in El Salvador," *Journal of Latin American Studies* 35, no. 4 (2003): 827, 849.

39. USAID includes rule of law work under the umbrella of "democracy and governance." See Chapter 2.

40. United Nations, *In Larger Freedom,* paras. 148–151.

41. For an overview of the division's work, see http://www.un.org/depts/dpa/ead/overview.html.

42. United Nations, *In Larger Freedom,* para. 151. The UN Democracy Fund was established within the UN Fund for International Partnership in March 2006; see http://www.un.org/democracyfund.

43. Preamble to *Universal Declaration of Human Rights,* General Assembly Resolution 217 A (III), UN Doc. A/810 (December 10, 1948), recital 3.

44. A list of core international human rights instruments is available at http://www.ohchr.org/english/law/index.htm.

45. Other principles adopted by the United Nations are fundamental elements of a system based on the rule of law. See, for example, *International Covenant for Civil and Political Rights,* esp. art. 2, which prohibits discrimination; art. 16, which establishes the right to be recognized as a person before the law; and art. 26, which establishes the principle of equality before the law.

46. UN General Assembly Resolution 48/132 (1993).

47. UN General Assembly Resolution 49/194 (1994); UN General Assembly Resolution 50/179 (1995); UN General Assembly Resolution 51/96 (1996); UN General Assembly Resolution 52/125 (1997); UN General Assembly Resolution 53/142 (1998); UN General Assembly Resolution 55/99 (2000); UN General Assembly Resolution 57/221 (2002).

48. United Nations, *The Rule of Law and Transitional Justice,* para. 8.

49. UN Security Council Resolution 808 (2003); UN Security Council Resolution 955 (1994).

50. United Nations, *The Rule of Law and Transitional Justice,* para. 44. See also OHCHR, *Rule of Law Tools for Post-Conflict States: Prosecution Initiatives* (Geneva, 2006).

51. Thomas Carothers, "The Many Agendas of Rule of Law Reform in Latin America," in *Rule of Law in Latin America: The International Promotion of Judicial Reform,* edited by Pilar Domingo and Rachel Sieder (London: Institute of Latin American Studies, 2001), pp. 11–12.

52. Albert Venn Dicey, *An Introduction to the Law of the Constitution,* 8th ed. (London: Macmillan, 1915). For an overview of the term in Germany, France, the United Kingdom, and the United States, see Rainer Grote, "Rule of Law, Rechtstaat, and Etat de Droit," in *Constitutionalism, Universalism, and Democracy: A Comparative Analysis,* edited by Christian Starck (Baden-Baden: Nomos, 1999), p. 271.

53. Brian Tamanaha, *On the Rule of Law: History, Politics, Theory* (Cambridge: Cambridge University Press, 2004), p. 3; Lord Bingham of Cornhill, "The Rule of Law," pp. 2–3.

54. See, for example, José María Maravall and Adam Przeworski, eds., *Democracy and the Rule of Law* (Cambridge: Cambridge University Press, 2003).

55. See Chapter 2 of this volume. The distinction between the "rule-book" and the "rights" conception is proposed in Ronald Dworkin, *A Matter of Principle* (London: Harvard University Press, 1987), pp. 11–12; Kleinfeld Belton, "Competing Definitions of the Rule of Law," p. 14.

56. United Nations, *The Rule of Law and Transitional Justice,* para. 6.

57. Maravall and Przeworski, *Democracy and the Rule of Law.*

58. C. Biebesheimer and J. Payne, "IDB Experience in Justice Reform: Lessons Learned and Elements for Policy Formulation," Technical Paper Series (Washington, D.C.: Inter-American Development Bank, 2001); Harry Blair and Gary Hansen, "Weighing In On the Scales of Justice: Strategic Approaches for Donor-Supported Rule of Law Programs," Assessment Report no. 7 (Washington, D.C.: US Agency for International Development, 1994); David Pedro, "Technical Cooperation in Strengthening the Rule of Law in Latin America: Applicability of United Nations Standards and Norms in Crime Prevention and Criminal Justice to Facilitate Access to Justice," in *The Application of United Nations Standards and Norms in Crime Prevention and Criminal Justice* (Vienna: UNODC, 2003), http://www.unodc.org/pdf/crime/publications/standards%20&%20norms.pdf; Lynn Hammergren, "Do Judicial Councils Further Judicial Reform? Lessons from Latin America," Democracy and Rule of Law Project, Rule of Law Series no. 28 (Washington, D.C.: Carnegie Endowment for International Peace, 2002).

59. Carothers, "The Many Agendas of Rule of Law Reform in Latin America," pp. 4–5; Luis Salas, "From Law and Development to Rule of Law: New and Old Issues in Justice Reform in Latin America," in Domingo and Sieder, *Rule of Law in Latin America,* pp. 17, 20.

60. Salas, "From Law and Development to Rule of Law," p. 25.

61. Erik Jensen and Thomas C. Heller, Introduction to *Beyond Common Knowledge,* p. 2.

62. Thomas Carothers, ed., *Promoting the Rule of Law Abroad: In Search of Knowledge* (Washington, D.C.: Carnegie Endowment for International Peace, 2006).

63. Frank Upham, "Mythmaking in the Rule of Law Orthodoxy," Democracy and Rule of Law Project, Rule of Law Series no. 30 (Washington, D.C.: Carnegie Endowment for International Peace, 2002) http://www.carnegieendowment.org/files/wp30.pdf.

64. Stephen Golub, "Beyond Rule of Law Orthodoxy: The Legal Empowerment Alternative," in Carothers, *Promoting the Rule of Law Abroad,* p. 161.

65. Kleinfeld Belton, "Competing Definitions of the Rule of Law," p. 6.

66. See Neil Kritz, ed., *Transitional Justice: How Emerging Democracies Reckon with Former Regimes,* 3 vols. (Washington, D.C.: US Institute of Peace, 1995); William A. Schabas, *Introduction to the International Criminal Court* (Cambridge: Cambridge University Press, 2001); Cherif M. Bassiouni, ed., *Post-Conflict Justice* (Ardsley, N.Y.: Transnational, 2002); Priscilla Hayner, *Unspeakable Truths* (London: Routledge, 2002); William A. Schabas, *The UN International Criminal Tribunals: The Former Yugoslavia, Rwanda, and Sierra Leone* (Cambridge: Cambridge University Press, 2006). For an overview of publications from the International Centre for Transitional Justice since 2002, see http://www.ictj.org/en/news/pubs/index.html.

67. See, for example, Lone Lindholt, Paulo de Mesquita Neto, Danny Titus, and Etannibi E. Alemika, eds., *Human Rights and the Police in Transitional Countries* (The Hague: Kluwer Law International, 2003); Robert Perito, Michael Dziedzic, and Beth C. DeGrasse, "Building Civilian Capacity for US Stability Operations: The Rule of Law Component," Special Report no. 118 (Washington, D.C.: US Institute of Peace, 2004); Laurel Miller and Robert Perito, "Establishing the Rule of Law in Afghanistan," Special Report no. 117 (Washington, D.C.: US Institute of Peace, March 2004); Robert M. Perito, "Establishing the Rule of Law in Iraq," Special Report no. 104 (Washington, D.C.: US Institute of Peace, April 2003). All of these US Institute of Peace reports are available at http://www.usip.org. See also Martina Huber, "Monitoring the Rule of Law: Consolidated Framework and Report," Conflict Research Unit occasional paper (The Hague: Clingendael Institute of International Relations, 2002); Anja Kaspersen, Espen Barth Eide, and Annika Hansen, *International Policing and the Rule of Law in Transition from War to Peace,* Working Paper no. 4 (Oslo: Norwegian Institute of International Affairs, October 2004); William G. O'Neill, "Rebuilding the Rule of Law in Iraq: Ten Tips from Recent Experience" (Washington, D.C.: Henri Stimson Center, 2003); Hansjörg Strohmeyer, "Collapse and Reconstruction of a Judicial System: The United Nations Mission in Kosovo and East Timor," *American Journal of International Law* 95, no. 1 (2001): 46–63; Jamal Benomar, "Justice After Transitions," in Kritz, *Transitional Justice;* Jamal Benomar, "Rule of Law Technical Assistance in Haiti: Lessons Learned," in *Empowerment, Security, and Opportunity Through Law and Justice,* World Bank conference, St. Petersburg, Russia, July 8–12, 2001, http://haiticci .undg.org/uploads/lessons%20learned%20justice_2001.pdf.

68. Call, *Constructing Justice and Security After War,* p. 5.

69. Jane Stromseth, David Wippman, and Rosa Brooks, *Can Might Make Rights? Building the Rule of Law After Military Interventions* (Cambridge: Cambridge University Press, 2006).

70. UN General Assembly Resolution 60/180 (2005).

PART 1

The Rule of Law: Conceptual Perspectives

2

Exploring the Rule of Law in Theory and Practice

Rama Mani

The concept of the rule of law is practically as old as philosophy itself. From Aristotle, who saw the rule of law as superior to the rule of man, to contemporaries like Ronald Dworkin and Judith Shklar, it has been debated through the years, alternately rising and fading from prominence. Yet the concept of the rule of law remains a conundrum. It is seen at once as a distant aspiration or ideal, and a concrete objective; as a political goal or a legal institution.[1] The term is bandied about nonchalantly in academic literature, policy papers, and political declarations as though its meaning were unequivocal; however, there is neither clarity nor unanimity around its definition or component elements.

While rule of law "reform" is the buzzword in policy discussions today, buoyed by newfound enthusiasm and support from donors and international organizations, there is less discussion about the continuing confusion over the definition of the rule of law itself. Likewise, there is either benign or willful ignorance of the parallel divergence between proclaimed definitions and objectives of the rule of law proffered by organizations and donors on the one hand and, on the other hand, the technical and operational programs implemented on the ground, which fall short of either embodying the definitions or delivering on the stated objectives of the rule of law.

I argue in this chapter that despite the age-old debates and discussions on the concept of the rule of law, there remains a fundamental divide in its understanding both in theoretical terms and in practice. This divide is reflected in theory between two opposed views, described here as "maximalist" and "minimalist." In practice, this divide reflects itself in the divergence between stated rationales and objectives put forward by organizations, and the programs implemented on the ground. Despite some rhetoric among operational organizations that propose what would amount to "maximalist" definitions, in practice most agencies focus on the "minimalist" institutions, form, and function of the rule of law rather than on ensuring that it delivers on its substance. This divergence is highlighted today in the gap between normative definitions and far-reaching overambitious rationales put forward by the major organizations involved in this area, and their minimalist and functionalist practice. Due to this gap, programs on the ground that are billed as rule of law, despite good intentions and public commitments, are unlikely to deliver on the grandiose aims proclaimed in these optimistic, normative definitions, nor on the benefits that are supposed to accompany the rule of law. In effect, then, the theoretical divergence in the concept has a very tangible reflection in the divergence that is witnessed in practice.

We face a conundrum between the *need* for a normative ambitious concept of the rule of law that delivers justice and protection to people, and the *reality* of programs that are unable to deliver on these ambitious objectives. The choice is between downsizing definitions of the rule of law to "fit" the minimalist reality of current rule of law programs, or significantly upsizing programs—effectively radically overhauling them—to meet at least some of the high aspirations and declared objectives of definitions like the one put forth by UN Secretary-General Kofi Annan in 2004.[2]

Despite the difficulty of the latter option, I argue strongly in its favor. Rule of law programs based on a minimalist conception have not proven themselves to be effective in delivering on any of their objectives, whether development, democracy, or security. Further, minimalist rule of law shies away from the needs and aspirations expressed by most people in most societies emerging from brutal, lawless conflict, and surrenders them to legal institutions that might eventually deliver order but are unlikely to deliver justice.

This chapter explores the concept of the rule of law and its application in practice. I begin by exploring the backdrop to and divergent definitions of the rule of law in theory, and then identify and examine the main rationales proposed by some of the major operational actors for undertaking rule of law reform. Next I explore some of the causes of these gaps between expressed organizational rationales and the reality on the ground. Finally, I argue in favor of a changed approach—restoring a measure of rationality to rule of law reform—and propose some policy recommendations and directions for further research.

Defining the Rule of Law: Mapping Divergence

A venerable concept in philosophical and legal discourse for centuries, the "rule of law" has become practically a household term in international diplomatic and donor circles, especially since 1989. Given the UN Secretary-General's August 2004 report on the subject, and the March 2005 report on UN reforms, it could be said that the rule of law has come of age in the international community and won its pride of place, alongside more established notions and practices like peacekeeping and conflict prevention.[3]

Despite its frequent use for centuries, and notwithstanding over fifteen years of experience in this newly redefined venture, practitioners and theorists alike avow that there is "no single template," and "no fixed meaning," for the rule of law. Renowned legal scholars concur on the imprecision and vagueness of the term, despite its frequent use.[4] It has been noted, for instance, that in China today "[the] rule of law is one of the much said but little understood concepts in popular press and daily conversations."[5]

The definition of the rule of law is at once confused and contested. A host of often inconsistent definitions are adopted both by academics and by operational agencies acting in the area of rule of law, often with the caveat that there is no consensual definition. However, scholars have acknowledged, in different ways, that there is not just confusion, but also a significant divergence between different schools of thought on the definition and content of the rule of law.

The varying scholarly definitions and depictions of the rule of law offered through the years can be separated into two broad categories based on their content and emphasis. I refer to these two categories as the "maximalist" and "minimalist" conceptions of the rule of law.[6] This divergence harks back to the fundamental and age-old dichotomy in legal philosophy between the traditions of natural law and positive law. The natural law tradition insists that "what the law is depends in some way on what the law must be," and that the law has a necessary correlation to morality.[7] In contrast, legal positivists stress what the law is, rather than what it ought to be. For positivists, it is the source and formal criteria that are determinant, rather than the content. If law fulfills established criteria of legality, even a bad law is still a law. Legal positivists clarify that they do not disregard morality, but simply place it afterward. Despite the subsequent emergence of many other legal traditions and theories, this dichotomy continues to mark legal philosophy. It has particular significance for our purposes in the understanding of the rule of law.

Definitions of the rule of law that fall within the minimalist perspective are those that divest the rule of law of its substantive and moral content. In this view, the concept is restricted to its historical genesis as a means of protection from the arbitrariness of "rule by man" and from the abuse of power by the state. Thus it primarily encompasses a government governed by and subject to rules. Friedrich von Hayek's definition still best describes this position: "Stripped of all its technicalities, this means that government in all its actions is bound by rules fixed and announced beforehand—rules which make it possible to foresee with fair certainty how the authority will use its coercive powers in given circumstances, and to plan one's own individual affairs on the basis of that knowledge."[8] For Hayek, the predictability offered by the rule of law, even if oppressive, brings with it security; unpredictability and arbitrariness, in his view, produce insecurity and hamper individual freedom.

The *Rechtsstaat* or *état de droit* (state of law) that developed in continental Europe in the nineteenth century could be seen as an extreme form of minimalist rule of law. However, its excessive administrative control and consequent in-equities led prominent legal scholars like Albert Venn Dicey, Michael Oakeshott, and even Hayek himself to dismiss it as an expression of the rule of law.[9] Nevertheless, in the minimalist view, the rule of law could be consistent with a variety of political systems besides liberal democracy, such as a theocracy or monarchy that follows established and regular procedures.[10]

The definitions of the rule of law that fall within the maximalist perspective are closer to the natural law position. They would see the rule of law as an umbrella encompassing structural, procedural, as well as substantive elements. Dicey captured the threefold dimensions of the rule of law in his depiction: "The rule of law has three meanings. It means in the first place the absolute supremacy or predominance of regular law as opposed to the influence of arbitrary power; [second] equality before the law; [third] the laws of the constitution are . . . the consequence of the rights of individuals."[11]

Definitions within the maximalist perspective would not find it possible to separate substantive justice from formal justice: law *is* about justice. A contemporary political articulation of this view was provided by the Organization for Security and Cooperation in Europe (OSCE): "[The participating states] consider that the rule of law does not merely mean formal legality which assures regularity and consistency in the achievement and enforcement of democratic order, but justice based on the recognition and full acceptance of the supreme value of the human personality and guaranteed by institutions providing a framework for its fullest expression."[12]

Drawing such a clear distinction between these two opposing views of rule of law is neither radical nor new. Several scholars have drawn attention to such divergent perspectives, using different terms and categories of distinction. Renowned jurisprudence scholar Ronald Dworkin famously distinguished the "rule book" or formalistic approach from the "rights"-based approach to the rule of law, and is an ardent advocate of the latter.[13] Judith Shklar points to the difference between Montesquieu's and Aristotle's conceptions of the rule of law.[14] In the African context, H. Kwasi Prempeh distinguishes between the jurisprudence of executive supremacy on the one hand, and of constitutionalism on the other.[15] An illuminating recent depiction of this definitional distinction is drawn by Rachel Kleinfeld Belton.[16] She divides the multiple definitions proposed for the rule of law into those focusing on the "institutional attributes" considered necessary for the rule of law, as opposed to the "ends" delivered by the rule of law. While each scholar uses a different set of criteria to base their distinction, in each case there is a roughly comparable distinction drawn between the formalistic and institutional dimension of rule of law, and the normative and substantive dimension. My depiction of "maximalist" and "minimalist" seeks to categorize this divergence in simple, broad, and generally unequivocal terms.

This does not imply, however, that the two views share nothing in common. On the contrary, both views require adherence to the principles of legality, namely that laws be general, promulgated, clear and open, noncontradictory, prospective, constant and relatively stable, and possible, and that official action be congruent with declared rule.[17] Both also agree largely on the need for accessibility of courts, and on the observance of principles of natural justice as well, namely open and fair hearing, absence of bias, due process, impartiality and regular functioning of the law, and judicial review of courts over legislative action.[18] Like positivists, those defending minimalist views of the rule of law would clarify that they do not deny the importance of justice or rights, but view them as distinct and outside the realm of the rule of law.

The fundamental difference between the two, then, is qualitative: the distinction between the *form* emphasized by minimalists and the *substance* underlined by maximalists. This divide remains difficult to breach, as minimalists will rarely concede that substance is a part of the rule of law, while maximalists will be loath to backtrack from their insistence on substance as essential.

The UN Secretary-General's August 2004 report on the rule of law sought to cut short the definitional confusion by proposing the following working definition: "[The rule of law] refers to a principle of governance in which all persons, institutions and entities, public and private, including the state itself, are accountable to laws that are publicly promulgated, equally enforced, and independently adjudicated, and which are consistent with international human rights norms and standards."[19] The behind-the-scenes effort undertaken to synthesize and articulate a single succinct definition for the United Nations is substantial and commendable. However, the question is whether this definition takes into account the divergent views on the rule of law, and more importantly whether it bridges this divide once and for all. A surface reading might suggest that it does indeed link—if not wed—the two divergent views. The Secretary-General's definition chooses to highlight two aspects of the rule of law. First, it supports the typically minimalist insistence, underlined by Hayek, on subjecting government and all its institutions to law. It goes further, however, by also extending accountability to individuals and to "entities" alongside institutions. Further, it emphasizes that accountability is equally applicable to "public and private" actors and organizations.

Second, it adopts the maximalist leaning toward the rule of law, by stipulating "consistency" with human rights norms and standards. It is critically important that the UN Secretary-General's definition underlines such adherence to human rights, as the United Nations is the primary birthing place and custodian of human rights at the international level. Nevertheless, this definition falls short of actually making the causal and inseparable association between justice, morality, and the law that the maximalist view defends. Human rights standards are depicted here as another procedural requirement alongside the standard principles of legality and due process, rather than as a definitional and normative requirement whereby law only qualifies as law if it embodies justice and, consequently, the rights that seek to deliver justice. To sum, the Secretary-General's definition moves us forward slightly, but does not serve to bridge the divergent views in any definitive manner. It will not end either the confusion or the contestation around the definition of the rule of law, as it is not clear enough in its articulation. It is largely a minimalist definition, albeit with the important addition of adherence to human rights norms and standards.

A potential value-added of the Secretary-General's definition is its subtle yet unmistakable emphasis on accountability and on equality before the law, at a time when impunity in conflict areas and on the global scene threaten to undermine the credibility of the rule of law. This emphasis is morally valuable, even if it is unclear whether it will have any demonstrable effect. Using Kleinfeld Belton's depiction, the Secretary-General's definition is neither clearly "ends based" nor focused on "institutional attributes." It falls somewhere in between. By describing the rule of law as a "principle of governance" but not naming within the definition any of the specific institutions it is embodied in, nor the purposes it might serve or ends it might deliver, this definition still leaves the field open for doubt and equivocation. The divergence between the two predominant conceptions of the rule of law will continue to be reflected in international discourse and to shape and influence practice.

The Consequences of Divergence: Implications for Human Rights, Development, and Security

This simple depiction of the divergence itself suggests some of the further confusions raised, depending on which view one adopts. What is the relationship of the rule of law to human rights: are they synonymous or at least overlapping, in the maximalist view, or instead entirely distinct and unrelated, in the minimalist view? Is the rule of law primarily a tool to deliver security and order, through its attributes of predictability and reliability in its form and functioning, or rather a framework for the protection and progressive realization of human rights and justice? Is it a policy instrument for development and economic growth, or a security instrument for law enforcement?

The relationship between the rule of law and human rights is rendered particularly problematic due to the conceptual divergence described above. While rarely discussed, this confusion has existed since the crafting of the Universal Declaration of Human Rights itself, if not clearly enunciated earlier. The preamble of the Universal Declaration states: "It is essential, if man is not to have recourse, as a last resort, to rebellion against tyranny and oppression, that human rights should be protected by the rule of law."[20] International treaties and declarations draw a clear link, therefore, between human rights protection and the provision of a rule of law framework to safeguard these rights.

Some human rights proponents go further in making a more sweeping link between the rule of law and all aspects of human rights. The International Commission of Jurists, at its 1959 conference in Delhi, adopted the Declaration on the Rule of Law in a Free Society, in which it recognized that the rule of law was "a dynamic concept . . . which should be employed not only to safeguard and advance the civil and political rights of the individual in a free society, but also to establish social, economic, educational and cultural conditions under which his legitimate aspirations and dignity may be realized."[21]

Chapter 3 subjects this relationship to deep and much needed critical scrutiny. Here, for the purposes of the present discussion on the two divergent conceptions, it will suffice to underline the confusion this raises in both theory and practice regarding the relationship between the two concepts. The minimalist view regards human rights as entirely separate from and unrelated to the rule of law; the maximalist view considers human rights and values to be a fundamental underpinning of the rule of law. Consequently, a donor or implementing agency that follows a minimalist view of the rule of law would not see human rights as a part of its purview, whereas one following a maximalist perspective would consider human rights protection and promotion a natural and inevitable part of its mandate.

The rule of law has also become a popular mantra among economic and development actors. This linkage between the rule of law and economic development is not new. It was already drawn in the early era of postcolonial development practice.[22] A maximalist reading of the rule of law in the development arena would imply ensuring that all are equal before the law and have access to it, and would try to empower people to participate socially and economically as well as politically as development actors.[23] A minimalist attitude would not be concerned with distribution, equality, and justice but rather with functional and efficient institutions in the economic arena, much along the lines currently followed by the World Bank.[24] Minimalists would, for example, focus on commercial and investment laws, and the protection of property, and provide training in such laws and procedures to commerce and trade officials, with the aim of enhancing the efficiency of the economic system. Thus rule of law reform programs in the economic arena would be entirely different in their scope, design, and objectives, and consequently in their outcomes, depending on the view of the rule of law they adopted and were framed within.

The most recent linkage in terms of policy and practice is that between the rule of law and security, particularly as rule of law reform is taken to countries emerging from conflict or in political transition. The rule of law is seen as a critical tool from the security point of view, particularly in countries in transition. In states undergoing or emerging from conflict, or at risk of collapse, the rule of law is seen to provide a bulwark of governance and a mechanism for the nonviolent settlement of disputes. It offers the option that grievances could be addressed within the ambit of the law and existing politically accepted avenues, rather than through the resort to force. This rationale has been reinforced in recent years with the emergence of what is now referred to as "security sector reform" or "security sector governance."[25] On the whole, the rule of law has come to be seen as a subset of the wider security sector, which also includes the military, the intelligence apparatus, and inter alia the many parliamentary and civil oversight bodies responsible for military policy. This subsuming of the rule of law to the security sector has mixed, and sometimes negative, ramifications.[26]

However, the divergence in the understanding of the rule of law leads to confusion once again. For those who adopt a minimalist view, the rule of law is primarily embodied in security institutions—mainly the police and penal authorities. Rebalancing the relationship between police and armed forces, and the need to civilianize the police and wean them away from military dominance, is often considered a priority in highly militarized societies.[27] The continuing violence, threat of relapse into conflict, high levels of crime, and other risk factors often tempt rule of law reformers to focus on the hard security end of rule of law reform particularly in police training, such as riot control and training border guards. However, those adopting a maximalist view are not better off: while their aspiration might lean in the direction of providing more comprehensive human security rather than strictly state or military security, they are faced with the reality of long-corrupt and manipulated institutions on the one hand, and the volatility of the transitional situation on the other, and are often unable to bridge the gap. Thus, while minimalist rule of law runs the risk of turning toward recidivist authoritarianism, maximalist rule of law becomes a victim of its own normative ideals in volatile situations.

These confusing realities based on divergent conceptions of the rule of law are not just a matter for academic reflection, but also have real and tangible consequences. They can be witnessed in the disparity between the vehemently stated rationales and objectives provided by some of the leading international actors in the rule of law arena and their programs and practices on the ground.

Rationales or Irrational Promises?
International Justifications for Rule of Law Strategies

The rule of law has been a tool in the donor agency arsenal since the beginning of the postdecolonization development era in the 1960s. However, the international fascination with the rule of law has both intensified and broadened since 1989. It is with this post–Cold War period that the analysis of stated rationales is primarily concerned, just as this volume is interested in rule of law programs and civil war. Through the post–Cold war years, a plethora of diverse organizations have become involved at different times and in different ways in rule of law programming. They have stated their rationales for undertaking programs in the rule of law area in increasingly emphatic and categorical terms. These stated rationales indicate the objectives or outcomes they believe, presume, or claim that the rule of law will deliver. What is fascinating to note, then, is how, over time, the rule of law has become an elixir for many ills and a panacea delivering many desirable goods. Three distinct but ultimately overlapping rationales and motivations can be distinguished: economic development and market economy, democracy and governance, and security.

For several organizations, economic growth and development remained, as in the 1960s, the main purpose for pursuing rule of law reform. In the World Bank's view, "sound legal frameworks are *prerequisites* for economic growth and social development."[28] This is the goal underlined in the individual rationales for the rule of law projects undertaken by the World Bank, which span the areas of access to law and justice, personal and property rights, legal services, legal reform, judicial and other dispute resolution mechanisms, legal institutions for a market economy, and law reform. The Bank has gone far to proclaim this linear causal link between the rule of law and economic development. For example, in 2001, then–World Bank president James D. Wolfensohn called on governments and the international community to recognize that "an effective legal and judicial system is not a luxury, but a key component of a well-functioning state and an essential ingredient in long-term development." He publicly went on record to cite concrete empirical evidence of a "large, significant and causal relationship between improved rule of law and income of nations, rule of law and literacy, and rule of law and reduced infant mortality." He claimed that the difference in income per capita and in reduced infant mortality can be about three to one between a country with relatively good rule of law institutions and one with inadequate institutions.[29]

The second rationale put forward for undertaking rule of law reform is democracy promotion. This is the rationale categorically defended by the US State Department and promoted actively by its development agency, the US Agency for International Development (USAID), and also by other US-based organizations. For the United States, this rationale of democracy promotion is intricately and immiscibly linked to the previous rationale of promoting a market economy. It is often expressed as a dual and, in their view, mutually reinforcing rationale. These twinned motivations led to the flourishing of US-sponsored rule of law reform agendas and programs, especially with the simultaneous political-economic transitions in Eastern and Central European countries from authoritarian single-party rule to multiparty democracy, and from centrally planned command economies to market economies. For the United States, this was not just common sense, but also a vital part of national interests. As stated by USAID: "The rule of law is the cornerstone of democracy and essential to a well-functioning market economy. [In Latin America] these projects are essential to strengthen democracies in that region, create greater stability and security, and attract greater inflows of foreign investment. *In effect, USAID's rule of law program serves several vital and strategic US interests.*"[30] While promoting the economic goal of market economy and the political goal of democracy did not pose a problem for USAID, organizations like the World Bank, with their mandate to be apolitical, could not undertake the political agenda of democracy promotion, and restricted their rationale to promoting open market economies and fostering economic growth and development through rule of law reform.

What enabled the World Bank and other financial and development agencies to link the economic and democratic rationales without betraying their apolitical mandates was the appearance of the mantra of "governance" on the development agenda. Although the concept of good governance predated 1989, with rising evidence of the failure of development aid practices and aid fatigue, it was catalyzed by the Iron Curtain's demise.[31] With the dissolving of bipolar motivations behind aid to often dictatorial and badly governed client states, the importance of shoring up functioning governments to provide services and basic goods reemerged. The concept of "good governance" began to gain currency and it became easier to use good governance criteria as an element of conditionality in aid—without appearing to interfere directly in politics. Increasingly, the rule of law began to be seen, alongside democratic government, as a key component of good governance. The World Bank could therefore establish an entire governance program and state its "key objective" in this area as follows:

> A fundamental role of the Bank is to help governments work better in our client countries. The Public Sector Group's objectives are based on the view that the Bank must focus more of its efforts on building efficient and accountable public sector institutions—rather than simply providing discrete policy advice. A main lesson from East Asia (and to some extent Russia) is that good policies are not enough—that the Bank cannot afford to look the other way when a country is plagued by deeply dysfunctional public institutions that limit accountability, set perverse rules of the game, and are incapable of sustaining development.[32]

The UN Development Programme (UNDP) reframed its focus around governance by the late 1990s, and unequivocally declared the following causal link between human development, governance, and the rule of law: "[The] UNDP believes that human development is unattainable without creating a system of good government. . . . Good governance has many attributes. It is participatory, transparent, accountable, and it promotes the rule of law."[33]

The third rationale was the security motivation that emerged with the exigencies of postconflict peacebuilding, forcing international organizations and particularly the UN system to pay attention to the rule of law. The year 1989 ushered in a period of rapid resolution of many long-standing conflicts, several of which were tied to Cold War politics, such as in Namibia, Cambodia, El Salvador, and Mozambique. In those early years of postconflict peacebuilding, peace agreements often stipulated a rapid election and democratic transition, adding additional pressure. The Cambodian case lent particular urgency to the need to bolster the rule of law as a buffer against continuing insecurity, impunity, and violence in the country, despite the signing of a peace agreement and an international presence in the country to implement it. Based on his experiences in Cambodia, an international lawyer emphatically asserted: "A young democracy without a rule of law may soon degenerate into a people ruled by warlords and tribalism. A fragile government without an independent and adequately resourced judiciary may soon perish. A lasting peace is not achievable unless it carries with it the imperative of law."[34]

It was in Cambodia, too, that the idea was first floated by legal experts of introducing "justice packages" into volatile postconflict countries for application during transitions by the international operation responsible for implementing the peace agreement.[35] This led to several different experiments in the transitional administration of justice, most recently in Timor-Leste and Kosovo, and finally to the proposed "model transitional codes for postconflict criminal justice," the result of a joint project undertaken by the Irish Centre for Human Rights, at the University of Galway, and the US Institute for Peace.[36] A novel initiative was the European Union's recent rule of law mission in Georgia in July 2004, launched as a flagship in the context of its new European Security and Defense Policy.[37]

While the immediate and pressing rationale for rule of law reform in postconflict countries was that of security, to this was added the other rationales that might deliver other aspects of postconflict peacebuilding, such as reconstruction and economic and social development. Thus, for example, the ongoing rationale of the Canadian International Development Agency (CIDA) for promoting the rule of law in the Balkans: "The establishment of the rule of law in these (post-conflict) states is a cornerstone for economic development and social justice. Sustainable economic development relies on clear and balanced rules and regulations, and social justice cannot be realized without the achievement of democratic rule of law."[38]

Of note in each of these cited rationales is the emphatic nature of the linear, two-way, direct causal relationship drawn by each institution between the rule of law and a particular set of "goods" that constitute their primary business. Thus, USAID claims that the rule of law will deliver democracy and a market economy, and that neither is possible in its absence. The World Bank promises that the rule of law will deliver economic growth and development, which likewise would not be possible without it. The UNDP proclaims that the rule of law will produce human development and good governance, and that neither will transpire without it. International lawyers in postconflict situations predict violent chaos and insecurity without the rule of law, and security and order with. The new catchphrase of "human security," highly popular in certain policy circles and championed by Canada among other countries, has not been immune to rule of law "contagion." Thus CIDA also links the rule of law and governance to the delivery of human security: "Public service reform and rule of law are necessary to the efficient and effective delivery of social services, human security and other public goods."[39] Likewise, reference to a "human rights" rationale for rule of law promotion can be found in the strategies of certain donors and agencies, such as the European Union, the OSCE, and CIDA.

Each of these three rationales can be distinguished from the others, and the trajectory of its particular emergence can be traced back to particular political events and catalytic contexts. Each can also be traced back to one or few specific organizations that proposed that particular rationale initially. This could have led to separate actors following parallel, distinct, and unrelated programs to achieve different strategic aims in different contexts—USAID pursuing democratization, the World Bank promoting economic growth, and the UNDP promoting human development and governance for example—all using the rule of law as means or ends. Instead, each organization's expression of its compelling rationale has become increasingly overlapping, mired, and confused over time. Actors have begun to profess several of these rationales and engage in more than one aspect of the rule of law simultaneously—economic development, democratization, governance and postconflict peacebuilding, and even conflict prevention. The rationale proposed by the United Kingdom's Department for International Development (DfID), one of the most progressive, "avant-garde," and integrated or "joined-up" donors, illustrates how lead agencies in this area have begun to articulate all-encompassing rationales for their rule of law strategies:

> The provision of law and order is a core government responsibility and is part of the necessary framework for economic and social development:
>
> - The rule of law is correlated with economic growth and investment. An effective justice sector provides better livelihoods for poor people;
> - The rule of law is necessary for the protection of economic and social as well as civil and political rights;
> - A strong independent judiciary is necessary to constrain the arbitrary exercise of state power;
> - An effective justice sector is a safeguard against corruption;
> - The justice sector offers one means of resolving disputes and preventing conflict.[40]

When a single agency declares unequivocally that the rule of law will deliver on everything from governance to economic development to social justice to conflict prevention, it signals that the concept has been overloaded. Further, by making the rule of law central to each dimension of the organization's core business, it also raises the stakes by predicating that "success" will be judged based on whether the rule of law delivers on this gamut of ends. It is simply unrealistic for a single concept—even if it were not as confused, contested, and divergent as the rule of law—to deliver on such a panoply of promises. (Furthermore, it is ill-advised for organizations, however committed, to set themselves up to deliver so many goods from a single concept.) However well-intentioned and carefully planned, no rule of law program could generate so many diverse goods in entirely different contexts.

From Rationales to Effectiveness: Do Rule of Law Programs Deliver?

As Thomas Carothers reports, international organizations and donor countries have spent over US$1 billion over the past two decades in efforts to bring the rule of law to countries transitioning toward democracy or trying to escape poverty.[41] This does not include the further many billions of dollars spent in postconflict peacebuilding since 1989, much of which has also been devoted at least ostensibly to rule of law reform. Has this been money well spent? Have any of the promised fruits been harvested, and if not, for what reasons?

The many studies emerging from recent postconflict transitions suggest that the success rate is not high, neither of rule of law programming specifically nor of postconflict peacebuilding itself more generally. It is now acknowledged that the rate of relapse into violent conflict in postconflict countries is about 50 percent.[42] In other words, despite the importance attributed by several international organizations to rule of law reform as the linchpin of stability and security since 1992, half of all countries that have ended conflict will fall back into conflict.

It would be erroneous, naturally, to attribute peacebuilding's failure and return to conflict solely to the failure of rule of law programs, for the reasons are far more numerous and complex.[43] Nonetheless, it is noteworthy that some of the postconflict countries where international actors undertook rule of law programs with the explicit purpose of achieving security and stability and avoiding a relapse into conflict have not demonstrated the promised results, but rather continue to suffer from weak rule of law, weak development, and weak democracy. Haiti, Guatemala, and Afghanistan offer three different but revealing examples of the outcomes of internationally driven rule of law initiatives.

Haiti is an important case in this regard. Donors, particularly the United States and Canada, invested massively in rule of law reform after the overthrow of dictator Raoul Cedras and the return of President Jean-Bertrand Aristide, hoping to move Haiti toward security, development, and democracy. The old, discredited security forces were entirely disbanded—on President Aristide's command. A brand-new police force was recruited and trained, and the dysfunctional phantom judiciary was brought back to life. Close observers and involved legal reform practitioners noted early progress.[44] From 1994 to 1996 alone, donors spent over US$100 million in this area. Yet despite the international efforts and

an ambitious and promising beginning, the tragic and violent events that un-
folded in Haiti in 2004–2005, leading to the forced ouster of Aristide, cast into
doubt whether any of the rule of law investments had borne fruit. The UNDP's
2002 report on human development, which focused on democracy and included
indicators for governance, rule of law, and democratization, gave a bleak assessment of the situation. According to the report, based on World Bank governance
indicator datasets and utilizing a scoring scale of −2.50 to +2.50, Haiti scored
−1.45 on the rule of law (based on diverse factors such as the existence of black
markets, crime, and corruption, enforceability of contracts, and the unpredictability of the judiciary), while it scored −0.38 on political stability and lack
of violence (based on perceptions of likelihood of destabilization).[45]

In Guatemala, a return to violent conflict has so far been avoided, if barely.
A spiralling proliferation of small arms and the spread of violent crime and
petty gangs have reduced personal security to a low point, despite the long-
standing presence of the UN Verification Mission in Guatemala (MINUGUA),
which monitored the implementation of the peace agreements.[46] Guatemala's
peace settlement of December 1996 was seen at the time as one of the most far-
reaching, anchored around detailed reforms of the security sector and the rule
of law, as well as other social and institutional transformation and an international truth commission.[47] Yet, in 2003, Guatemala risked a return to power of
former dictator Rios Montt, despite the many ostensible transitional justice
measures undertaken under the peace agreements to address former abuses.
Luckily this was avoided, and Montt's potentially volatile remobilization of
former militia to rally to his cause did not result either in his election victory or
in the feared outcome of a renewed civil war.

Although careful arrangements were included in the peace agreements to
reduce the size, budget, and political influence of the military, international
and nongovernmental observers in the country note that the Guatemalan military still remains largely unreformed and powerful. It only signed on to the
peace agreements to win political leverage at a time when the country was
under heavy international pressure to end the war, but did not have the requisite political will to undertake any reform reducing its power.[48] Furthermore,
human rights and civil society activists report being increasingly threatened in
their work, citing frequent break-ins, death threats, and assassinations, while
impunity for violators and general lawlessness prevail. Thus, despite major international investment in rule of law reform in Guatemala, in 2002 the country scored −0.63 for rule of law and, more chillingly, −0.77 for political stability and lack of violence, based on UNDP human development criteria.[49]

In Afghanistan, after decades of unremitting conflict, the primary demand
of ordinary people after the Taliban's removal from power was a return to the
rule of law to replace what they referred to as "the law of the jungle."[50] Yet despite the rhetorical attention given to the rule of law by international donors,
progress has been very limited, for a host of political reasons. One indicator is

that the post of Special Adviser on the Rule of Law within the UN Assistance Mission in Afghanistan (UNAMA) remained empty for many of the early years of the post-Taliban reconstruction, despite the importance given in UNAMA statements to the rule of law. A new lead-country approach to the rule of law and security sector was adopted to ensure longer-term investment by donors. Italy was given the lead on judicial reform, Germany on police reform, and the United Kingdom on intelligence, while the United States took the lead on military reform. However, this approach appears not to have paid the dividends expected. Despite the seminars and training programs on the ground in each of these areas, in reality political factors, including the weak control of the central government outside Kabul and the reigning insecurity and lawlessness across the country, have meant that there has been no translation into rule of law on the ground.[51] Furthermore, despite the establishment of a national body, the Judicial Commission, under the Bonn Agreement, none of the rule of law processes, whether international or national, have significantly engaged the participation of the local population. This compares negatively with, for example, the work of the Constitutional Commission and the Independent Human Rights Commission, both of which expended considerable efforts at least to consult with and seek the views of Afghans across the country, despite prevailing insecurity and limited access to certain provinces. While, again, many factors are involved, the prioritization of security, and the downplaying of the rule of law and justice, might be largely responsible.[52]

Avoidable or Inevitable? Tracing the Causes of Failure

What might be the reasons for the poor performance to date of rule of law programs, when measured against the rhetoric and proclaimed rationales of their organizational proponents? To answer this question, it is necessary to go back to the first attempted legal reform in post–World War II donor practice, and put the current post–Cold War experience in perspective. In the 1960s, in the first flush of the development enterprise, the leading donors, particularly in the United States, led by USAID and the Ford Foundation, began a far-reaching initiative to reform both judicial institutions and the substantive laws of countries across three developing continents: Asia, Africa, and South America. This became known as the "law and development movement," and was premised on the notion that law reform was essential for economic development, and furthermore that legal reform and education could serve as a vector for change and development. Senior scholars from leading US universities like Harvard, Yale, and Stanford were taken onboard, and generated a wealth of literature on the subject.[53] Yet within a decade, the movement was declared a failure by its own academic founders. Four principal reasons have been put forward for this failure. First, there was neither theory nor evidence tracing the impact that law had or might have on development, which led to an inability to prioritize and sequence reforms or predict and measure outcomes. Second, the movement failed to engage the participation of lawyers and other actors in the countries concerned, but instead relied on foreign consultants who determined the nature and pace of reforms. Third, the movement only targeted the formal legal system, ignoring customary and traditional law. Fourth and most important, according to critics, was the dependence on and unsuccessful importing of US legal models and the US culture of "liberal legalism," which was not necessarily suitable to other contexts.[54]

Despite the well-documented failure of the law and development movement, the major donors and economic development actors, led by USAID and the World Bank, reentered the field of rule of law reform only a few years later. Admittedly, their rationales this time around were subtly different: they no longer aimed for large-scale social transformation and development. It is perhaps their earlier experience that led the World Bank and USAID to steer clear of politics and government, and to restrict their interventions to the areas of commercial, property and investment law, and other areas they consider likely to yield a high return on economic growth and to promote Western-style market economies. However, agencies like the DfID and the UNDP openly declare in their stated rationales the intent to promote broader economic, social, and human development, not dissimilar from the aims of the law and development movement.

The World Bank closely follows and commissions research on the lessons learned from past "law and development" as well as from legal reform experience.[55] It is open to the examination of its flaws, and attempts to demonstrate that it is managing to evade repeating old mistakes this time around. The current proclivity for rule of law programming would appear then to be fully informed and strengthened by past experiences and lessons and therefore destined to avoid earlier pitfalls.

In 1995, the British Council sponsored a meeting to assess whether the new round of attention to the rule of law would manage to avoid the mistakes of the law and development movement. While some scholars were fairly optimistic that the World Bank appeared to have learned from the past, others were more pessimistic, and already observed some evidence that contemporary donors and actors were proceeding in their predecessors' footsteps. Julio Faundez noted that all the earlier uncertainties regarding the relationships and complex causalities between politics, development, and formal and informal law still remain. Joseph Thome observed that the earlier false premises of the law and development movement has not significantly shifted, including the reliance on and importing of the US-style legal framework.[56]

All four lessons cited earlier for the failure of the law and development movement in the 1970s are still valid today. And in the middle to late 1990s, when attention to rule of law programs began to grow, researchers and program evaluators began to document very similar concerns.[57] Even as rule of law reform finally comes of age on the international security agenda, the authoritative analyses of leading legal scholars Frank Upham and Thomas Carothers throw a serious spanner in the works. They point out that the glib presumptions and increasingly unambiguous assertions that without rule of law there can be no peace, no security, no democracy, no governance, and no development may be just that—assertions. There is little evidence to back them up in practice.[58]

Upham uses the United States and Japan as examples. In the former case, he uses the atypical legal system in the United States to show that it is possible to have a fully functioning and highly prosperous system without most of the characteristics that are considered within rule of law programming to be the "essential" elements of the rule of law. In the latter case, he demonstrates that it is possible to have astounding economic growth without the rule of law. At present, China's economic emergence would seem to strengthen this argument. This would seem to indicate that, after all, the rule of law is not such a "prerequisite" or "cornerstone" for the achievement of either democracy or economic development, the two most favored goals of rule of law proponents.

Carothers points out that "even when aid programs are able to facilitate fairly specific changes in relevant institutions, it is rarely clear what the longer term effects of those changes are on the overall development of the rule of law in the country in question."[59] He affirms that "the axiomatic quality of the core rationales of the current wave of rule of law assistance efforts—that the rule of law is necessary for economic development and democracy—is misleading when used as a mechanistic, causal imperative by the aid community."[60]

This is cause for serious circumspection in charging ahead with the current rule of law agenda without critical reexamination. In referring to the mechanistic application of the rule of law by most donors, Carothers has put his finger on a persistent, long-diagnosed but unresolved problem that is significantly responsible for these recurrent failings. Writing in 1998, I had underlined the "apolitical" and "technical" nature of rule of law reform programs, which therefore missed their mark.[61] In 2002, I described this approach as "programmatic minimalism": rule of law actors adopted a minimalist conception of the rule of law and applied a mechanistic, technical, politically insensitive, programmatic approach, which therefore failed to produce results.[62]

Writing in 2005, Rachel Kleinfeld Belton indicates that little has changed as yet. She observes that practitioners involved in rule of law programs tend to use definitions of the rule of law based on institutional attributes rather than on ends. "Defining the rule of law by its institutions also slants practitioners towards overly technocratic models of reform," but "achieving rule of law ends requires political and cultural, not only institutional, change."[63] As Upham insists, the very foundation of his argument is that "law is deeply contextual and cannot be detached from its social and political environment."[64] Yet when confronted with a sui generis situation requiring a highly politically sensitive and tailored response, "practitioners are tempted to move directly towards building institutions that look like those reformers know."[65] Kleinfeld Belton explains the problem with an economic rationale: "Practitioners often confuse 'building the rule of law' with enacting a particular vision of economic life."[66]

A parallel tendency of international practitioners is to focus on restoring legal material, rebuilding or refurbishing courthouses, or at best providing "seminars" for law officers, rather than engaging in substantive and sometimes politically contentious reform. In 1998 a senior UN official explained only half-jokingly how in Rwanda, "restoring justice became a question of how to give computers to the Justice Ministry."[67] In mid-2003, during an interview with a senior Supreme Court official in Kabul, one could not help but notice the pristine computer still wrapped in its plastic sitting untouched in the corner of his office, while the corridors of the building were being given a new coat of paint. In Kunduz, the police chief, a former mujahid, proudly listed the number of donor-sponsored seminars on police reform he had attended in the past year, then sheepishly confessed that they had little relevance or applicability to the enormous law and order problems he faced daily; he wished that more seminars could be conducted locally for his junior and inexperienced officers rather than multiplying trainings for senior chiefs in faraway Kabul.[68] These reforms therefore tend to be piecemeal, although Kleinfeld Belton cautions that "poorly devised reforms of rule of law institutions can undermine rule of law ends," and underscores that improving the rule of law generally and law and order specifically require cooperation across all rule of law institutions.[69]

Hand in hand with a politically insensitive, technical, imported, and thus external legal framework is the estrangement of any meaningful local participation and ownership in the process and final outcome—exactly the failing of the law and development movement with its overreliance on US experts and legal models.

The discussion of these weaknesses and failings of rule of law programs is no longer only restricted to academic conferences and journals, but has come to the attention of senior policymakers as well. The UN Secretary General's 2004 report on the rule of law and transitional justice avowed, "The international community has not always provided rule of law assistance that is appropriate to the country context. Too often, the emphasis has been on foreign experts, foreign models and foreign conceived solutions." It then assured that the UN is now looking to "nationally led strategies of assessment and consultation carried out with the active and meaningful participation of national stakeholders" across the spectrum.[70] The road to accomplish this systematically in practice is still long, however. For the time being, while rule of law reform has finally come of age, it has done so at a time when its weaknesses and failures are more apparent than ever before. Furthermore, we now know that the causes of these failings were at least partly foreseeable and hence avoidable, but that despite evidence and diagnosis, and despite notable policy changes, little effective change has happened on the ground.

Policy Recommendations:
Restoring Rationality to Rule of Law Reform

At the United Nations, it took the persistent efforts of a handful of committed diplomats and senior UN officials to raise the profile of the rule of law to its current status, and this is to be commended. In light of the many difficulties, ranging from divergent conceptions to unrealistic rationales and poor performance on the ground, the signal concern today is how to proceed. The more cynical critics might ask whether to proceed at all with rule of law reform.

This cynical perspective is not appropriate. Admittedly, past approaches have not yet demonstrated sustained positive effect over the medium term, and in some cases, as documented by Kleinfeld Belton, have been counterproductive. Business as usual in the rule of law is not an option. If the baby is not to be thrown out with the bathwater, there is serious and urgent need for a major overhaul of strategy—indeed for nothing short of restoring rationality to the currently irrational pursuit of this still confused and diffused aim.

Actors in the international community who are involved in rule of law reform should acknowledge and address head-on the cognitive dissonance and considerable human and material costs of their present approach. They should recognize the divergent conceptions and costs of ignoring these aspects and the accompanying divergence between their stated rationales and their actual program outcomes. While proclaiming grandiose ambitions, in practice most rule of law programs have been minimalist, technical, and focused on programs or projects—such as refurbishing courthouses, or holding seminars and training for police officers. They have not taken on a more holistic, "maximalist" view of rule of law or longer-term programs that seek incrementally to achieve this ethos of a rule of law embedded in justice. Yet this minimalistic approach has failed to deliver results.

International actors should therefore reject their minimalist approaches, and consciously adopt a "maximalist" conception of the rule of law as their definition, with incremental programming that seeks to achieve this vision over the long term. In practical terms this would require adopting, in Kleinfeld Belton's terms, an "ends-based" definition when they plan their rule of law strategies, to avoid focusing on institutional attributes and reforms that replicate Western-style institutions in non-Western contexts. This would also mean that measurement of outcomes should be based on ends rather than on institutions "reformed" or programs implemented. This would imply a deliberate move away from technical and apolitical "programmatic minimalism," which often causes as much harm as good.

Alongside this, it would be necessary for the major organizations involved to review their flamboyant rationales in light of evidence or lack thereof to back their assertions. While adopting a maximalist ends-based definition grounded in justice and norms, they should nevertheless define more modest and realistic rationales and programs to implement them incrementally and realistically over time. They should withdraw from exaggerated claims of delivering a series of goods that the rule of law is unlikely to deliver. Instead they should aim to foster the rule of law as an end in itself, rather than a means to a series of other ends and motivations generated by their own institutional mandates or political agendas—a rule of law that both generates and embodies justice and protects the rights of all residents, including the most vulnerable.

Translating the above into policy recommendations for principal actors and donors involved in rule of law reform, several priorities emerge:

- The overriding priority should be to move from rhetoric to real progress in fully engaging the diverse and heterogeneous local population at all levels in the process of generating their own country's rule of law according to their needs, culture, and context. Both local and international actors should recognize that this is a long-term process that must be built on local needs and input in order to be acceptable to the local population.
- Basing the rule of law on local participation and their articulation of needs leads almost automatically to a requirement to embed rule of law programs firmly in justice, the full spectrum of human rights, and human dignity. Thus rule of law programs should be more concerned with protection of citizens than with enforcement of laws as an end, although the latter is a necessary means to deliver the former.
- Rule of law reform requires the adoption of a politically astute and realistic rather than a technical approach to rule of law programming. Attention must be given to the volatile political context and the different political interests involved. Attention must also be given to fostering and nurturing political will and commitment to rule of law reform at the highest political level.
- Rule of law reform should lead, ideally, to greater convergence in the divergent rationales and approaches of different international actors, and to greater commitment to saving and sharing resources in clearly defined programs.
- Donors and practitioners—and scholars too—should adopt a less flamboyant, assertive, declaratory tone in claiming all the purported offspring of the rule of law, given the scant evidence we have to date. Yet this should not mean downscaling programs even further from their current minimalist technical focus, but rather upscaling current efforts so that programs meet at least some of the maximalist ends they seek to achieve incrementally.

We must be guided in our rule of law work by a sense of accountability to postconflict populations—to protect them as best we can, without promising what we can't deliver.

Notes

I express my gratitude to Katya Shadrina, my untiring faculty assistant, for her invaluable research assistance. I am grateful to the International Peace Academy and particularly to Agnès Hurwitz for her unfailing encouragement and her energy in carrying through this entire project.

1. Various definitions of rule of law are presented in Allan Hutchinson and Patrick Monahan, eds., *The Rule of Law: Ideal or Ideology?* (Toronto: Carswell, 1987).

2. United Nations, *The Rule of Law and Transitional Justice in Conflict and Post-Conflict Societies,* Report of the Secretary-General, UN Doc. S/2004/616 (August 23, 2004), para. 6.

3. United Nations, *The Rule of Law and Transitional Justice*; United Nations, *In Larger Freedom: Towards Development, Security, and Human Rights for All—Report of the Secretary General,* UN Doc. A/59/2005 (March 21, 2005).

4. Mark Ellis, "Strengthening Democracy: The Rule of Law and Institution Building," paper presented at the conference "InterAction: Strengthening African Democracy," Abuja, Nigeria, November 22–25, 2004; Matthew Stephenson, "The Rule of Law as a Goal of Development Policy," prepared for the World Bank, http://www1 .worldbank.org/publicsector/legal/ruleoflaw2.htm (last accessed November 15, 2007); see Barry Hager, "The Rule of Law: A Lexicon for Policy Makers" (Washington, D.C.: Mansfield Center for Pacific Affairs, 1999).

5. Bo Li, "What Is Rule of Law?" *Perspectives* 1, no. 5 (2000), http://www.oycf .org/perspectives/5_043000/what_is_rule_of_law.htm.

6. See Rama Mani, *Beyond Retribution: Seeking Justice in the Shadows of War* (Cambridge: Polity, 2002), pp. 25–31. Here I build and elaborate on the concept of rule of law as outlined in my *Beyond Retribution* analysis.

7. Ronald Dworkin, "'Natural' Law Revisited," in *The Nature and Process of Law,* edited by Patricia Smith (Oxford: Oxford University Press, 1993), p. 239; Martin Golding, *The Philosophy of Law* (London: Prentice Hall, 1975), pp. 24–51.

8. Friedrich von Hayek, *Road to Serfdom* (London: Ark, 1968), cited in Joseph Raz, *The Authority of Law: Essays on Law and Morality* (Oxford: Clarendon, 1979), p. 210.

9. See, for example, Richard Flathman, "Liberalism and the Suspect Enterprise of Political Institutionalisation: The Case of the Rule of Law," and Gerald Gaus, "Public Reason and the Rule of Law," in *The Rule of Law: Nomos XXXVI,* edited by Ian Shapiro (New York: New York University Press, 1994).

10. Raz, *The Authority of Law,* p. 221.

11. Albert Venn Dicey, *An Introduction to the Study of the Law of the Constitution* (Basingstoke: Macmillan, 1959), pp. 202–203.

12. Conference on Security and Cooperation in Europe, "Document of the Copenhagen Meeting of the Conference on the Human Dimension of the CSCE," Copenhagen, June 1990, http://www.ohchr.org/english/law/compilation_democracy/csce.htm. The OSCE was previously called the Conference on Security and Cooperation in Europe (CSCE).

13. Ronald Dworkin, "Political Judges and the Rule of Law," in *A Matter of Principle* (London: Harvard University Press, 1987), pp. 9–32.

14. Judith Shklar, "Political Theory and the Rule of Law," in Hutchinson and Monahan, *The Rule of Law.*

15. H. Kwasi Prempeh, "A New Jurisprudence for Africa," *Journal of Democracy* 10, no. 3 (1999): 135–149.

16. Rachel Kleinfeld Belton, "Competing Definitions of the Rule of Law: Implications for Practitioners." In *Promoting the Rule of Law Abroad: In Search of Knowledge,* edited by Thomas Carothers (Washington, D.C.: Carnegie Endowment for International Peace, 2006).

17. Lon Fuller depicts these eight points as the "inner morality of law" in *The Morality of Law* (London: Yale University Press, 1964), pp. 33–94. See also John

Rawls, *A Theory of Justice* (Oxford: Oxford University Press, 1971). Raz and Rawls used these as the basis for their articulation of the principles of the rule of law.

18. Raz, *The Authority of Law,* pp. 216–218; Rawls, *A Theory of Justice,* pp. 238–239.

19. United Nations, *The Rule of Law and Transitional Justice in Conflict and Post-Conflict Societies: Report of the Secretary-General,* UN Doc. S/2004/616 (23 August 2004), para. 6.

20. United Nations, Preamble to *Universal Declaration of Human Rights,* UN Doc. A/810 (December 10, 1948), recital 3.

21. International Commission of Jurists (ICJ), "The Rule of Law in a Free Society," declaration adopted at the ICJ Congress, New Delhi, January 5–10, 1959, http://www.icj.org/article.php3?id_article=3088&id_rubrique=11&lang=en. See also International Commission of Jurists, "Development, Human Rights and the Rule of Law," report of a conference held in The Hague, April 27–May 1, 1981, http://www.icj.org/article.php3?id_article=3092&id_rubrique=11.

22. Elliot M. Burg, "Law and Development: A Review of the Literature and a Critique of 'Scholars in Self-Estrangement,'" *American Journal of Comparative Law* 25 (1977): 492–530. See an interesting short analysis of the movement at http://www.worldbank.org.

23. See, for example, Swiss Development Cooperation (SDC), "SDC's Human Rights and Rule of Law Guidance Documents: Influence, Effectiveness, and Relevance within SDC," Evaluation no. 2004/1 (Berne, March 2004). The SDC, for example, sees human rights and rule of law as the basis and framework that should underpin all their programming.

24. See, for example, World Bank, *Legal and Judicial Reform: Strategic Directions* (Washington, D.C., 2003).

25. For an analysis of this emerging concept and sector, see, for example, Alan Bryden and Heiner Hanggi, eds., *Reform and Reconstruction of the Security Sector* (Geneva: Geneva Centre for the Democratic Control of Armed Forces, 2004); Heiner Hanggi and Theodor Winkler, eds., *Challenges of Security Sector Governance* (Geneva: Geneva Centre for the Democratic Control of Armed Forces, 2003).

26. See, for example, Rama Mani, "Contextualizing Police Reform: Security, the Rule of Law, and Post-Conflict Peacebuilding," in Tor Tanke Holm and Espen Barth Eide, eds., *Peacebuilding and Police Reform* (Portland: Cass, 2000), pp. 9–24.

27. Holm and Eide, *Peacebuilding and Police Reform.*

28. Emphasis added. World Bank, Law and Justice Institutions, "Law Reform," http://web.worldbank.org/wbsite/external/topics/extlawjustinst/0,,contentmdk:20745866~menupk:1989592~pagepk:210058~pipk:210062~thesitepk:1974062,00.html (last accessed November 15, 2007).

29. World Bank, "Rule of Law Central to Fighting Poverty," Press Release no. 2002/013/S (July 9, 2001), http://econ.worldbank.org/wbsite/external/extdec/extresearch/extprograms/exttraderesearch/0,,contentmdk:20011894~menupk:162686~pagepk:210083~pipk:152538~thesitepk:544849,00.html.

30. USAID, "USAID Promotes the Rule of Law in Latin American and Caribbean Democracies," http://www.usaid.gov/locations/latin_america_caribbean/democracy/rule/index.html, emphasis added; USAID, "USAID/Russia: Strategy Amendment (1999–2005)," February 2002, p. 36, russia.usaid.gov/en/more_info/publications/strategy-public_version.doc.

31. For a critical evaluation of the governance debate, see Mark Duffield, *Global Governance and the New Wars: The Merger of Development and Security* (London:

Zed, 2001). "Good governance" became and remains the buzzword with most donors and international financial institutions. See, for example, International Monetary Fund, "The IMF's Approach to Promoting Good Governance and Combating Corruption: A Guide," June 20, 2005, http://www.imf.org/external/np/gov/guide/eng/index.htm.

32. World Bank, "Public Sector and Governance," http://www1.worldbank.org/publicsector/index.cfm (last accessed November 15, 2007).

33. It was in 1999, under its newly instated administrator Mark Malloch Brown, that the UNDP undertook governance as its primary objective. See UNDP, *Rule of Law,* UNDP Programme on Governance in the Arab Region, http://www.undp-pogar.org/themes/ruleoflaw.html.

34. Mark Plunkett, "Re-establishing Law and Order in Peace-Maintenance," *Global Governance* 4, no. 1 (1998): 63.

35. Ibid. The Cambodian experience also led Gareth Evans to support Plunkett's idea in the former's book *Cooperating for Peace: The Global Agenda for the 1990s and Beyond* (St. Leonards: Allen and Unwin, 1993).

36. National University of Ireland, Galway, Irish Centre for Human Rights, "Model Transitional Codes for Post-Conflict Criminal Justice Project," http://www.nuigalway.ie/human_rights/projects/model_codes.html.

37. European Union, "Conclusions of the General Affairs and External Relations Council," Doc. No. 10191/04, June 14, 2004, p. 14, http://www.consilium.europa.eu/ueDocs/cms_Data/docs/pressData/en/gena/80952.pdf.

38. Canadian International Development Agency, "Balkans," http://www.acdi-cida.gc.ca/Balkans-e.

39. Canadian International Development Agency, "Estimates: 2004–2005 Part III—Report on Plans and Priorities," Minister for International Cooperation, Ottawa, http://www.acdi-cida.gc.ca/inet/images.nsf/vluimages/publications2/$file/cida-rpp-2004-05.pdf.

40. DfID, *Safety, Security and Accessible Justice: Putting Policy into Practice* (London, July 2002), p. 13.

41. Thomas Carothers, "The Rule of Law Revival," *Foreign Affairs* 77, no. 2 (1998): 95–106. See also Kleinfeld Belton, "Competing Definitions of the Rule of Law," p. 1.

42. Of the emerging literature on this subject, see, for example, the collection of scholarly articles in Havard Hegre, ed., "Special Issue on Duration and Termination of Civil War," *Journal of Peace Research* 41, no. 3 (2004).

43. See, for example, Barbara Walter, "Does Conflict Beget Conflict? Explaining Recurring Civil War," *Journal of Peace Research* 41, no. 3 (2004): 371–388.

44. Of the many analysts on Haiti, Rachel Nield has meticulously traced, analyzed, and documented Haiti's rule of law progress over more than a decade, and her reports for the Washington Office on Latin America are particularly edifying in following Haiti's ride up and down the rule of law roller coaster. See Rachel Nield, "Can Haiti's Police Reforms Be Sustained?" (Washington, D.C.: Washington Office of Latin America, 1998). See also Melissa Ziegler and Rachel Nield, "From Peace and Governance: Police International Community" (Washington, D.C.: Washington Office of Latin America, 2002).

45. UNDP, *Human Development Report 2002: Deepening Democracy in a Fragmented World* (New York: Oxford University Press, 2002), tab. A1.1, p. 40.

46. While echoed in MINUGUA's reports and other sources, this is my personal analysis, based on field research and extensive confidential interviews with national, civil, and international actors in the security, justice, and human rights sectors that I conducted in Guatemala in August–September 2003 for a case study commissioned by

the Small Arms Survey, Geneva (unpublished). Note that MINUGUA ceased its operations in November 2004.

47. See "Guatemala Peace Agreements" at http://www.usip.org/library/pa/guatemala/pa_guatemala.html. Particularly see two detailed accords that specifically focused on questions of human rights, the rule of law, and security sector reforms: "Acuerdo global sobre derechos humanos" (Global Human Rights Accord), signed in Mexico City on March 29, 1994; and "Acuerdo sobre fortalecimiento del poder civil y function del ejercito en una sociedad democratica" (Agreement on the Strengthening of Civilian Power and on the Role of Armed Forces in a Democratic Society), signed in Mexico City on September 19, 1996.

48. This was the view of Guatemalan civil society, human rights activists, and MINUGUA experts. A particular tribute should be paid to MINUGUA's highly committed staff, for remaining closely involved as vigilant observers and analysts, despite MINUGUA's lack of political clout in its mandate to leverage changes in this deteriorating situation.

49. UNDP, *Human Development Report 2002,* tab. A1.1, p. 40.

50. This common desire for the rule of law was the unambiguous finding of my extensive interviews with Afghan individuals and focus groups around the country in 2003. See Rama Mani, "Ending Impunity and Building Justice in Afghanistan" (Kabul: Afghanistan Research and Evaluation Unit, December 2003).

51. See, for example, the penetrating analysis of the failures in the critical early period of windows of opportunity provided in International Crisis Group, *Judicial Reform and Transitional Justice* (Brussels, January 2003); Mark Sedra, "Challenging the Warlord Culture: Security Sector Reform in Post-Taliban Afghanistan," Paper no. 25 (Bonn: Bonn International Centre for Conversion, 2002).

52. I make this argument in Mani, "Ending Impunity and Building Justice in Afghanistan."

53. Burg, "Law and Development."

54. David Trubek and Marc Galanter, "Scholars in Self-Estrangement: Some Reflections on the Crisis in Law and Development," *Wisconsin Law Review* (1974): 1062–1101.

55. See Patrick McAuslan, "Law, Governance, and the Development of the Market: Practical Problems and Possible Solutions," and Joseph R. Thome, "Comment on McAuslan's 'Law, Governance, and the Development of the Market: Practical Problems and Possible Solutions,'" in *Good Government and Law: Legal and Institutional Reform in Developing Countries,* edited by Julio Faundez (New York: St. Martin's, 1997).

56. See chapters by Julio Faundez and Joseph Thome in Faundez, *Good Government and Law.*

57. When I began investigating rule of law reform and conducting extensive interviews with legal experts and UN officials in 1997–1998, I was certainly not the first or only researcher to highlight some of the failings, risks, and dangers of these approaches. See, for example, Rama Mani, "Conflict Resolution, Justice, and the Law: Rebuilding the Rule of Law in the Aftermath of Complex Political Emergencies," *International Peacekeeping* 5, no. 3 (1998): 1–25. The most recent studies on the subject identify the same problems; see, for example, Kleinfeld Belton, "Competing Definitions of the Rule of Law."

58. Frank Upham, "Mythmaking in the Rule of Law Orthodoxy," Working Paper no. 30 (Washington, D.C.: Carnegie Endowment for International Peace, September 2002); Thomas Carothers, "Promoting the Rule of Law Abroad: the Problem of Knowl-

edge," Working Paper no. 34 (Washington, D.C.: Carnegie Endowment for International Peace, January 2003).

59. Carothers, "Promoting the Rule of Law Abroad," p. 11.

60. Ibid., p. 7.

61. Mani, "Conflict Resolution."

62. Mani, *Beyond Retribution,* pp. 76–81.

63. Kleinfeld Belton, "Competing Definitions of the Rule of Law," pp. 18, 21.

64. Upham, "Mythmaking in the Rule of Law Orthodoxy," p. 7.

65. Kleinfeld Belton, "Competing Definitions of the Rule of Law," p. 18.

66. Ibid., p. 23.

67. Mani, *Beyond Retribution,* p. 69.

68. These interviews were conducted in Afghanistan between March and August 2003, as part of my research toward Mani, "Ending Impunity and Building Justice in Afghanistan." I am grateful to the Afghanistan Research and Evaluation Unit for fully underwriting this research.

69. Kleinfeld Belton, "Competing Definitions of the Rule of Law," p. 12.

70. United Nations, *The Rule of Law and Transitional Justice,* para. 15.

3

Invoking the Rule of Law: International Discourses

Balakrishnan Rajagopal

E stablishing the rule of law is increasingly seen as the panacea for all the problems that afflict many non-Western countries. Development experts prescribe it as the surest shortcut to market-led growth; human rights groups advocate the rule of law as the best defense against human rights abuses; and in the area of peace and security, the rule of law is seen as the surest guarantee against the (re)emergence of conflicts and the basis for rebuilding postconflict societies. Indeed, the rule of law has occupied this central position at least since the early 1990s, as Thomas Carothers recognized in a well-known article on the revival of the rule of law some years ago.[1] Therefore, in a superficial sense, the rule of law could be seen as the common element that development experts, security analysts, and human rights activists agree on, and as the mechanism that links these disparate areas.

In this chapter I argue that this newfound fascination with the rule of law is misplaced. Underlying this "linkage" idea is, I would suggest, a desire to escape from politics, by imagining the rule of law as technical, legal, and apolitical. In other words, there is a tendency to think that failures of development, threats to security, and human rights violations could all be avoided or managed by a resort to law. I trace the characteristics of this idea and the different strands of policy and disciplinary discourses that have led to this conclusion, and argue that there is in fact a need to retain politics at the center of the discussions of development, human rights, and security. In addition, I argue that the invocation of the rule of law hides many contradictions between the different policy agendas themselves (such as between development and human rights or between security and human rights) that cannot be fully "resolved" by invoking the "rule of law" as a mantra. It is far more important to inquire into the real consequences of these agendas on ordinary people. Focusing attention on the rule of law as a broad if not lofty concept diverts attention from the coherence, effectiveness, or legitimacy of specific policies that are pursued to ensure security, promote development, or protect human rights. The rule of law agenda threatens to obfuscate the real trade-offs that need to be made in order to achieve these worthy goals.

The post–Cold War consensus on the rule of law must be seen against the background of two macro-level developments. First, an increasing number of intrastate conflicts around the world have led to concerns of state failure, prompting new generations of peace operations sanctioned by the UN Security Council as well as situations of classic military occupations, such as the situation of Iraq. Second, the structurally violent and divisive nature of development interventions has resulted in human rights violations and other social costs, through such devices as the privatization of key national industries and increased unemployment, and speculative bubbles in international financial transactions that have massive impact on real estate and housing markets, contributing to poverty, mass population displacement and urban migration, the elimination of subsidies for food and services, and the introduction of user fees for infrastructure. Against this background, the relationship between the disparate agendas of development, security, and human rights cannot be underestimated, and the invocation of the rule of law will not substitute for an honest evaluation of the costs and benefits of different policies, norms, and institutions.

I begin by tracing the historical origins of the links between security, development, and human rights discourses since World War II and identify some recurring themes despite real differences between them. I point out the ways in which the lines between these discourses began blurring since the 1970s, and during the post–Cold War period, especially in the context of peace operations. I next discuss the convergence between the human rights and rule of law discourses in the post–Cold War period, but point out the continuing differences between the two, and turn to an examination of the rule of law in the context of development, finding that it is no substitute for human rights, and questioning whether it is even a key requirement for successful economic growth. I also examine the rule of law in the context of security, and find that reliance on this concept cannot hide the more fundamental question of legitimacy in the post–September 11 world. In the field of security, it would not be prudent to lessen the reliance on the discourse of human rights for the fuzzier discourse on the rule of law. In conclusion, I offer some reflections on the lessons that have been learned about how best to capture the synergy that may exist between different fields of international interventions in the security, development, and human rights domains.

Security, Development, and Human Rights: Origins and Relationships

The discourses of security, development, and human rights have diverse origins but multiple, often unrecognized intersections. Briefly put, the discourse of security emerged from the realist critiques of international relations. Influenced by scholars such as Hans Morgenthau, it was primarily conceived in statist terms and was focused on managing the conflicts that arose between nation-states.[2] This notion of security was predominant during the Cold War when threats to the interstate system were perceived to be severe. The security studies scholarship was also correspondingly dominated by political scientists who began by acknowledging the centrality of the doctrine of national security.

The discourse of development, which has been much contested since its emergence in the 1940s, had its origin in colonial rule, development economics, and political development theory, and focused on the economic growth of "new" nation-states after decolonization.[3] Largely utilitarian in its calculus, the discipline of development tended to focus on measurement of aggregate indexes of welfare, drawing on national income estimates from the 1940s.

As can be readily seen, the discourses of security and development were natural allies. Both discourses relied heavily on the notion of the territorial nation-state, and drew their force from their ability to supply content to aspects of nationalism, both territorial and developmental. The welfare of individuals or of substate entities did not figure prominently in the study of either security or development. In addition, the two discourses were interlinked from the beginning for different reasons. Development interventions tended to be seen by Western leaders as one of the best tools available to fight the communist menace, offering incentives for restive rural peasant populations not to rebel, while cementing the patron-client relationships between friendly regimes in power and their key domestic constituencies. As US secretary of state John Foster Dulles stated in 1956, "East and West are in a contest in the field of development of underdeveloped countries. . . . Defeat . . . could be as disastrous as defeat in the arms race."[4] When radical communist movements swept to power in several third world states during the 1950s, the response by the West was swift: the iron fist of repression and foreign intervention was brought down heavily on these countries, while the velvet glove of development was applied to pacify the restive rural masses. For example, these events forced the demotion of Latin America by the United States as an "underdeveloped area," from its prewar status as a region with a range of "advanced" economies, in order to justify its foreign assistance (and therefore security) rationale.[5] Indeed, the different paradigm shifts in development discourse—for example, from growth with redistribution to poverty alleviation and basic needs in the 1970s—were explicable by the proxy wars in the third world between the Cold War blocs.[6] The "war on poverty" announced by Robert McNamara at the World Bank in 1972 had a distinct security rationale to it. Political development theorists provided theoretical support for this by justifying the importance of political stability and repression for economic growth that would prevent the countries concerned from falling to the communists.[7] This focus on the linkage between security and development continues to this day, as demonstrated by the emphasis on development in the US

National Security Strategy, released in 2002, though with a focus on "failing states" and "the embittered few" rather than the communists.[8] Thus the language has changed but not the rationale.

The emergence of the human rights discourse did not fundamentally threaten this symbiotic relationship, at least not at first. Conceived as a set of state obligations toward citizens, the human rights system fit easily into the nation-state-focused world of security and development. The system of human rights did not pose any radical challenges to the state-centric world order—such as by pushing for extranational obligations of states or obligations of nonstate actors—and reaffirmed the same goals that development and security regimes set for themselves. To the extent that there appeared to be any contradictions, human rights law provided for exemptions within the terms of the treaties themselves. For example, the law itself allowed violations where these were needed to preserve political stability, through the concept of public emergency laid down under Article 4 of the International Covenant on Civil and Political Rights. Economic and social rights were conceived of in promotional terms under the International Covenant on Economic, Social, and Cultural Rights that did not seriously threaten the dominant role of the state in the economy by imposing legal limits on the state's ability to guide economic development. Many states in the West (especially in Europe) and the newly independent third world countries widely subscribed to this position during the 1960s. Given the largely voluntarist premises of international human rights law, states could choose to undertake limited obligations that they were comfortable with. Despite this compatibility, the human rights discourse remained largely isolated from the discourses of security and development until the 1970s, and was largely dominated by lawyers.

Significant changes since the 1970s began blurring the lines between the discourses of development, security, and human rights. The story of the relationship between development and human rights is well chronicled elsewhere,[9] but the following key developments in that relationship should be noted:

• The notion of development expanded to include human development measures at the level of the family and the household, chiefly evidenced through reports of the UN Development Programme (UNDP).

• The language of social progress and development emerged from the Declaration of Tehran in 1967 and culminated in the UN General Assembly's Resolution on the Right to Development in 1987. This move followed two decades of attempts by third world countries to elevate development as an international legal norm that would impose legal obligations on rich countries, both to abstain from intervening in third world developmental strategies (such as the pursuit of an industrial policy), and to provide more development assistance.

• The governance agenda in development policy emerged in the late 1980s, focusing attention on governmental failures as the reason behind developmental failures. Arising from the experience of sub-Saharan Africa, this move saw the failure of development as the result of the absence of adequate institutions, both political and economic. At issue were the lack of transparency and accountability of government. This contrasted with the early explanations for the failure of development, which had focused on the absence of the right capital and prices and the absence of an appropriate policy framework for economic growth. This new focus on governance—or "good governance" in the literature of the World Bank—neatly coincided with the rise of the institutionalist turn in development economics, which came to see the legal frameworks of property and contracts as the source of economic growth. This newfound interest in institutions and legal norms had the effect of bringing human rights (which also focused primarily on legal reform) closer to development.

• Rights-based approaches to development emerged in the 1990s in multilateral and bilateral development agencies, combined with a new interest in economic, social, and cultural rights. The move toward a rights-based approach was driven by a paradigm shift within development that began to see development itself as freedom, while retaining a belief that such a new paradigm could lead to changes at the project level, where development is "delivered" to its beneficiaries. The new interest in economic and social rights was driven in large part by the constitutionalization and judicialization of these rights, as part of a wave of democratic transitions and constitution-making across the world.

• High-profile global civil action campaigns arose in countries like Brazil and India, focused on issues of displacement and damage to the environment, which led in turn to the adoption in the 1980s of better standards by the World Bank on internal displacement and respect for indigenous peoples' rights, and to the establishment in the early 1990s of the World Bank Inspection Panel. These mobilizations, which were simultaneously global and local, provided the political background to the move to bring human rights and development closer together.[10]

The discourse of security, too, began to change. First, it was expanded to include understandings of environmental security, focusing attention on environmental damage as the cause and consequence of violent conflicts, including conflicts relating to natural resources.[11] The traditional notion of security was also increasingly challenged by new notions of human security that emphasized human beings over states. Second, the notion of international security was expanded to include intrastate conflicts, which were proliferating rapidly after the end of the Cold War. As the International Commission on Intervention and State Sovereignty reported in 2001, the changing nature of armed conflict in the world was reflected in the fact that 90 percent of the people killed in armed conflicts in the late twentieth century were civilians, compared to only one out of ten at the beginning of the century.[12] Third, the source of threats to world order also changed, from classic state-based threats to non-state threats including terrorism, drug trafficking, and transnational organized crime. This expanded understanding of security shared many common elements with the most evolved thinking in development, which together indicated that the older consensus on the development-security linkage had broken down and been replaced with a new one that had human rights at its core.

This was problematic, however. The language of human rights had been appropriated as part of numerous peoples' struggles around the world, and it could not so readily be deployed as a tool of governance in the fields of development or security. In other words, development and security experts were working with relatively conflict-free notions of human rights that could be used to program activities in their respective fields, and this proved to be a problem. For every attempt to engage in "rights talk" by a development agency, a local actor such as a nongovernmental organization (NGO) or a social movement would offer an oppositional reading of rights. Rights discourse is in fact constantly appropriated for oppositional struggles, which makes it a particularly difficult device for governance strategies. For example, the World Commission on Dams attempted to build a new set of prescriptions for better dam building based on a human rights–influenced "rights and risks" approach.[13] For large dam-building states like India and China, this attempt to use human rights as a basis of governance proved to be too discomforting and they ended up rejecting the commission's report. However, for the NGOs and social movements of the people displaced by dams, the "rights and risks" approach provided a minimal political safeguard that their interests would be taken into account. This "counterhegemonic" function of rights, as I have called it elsewhere,[14] proved sufficiently problematic for the fields of development and security. Thus the links with the human rights discourse may, as a result, be in the process of being replaced with another more malleable discourse on the rule of law, as will be elaborated below. The relationship between development, security, and human rights had become confusingly self-referential and circular, each discourse pointing to the other as either the precondition for its own success or the reason for its failure. Notions such as human development and human security also muddied the waters by often equating their meaning to the full achievement of human rights, without being clear about how each is distinct.[15]

The new post–Cold War consensus on development, security, and human rights could be said to have the following characteristics. First, there has been a move away from the nation-state as the focus of development and toward the individuals and various subgroups (women, children, small farmers, etc.) living within it. Second, state failure is regarded as responsible for common and grave challenges in the fields of security, development, and human rights, and therefore saving "failed states" is seen as a priority for the international community. Third, there has been a corresponding redefinition of sovereignty from that of a right of a state to exclusive domestic control, to a responsibility of a state to protect its citizens. Finally, there is now a focus on the rule of law as the tool that will help achieve the goals of development, security, and human rights.

Human Rights and the Rule of Law: Conceptual Convergence or Divergence?

The new focus on human rights in the fields of development and security was proving to be rather uncertain for the reasons advanced above, including the open-ended nature of human rights and their use by opposing actors, the persisting tensions and trade-offs between the goals of development, security, and human rights, and the circular, self-referential nature of the convergence between the three discourses. While it was clear that development needed to transform itself from macro-level aggregates of human welfare computed according to a utilitarian calculus to focus on individuals, voice, and accountability, the language of human rights was proving to be highly contentious as a means toward that end. Similarly, while it was clear that traditional state-based notions of security were unhelpful, the notion of human security was proving difficult to realize, partly because it did not seem to have an agreed core of meaning and often simply came to mean a respect for human rights.

The rule of law came to be seen, in many ways, as a convenient substitute for human rights. Unlike human rights, the rule of law does not promise the achievement of any substantive social, political, or cultural goal. It is much more empty of content and capable of being interpreted in many diverse, sometimes contradictory ways. The human rights discourse is a discourse of social transformation and even emancipation, whereas the rule of law discourse does not have that ambition and may be seen as inherently conservative. This is largely, but not only, due to the association of the rule of law with a culture of law and order of the state, whereas the human rights discourse has conventionally been seen as articulating the entitlements of individuals and groups to be free from violence of various types. Especially in its nonlegal forms, the human rights discourse is a powerful tool for social change due to its normative commitment. By contrast, the rule of law discourse is far more compatible with the discourse of development, which retained its aversion to normative talk due to its roots in economics. Besides, since the 1980s, an important part of the development discourse had come to emphasize the importance of institutions, including legal norms, for achieving economic growth. Known as the "new institutionalists," these economic historians and rational choice institutionalists increasingly pointed to the importance of property rights, contract rights, and an independent and impartial judiciary for achieving economic growth.[16] This had a major impact on development policy and practice, and led to an exponential increase in the resources available for rule of law programming.[17] More important, the role of legal norms and institutions (both formal and informal) became much more central to the development discourse, and the rule of law became almost a "trope" for the many different things that the new institutionalists thought law could do to foster development. The rule of law discourse was also much more compatible with this strand of development theory, with its more neutral focus on formal realizability, the supremacy of law, and the emphasis on process. Despite the seminal work of Amartya Sen[18] and the significant efforts to mainstream it within the development discourse,[19] the human rights discourse has never been obviously compatible with conventional development approaches.

Yet in recent years the rule of law and human rights have been used in conjunction, as if they were indissociable. Alternatively, an expanded understanding of the rule of law is also being used, encompassing some notions of "rights" or "justice." Throughout the 1990s, one could see this tendency in the field of security, especially in the area of peacebuilding.[20] In the development realm, this expanded approach to the rule of law could be seen in the rhetoric of the World Bank, which in a 2002 policy document stated that the rule of law prevails where: (1) the government itself is bound by the law, (2) every person is treated equally under the law, (3) the human dignity of each individual is recognized and protected by law, and (4) justice is accessible to all.[21]

However, this ostensible convergence between the rule of law and human rights is more apparent than real. Historically, the connection between the human rights discourse and the rule of law was relatively tenuous. Despite the reference to the rule of law in the preamble of the Universal Declaration of Human Rights (1948),[22] the relationship between the rule of law and human rights has been unclear and is in fact one of the least-analyzed from a theoretical perspective. In fact, the notion of the rule of law was fundamentally challenged after the experience of the Nazi regime, which was, after all, a regime based on a fairly scrupulous commitment to legal rules and administrative regulations. Despite the seminal German contribution to the rule of law since the nineteenth century, including through the concept of *Rechtstaat,* the idea that the rule of law could prevent barbarities was discredited after the Nazi experience. The human rights discourse in fact reflects this ambivalence. The Universal Declaration itself invokes the rule of law only as a defensive mechanism against self-help and mob justice, but not as a precondition or necessity for the realization of human rights. There is in fact no general right of access to or enjoyment of the rule of law in international human rights law. The human rights covenants do not require that human rights should, under all circumstances, be guaranteed only through law, but only that law is one of many other "measures" that may be necessary to realize rights.[23] At the core of this debate is a larger jurisprudential question that has divided scholars since the Nazi atrocities, as to whether or not the rule of law has a moral core (see Chapter 2). Given this complex history and the ambivalence of human rights instruments, it is not accurate to speak, as many often do, of the rule of law and human rights as synonymous concepts.

In the end, despite some convergences, the rule of law remains sufficiently distinctive from human rights conceptually and practically. The human rights discourse remains a language of counterhegemonic resistance or even social emancipation, easily appropriated by myriad forms of popular struggles around the world or a language of hegemony and discipline, a facade that hides the agendas of powerful elites. The rule of law discourse has neither such linkage with popular politics nor sufficient distance from the agendas of the powerful. The centrality of the rule of law in the 1990s had more to do with a focus on security issues in peace agreements and the development discourse's new emphasis on institutions, than its convergence with human rights.

Rule of Law and Development: Problems of Coherence

The idea that law matters for economic performance has been around for a long time. At least since the late nineteenth century, and certainly since Max Weber, the German contribution to this idea has been central.[24] Weber stressed that the rise of modern capitalism was intimately linked to the rise of a particular form of law that he called "formal rationality."[25] He discussed this notion of ideal-type formal rationality in the context of his well-known discussion about the bureaucracy.[26] This Weberian insight lies at the core of today's prescriptions for rule of law reforms as the prerequisite for economic development. Whatever the rule of law may have meant in German legal thought or in Weber's writings, that concept has come to mean something much narrower and technical in the economic discourse emanating from development institutions such as the World Bank,[27] as well as in the influential writings of Hernando De Soto.[28] Under this much narrower definition, the rule of law has come to mean simply those institutions that are important for the creation and operation of an ideal-type free market *and nothing more.* Prescriptively, this means that rule of law rhetoric in economic development usually focuses on the creation of "clear" property and contract rights,[29] on formal law and on formalization of informal or social norms,[30] and on the centrality of the judiciary as a dispute resolution mechanism that will apply rules mechanically and without discretion, creating predictability for economic actors.[31] It is not concerned with the distributional outcomes of the market itself, which it leaves to other domains such as politics to deal with. The rule of law then becomes, as David Kennedy has noted, a substitute for development rather than a means leading to it.[32] Nor is it concerned with the idea that the rule of law might mean something more than a toolkit for marketization. I would suggest that this definition of the rule of law in the context of development raises serious problems of coherence and may hide contradictions between development and security or human rights agendas themselves.

This could be illustrated by taking the dominant prescriptive strands of development policy on the rule of law. First, the emphasis on "clear" property and contract rights sounds intuitively good. But this easy consensus hides the discomforting fact that clear property rights—in the sense of clear rights to exclude, for example—may not be needed for fast economic development. The economic record of China is certainly not attributable to clear property rights, and yet it is hailed as an economic miracle due to its record-setting rates of growth. At the micro level, there is increasing evidence that vigorous markets in areas like housing and land are possible even in the absence of clear, rigid, and formal property rights.[33] Indeed, creating too many clear and rigid property rights may even impede the growth of markets, especially in contexts of economic transition.[34] Also, the emphasis on clear property rights hides the question of distributional consequences—in other words, who should benefit or lose from the new and clear property rights. From a security and human rights perspective, these are key questions. A property rights regime that ends up concentrating land or other productive assets in the hands of a minority, especially if that minority is from a different ethnic, racial, or religious group, may very well alter the character of the state itself and lead to violent responses or discriminatory policies.[35] In a postconflict situation, a rigid approach to property rights may also end up preventing a new government from pursuing effective policies for reconciliation and even reparation through effective land reform, as happened in South Africa.[36]

A response to this critique may be that development institutions, such as the World Bank, are prevented from prescribing policies that touch on political considerations,[37] and that distributional questions are the domain of domestic politics. Such a response would not be convincing in the final analysis, for at least a couple reasons. First, in legal literature, questions of distribution have been long recognized as central to the efficient (not just fair) operation of a market economy in the West.[38] This makes questions of distribution intrinsically important for achieving effective progrowth policies, and not merely as an afterthought or charity. Second, external actors (including development actors) cannot take the position that they are not responsible for the social impacts of market-related policies such as the push for "clear" property rights, if such policies undermine security or human rights. Rwanda and the Balkans, for example, are well-known examples where unwise macroeconomic policies significantly contributed to ethnic violence and state failure.[39] This raises important questions about the accountability and responsibility of external actors for their policies within developing countries or countries in so-called transition.

A second prescriptive strand of rule of law strategies in development policy focuses on formal rules as the core of the rule of law. Despite the obvious appeal of thinking of formal rules as superior to informal rules—they are written, known in advance, capable of being understood more precisely, and therefore lead to greater predictability in economic exchanges, among other things—the formalization focus seems misplaced or ideological, for several reasons. First, it has long been recognized in legal thought, at least since the legal realist school of the early twentieth century, that the legal system is not a complete regime of formal norms, but allows the interplay of informal norms in ordering social relations including in the economic sphere. In private law adjudication of torts, contracts, and property, this phenomenon is rampant and manifests itself in many ways, including through the distinction between rules and standards.[40] Given this, the advocacy of a purely formal law approach has a kind of Alice-in-Wonderland feel to it. Second, the advocacy of formal law implicitly (and often explicitly) equates informality with illegality, and advocates the replacement of illegal, informal norms with formal, legal norms, a line of argument famously popularized by Hernando De Soto, for example.[41] This completely overlooks a very rich literature on informal norms and institutions in sociolegal studies and on pluralism in legal anthropology, which has long documented the coexistence of multiple legal and normative orders in which the statist, formal legal order is only one of many.[42] In addition, more recent research has also begun to problematize the neat dichotomy between, on the one hand, state, legal, and formal, and on the other hand, nonstate, illegal, and informal.[43] Instead, this literature has posited that legal and illegal norms and institutions are often deeply intertwined with each other, in a process wherein one could see the state as very much involved in the production of illegality while illegal norms and processes shape the very structures of the state itself. This focus on what has been called the "empirical state," a view that attempts to see "states from below and from within as much as from above,"[44] problematizes the typical understanding of the illegal and informal as deviant behaviors that will eventually be replaced by state law, while avoiding the romanticism of informal legal orders that are sometimes typical of the legal pluralism literature.

The third strand of rule of law strategies in development policy focuses on the judiciary and imagines adjudication as a mechanical exercise wherein typical bureaucratic discretion is eliminated. In this approach the rule of law is idealized as a relief from rent-seeking activities of the executive or the interest-group balancing of the legislative branches. It also pictures the judiciary purely as a dispute resolution mechanism (in reality, perhaps only in commercial cases). This image of the judiciary dominates much of the current literature, for example in law and economics.[45] This emphasis on the mechanical nature of judicial processes also often leads to the advocacy of simple formal norms, resting on the idea that complex norms may call for complex judicial techniques, such as interest balancing or efficiency analysis, that judges in poor countries may not be competent to undertake.[46] The mechanical nature of adjudication has little to do with the nature of the legal system itself—for example, common law or civil law—which may in fact differ less than is commonly assumed.[47] Many of these beliefs seem to overlook elementary lessons of legal thought while sometimes asserting highly contradictory ideas. The mechanical image of the judge certainly cannot be squared with the knowledge, shared by almost all legal thinkers, that rules are always incomplete, inconsistent, and ambiguous, and that the role of the judge is to resolve this through a process of interpretation. Legal realists argued that the law-politics distinction becomes blurred in this process of interpretation, while the critical legal theorists have argued that judicial reasoning may show a bias or ideology that may systematically lead to domination by elites.[48] Liberals like Ronald Dworkin see judicial interpretation as leading to the introduction of principles to fill gaps and resolve conflicts between the rules themselves.[49] Early US legal thinkers, from Karl Llewellyn to Oliver Wendell Holmes (who espoused the sociological jurisprudence method), would not have shared this mechanical view of the judge's role. Even modern law could be said to share a very pragmatic orientation to adjudication, in its call to judges to look outside the law (though only to economics) to find solutions to legal problems.[50] In fact, emerging literature in economics is itself beginning to cast doubt on whether the introduction of formal norms and a mechanical judiciary is actually leading to economically efficient outcomes.[51]

It is clear that this idealized—and ideologized—image of the rule law does not lead to development, even narrowly conceived as economic growth. But it has problematic implications for human rights and security as well. A narrow conception of the judge, for example, often leads to arguments by scholars like Richard Posner that human rights laws should not be introduced in developing countries if economic growth is to be favored.[52] Indeed, a call for the rule of law in the context of plural legal orders is often a call for the assertion of the superiority of state law over nonstate law, through the coercive power of the state to achieve particular outcomes that favor some. This can be seen in the advocacy to override customary property rights with "registered land titles" in countries like Kenya, for example,[53] which may create problems from a security or human rights perspective in postconflict or transitional contexts. Finally, as I have argued above and elsewhere,[54] the human rights discourse has a political and counterhegemonic function that makes it much more critical than the development discourse. The rule of law discourse will not easily replace it, for this very reason. Thus the call for the rule of law discourse is a call to use state law to prefer some methods and consequences relating to development, human rights, and security, and must not be interpreted as a call to respect human rights. Rather, there needs to be a more critical evaluation of the uses of the rule of law in particular contexts.

The Rule of Law and Security: Problems of Legitimacy

As explained earlier, the concept of international security has fundamentally changed in recent years—the former state-based, territorial notion of security has now been supplanted by a more comprehensive notion of security. The 2004 report of the High-Level Panel on Threats, Challenges, and Change, created by the UN Secretary-General, describes this as follows: "any event or process that leads to large scale death or lessening of life chances and undermines States as the basic unit of the international system, is a threat to international security."[55] It then goes on to include six clusters of threats within this definition: environmental and social threats including poverty, infectious disease, and environmental degradation; interstate conflict; internal conflict, including civil war, genocide, and other large-scale atrocities; nuclear, radiological, chemical, and biological weapons; terrorism; and transnational organized crime.[56] With this holistic approach, the report joins a chorus of calls to expand the narrow definition of state security, to include environmental security and human security.[57] Indeed, the National Security Strategy of the United States makes this linkage between poverty and security quite clear and asserts that poverty can make weak states vulnerable to terrorist networks and drug cartels within its borders.[58] With this move, poverty itself becomes a security threat, so that the means of responding to it become more militarized. Poverty alleviation—through the Millennium Development Goals, for example—becomes a means of addressing a security threat, as opposed to a set of tools that are required either because of moral duties toward the poor or because of a broad-based economic development strategy.[59] Therefore, a logical conclusion from this new approach would be that military interventions to secure development goals or to deal with environmental catastrophes would be legitimate and perhaps even lawful. This is not a fanciful line of thinking: one could recall the important, perhaps unwitting, role that the UNDP's 2002 report on Arab human development played in supporting the neoconservative argument for the Iraq war, by pointing to the role of gender inequality and poverty in Arab "backwardness."[60] The timing of that report did not hurt the broad US agenda of modernizing the Middle East by force. Rather, to the contrary, it helped generate a hegemonic consensus that forcible intervention was for the good of the Arab people. Of course, human rights–based arguments have been used many times by hegemonic states to justify their interventions, in the form of the doctrine of humanitarian intervention.[61] Human rights groups such as Human Rights Watch were similarly inadvertent allies of the Iraq war effort by refusing to evaluate the legality of the war effort itself, while highlighting the terrible human rights record of the Iraqi regime, thereby bolstering the argument of the war hawks that the use of force was justified against the Baghdad dictator. Similarly, the aftermath of the Asian tsunami in early 2005 saw a tremendous level of military intervention and jockeying between states that were eager to show how capable their respective military forces were in responding to natural disasters. This "securitization of everything" is, in this sense, not new, though it is the first time that a UN-appointed panel is endorsing such a broad definition. What does one make of this move, and how is this related to the rule of law?

One could begin by noting that the term "rule of law" is not used in the High-Level Panel's report itself. The sections of the report that seem most pertinent to the issue are Parts 3 and 4, which deal, inter alia, with the role of the

Security Council. Here, the report firmly supports the view that the Security Council must be the sole authority to authorize the use of force in cases that fall outside the purview of Article 51 of the UN Charter.[62] This commitment to multilateralism is coupled with an acknowledgment that the Council needs to be reformed, and with two proposed models for change in its membership. While this commitment to seek structural change in the way the current international order is managed is to be welcomed, the report is silent on the question of the Council's compliance with international law, and only refers to the Council's lack of accountability through the rather weak call for "civil society engagement."[63] Similarly, though the report recognizes that the "war on terror" within many countries has itself emerged as a major threat to human rights and the rule of law,[64] it offers no concrete recommendations for making the "war on terror" conform to human rights or the rule of law. The Secretary-General's own report, building on the High-Level Panel's report, continues in the same vein, by failing to address the Security Council's own history of noncompliance with human rights standards, or the problematic aspects of the "war on terror."[65] The Council's record since the end of the Cold War has raised problematic questions about its commitment to human rights, ranging from policy failures (such as the failure to take action in specific human rights crises) to active collaborations in human rights violations (imposing economic sanctions that lead to large numbers of deaths, providing the cover of legitimacy to wars of aggression). The key problem here arises from the fact that the Secretary-General uses the term "rule of law" to mean many things, including multilateralism, a commitment to the UN Charter, and human rights principles. While this maximalist approach to the meaning of the rule of law may be, and indeed is, laudable, the Security Council will find it almost impossible to comply with such an expanded notion of the rule of law in its own actions, at least as judged by its past record. In addition, the implications of a broad approach to defining security are not readily apparent, especially relating to the role of the Security Council. Would the Council be expected to act under Chapter VII of the Charter to end massive human insecurity of any kind, including insecurity caused by poverty or natural disasters? That seems unlikely and even unwise, as it would multiply the grounds—and pretexts—for use of force in international relations at a time of hegemonic relations between states.

These two related failures—a failure to critically focus on the Security Council and a failure to critically evaluate the "war on terror"—are in fact very much interrelated. They undermine the whole attempt to articulate a broad notion of security as they raise concerns that an unaccountable Security Council (even if it is expanded numerically) may end up flouting human rights and the rule of law in the name of responding to myriad nontraditional threats. They also raise important questions of the legitimacy of Security Council actions under Chapters VI and VII of the Charter to pursue rule of law programs in peace operations, when the Council itself overlooks the rule of law in its own functioning. The former Secretary-General in fact sees this connection quite clearly. In his speech at the opening of the fifty-ninth session of the General Assembly in 2004, Kofi Annan stated: "Those who seek to bestow legitimacy must themselves embody it; and those who invoke international law must themselves submit to it." He further added that "every nation that proclaims the rule of law at home must respect it abroad; and every nation that insists on it abroad must enforce it at home."[66] These Delphic pronouncements point to an important truth: that the absence of the rule of law (however one may define it) in domestic contexts has to be linked with the absence of the rule of law at the international level. This absence of the rule of law is not merely evidenced by the more obvious example of the US decision to sidestep the Security Council in its war against Iraq. More problematically, it relates to the actions of the Security Council itself as it authorizes what many consider to be arbitrary if not unlawful actions through its counterterrorism committee, created under Security Council Resolution 1373.[67] Many of its actions arguably flout basic protections extended under human rights treaties, and available under customary international law, such as the presumption of innocence, the right to confront one's accusers, and even the right to a remedy, which are not automatically available under the Council's procedures. The perceived absence of the rule of law, especially in its expanded meaning that includes human rights, in the actions of the Security Council, makes it more difficult to advance those notions within domestic contexts, especially through peace operations authorized by the Council itself. This "legitimacy deficit" is compounded by a gathering sense that for all the talk about "comprehensive security" in the High-Level Panel's report, it remains overwhelmingly focused on the idea that the proper response to terrorism consists of rebuilding and strengthening so-called weak or failed states.[68] In this new world of strong states, softer goals such as development, environmental protection, and human rights are likely to take a back seat, while nation-building strategies are likely to focus on the imposition of order from the outside,[69] evoking concerns about the return of formal colonialism. Such an externally driven approach is unlikely to elicit much concern for the rule of law (however narrowly or broadly it is defined). These concerns, which matter for the legitimacy of the rule of law in the domain of security, need to be addressed much more robustly.

Conclusion

The discourses of security, development, and human rights have gradually merged. The key challenges to security are now seen to come not from invading armadas of strong states but from well-organized groups of transnationally linked terrorists who operate in "failed" or weak states that are unable or unwilling to stop them. Security is also now more broadly conceived to mean human and state security. Development challenges are currently thought to arise from the absence of viable state institutions, including a judiciary and formal laws that protect property and contracts. Human rights challenges are also increasingly seen as particularly acute in situations where states have failed or are too weak to stop massive abuses. There is in other words a consensus that state failure or failure of governance is the root of all the problems in these disparate areas of security, development, and human rights. This consensus has in turn led to a focus on the rule of law as a way of rebuilding or strengthening the state. But using the rule of law as a way to build up states will not resolve the tensions between the disparate agendas of development, security, and human rights themselves. It is not my argument here that the rule of law is a pernicious idea or a Trojan horse. Effective governance of any society cannot rest on any basis other than law. But the term "rule of law" is currently capable of too many disparate meanings depending on the international policy agenda in which it is invoked.

The invocation of the rule of law will be of limited relevance if there are conflicts between the agendas themselves—for example, between human rights and development or between human rights and security—and will not resolve fundamental contradictions between these various agendas. The current discourse, reflected in the High-Level Panel's report and the Secretary General's reports, is remarkably conflict-free and assumes a harmonious and mutually reinforcing relationship between development, human rights, and security. This assumption is unwarranted and even perhaps ideological. Promoting the rule of law as part of disparate policy agendas also creates uncertainty in terms of the outcomes of programmatic approaches—in other words, it is not clear who will be the losers and who will be the beneficiaries as a result of the implementation of these various policy agendas. A commitment to the formalization of informal property may mean, for example, that foreign investors are able to buy more land in an urban area and that local entrepreneurs are bought out. It may indeed be the outcome that a particular society and government desires to achieve. But it does not help to camouflage that outcome in the language of the rule of law as though it is justified by the very rationality and objectivity of the law itself.

Neither does a commitment to the rule of law as a way to rebuild or strengthen the state answer the question of how large or small the state needs to be. Nor does it resolve the question of whether the state needs to be strong in some areas while weak in others. The answers to these questions are likely to vary dramatically depending on the local and national contexts and the particular policy components of the agendas themselves. Finally, the commitment to establish the rule of law within failed states will be fundamentally undermined if the international rule of law is not given greater consideration, especially where rule of law programs are pursued through peace operations authorized by the Security Council. It is most unfortunate that the recent flood of UN reports do not deal with this issue with the seriousness it requires.

Notes

I thank the participants in the workshops organized by the International Peace Academy in New York for their comments on a very early draft of this chapter. I also thank Diane Davis and Mike Pugh for comments on a previous draft. Special thanks are due to Agnès Hurwitz, the volume editor, for her comments, warmth, and enthusiasm. Responsibility for all errors is mine.

1. Thomas Carothers, "The Rule of Law Revival," *Foreign Affairs* 77 (March–April 1998): 95–106.

2. See Hans J. Morgenthau, *Politics Among Nations: The Struggle for Power and Peace* (New York: Knopf, 1978).

3. See Arturo Escobar, *Encountering Development: The Making and Unmaking of the Third World* (Princeton: Princeton University Press, 1994); Wolfgang Sachs, ed., *Development Dictionary: A Guide to Knowledge as Power* (Atlantic Highlands, N.J.: Zed, 1992); Ha-Joon Chang, *Kicking Away the Ladder: Development Strategy in Historical Perspective* (London: Anthem, 2002).

4. Cited in Clifton Daniel, ed., *Chronicle of the 20th Century* (Mount Kisco, N.Y.: Chronicle, 1987), p. 776.

5. Devesh Kapur, John P. Lewis, and Richard Webb, *The World Bank: Its First Half Century* (Washington, D.C.: Brookings Institution, 1997), p. 143.

6. For a discussion, see ibid.

7. See Samuel Huntington, *Political Order in Changing Societies* (New Haven: Yale University Press, 1968).

8. US Department of State, *The National Security Strategy of the United States of America,* http://www.whitehouse.gov/nsc/nss.html.

9. Balakrishnan Rajagopal, *International Law from Below: Development, Social Movements, and Third World Resistance* (New York: Cambridge University Press, 2003), chap. 7.

10. Ibid.

11. There is a very rich and complex literature on environmental security. A good source is the Environmental Change and Security Project at the Woodrow Wilson Center for International Scholars; see http://www.wilsoncenter.org/index.cfm?fuseaction=topics.home&topic_id=1413. Two recent samples of the literature are Ken Conca and Geoffrey D. Dabelko, eds., *Environmental Peacemaking* (Baltimore: Johns Hopkins University Press, 2002); and Nancy Lee Peluso and Michael Watts, *Violent Environments* (Ithaca: Cornell University Press, 2001).

12. International Development Research Centre, *The Responsibility to Protect: Report of the International Commission on Intervention and State Sovereignty* (Ottawa, December 2001), p. 13.

13. See World Commission on Dams, *Dams and Development: A New Framework for Decision-Making* (Sterling, Va.: Earthscan, 2000).

14. Rajagopal, *International Law from Below,* chap. 8.

15. See, for example, UNDP, *Human Development Report 2000* (New York: Oxford University Press, 2000). See also Commission on Human Security, *Human Security Now* (2003), http://www.humansecurity-chs.org/finalreport/index.html.

16. See, for example, Douglas North, *Institutions, Institutional Change, and Economic Performance* (New York: Cambridge University Press, 1990); World Bank, *World Development Report: Building Institutions for Markets* (New York: Oxford University Press, 2002); Christopher Clague, *Institutions and Economic Development: Growth and Governance in Less Developed and Post-Socialist Countries* (Baltimore: Johns Hopkins University Press, 1997).

17. On the impact on development policy, see, for example, World Bank, *World Development Report: Building Institutions for Markets;* Hernando De Soto, *The Mystery of Capital: Why Capitalism Triumphs in the West and Fails Everywhere Else* (New York: Basic, 2000).

18. See, for example, Amartya Sen, *Development as Freedom* (New York: Knopf, 1999).

19. For a discussion, see Rajagopal, *International Law from Below,* chap. 7.

20. United Nations, *Supplement to An Agenda for Peace: Position Paper of the Secretary-General on the Occasion of the Fiftieth Anniversary of the United Nations,* UN Doc. A/50/60 (January 3, 1995). See also United Nations, *Report of the Panel on UN Peace Operations* (Brahimi Report), UN Doc. A/55/305-S/2000/809 (August 21, 2004).

21. World Bank, "Legal and Judicial Reform: Observations, Experiences and Approach of the Legal Vice Presidency" (Washington, D.C., July 2002).

22. United Nations, *Universal Declaration of Human Rights,* Preamble, recital 3: "Whereas it is essential, if man is not to be compelled to have recourse, as a last resort, to rebellion against tyranny and oppression, that human rights should be protected by the rule of law."

23. United Nations, *International Covenant on Economic, Social, and Cultural Rights,* art. 2(1); United Nations, *International Covenant on Civil and Political Rights,* art. 2(2), referring to "legislative or other measures."

24. David Trubek, "Max Weber on Law and the Rise of Capitalism," *Wisconsin Law Review* 3 (1972): 720–753.

25. Max Weber, *Economy and Society: An Outline of Interpretive Sociology* (New York: Bedminster, 1968).

26. Ibid., pp. 217–223.

27. A classic introduction is World Bank, "Legal Institutions and the Rule of Law" in *World Development Report: From Plan to Market* (New York: Oxford University Press, 1996). A more recent, and more nuanced, example that shows the influence of the new institutional economics literature is World Bank, Introduction to *World Development Report: Building Institutions for Markets.*

28. De Soto, *The Mystery of Capital.*

29. World Bank, "Legal Institutions and the Rule of Law."

30. De Soto, *The Mystery of Capital;* World Bank, *World Development Report: Building Institutions for Markets,* chap. 9.

31. World Bank, *World Development Report: Building Institutions for Markets,* chap. 6. For an example of the interest among economists about the role of courts, see Simeon Djankov, Rafael La Porta, Florencio Lopez-De-Silanes, and Andrei Shleifer, "Courts," *Quarterly Journal of Economics* 118, no. 2 (May 2, 2003): 453–517.

32. David Kennedy, *The Dark Sides of Virtue: Reassessing International Humanitarianism* (Princeton: Princeton University Press, 2004).

33. See, for example, Omar Razzaz, "Land Disputes in the Absence of Ownership Rights: Insights from Jordan," in *Illegal Cities: Law and Urban Change in Developing Countries,* edited by Edesio Fernandes (New York: St. Martin's, 1998); Mona Fawaz, "Strategizing for Housing: An Investigation of the Production and Regulation of Low-Income Housing in the Suburbs of Beirut," PhD diss., Cambridge, Massachusetts Institute of Technology, 2004.

34. See Michael A. Heller, "The Tragedy of the Anticommons: Property in the Transition from Marx to Markets," *Harvard Law Review* 111, no. 3 (1998): 621.

35. For a provocative argument that this has happened with alarming regularity when free-market policies have been simultaneously introduced with democratization as joint recipes for political and economic transition, see Amy Chua, *World on Fire:*

How Exporting Free Market Democracy Breeds Ethnic Hatred and Global Instability (New York: Doubleday, 2003).

36. For an early warning, see Shadrack B. O. Gutto, *Property and Land Reform: Constitutional and Jurisprudential Perspectives* (Johannesburg: Butterworths, 1995).

37. This has been a standard response by the World Bank's legal counsel over several decades, based on the prohibition contained in Article 4 of its Articles of Agreement. But the World Bank is increasingly adopting frameworks of analysis that openly acknowledge and advocate political and institutional changes as key prerequisites of reform in many areas. For example, the World Bank has advocated a significant role of the state to secure socially desirable land use, especially in postconflict settings. See Klaus Deininger, *Land Policies for Growth and Poverty Reduction* (Washington, D.C.: World Bank and Oxford University Press, 2003), chap. 4. It is not clear if this new turn to politics means that the World Bank has abandoned strict compliance with Article 4 of its Articles of Agreement, or whether it is simply a sign of plural voices within a large and complex bureaucracy.

38. See, for example, Frank Michelman, "Possession vs. Distribution in the Constitutional Idea of Property," *Iowa Law Review* 72, no. 5 (July 1987): 1319.

39. R. Andersen, "How Multilateral Development Assistance Triggered the Conflict in Rwanda," *Third World Quarterly* 21, no. 3 (2000): 441–456; Anne Orford, "Locating the International: Military and Monetary Interventions After the Cold War," *Harvard International Law Journal* 38 (1997): 443–485, relying on Susan Woodward, *Balkan Tragedy: Chaos and Dissolution After the Cold War* (Washington, D.C.: Brookings Institution, 1995).

40. See Duncan Kennedy, "Form and Substance in Private Law Adjudication," *Harvard Law Review* 89 (1976): 1685. This is also recognized by legal scholars writing in different legal traditions including law and economics. See, for example, Carol Rose, "Crystals and Mud in Property Law," *Stanford Law Review* 40, no. 3 (1988): 577.

41. De Soto, *The Mystery of Capital.*

42. See, for example, Boaventura de Sousa Santos, "The Law of the Oppressed: The Construction and Reproduction of Legality in Pasagada," *Law and Society Review* 14, no. 3 (1977): 279–302; Lauren Benton, "Beyond Legal Pluralism: Towards a New Approach to Law in the Informal Sector," *Social and Legal Studies* 3, no. 2 (1994): 223–242. See also Sally Engle Merry, "Legal Pluralism," *Law and Society Review* 22, no. 5 (1988): 869–896; Omar Razzaz, "Land Disputes in the Absence of Ownership Rights: Insights from Jordan," in Fernandes, *Illegal Cities.*

43. See Josiah Heyman, *States and Illegal Practices* (New York: Berg, 1999). See also Fernandes *Illegal Cities.*

44. See Heyman, *States and Illegal Practices,* p. 20.

45. See Richard Posner, "Creating a Legal Framework for Economic Development," *World Bank Research Observer* 13, no. 1 (1998): 1–11.

46. Ibid.

47. See Martin Shapiro, "The Success of Judicial Review," in *Constitutional Dialogues in Comparative Perspective,* edited by Sally J. Kenney (New York: St. Martin's, 1999).

48. See Duncan Kennedy, *A Critique of Adjudication* [fin de siècle] (Cambridge: Harvard University Press, 1997).

49. Ronald Dworkin, *Law's Empire* (Cambridge, Mass.: Harvard University Press, 1986).

50. See Richard Posner, *The Problems of Jurisprudence* (Cambridge, Mass.: Harvard University Press, 1990).

51. See Djankov et al., "Courts."

52. See Posner, *The Problems of Jurisprudence.*

53. For a detailed analysis, see Joel Ngugi, "Re-examining the Role of Private Property in Market Democracies: Problematic Ideological Issues Raised by Land Registration," *Michigan Journal of International Law* 25, no. 2 (2004): 467–527.

54. Rajagopal, *International Law from Below,* chap. 8.

55. United Nations, *A More Secure World: Our Shared Responsibility—Report of the Secretary General's High-Level Panel on Threats, Challenges, and Change,* UN Doc. A/59/565 (December 1, 2004), 25.

56. Ibid., pt. II.

57. Commission on Human Security, *Human Security Now.*

58. See US Department of State, Introduction to *National Security Strategy of the United States.*

59. Indeed, this could be said to be one of the weaknesses of the UN report on the Millennium Development goals, to the extent that the report advocates what could be termed as a "Washington Consensus Plus" approach to poverty alleviation rather than encouraging plural paths of economic development. See UN Millennium Project, *Investing in Development: Practical Plans to Achieve the Millennium Development Goals* (New York: Millennium Project Secretariat, 2005).

60. UNDP, *Arab Human Development Report: Creating Opportunities for Future Generations* (New York, 2002). For a commentary, see Thomas Friedman, "The Arabs at the Crossroads," *New York Times,* July 3, 2002.

61. See, for example, Fernando Teson, *Humanitarian Intervention: An Inquiry into Law and Morality* (Irvington-on-Hudson, N.Y.: Transnational, 1997).

62. UN Charter, art. 51: "Nothing in the present Charter shall impair the inherent right of individual or collective self-defence if an armed attack occurs against a Member of the United Nations, until the Security Council has taken measures necessary to maintain international peace and security. Measures taken by Members in the exercise of this right of self-defence shall be immediately reported to the Security Council and shall not in any way affect the authority and responsibility of the Security Council under the present Charter to take at any time such action as it deems necessary in order to maintain or restore international peace and security."

63. See United Nations, *A More Secure World,* p. 83.

64. Ibid., p. 48.

65. United Nations, *In Larger Freedom: Towards Development, Security and Human Rights for All—Report of the Secretary General,* UN Doc. A/59/2005 (March 21, 2005).

66. United Nations, *Rule of Law at Risk Around the World, Says Secretary-General in Address to General Assembly,* Press Release no. SG/SM/9491 (September 21, 2004).

67. See, for example, Human Rights Watch, "Hear No Evil, See No Evil: The U.N. Security Council's Approach to Human Rights Violations in the Global Counter-Terrorism Effort," briefing paper, August 10, 2004. For a review of some of the problems of legitimacy and the level of contention at the Security Council, see Jose Alvarez, "The Security Council's War on Terrorism: Problems and Policy Options," in *Judicial Review of the Security Council by Member States,* edited by Erika de Wet and André Nollkaemper (Amsterdam: Amsterdam Center of International Law, 2003); Edward Luck, "Tackling Terrorism," in *The UN Security Council: From the Cold War to the 21st Century,* edited by David M. Malone (Boulder: Lynne Rienner, 2004).

68. This is not surprising since the discourse of failed or weak states had already emerged as part of the mainstream policy and legal discourse in the 1990s and the link between weak states and US national security had been well recognized. For a critical

review of the failed states idea, see Ruth Gordon, "Saving Failed States: Sometimes a Neocolonialist Notion," *American University Journal of International Law and Policy* 12, no. 6 (1997): 903. On weak states, and US national security, see Center for Global Development, *On the Brink: Weak States and US National Security* (Washington, D.C., 2004), http://www.cgdev.org/content/publications/detail/2879.

69. See Neclâ Tschirgi, "Post-Conflict Peacebuilding Revisited: Achievements, Limitation, Challenges," prepared for the WSP International and IPA "Peacebuilding Forum" conference, New York, October 7, 2004, http://www.ipacademy.org/pdfs/post_conflict_peacebuilding.pdf, pp. 17–18.

PART 2

Conflict Prevention, Peacekeeping, and Peacebuilding

4

Prevention and the Rule of Law: Rhetoric and Reality

Chandra Lekha Sriram

While there were many factors, both internal and external, that explain the cause of the civil war, the Commission came to the conclusion that it was years of bad governance, endemic corruption, and the denial of basic human rights that created the deplorable conditions that made conflict inevitable.
—*Final Report of the Sierra Leone Truth and Reconciliation Commission*[1]

It is frequently observed that the prevention of violent conflict is the first promise in the UN Charter, and the one most frequently betrayed.[2] For much of the Cold War, this was perhaps most notably the case, as deadlock in the Security Council prevented UN action when conflict was already raging, much less when there was a mere risk of conflict. The end of the Cold War saw a proliferation in internal armed conflicts, as well as in UN peace operations after conflict had broken out. In the 1990s, the need to prevent violent conflict also gained profile in the United Nations, but implementation of preventive practice, while gaining ground, has consistently lagged behind the rhetoric.[3] This chapter examines the norm and discourse of conflict prevention at the United Nations and several other key donors, tracing its development from a general idea to a policy formulation with multiple foci, actors, and priorities. It examines, in particular, the inclusion of the rule of law as a tool for conflict prevention, and its priority in development assistance. I suggest that while the rule of law has had an important place in the practice of development assistance, and is increasingly present in the rhetoric of conflict prevention, it is as yet unclear whether conceptualizing rule of law as important to prevention has altered priorities for development assistance. To some, this may present an "old wine in new bottles" problem—simply labeling traditional practices with new labels as preventive does not necessarily change the content.[4] I suggest that this is in part true, but that perhaps as the norms develop and policy priorities shift, what we are seeing is not old wine, but the creation of new wine that has simply yet to mature.

The Rule of Law and Conflict Prevention

As prevention became a greater priority in UN circles in the 1990s, it also became the subject of extensive work by a host of academics and policy-oriented think tanks.[5] I draw on these scholarly contributions throughout this chapter, but do not address them in detail. I examine instead only the report of the Carnegie Commission on Preventing Deadly Conflict as a key formulation of policy options for the prevention and resolution of conflict, as well as a number of landmark documents in the UN's development of the prevention agenda: *An Agenda for Peace,* the *Report of the Panel on United Nations Peace Operations* (Brahimi Report), and Secretary-General Kofi Annan's report, *Prevention of Armed Conflict.*[6] I also deal briefly with the ramifications of the 2004 report of the UN Secretary-General's High-Level Panel on Threats, Challenges, and Change.[7]

An Agenda for Peace, the 1992 report of UN Secretary-General Boutros Boutros-Ghali, is perhaps the first important statement in the post–Cold War era of UN policy on conflict prevention, though in that report it was treated as preventive "diplomacy."[8] While the report emphasized the importance of easing tensions before they escalate into conflict, and of responding to nascent conflict rapidly, it did not address what is now more commonly described as "structural" prevention. For the purposes of the United Nations in the 1990s, the goal of prevention was to address relatively immediate causes of conflict—even the "early warning" described in the *Agenda* has this focus—rather than longer-term, embedded causes of conflict. As we shall see, it is with the rise of the latter, structural prevention, that a role for development actors and development assistance can be increasingly discerned.[9]

The Brahimi Report of 2000 largely examined peacekeeping operations and postconflict peacebuilding, including transitional administrations, reserving only a few substantive paragraphs for discussions of preventive action. These paragraphs focused largely on conflict prevention as an element of peacekeeping or peacebuilding operations, rather than on longer-term, structural prevention. While this extensive report did refer to the importance of upholding the rule of law, it did so in the context of postconflict settings, and with few articulated roles for development actors. The rule of law in this context was understood in a limited fashion, as aspects of law pertaining to civilian police operations, or human rights and reconciliation concerns in postconflict settings.[10]

While the Brahimi Report represented a modest advancement in the definition of conflict prevention for the UN system, the official discourse had not yet embraced a fundamental distinction emerging in the academic and policy literature on conflict prevention—that between operational and structural prevention—much less the finer gradations of conflict being examined by that literature. This distinction was set out in the final report of the Carnegie Commission on Preventing Deadly Conflict, released in 1997.[11] On this account, operational prevention encompassed the types of prevention envisioned in *An*

Agenda for Peace: preventive diplomacy and preventive deployment, in contexts where conflict was imminent or had already broken out and required containment. Structural prevention, on the other hand, was understood to address the deeper sources of conflict, including horizontal inequality, systematic discrimination, failures of the rule of law, and the like. The introduction of this category opened the way for a discussion of the roles that could be played by development actors in places at risk of conflict. The subsequent years saw increasing discussion of development aid as a tool for conflict prevention, and of specific programming for such an end.[12]

It was not until the release of the UN Secretary-General's report *Prevention of Armed Conflict,* in 2001, that the concept of structural prevention was officially embraced by the entire UN system, although many bodies active in preventive policy and practice, particularly the UN Development Programme (UNDP), had for years sought to refine development to be conflict-sensitive and conflict-preventive.[13] The report explicitly recognized that the early signs of conflict could be best recognized and often addressed through country teams, largely development actors.[14] The report placed a strong emphasis on system-wide coordination, and the importance of the work of the UNDP, through its support (along with the Electoral Assistance Division of the UN Department for Political Affairs) to local electoral processes.[15] In addition to support for democratization, the report also emphasized the importance of strengthening respect for human rights as part of a long-term strategy of conflict prevention, and more generally emphasized the role of development assistance, by the UNDP and the Bretton Woods institutions, for conflict prevention.[16] The report noted the significant proportion of UNDP expenditures in conflict-prone countries that target governance and rule of law concerns.[17] This emphasis on such development activities as central to prevention was a marked shift from earlier reports.[18]

Prevention was also addressed in the report of the High-Level Panel on Threats, Challenges, and Change, a panel of eminent persons established by the UN Secretary-General to examine the UN's future role in addressing global threats. This report, released in December 2004, examined not just conflict prevention, but threats such as poverty and infectious disease as well.[19] The report's consideration of the prevention of armed conflict took up threats of both interstate and international armed conflict. However, its discussions of internal armed conflict per se composed only five paragraphs, and while some space was devoted to the importance of early warning and analysis, greater importance was granted to preventive diplomacy and mediation, and preventive deployment.[20] Greater emphasis, for the prevention of both internal and interstate conflict, was placed on international regulatory frameworks and norms, ranging from the International Criminal Court to mechanisms for regulating natural resource extraction and transfer of small arms and light weapons.[21] The attention given to the international rule of law, beyond the domestic rule of law, may prove an important advance.[22] Similar focus on both domestic and international rule of law appeared in the Secretary-General's March 2005 report *In Larger Freedom: Towards Development, Security, and Human Rights for All*.[23] Several paragraphs were devoted to the reduction and prevention of war, with an emphasis on peacekeeping and peacebuilding.[24] In discussing prevention, however, the report only directly referenced the rule of law as it applied to UN administrators and peacekeepers in light of recent allegations of misconduct by both.[25] The establishment of the UN Peacebuilding Commission is a promising step, but again the emphasis is on situations where conflict has already occurred, not where it is simply at risk of occurring.[26]

As the policy priorities for conflict prevention have become more refined, a number of areas of concern have been emphasized not merely as important goals in themselves, but also as tools of conflict prevention. These include reform of the security sector and disarmament, demobilization, and reintegration (DDR) of former combatants; democratic reform and improved governance; and human rights and the rule of law. Clearly, none of these concepts can be kept conceptually distinct—each of these areas is clearly tightly linked to the others. However, for the purposes of policy elaboration, such concepts often must be disaggregated. To that end, I offer a brief definition of the rule of law for the purposes of the United Nations and conflict prevention, though it is clearly not the only possible definition.

Defining the Rule of Law

Myriad definitions of the "rule of law" exist in legal and policy circles. As noted above, even distinguishing the rule of law from other policy priorities is quite difficult. For example, reports of the UN Secretary-General have included, as priorities for strengthening the rule of law, strengthening democratic institutions, human rights training and support to multiple national institutions, constitutional reform and legislative assistance, strengthening judicial capacity, and the like.[27] The Secretary-General's report on strengthening the rule of law in transitional societies offers both a general and an all-encompassing definition:

> The "rule of law" is a concept at the very heart of the Organization's mission. It refers to a principle of governance in which all persons, institutions, and entities, public and private, including the State itself, are accountable to laws that are publicly promulgated, equally enforced and independently adjudicated, and which are consistent with international human rights norms and standards. It requires, as well, measures to ensure adherence to the principles of supremacy of law, equality before the law, accountability to the law, fairness in the application of the law, separation of powers, participation in decision-making, legal certainty, avoidance of arbitrariness and procedural and legal transparency.[28]

This is an extremely procedurally focused definition of law, one that comports relatively well with H. L. A. Hart's positivist approach. The emphasis here is not on the content or conception of "justice," but rather on the presence of appropriately constituted authorities, public creation of laws, and accountability of the state apparatus.[29] Aside from the reference to international human rights norms and standards, the definition may offer relatively little in the way of insights for conflict prevention and management. For the purposes of this chapter I use this definition as an important baseline, but I supplement it, for the purposes of conflict management and prevention, with the activities mentioned in the report itself, as well as the earlier reports cited here, such as support to national justice systems, democratic institutions, and human rights institutions. This definition largely excludes major aspects of governance, economic security, or physical security, and focuses on legislation, the judiciary, and human rights institutions, including as a subsidiary problem that of transitional justice, as concerns the rule of law.[30]

The Rule of Law as a Prevention Priority

Just as conflict prevention evolved as a development priority during the 1990s, so too did concerns with the rule of law and human rights as tools of conflict prevention. The inclusion of such structural concerns as a functional judiciary, protection of human rights, and constitutional or legal reforms developed gradually, and remains of greater interest to some organizations than others. Great emphasis is currently placed on the rule of law as a tool in postconflict or transitional settings, while relatively little is placed at the level of policy development on the rule of law as preventing conflict from starting in the first place.[31] This means that the rule of law agenda remains confined, largely, to the postconflict peacebuilding segments of conflict prevention, rather than being applied to all phases of potential conflict. This does not mean that significant rule of law programming does not take place, particularly through the UNDP, or that much of it is not conceptualized as preventive by programmers, but rather that most policy discussions do not emphasize these features as yet. UNDP policy, however, is also evolving.

The Evolving Role of the Rule of Law

While it would be a mistake to suggest that the emergence of rule of law concerns in conflict analysis and prevention discourse is new, they have only relatively recently begun to be prioritized at a policy level. Several resolutions of the UN General Assembly and reports of the UN Secretary-General since the 1990s have sought to prioritize the rule of law as a UN activity, but these largely viewed it as protecting human rights and fundamental freedoms and, as such, primarily a priority for the UN Office of the High Commissioner for Human Rights.[32] However, as the centrality of the corruption, collapse, or distortion of the rule of law as conflict-creating, enabling, or escalating became apparent, it began to be viewed as a priority across the UN system, particularly but not solely in peace operations,[33] and for the World Bank, the European Union, and bilateral donors.

The importance of the rule of law in peace operations in conflict and post-conflict societies was further addressed by a task force of the Executive Committee on Peace and Security on Rule of Law in Peace Operations.[34] The task force, comprising representatives from eleven UN departments and agencies involved with rule of law activities, found significant expertise across the UN system, but also a general failure to centralize or coordinate that expertise through one lead department or agency in preparation for peace operations.[35]

In September 2003 the UN Security Council first sought to address the issue of the rule of law in postconflict societies, through a ministerial-level meeting, followed by an open Council debate.[36] Those discussions highlighted the importance of the rule of law to enable peaceful settlement of disputes, and the centrality of including these elements in peace operations as well as in postconflict peacebuilding.[37] Building on those discussions, as well as further discussions held in January 2004 on the role of the United Nations in postconflict national reconciliation, the Secretary-General issued a report in August 2004 on the rule of law and transitional justice in conflict and postconflict societies.[38]

This 2004 report was comprehensive, and did focus primarily on the rule of law and transitional justice in states in conflict or emerging from conflict, but not on those merely at risk of engaging in conflict. As such, priorities included developing a clear role for peace operations, supporting transitional justice and criminal prosecutions, establishing truth-telling mechanisms such as truth commissions, vetting, and reparations. Many of these foci are clearly tailored to conflict and postconflict settings only, and are not of great relevance for countries that are at risk of conflict, or for development actors that seek to assist them.[39]

However, several elements of the report are relevant for those who seek to prevent conflict through rule of law programming before it has actually emerged. In particular, the discussions of the need to assess national needs and capacities, support domestic reform constituencies, fill the rule of law vacuum, and develop national justice systems have policy relevance for prevention, and some of these elements have already been embraced in programming by development actors.[40] The sections of the report on identifying underlying causes of tension and conflict, specific vulnerable groups, and the condition of both the formal and the informal justice sectors could easily be employed by those engaged in structural prevention to identify both the specific risks of conflict and the relevant sectors of society that might be empowered to mitigate that risk; the report rightly emphasizes the danger of foreign models and foreign-designed solutions.[41] While the report's discussions of the rule of law vacuum focus on postconflict conditions, it could easily be describing crisis and pre-conflict situations when it points out that "legislative frameworks often show the accumulated signs of neglect and political distortion, contain discriminatory elements and rarely reflect the requirements of international human rights and criminal law standards."[42] Such conditions are clearly early warnings of the risk of conflict, not simply the result of it. They may require a host of responses, from support for judicial, legislative, and police reform, to support for reform of the closely related security and corrections sectors. Clearly these will be difficult where governments are resistant to donor interference, but should remain priorities where conflict has not yet emerged.[43]

In October 2004 the UN Security Council held a public debate on the Secretary-General's August report, and expressed strong general support for the latter's findings.[44] The debate, like the report, focused primarily on responses in postconflict countries, not countries at risk of conflict. Some delegates stressed the potential errors made by "well-meaning outsiders," highlighting the challenge of gaining acceptance of international interference even after conflict, much less prior to its emergence.[45]

The Council debate highlighted a key obstacle to coherent rule of law policies and programming already recognized by the aforementioned task force—that UN work in the fields of transitional justice and rule of law is divided among eleven departments and agencies.[46] No single department or agency has the lead in this issue area, as a result of which there has been a lack of coordination and an absence of common policies. A number of governments offered a "nonpaper" to address this issue.[47] That discussion, however, emphasized the importance of better coordination particularly in the area of peace operations; only Sweden explicitly discussed the role of the rule of law in prevention, emphasizing peacebuilding as but one arena of conflict prevention.[48]

In his March 2005 report *In Larger Freedom,* the Secretary-General announced the intention to create a rule of law assistance unit in a proposed peacebuilding support office, "to assist national efforts to re-establish the rule of law in conflict and post-conflict societies."[49] The definition of rule of law per se was not revised from that in the August 2004 report, and emphasis was again placed on compliance with international law, and responses to gross violations of international humanitarian law in particular.[50] The demands of human rights and democracy, concepts linked to the rule of law in the August document, were treated in separate sections. While the human rights section did address the need for national capacity building and support for mechanisms such as national human rights institutions, as well as the need for a human rights field presence during crises, little more was said bearing direct import for the rule of law or prevention.[51]

Much rule of law programming is of course carried out in the field by the UNDP, which has treated it as an underpinning of development but also, as former UNDP administrator Mark Malloch Brown emphasized in the October 2004 open debate, as vital for postconflict societies.[52] The UNDP recognizes the rule of law as an element of democracy promotion and postconflict peacebuilding, but also, increasingly, as an element of conflict prevention. In its justice sector work, the UNDP emphasizes access to justice for the disadvantaged as an element of development and democratization, but also as a tool of conflict prevention.[53] Its justice and security sector reform priorities place conflict squarely in the development agenda, as a key cause of human insecurity, and emphasize the importance of accountability of the judiciary and security structures to democratic control for the promotion of human security and development.

Conflict Prevention and Other International Actors

As the Secretary-General's 2001 report on conflict prevention noted, the United Nations is not the only, and often not the most important, actor in conflict prevention. The relevant actors for prevention are too numerous to be comprehensively listed here, but include regional organizations, member states, bilateral donors, local and international nongovernmental organizations (NGOs), and many more.[54] I focus here only on the United Kingdom as a major bilateral donor, the World Bank, and the European Union as illustrations of key actors in conflict prevention.

The United Kingdom's Department for International Development (DfID) has increasingly recognized the need to shift from traditional approaches to development to ones that are more conflict-sensitive, developing within the DfID the Conflict and Humanitarian Affairs Division, and developing across UK policy, through the Global Conflict Prevention Pool, a strategy for prevention that includes the DfID, the Ministry of Defence, and the Foreign and Commonwealth Office.[55] Attempts at a joint approach to conflict prevention signaled recognition of the blurring of lines between activities in development and those in security. In particular, DfID policy has regularly pointed to three donor approaches to conflict—working *around* it, working *within* it, and working *on* it—and has increasingly pursued the latter, attempting to focus development programming on root causes of conflict.[56] In comparison to this last approach, working *around* conflict has been understood as conducting programming in ways that avoid conflict and its causes, while working *within* conflict has involved programming in the midst of conflict without seeking to directly address it.

While the Global Conflict Prevention Pool strategy does recognize the importance of rule of law programming, its emphasis in the area of conflict prevention has largely been on security sector reform and DDR, areas that, while clearly linked to rule of law reform, are not the same.[57] Specifically, the Global Conflict Prevention Pool strategy, while operating in important conflict zones or conflict-prone zones globally, emphasizes security sector reform and small arms and light weapons.[58] However, for UK strategy, this does include civil authorities meant to control the security sector, such as the legislature and judiciary.[59]

The World Bank has increasingly sought to address conflict and the risk of conflict following its recognition during the early 1990s that civil wars, particularly those in Africa, were a challenge to traditional development programming.[60] The Bank, like bilateral donors, increasingly realized that it could not simply operate in conflict or postconflict zones, but should develop strategies to deal with the specific challenges of these areas, such as the need for DDR of former combatants. To that end, in 1997 the Bank created the Post-Conflict Unit (now the Conflict Prevention and Reconstruction Unit).[61] The Bank's own reporting indicates that it has an evolving agenda or approach with regard to assistance in conflict, conflict-prone, and postconflict countries, with an increasing presence, in particular, in rehabilitation and reconstruction in postconflict settings. As with the DfID, the Bank has increasingly come to work on and within conflict, not merely around it, nor even, as was once the case, absent from conflict or postconflict zones.[62] It has further sought to gear its programming away from *post*conflict reconstruction (as the first name of the conflict-focused unit indicated) and toward greater sensitivity to the risk of conflict and conflict "prevention" (as the unit's current name emphasizes).[63] The World Bank's evolving conception of conflict prevention now acknowledges the importance of the rule of law, but is focused primarily on its relationship to functional governance, and also the relationship of functional legal systems to effective control over property and attractiveness to foreign investment; greater emphasis is still placed on aspects of security such as DDR programs.[64]

The European Union has increasingly sought to prioritize conflict prevention as an element of its European Security and Defense Policy and Common Foreign and Security Policy.[65] In a 2001 communication, the European Commission noted the UN's primary role in conflict prevention under the Charter, but also delineated key areas of activity for the European Union. Chief among the European Union's tools has been the promotion of integration, first in the EU region and surrounding countries, but also through the Euro-Mediterranean partnership and support to other regional groupings, such as Mercosur, or through arrangements such as the Cotonou Agreement with the states of Africa, the Caribbean, and the Pacific.[66] In addition to general support through trade links and support for regional integration, the European Commission's 2001 communication focused on tools to address the root causes of conflict through development policy and other cooperation programs, including support for democracy, the rule of law, civil society, the media, security sector reform, and DDR.[67] The communication highlighted the importance of using country strategy papers to identify signs of early warning of conflict potential, and to develop programming tools that include preventive measures.[68] The communication was followed by the EU Program for the Prevention of Violent Conflicts, proposed by the Swedish EU presidency and endorsed at the European Council of Göteborg in June 2001, and more importantly, by a 2002 review of the Commission's prevention policy, which insisted on the value of greater investments in this area in the wake of the attacks of September 11, 2001.[69] Conflict prevention assessment missions have also been conducted in Sri Lanka, the South Pacific, Indonesia, and Nepal.

EU programming emphasizes the special importance of several tools of conflict prevention, which include support for democracy, the rule of law, and civil society.[70] The rule of law, or rather the lack thereof, for example, is one of the criteria in the Commission's checklist for root causes of conflict and early warning indicators.[71] On the other hand, the rule of law does not seem to be a priority in the basket of development activities mentioned in the 2001 communication; rather, emphasis is placed on democratic transition and elections, good governance generally, parliamentary activities, and freedom of the media. The communication's only citation of specific rule of law activities, under the definition employed in this chapter, concerns support to victims of human rights violations. While the discussions in the communication are illustrative rather than comprehensive, the relatively narrow policy priority of the rule of law per se seems apparent. A further challenge is that, the language of the communication notwithstanding, the traditional focus of EU cooperation in this area has been poverty reduction and development, rather than conflict prevention. The capacity of development policy to address the rule of law as a preventive strategy is further limited by the donor dilemma discussed above—that is, the need to secure host-government consent to provide assistance. This does not make such preventive development policy impossible, but clearly hampers it.[72]

The European Union is not the only European institution whose policies deal with rule of law issues. The Organization for Security and Cooperation in Europe (OSCE) addresses rule of law concerns as part of its human rights and democratization programming, and in some instances does highlight the preventive nature of its activities. Rule of law policies are promulgated by the Office for Democratic Institutions and Human Rights, the Office of the High Commissioner on National Minorities, and relatedly, the Strategic Police Matters Unit.[73] The work of the High Commissioner, in particular, has been expressly conceptualized as conflict-preventive.[74]

Policy Options for Preventive Rule of Law

While the majority of discourse on the rule of law and conflict has focused on postconflict peacebuilding, much can be gleaned from these discussions for application to preventive policy as well. Again, one caveat is of course the donor dilemma—in postconflict settings it will be far easier for the international community to encourage or even compel reforms that governments of countries at risk of conflict will be loath to introduce.[75]

Judicial Reform

While great efforts are made to reform the judiciary and all its attendants, including judges, prosecutors, defense attorneys, and clerks, severe corruption in this sector can aggravate tensions in a society and result in serious victimization and human rights abuses. As such, it is a logical subject of preventive policies and development assistance. Similarly, in many conflict-prone societies, even where the formal legal sector is weak at best, traditional justice mechanisms may have more traction and coverage, so support for them might also be a viable option. Further, security institutions such as the police and military, and corrections, need to be addressed simultaneously. Among relevant policies for all of these institutions will be reform of procedures and doctrines, and vetting of membership in many cases. More generally, broad institutional capacity building, including judicial training, may well be of great utility.[76]

Strengthening of Legislatures

Clearly, if access to the legislature, as a representative or as a citizen, is limited or systematically biased, this is also a potential source of conflict. Support for the democratization of legislatures, or more generally the increase of access to these, is an important goal in itself. Further, as these institutions often also maintain control over the judiciary and other legal institutions, ensuring their proper functioning becomes doubly important. The same might be said of a host of executive ministries or agencies, such as any justice ministry.

Monitoring Mechanisms and Civil Society

A host of monitoring and regulatory bodies can also help to ensure the proper functioning of the rule of law. These may include human rights monitoring institutions and ombudspersons, law reform commissions, bar associations, NGOs, the media, academics and think tanks, and judicial-training programs. These are common foci of postconflict programming, but support for them would clearly be useful in preventing conflict from emerging.[77]

Constitutional and Legal Reform

During transition, or after conflict, many countries engage in a protracted process of constitutional and legal reform. This is not surprising, as unfair constitutional arrangements concerned with power or resources, or even those perceived as unfair, are often at the root of conflict.[78] Support and encouragement for the reform of inequitable constitutional or legal provisions may help to mitigate potential sources of conflict. Naturally, such support may be viewed as intrusive; one possible, if limited, model is the type of quiet diplomacy engaged in by the OSCE High Commissioner on National Minorities to address such sources of potential conflict discreetly.[79]

Anticorruption

Anticorruption and transparency and accountability measures are clearly vital in the sectors discussed above, such as the judiciary, but also must be supported in all sectors of public administration and regulation, down to such mundane regulations as tax collection and car registration, in order to combat

a broader culture of lawlessness.[80] As with many of the other measures discussed here, to the degree that corruption is embedded in administration and
broader political culture, it will be difficult to address except in a postconflict
setting, yet it ought in theory to remain an important preventive priority as
well.

Mainstreaming Human Rights and Conditionality:
Conflict-Preventive or Conflict-Promoting?

Any discussion of the rule of law and conflict prevention in contemporary UN
and bilateral policies would be incomplete without addressing the contempo-
raneous "mainstreaming" of human rights in development policy, in some instances through the use of aid conditionality as a tool to promote human rights.
While in theory these developments might be expected to be consistent with
broader rule of law programming, they may be demonstrably inconsistent with
the goal of conflict prevention. Further, some studies suggest that even if such
approaches do not have conflict-inducing effects, they may simply not be very
effective.

The goal of mainstreaming human rights was highlighted by the UN
Secretary-General in his 1997 reform program, which refers to "the concept of
enhancing the human rights programme and integrating it into the broad range
of United Nations activities, also in the areas of development and humanitarian action."[81] Mainstreaming human rights into programming need not necessarily lead to conditionality per se, but the integration of human rights in UN
development policy, as well as the rise of "good governance" conditionality by
international financial institutions (IFIs) and conditionality by bilateral donors
such as the DfID, collectively lead to a type of rights conditionality, with the
attendant difficulties associated with more traditional conditionality based on
economic criteria.

The 1997 reform program consolidated activities in the Office of the High
Commissioner for Human Rights, and tasked it with mainstreaming human
rights. The office's primary mainstreaming tools were development-oriented,
including the UN Development Assistance Framework (UNDAF) and common country assessments.[82] These tools are central to the UNDP's formulation
of development policy, traditionally taking into account basic development indicators with the goal of addressing poverty, but increasingly are being used
to address such related concerns as human rights and potential conflict.

The mainstreaming of human rights was thus necessarily also taken up by
the UNDP, which in 1998 issued a policy document on its own efforts to develop a human rights approach to development.[83] The document contended
that human rights and sustainable development were mutually reinforcing, and
took note of the ways in which human rights violations contributed to underdevelopment. It further contended that "poverty is a human rights violation,

and freedom from poverty is an integral and inalienable human right."[84] Mainstreaming human rights, according to the document, would involve the use of several extant UNDP development strategies: sustainable development with a goal of eliminating poverty, targeting disadvantaged or excluded groups, promoting partnerships with civil society, and strengthening institutions of governance. Perhaps the most important element lay in the governance agenda, as the policy document noted the need for "addressing governance issues (such as corruption, the rule of law, participation, democratization, and accountability) in which human rights have been integral but, all too often, not explicitly spelled out."[85] The UNDP's policy focus was thus expanded, refining a governance agenda that had focused on access to governance and corruption, to include concerns with human rights violations, the development of national human rights and juridical institutions, as well as support for civil society organizations working in this area.

The UNDP's policy document highlighted specific areas of programming and technical support. It did not, unlike bilateral donors or IFIs, explicitly adopt a conditionality approach. By contrast, IFIs, bilateral donors such as DfID, and members of the Group of Eight have adopted policies of greater or lesser conditionality, not always concerned with human rights per se, but with "good governance," which might or might not include respect for human rights.[86] The Group of Eight, at the July 2001 Genoa Summit, articulated the reasoning for the focus on good governance: "Open, democratic and accountable systems of governance, based upon respect for human rights and the rule of law, are preconditions for sustainable development and robust growth."[87]

However, conditionality is a highly controversial tool. As disputes over structural adjustment and conditionality during the 1980s demonstrated, rigid criteria can have unintended and destabilizing effects, particularly on vulnerable states and markets.[88] The same may be the case for rigid governance criteria as conditions for aid. Rather than improving the developmental and human rights situation in a country, aid may have exactly the reverse effect—those least able to reform are punished with the withdrawal of aid. Yet governance conditions as elements of conditionality have grown, and now constitute over half of the aid conditions for many recipients of International Monetary Fund support.[89] It is for this reason that the DfID, in 2004, issued a policy paper seeking to alter aid conditionality. It sought not to eliminate it, but to lessen the burden, in part by making the results of conditionality more predictable in order to ensure that sanctions for failure to meet certain governance benchmarks do not further destabilize fragile states.[90]

There is additional cause for concern in that conditionality has not been proven to "work." Some studies have suggested that, beyond potentially destabilizing effects, conditionality on the basis of governance or rights has little or no effect on state practice.[91] Instead, as Jeffrey Checkel suggests with reference to conditionality based on membership in key European institutions, it may be the case that conditionality alone does not result in compliance or behavioral change, but that dialogue and discursive approaches are important as well.[92] Checkel suggests that a two-track approach combining conditionality and dialogue would be the most effective. And this might well be the case provided that such an approach does not cause destabilization, as would be possible in many of the most conflict-prone states. In such instances the more cautious approach of the UNDP, prioritizing support to rights-oriented institutions rather than conditionality, may prove wise, lest human rights programming prove to actually promote conflict rather than serve to prevent it.

Policy Recommendations

Since 1998, conflict prevention has progressively become a priority for the United Nations, the European Union, the World Bank, and the United Kingdom (as a key bilateral donor). At the same time, commitments to the rule of law have risen in prominence, at least in postconflict peacebuilding if not specifically in wider, structural conflict prevention. We have found that while there is a trend toward using rule of law programming for conflict prevention, practice is still developing and is far from consistent. While it is expressly understood that the failures of the rule of law often contribute to the initiation of conflict, supporting rule of law reforms only in places at risk of conflict has not been strongly advocated. What emerges is progressive but uneven policy development; for the most part, the rule of law is conceptualized as a development tool, or as a tool largely of postconflict peacebuilding. Where it is included in the basket of preventive tools, as with support for legislative reform, the rule of law is often overshadowed by the important and linked, but distinct, goals of security sector reform. Thus, while an apparent norm is developing that highlights the importance of the rule of law as preventive, it is unclear that this norm has yet crystallized. Where the rule of law is largely still conceptualized as a development tool, as in the policy statements of the World Bank, and in many of the policy statements by the United Nations until recently, the use of preventive and peacebuilding language often appears to be a later addition. The Organization for Economic Cooperation and Development, not discussed in this chapter, treats the rule of law purely as a tool for development, strengthening property rights, and helping to attract international capital.[93] But another normative trend is emerging, one that encompasses the rule of law as part of a conflict-limitation and conflict-prevention strategy.

The primary, and perhaps obvious, policy recommendation that emerges from this chapter is that the same attention to the importance of the rule of law *after* conflict might be paid to its importance *before* conflict. This means that many of the peacebuilding tools identified here and in the many policy documents discussed—judicial, legislative, and constitutional reform, support for traditional justice mechanisms where appropriate, combating corruption and human rights abuses, and the like—might be included in preventive efforts as well. Here the OSCE High Commissioner on National Minorities is a rare, if also relatively limited, example of preventive rule of law work. Unfortunately, preventive rule of law work is predictably likely to be more challenging, as governments not emerging from conflict, or profiting from fomenting certain types of internal strife, are unlikely to permit international interference of the sort so common in peacebuilding.[94]

Notes

1. Sierra Leone Truth and Reconciliation Commission, *Final Report,* October 2004, http://trcsierraleone.org/drwebsite/publish/index.shtml.

2. Karin Wermester, "From Promise to Practice? Conflict Prevention at the UN," in *From Promise to Practice: Strengthening UN Capacities for the Prevention of Violent Conflict,* edited by Chandra Lekha Sriram and Karin Wermester (Boulder: Lynne Rienner, 2003), p. 375.

3. Fen Osler Hampson, Karin Wermester, and David M. Malone, "Introduction: Making Conflict Prevention a Priority," in *From Reaction to Conflict Prevention: Opportunities for the UN System,* edited by Fen Osler Hampson and David M. Malone (Boulder: Lynne Rienner, 2002), pp. 2–4.

4. For a powerful critique of the concept of conflict prevention generally, raising similar concerns, see Edward C. Luck, "Prevention: Theory and Practice," in Hampson, *From Reaction to Conflict Prevention,* pp. 257–259.

5. Key works arising from prevention research include Barnett Rubin, "Cases and Strategies for Preventive Action," report of the 1996 Center for Preventive Action annual conference (New York: Century Foundation, 1998); Michael Lund, *Preventing Violent Conflicts: A Strategy for Preventive Diplomacy* (Washington, D.C.: US Institute of Peace, 1996); Peter Wallensteen, *Preventing Violent Conflicts: Past Record and Future Challenges* (Uppsala: Uppsala University Department of Peace and Conflict Research, 1998); Carnegie Commission on Preventing Deadly Conflict, *Preventing Deadly Conflict: Final Report* (New York, 1997); Hampson and Malone, *From Reaction to Conflict Prevention;* Sriram and Wermester, *From Promise to Practice.*

6. United Nations, *An Agenda for Peace: Preventive Diplomacy, Peacemaking, and Peacekeeping: Report of the Secretary-General,* UN Doc. A/47/277-S/24111 (June 17, 1992); United Nations, *Report of the Panel on United Nations Peace Operations* (Brahimi Report), UN Doc. A/55/305-S/2000/809 (August 21, 2000); United Nations, *Prevention of Armed Conflict: Report of the Secretary-General,* UN Doc. A/55-985-S/2001/574 (June 7, 2001).

7. United Nations, *A More Secure World: Our Shared Responsibility—Report of the Secretary General's High-Level Panel on Threats, Challenges, and Change,* UN Doc. A/59/565 (December 1, 2004), http://www.un.org/secureworld.

8. United Nations, *An Agenda for Peace,* paras. 23–33.

9. On the various "phases of conflict" and prevention, and specific tools, including development assistance, see Chandra Lekha Sriram, "From Risk to Response: Phases of Conflict, Phases of Conflict Prevention," in Sriram and Wermester, *From Promise to Practice,* pp. 13–34. A skeptical view of structural prevention is offered in Luck, "Prevention."

10. United Nations, *Report of the Panel on United Nations Peace Operations,* paras. 29–34 specifically, and paras. 29–47 generally.

11. Carnegie Commission on Preventing Deadly Conflict, *Preventing Deadly Conflict*. See also Anne-Marie Gardner, "Diagnosing Conflict: What Do We Know?" in Hampson, *From Reaction to Conflict Prevention*.

12. See, for example, Mukesh Kapila and Karin Wermester, "Development and Conflict: New Approaches in the United Kingdom," and Patricia Cleves, Nat Colletta, and Nicholas Sambanis, "Addressing Conflict: Emerging Policy at the World Bank," in Hampson, *From Reaction to Conflict Prevention*. See also Nat J. Colletta and Michelle L. Cullen, *Violent Conflict and the Transformation of Social Capital: Lessons from Cambodia, Rwanda, Guatemala, and Somalia* (Washington, D.C.: World Bank, 2000).

13. United Nations, *Prevention of Armed Conflict*. Specific policy and institutional developments are summarized in the report itself, particularly paras. 65–80, and are also discussed in detail in Wermester, "From Promise to Practice?"

14. United Nations, *Prevention of Armed Conflict,* paras. 69–70.

15. Ibid., para. 79.

16. Ibid., paras. 94–107.

17. Ibid., paras. 102–103.

18. United Nations, *Security Council Resolution on Prevention of Armed Conflict,* UN Doc. S/RES/1366 (August 30, 2001); UN General Assembly Resolution 57/337 (2003).

19. United Nations, *A More Secure World,* paras. 44–73.

20. Ibid., paras. 84–88, 98–106.

21. Ibid., paras. 89–97.

22. This may not suffice. At the International Peace Academy authors' meeting for this volume, it was repeatedly suggested that so long as there was weak international rule of law, which some suggested was demonstrated by current US involvement in Iraq, domestic rule of law could hardly be expected to follow.

23. See, generally, United Nations, *In Larger Freedom: Towards Development, Security, and Human Rights for All—Report of the Secretary General,* UN Doc. A/59/2005 (March 21, 2005).

24. Ibid., paras. 106–121.

25. Ibid., para. 113.

26. Ibid., para. 137.

27. United Nations, *Strengthening the Rule of Law: Report of the Secretary-General,* UN Doc. A/52/475 (October 16, 1997); United Nations, *Strengthening the Rule of Law: Report of the Secretary-General,* UN Doc. A/55/177 (July 20, 2000). Compare Agnès Hurwitz and Gordon Peake, *Strengthening the Security-Development Nexus: Assessing International Policy and Practice Since the 1990s* (New York: International Peace Academy, April 2004). Compare also Martina Huber, "Monitoring the Rule of Law: Consolidated Framework and Report," Conflict Research Unit occasional paper (The Hague: Clingendael Institute, July 2002).

28. United Nations, *The Rule of Law and Transitional Justice in Conflict and Post-Conflict Societies: Report of the Secretary-General,* UN Doc. S/2004/616 (August 23, 2004), para. 6.

29. H. L. A. Hart, *The Concept of Law* (Oxford: Clarendon, 1961). See also Rachel Kleinfeld Belton, "Competing Definitions of the Rule of Law: Implications for Practitioners," in *Promoting the Rule of Law Abroad: In Search of Knowledge,* edited by Thomas Carothers (Washington, D.C.: Carnegie Endowment for International Peace, 2006).

30. I do not suggest more generally that these can or ought to be pursued in a vacuum. As I have illustrated in the context of transitional justice, it is impossible to address transitional justice, or judicial and security reform, without considering their ef-

fects on each other and performing a balancing act of sorts. See Chandra Lekha Sriram, *Confronting Past Human Rights Violations: Justice vs. Peace in Times of Transition* (London: Cass, 2004).

31. See, for example, the excellent overview of the justice sector and conflict, focusing primarily on postconflict settings, in UN Office of the High Commissioner for Human Rights (OHCHR), *Rule-of-Law Tools for Post-Conflict States: Mapping the Justice Sector* (Geneva, 2006)). See also Shelley Inglis, *Legal Systems Monitoring Tool,* 2006 (on file with author); William O'Neill, "Draft Statement to Security Council Arria meeting" (September 30, 2004) (draft on file with author).

32. United Nations, *Strengthening the Rule of Law* (October 16, 1997); United Nations, S*trengthening the Rule of Law* (July 20, 2000).

33. OHCHR, *Rule-of-Law Tools for Post-Conflict States.*

34. O'Neill, "Draft Statement to Security Council Arria Meeting," September 30, 2004; Nina Lahoud, *ECPS Task Force for Development of Comprehensive Rule of Law Strategies for Peace Operation* (on file with author).

35. O'Neill, "Draft Statement to Security Council Arria Meeting."

36. United Nations, *Justice and the Rule of Law: The United Nations Role,* Press Release no. *SC/7880* (September 24, 2003), http://www.un.org/news/press/docs/2003/sc7880.p2.doc.htm.

37. European Union Presidency, "Justice and the Rule of Law: The UN Role," statement delivered to the UN Security Council (September 30, 2003), http://www.europa-eu-un.org/articles/en/article_2844_en.htm. It is worth noting that these discussions coincided with the release of a report designed to address other elements of transitional reform, specifically consolidation of democratic control: United Nations, *Support by the United Nations System of the Efforts of Governments to Promote and Consolidate New or Restored Democracies: Report of the Secretary-General,* UN Doc. A/58/392 (September 26, 2003).

38. United Nations, *The Rule of Law and Transitional Justice.* For the statement emerging from the January 2004 discussions, see United Nations, *Statement by the President of the Security Council,* UN Doc. S/PRST/2004/2 (January 26, 2004).

39. United Nations, *The Rule of Law and Transitional Justice*, paras. 2–4, 11–13, 38–55, in particular, have the most relevance for postconflict settings.

40. Ibid., paras. 14–18, 27–37.

41. Ibid., esp. para. 17.

42. Ibid., para. 27.

43. This is not to make light of the so-called donors' dilemmas, which make it difficult for donors to always speak forthrightly about abuses that may be perpetrated by governments, whose permission such donors require to operate in-country. See, for example, Stephen Brown, "Quiet Diplomacy and Recurring 'Ethnic Clashes' in Kenya," in Sriram and Wermester, *From Promise to Practice.*

44. United Nations, *Security Council Stresses Importance, Urgency, of Restoring Rule of Law in Post-Conflict Societies: Statement by the President of the Security Council,* UN Doc. S/PRST/2004/34 (October 6, 2004), http://www.un.org/news/press/docs/2004/sc8209.doc.htm.

45. Ibid., statement of the delegate of the Philippines.

46. Ibid., statement of the delegate of Germany.

47. Ibid., statement of the delegate of Finland. Finland, Germany, and Jordan presented a "nonpaper" on the question of institutional coordination.

48. Ibid., statement of the delegate of Sweden.

49. United Nations, *In Larger Freedom,* para. 137.

50. Ibid., paras. 133–139.

51. Ibid., paras. 140–152, esp. paras. 142–143. As noted, the discussion of prevention made only one reference to rule of law, but it was to the need for UN employees to abide by it.

52. United Nations, *Security Council Stresses Importance, Urgency, of Restoring Rule of Law in Post-Conflict Societies: Statement of the Administrator of UNDP,* UN Doc. S/PRST/2004/34 (October 6, 2004).

53. UNDP, *Protecting and Promoting the Universal Values of Human Rights and Rule of Law*, 2005, www.undp.org/governance/sl-justice.htm; UNDP, *Justice and Security Sector Reform: BCPR's Programmatic Approach* (November 2002), http://www.undp.org/bcpr/jssr/index.htm (accessed January 15, 2007).

54. See, generally, United Nations, *Prevention of Armed Conflict.* On regional and subregional conflict prevention see, inter alia, Chandra Lekha Sriram and Zoe Nielsen, eds., *Exploring Subregional Conflict: Opportunities for Conflict Prevention* (Boulder: Lynne Rienner, 2004). See also Chandra Lekha Sriram, Albrecht Schnabel, John Packer, and Augustine Touré, *Sharing Best Practices on Conflict Prevention: The UN, Regional and Subregional Organizations, National and Local Actors* (New York: International Peace Academy, 2002); David Carment, *Creating Conditions for Peace: What Role for the UN and Regional Actors?* (New York: International Peace Academy, 2002). All of the above-cited International Peace Academy works are available at http://www.ipacademy.org/publications.

55. Kapila and Wermester, "Development and Conflict: New Approaches in the United Kingdom"; Department for International Development, Foreign and Commonwealth Office, and Ministry of Defence, *The Global Conflict Prevention Pool: A Joint UK Government Approach to Reducing Conflict,* August 2003, http://www.dfid.gov.uk/pubs/files/global-conflict-prevention-pool.pdf.

56. Jonathan Goodhand, *Conflict Assessments: A Synthesis Report: Kyrgyzstan, Moldova, Nepal, and Sri Lanka* (London: King's College Conflict, Security, and Development Group, 2001), http://www.dfid.gov.uk/pubs/files/conflictassessmentsynthesis.pdf.

57. Foreign and Commonwealth Office, "UK Global Conflict Prevention Pool," http://www.fco.gov.uk/servlet/front?pagename=openmarket/xcelerate/showpage&c=page&cid=1013618138445. See also Department for International Development, Foreign and Commonwealth Office, Ministry of Defence, and Cabinet Office, *Evaluation of the Conflict Prevention Pools; UK Government Response* (July 2004), http://www.dfid.gov.uk/aboutdfid/performance/files/ev647ukgovt.pdf.

58. Department for International Development, Foreign and Commonwealth Office, and Ministry of Defence, *The Global Conflict Prevention Pool,* pp. 30–35.

59. Ibid., p. 30.

60. Cleves, Colletta, and Sambanis, "Addressing Conflict," pp. 321–322.

61. World Bank, *The Role of the World Bank in Conflict and Development: An Evolving Agenda* (2004), http://lnweb18.worldbank.org/essd/sdvext.nsf/67bydocname/theroleoftheworldbankinconflictanddevelopmentanevolvingagenda1/$file/conflictagenda2004.pdf.

62. Ibid., pp. 3–5.

63. Ibid., p. 9.

64. Ibid., pp. 33–34.

65. European Union, "EU Programme for the Prevention of Violent Conflicts" (2001), http://www.eu2001.se/static/eng/pdf/violent.pdf; European Union, "Communication from the Commission on Conflict Prevention" (April 11, 2001), http://www.europa.eu.int/comm/external_relations/cfsp/news/com2001_211_en.pdf.

66. European Union, "Communication from the Commission on Conflict Prevention," pp. 8–9.

67. Ibid., pp. 9–10.

68. Ibid., pp. 11–12.

69. European Union, "One Year On: The Commission's Conflict Prevention Policy" (March 2002), http://ec.europa.eu/external_relations/cfsp/cpcm/cp/rep.htm.

70. European Union, "Communication from the Commission on Conflict Prevention," pp. 13–14.

71. European Union, "European Commission Check-List for Root Causes of Conflict," 2001, http://europa.eu.int/comm/external_relations/cpcm/cp/list.htm. Four distinct components of the rule of law are mentioned in the checklist: How strong is the judicial system? Does unlawful state violence exist? Does civilian power control security forces? Does organized crime undermine the country's stability? Also noteworthy are two other points of the checklist: legitimacy of the state (e.g., checks and balances, corruption) and respect for fundamental rights (e.g., civil and political freedoms, religious and cultural rights, and other basic human rights).

72. International Crisis Group, *EU Crisis Response Capability: Institutions and Processes for Conflict Prevention and Management* (June 26, 2001), http://www.crisisweb.org/home/index.cfm?id=1830&l=1, 37.

73. Organization for Security and Cooperation in Europe, "Activities: Rule of Law," http://www.osce.org/activities/13049.html (accessed November 13, 2007).

74. Walter A. Kemp, ed., *Quiet Diplomacy in Action: The OSCE High Commissioner on National Minorities* (The Hague: Kluwer Law International, 2001); John Packer, "The Work of the OSCE High Commissioner on National Minorities as an Instrument of Conflict Prevention," in Sriram et al., *Sharing Best Practices on Conflict Prevention.*

75. This section draws extensively on two mapping and monitoring documents: OHCHR, *Rule-of-Law Tools for Post-Conflict States,* and Inglis, *Legal Systems Monitoring.*

76. OHCHR, *Rule-of-Law Tools for Post-Conflict States.*

77. Ibid., pp. 17–24.

78. See, for example, Ralph Premdas, "Fiji: Peacemaking in a Multi-Ethnic State," in Sriram and Wermester, *From Promise to Practice,* pp. 133–159.

79. Kemp, *Quiet Diplomacy in Action.*

80. O'Neill, "Draft Statement to Security Council Arria Meeting."

81. United Nations, "Human Rights in Report of the Secretary-General on Renewing the United Nations: A Programme for Reform" (extracts from *Report of the Secretary-General to the General Assembly: Renewing the United Nations—A Programme for Reform,* UN Doc. A/51/950 [July 14, 1997]), http://www.unhchr.ch/html/hchr/unrefor.htm; Office of the High Commissioner for Human Rights, *Human Rights in Development: Mainstreaming Human Rights,* http://www.unhchr.ch/development/mainstreaming-01.html (accessed November 13, 2007).

82. "How Is OHCHR Mainstreaming Human Rights?" in Office of the High Commissioner for Human Rights, *Human Rights in Development,* http://www.unhchr.ch/development/mainstreaming-02.html.

83. UNDP, "Integrating Human Rights with Sustainable Human Development: A UNDP Policy Document" (January 1998), http://www.undp.org/governance/docs/hr_pub_policy5.htm.

84. Ibid., sec. 1.2: "How Human Rights Affect Sustainable Human Development."

85. Ibid., sec. 1.4: "UNDP and Human Rights."

86. Jeffrey T. Checkel, "Compliance and Conditionality," ARENA Working Paper no. 00/18 (n.d.), http://www.arena.uio.no/publications/wp00_18.htm; Carlos Santiso, "Governance Conditionality and the Reform of Multilateral Development Finance: The Role of the Group of Eight," G8 Governance no. 7 (n.d.), http://www.g7.utoronto

.ca/governance/santiso2002-gov7.pdf; Department for International Development, "Partnerships for Poverty Reduction: Changing Aid 'Conditionality'" (September 2004), http://www.dfid.gov.uk/pubs/files/conditionalitychange.pdf; Eurodad, "Partnerships for Poverty Reduction: Changing Aid Conditionality" (October 25, 2004), http://www.eurodad.org/whatsnew/reports.aspx?id=812.

87. Santiso, "Governance Conditionality," p. 8.

88. Ibid., pp. 9–11, 16–17.

89. Ibid., pp. 18–24.

90. Department for International Development, "Partnerships for Poverty Reduction," p. 12.

91. Checkel, "Compliance and Conditionality"; Gordon Crawford, "Foreign Aid and Political Conditionality: Issues of Effectiveness and Consistency," *Democratization* 4, no. 3 (1997): 69–108; Gordon Crawford, "Human Rights and Democracy in EU Development Co-operation: Towards Fair and Equal Treatment," in *European Union Development Policy,* edited by Marjorie Lister (London: Macmillan, 1998), pp. 131–178.

92. Checkel, "Compliance and Conditionality," pp. 6–7, 13–20.

93. See, for example, the following discussion by the head of the OECD's legal directorate: Christian Schricke, "How the OECD Promotes the Rule of Law" (1996), http://www.cipe.org/publications/ert/e19/E19_08.pdf. While this statement was made in 1996, more recent documents emphasize the same concerns.

94. This point is well made by Stephen Brown in "Quiet Diplomacy and Recurring 'Ethnic Clashes' in Kenya," in Sriram and Wermester, *From Promise to Practice.*

5

UN Peacekeeping Operations and Rule of Law Programs

William G. O'Neill

I have always been struck by how people in Haiti, Rwanda, Kosovo, Sierra Leone, Liberia, Cambodia, and elsewhere, wracked by conflict and lacking the most basic of human necessities—food, housing, medical assistance, jobs—often said that their most urgent priority was justice. This reflects a universal yearning: to have clear rules that apply equitably to all with avenues of redress when the rules are broken. These people know better than most how literally "deadly" the world becomes when rule by force usurps the rule of law.

Most conflicts in the world today spring from a fundamental denial of justice. Discrimination, exclusion, unequal access to resources and goods, and lack of basic freedoms lead to bloody conflicts that affect thousands of innocent civilians, most frequently women, children, and the elderly, the usual victims in modern wars. Furthermore, in most conflict contexts the legal system was, and was seen to be, biased, corrupt, and therefore illegitimate. Grievances, real and imagined, could not be resolved peacefully through the courts or other dispute resolution mechanisms, so they were addressed through violence. Reestablishing, or more accurately in most cases, establishing for the first time, the rule of law is an essential prerequisite for building a modicum of trust in war-torn societies. Among postconflict countries that did not make establishing free and transparent institutions to resolve conflicts and provide security a top priority, not a single country succeeded in preventing the recurrence of conflict.[1]

The UN Security Council's explicit acknowledgment in several of its recent resolutions of the importance of rule of law and transitional justice initiatives in peace operations reinforces this point. After years of denial, the Security Council now embraces the rule of law and recognizes that it is central to international peace and security.

However, the means given by the Security Council to work effectively in the rule of law domain are often insufficient. The resources do not match the rhetoric, leaving peacekeepers, national counterparts, and other stakeholders frustrated and demoralized. Moreover, while those working in the field have identified many "good practices" and "lessons," mistakes are repeated and many lessons go "unlearned." Capacity building, while often lauded and made the centerpiece of rule of law efforts, in reality remains poorly understood and often unrealized.

This chapter traces the evolution of rule of law programs in multidimensional peacekeeping operations. It seeks to examine the main challenges faced by the United Nations in the design and implementation of rule of law programs in the immediate aftermath of conflict, and in particular whether UN peacekeeping missions are adequately equipped to develop rule of law programs to effectively address existing needs. I argue that while important improvements have been made in policy and practice, the major challenge for the United Nations is to dedicate more resources and increase the efficiency and coherence of missions in a field that demands perseverance, vision, and accountability. The chapter concludes by proposing a set of concrete recommendations for current and future peacekeeping operations.

Historical Overview

Neither "peacekeeping" nor "rule of law" appear anywhere in the UN Charter. Peacekeeping doctrine, in its military and more recent civilian dimensions, has been developed over years of experience. Peacekeepers continually struggle to keep up with the changing demands and realities of complex, multidimensional peace operations.

During the Cold War, UN peacekeeping missions were military in nature and involved UN "blue helmets" standing between two warring parties, most often from two opposing countries. The UN troops' main task was to monitor a cease-fire and bide for time to allow a peace treaty to take hold. While the conflicts were interstate and relatively bloodless by the time the Security Council acted to interpose peacekeepers, these operations tended to last for years, even decades. Classic examples of UN peacekeeping in this era were Cyprus, the Indo-Pakistan cease-fire monitoring in Kashmir, and Sinai.[2] In this "traditional" peacekeeping, UN forces had rare and limited contact with civilian authorities and even less with nongovernmental organizations (NGOs), monitoring mostly from their watchtowers and patrolling the "no-man's land" on either side of cease-fire lines. These early peace operations also had relatively few civilian members. Restricted to administrative, financial, and logistical matters, they did not interact with government institutions such as the justice system, prisons, or the national police. UN Security Council resolutions of the 1960s to 1980s never mentioned a role for civilians in the peacekeeping efforts.

The conflicts and the UN's role changed with the end of the Cold War in the early 1990s. First, conflicts requiring UN peacekeeping overwhelmingly began to occur within one state, wreaking intense violence, causing millions of civilian casualties, and generating tens of millions of refugees and internally displaced persons. The state often had no functioning institutions, including police, judiciary, penitentiaries, or basic public administration. This represented a totally different landscape for military peacekeepers compared to the relatively orderly and peaceful context of the first thirty years of UN peacekeeping.

The Security Council was able to act more forcefully, authorizing more peacekeeping operations from 1994 to 2006 than it had for the previous thirty-five years.[3] Yet the Council persisted in the early 1990s in using the traditional model of peacekeeping designed for relatively static conflicts between two regular militaries with clear command and control capacities. The conflicts in El Salvador, Guatemala, Cambodia, and the former Yugoslavia did not fit this mold. Rather, these wars involved many irregular or insurgent groups, with sketchy command and control; all parties to these conflicts intentionally targeted civilians and saw control of the population as a sign of their power and legitimacy. Civilians suffered by far the greatest number of casualties, while uniformed soldiers and their insurgent foes escaped largely unscathed.

The Security Council mandates given to the peacekeeping operations of the early 1990s still reflected the old doctrine: peacekeepers were to "interpose" themselves between the warring factions. They were not supposed to take sides; "neutrality" was paramount. The only permissible use of force was in self-defense: if the peacekeepers themselves came under attack, they could defend themselves but were not to use force to protect others, even civilians, from violence. The Security Council did not anticipate peacekeepers' involvement in protecting civilians, nor did they see a role for peacekeepers to monitor or assess human rights observance.[4] Least of all, Security Council resolutions did not provide for civilians to work on reforming or, in many cases, building the institutions essential to the rule of law.

Real change started in the mid-1990s, particularly after the disastrous events in Srebrenica, Bosnia-Herzegovina, and Rwanda, where UN peacekeepers, with totally inadequate resources and mandates from the Security Council, and inadequate support from the UN Department of Peacekeeping Operations (DPKO), failed to protect civilians, leading to the massacre of seven thousand men and young boys in Srebrenica and hundreds of thousands in the Rwandan genocide.

After these failures, the Security Council and the Secretary-General embarked on a series of studies and reports to examine the state of peacekeeping, the changing nature of modern conflicts, and the need to protect civilians. In a landmark resolution in April 2000, the Security Council stated that it was gravely concerned at the "harmful and widespread impact of armed conflict on civilians, including the particular impact armed conflict has on women, children and other vulnerable groups," and further reaffirmed "the importance of fully addressing their special assistance and protection needs in the mandates of peacemaking, peacekeeping and peace-building."[5] The Security Council asserted that attacks on civilians are a direct threat to international peace and security, thus identifying violations of international humanitarian law and human rights as a threat to the peace. The Council was edging into the domain of the rule of law.

In parallel with traditional peacekeeping operations, the United Nations sponsored several "field operations" to monitor adherence to peace agreements: the UN Observer Mission in El Salvador (ONUSAL) starting in 1991, the International Civilian Mission in Haiti (MICIVIH) in 1993, and the UN Verification Mission in Guatemala (MINUGUA) in 1994.[6] Meanwhile, the UN Transitional Authority in Cambodia (UNTAC) was a different species entirely compared to both the traditional peace operations in Rwanda and Bosnia-Herzegovina and the missions in El Salvador, Haiti, and Guatemala.[7] UNTAC was a throwback to the old trusteeships by which the United Nations took direct control of key areas of government (foreign affairs, national defense, public security, and information) and essentially administered Cambodia until elections in mid-1993.[8] Yet UNTAC and the missions in El Salvador, Haiti, and Guatemala shared one common feature new to peace operations: human rights monitors.

All four had mandates authorizing them to monitor and report on the human rights situations, intervene with the authorities to convey concerns and complaints, and make recommendations toward a cessation of violations. The mandate for MICIVIH was typical:

> To obtain information on the human rights situation in Haiti and to make any appropriate recommendations to promote and protect human rights; . . . draw up official reports and communicate its official conclusions to the relevant international organizations. The Mission shall make known to the Haitian authorities its concerns about the human rights violations and shall take their response into account when preparing their reports and conclusions.[9]

It soon became apparent to the human rights field officers that merely monitoring and reporting human rights violations, while necessary, were not sufficient to address the causes of the violations and to prevent their recurrence. Justice systems were weak and subject to interference, police committed abuses instead of protecting citizens, and prisons were hellish. Also, human rights officers who only offered criticisms without solutions soon lost credibility and any chance to change behavior. While not yet using the term "rule of law," these human rights missions started to engage in institutional reform that would buttress respect for human rights, enhance accountability for perpetrators, and seek to involve nongovernmental organizations so that they would have a say in how their state operated.

The years 1994 to 1999 saw a concerted effort to combine monitoring human rights with initiatives to reform the core institutions we now see as fundamental to the rule of law in postconflict contexts: the judiciary, the police, the military, and the prisons. Human rights field officers in El Salvador, Haiti,

Guatemala, Rwanda, and Bosnia-Herzegovina did most of this work. Successive peace operations in Angola, Sierra Leone, the Democratic Republic of Congo, and Liberia had small human rights divisions whose officers, with extremely limited personnel and budgets, trained judges and prosecutors and worked with the increasing numbers of UN civilian police to reform or completely rebuild local police forces. In addition to a shortage of people and money, these peace operations often had weak mandates to engage in activity often deemed as "intrusive" by the host state and even by certain Security Council members. For example, the United States ended a successful program of judicial reform in Bosnia-Herzegovina in 2000 because several US senators did not consider this type of work to be "peacekeeping."[10]

Other UN agencies played almost no part in this early rule of law work. The UN Development Programme (UNDP), which has a long experience in institution building, participated sporadically. In Haiti, MICIVIH and the UNDP combined to implement a successful prison reform program from 1995 to 1997, but this is the proverbial exception that proves the rule. The Center for Human Rights, later renamed the Office of the High Commissioner for Human Rights (OHCHR), had little to offer. Although the office had conducted advisory or "technical cooperation" programs for forty years, this experience had little relevance in war-torn societies where institutions had barely functioned in the best of times.[11]

Since 1999 the centrality of the rule of law has become accepted in all peace operations. Kosovo and East Timor constitute important milestones on this largely unmarked path. The United Nations, as it had done in Cambodia nearly ten years before, took over governing these two territories. Yet much had changed. Institutional reform was low on UNTAC's list, while making the courts free and fair, the police respectful and effective, and the prisons humane were first-order priorities for the UN Interim Administration Mission in Kosovo (UNMIK)[12] and the UN Transitional Administration in East Timor (UNTAET).[13] Resources, while always fewer than needed, had greatly increased.

The Security Council was also catching up, helped along by the Brahimi Report, which emphasized the importance of the rule of law and recommended major increases in the UN's capacity to support the implementation of rule of law programs.[14] Since 2001, Security Council resolutions on peacekeeping have explicitly authorized peacekeepers to engage in core rule of law activities. One such example is Security Council Resolution 1542 of 2004, which established the UN Stabilization Mission in Haiti (MINUSTAH). The Council specified that the mission would monitor and report on the human rights situation; reestablish the corrections system and investigate violations of human rights and humanitarian law; help rebuild, reform, and restructure the Haitian national police, including vetting and certifying that its personnel had not committed grave human rights violations; develop a "strategy of reform and institutional development of the judiciary"; and "assist with the restoration and maintenance of the rule of law, public safety and public order." This clear and aggressive approach represented a quantum leap from MICIVIH's 1993 "terms of reference," which timidly called for "talks between the O.A.S. and the UN . . . and the Haitian authorities . . . with a view to establishing an agenda and schedule for instituting and effecting institutional reform."[15] This 2004 mandate captured crucial elements of rule of law reform in a postconflict setting: dealing simultaneously with key institutions like the judiciary, police, and corrections; vetting personnel as a way to reform institutions while insuring that past violators do not continue to wield power; and developing broad-based reform strategies for these institutions. At the same time, fundamental shortcomings appeared to remain in the UN's approach in light of the dramatic rise in violence in early 2005.[16]

Similarly, a Security Council resolution on Afghanistan specifically requested action to establish a fair and transparent judicial system while working to strengthen the rule of law.[17] In addition, the Security Council resolution that established the UN Operation in Burundi (ONUB) authorized ONUB to provide advice and assistance to carry out institutional reforms and "to complete the implementation of the reform of the judiciary and correction system."[18] For the UN Organization Mission in the Democratic Republic of Congo (MONUC), the Council called for a direct UN role to support the rule of law.[19] MONUC, in coordination with other UN agencies, donors, and nongovernmental organizations, was to provide assistance to reform the security forces and reestablish the rule of law.[20]

For the UN Observer Mission in Liberia (UNOMIL), early on, the Security Council mandated that the mission was only to investigate human rights violations and monitor the general situation. UNOMIL had no authority or means to support rule of law initiatives.[21] Ten years after these initial resolutions, the Security Council took a different approach, reflecting the evolution in peacekeeping doctrine. In 2003 the Council decided that the new operation, the UN Mission in Liberia (UNMIL) must support the implementation of the peace process, which required it to "assist the transitional government . . . in developing a strategy to consolidate governmental institutions, including a national legal framework and judicial and correctional institutions."[22]

The merging of military peacekeepers' capacity and willingness to protect civilians in civil wars, together with the enhanced presence of civilian peacekeepers to tackle some of the root causes of the violence, has generated a surge in attention to the rule of law in a manner unprecedented in UN peace operations. Unfortunately, Security Council mandates have outstripped the capacities of the UN Secretariat and major agencies to implement the resolutions' directives.

The Next Step:
Consolidating Practice and Improving UN Capacity

As demonstrated in the recent Security Council resolutions mentioned above, the rule of law now occupies a new and central role in international peacekeeping, at least at the rhetorical level. The UN Secretary-General's report to the Security Council in August 2004 reinforced this trend, which had been developing since the first large civilian deployments in peace operations began in 1993. This report, on the rule of law and transitional justice in conflict and postconflict societies, distills many of the principles, "lessons," and guidance, most learned through trial and error, in the eighteen peace operations deployed since the end of the Cold War.[23] Enthusiastically endorsed by the Security Council, some of whose members only a few years earlier had rejected the very notion that the rule of law had anything to do with peacekeeping, this report summarizes current UN doctrine on the paramount role of the rule of law in securing a lasting peace. The Secretary-General reinforced his commitment to the issue by making the rule of law the central theme in his speech at the opening of the fifty-ninth session of the General Assembly, noting that the rule of law is an essential element and guarantee of human dignity, especially for people who have endured war.[24]

The Secretary-General's report enunciating UN doctrine for rule of law programs in all phases of postconflict peacebuilding highlighted several needs in particular: improving methodology and adopting comprehensive approaches, shoring up greater resources for the rule of law, and aiming for local ownership of the reform process. While these principles and lessons had been identified in countless studies and conferences over the past decade, centralizing them and bestowing the Secretary-General's, and now the Security Council's, imprimatur have given them added power and influence. However, the UN's capacity to address the immensely complex rule of law challenges in situations where institutions have ceased to function and security is fragile remains patchy at best.

UN Capacity

The Brahimi Report recommended a steep increase in the UN Secretariat's capacity to analyze, plan, mobilize, and implement rule of law programs in peace operations. However, some member states continued to resist expanding UN capacity in this area, seeing the work as primarily "developmental," and worried that money spent on peacekeeping would not be spent on development. They also feared that peacekeeping was becoming increasingly "interventionist." It was therefore not surprising that the budgetary arm of the General Assembly refused to recommend funding for additional posts for the DPKO. All the DPKO could muster was two additional mid-level posts, one concentrating on judicial matters and the other on corrections.

Those who would say that money and personnel would be better used for development instead of peacekeeping fall into the trap of the "false dilemma." The two spheres are mutually reinforcing, rather than mutually exclusive. Helping to build the core rule of law institutions in a postconflict setting creates the conditions for long-term development to take root and be sustainable. Failing to address the rule of law challenge immediately may lead to renewed fighting, making development extremely difficult. Without the rule of law, development may remain in a humanitarian emergency phase and economic actors may be unlikely to invest in such an uncertain and dangerous environment.[25] The *Financial Times* editorial board got it right when, in commenting on the Secretary-General's reform package announced on March 21, 2005, it stated: "[The] key idea [of the reform package] is that development, security and human rights are not only imperative on their own, but are mutually reinforcing and should be pursued together."[26] The Secretary-General himself eloquently stated that "we will not enjoy development without security, we will not enjoy security without development, and we will not enjoy either without respect for human rights."[27]

While the haggling and back-room politicking continued in UN corridors, the Executive Committee on Peace and Security (ECPS) formed the Task Force for Development of Comprehensive Rule of Law Strategies for Peace Operations. Comprising senior representatives from eleven UN agencies and departments, the task force met during May–August 2002. It subsequently produced a report outlining how the United Nations could work more coherently and effectively on rule of law issues in all phases of peace operations.[28] It also produced massive annexes that identified existing UN expertise and experience in all aspects of the rule of law, reliable expertise outside the UN system and existing UN manuals, training materials, and guidelines. The task force discovered that the United Nations had a wealth of experience and useful tools to do rule of law work; the problem was that departments and agencies did not know about one another's expertise (and sometimes even their own) and rarely exchanged information.

The ECPS task force recommended creating a mechanism so that the United Nations could pool its experience and tools to maximize efficiency, coherence, and impact in the rule of law sector. "Focal points" representing the UNDP, the Department of Political Affairs (DPA), the DPKO, the UN Children's Fund (UNICEF), the UN High Commissioner for Refugees (UNHCR), and the OHCHR would meet, in person or electronically, to identify priorities and core rule of law challenges in a particular peace operation, ideally even before a mission began. Such premission planning helped accelerate UN work on rule of law issues in Afghanistan and Liberia. The focal points also contributed to discussions of mission mandates to ensure that they included rule of law priorities.

Greater awareness and lobbying for adequate funding and posts in mission budgets and staffing tables also fell to the rule of law focal points. No one wanted to arrive in a country and then realize that there was no money to vet the police or to pump in clean water to prisons, or that five more people were needed to train judges. And if detaining juveniles was a problem, the guidelines that UNICEF had prepared for Bosnia-Herzegovina could be adapted for Afghanistan or Liberia and not have to be reinvented. This accelerated the UN's impact on addressing these issues, so that time was not wasted in the early mission days.

It is too early to tell whether the newer peacekeeping missions in Burundi, Côte d'Ivoire, and Sudan, for example, will enjoy greater success than did the earlier missions. But there are encouraging signs. Based on recommendations made in the Brahimi Report and the report of the ECPS task force, the rule of law has gained much greater visibility. These recommendations led directly to the creation of three new posts in the DPKO's Criminal Law and Judicial Advisory Unit, and a fourth post will be filled soon. With specialists in judicial reform and corrections, this unit helped ensure that rule of law issues received early and intense attention from mission planners for Afghanistan, Iraq, Liberia, Congo, Burundi, and Haiti. It advocated strongly for proper staffing, mandates, and resources so that the real needs of the missions and of the host countries would be met. The unit has conducted numerous assessment missions either right before a peacekeeping mission deploys, or in its early stages; this was never done before.

With the exception of Iraq, each of the aforementioned missions contains dedicated rule of law officers who liaise closely with their military, police, human rights, humanitarian, and civil affairs counterparts. Their analyses and recommendations appear in the regular reports sent by the Special Representatives of the Secretary-General (SRSGs), via the Secretary-General, to the Security Council.[29]

The Rule of Law Unit in the UN Mission in Côte d'Ivoire (UNOCI) is fairly typical.[30] Rule of law officers working in Côte d'Ivoire, a divided country that still suffers from sporadic conflict, have identified several key activities: surveying the needs of the judiciary, monitoring the courts, improving prison conditions (especially in the north, where the insurgents have taken over all state functions), reforming the legislature, and combating sexual abuse and exploitation.[31] UNOCI's Rule of Law Unit has also implemented some quick-impact projects as recommended in the Brahimi Report.[32] For example, UNOCI financed a training course in hairdressing for women prisoners in Abidjan, and a woodworking course for juveniles in detention. The need to have some visible, concrete signs that the situation is improving is crucial to building momentum and confidence for more systemic rule of law initiatives.[33]

The rule of law received further impetus from two reports issued in the spring of 2005, the Secretary-General's *In Larger Freedom,* and the High Commissioner for Human Rights' own action plan, titled *Protection and Empowerment.*[34] The Secretary-General reiterated his support for the centrality of the rule of law in peace operations that he first stated in his August 2004 report on this subject. The High Commissioner's action plan called for a large increase in the number of field personnel deployed by her office, some of whom would be specifically assigned to the rule of law arena.[35]

Programmatic Challenges

There is no rule of law "blueprint," nor should there be. Many mistakes flow from the misconception that by marching down a checklist, one can achieve lasting peace and security and rule of law nirvana. At the same time, there are certain challenges that are common to most countries emerging from conflict—challenges that should be anticipated in advance so that adequate responses can be prepared. This section discusses some of the key hurdles to implementing rule of law programs and their implications for specific institutions and actors: the military, police, local actors, and nonstate actors.

Rule of law and the military. For rule of law programming, the major challenge in the peace implementation phase is to restore basic, immediate security, without which deeper engagement in rule of law reform is not possible. This usually means that international military peacekeepers must do police work in the early days, since UN civilian police do not arrive in time in the numbers necessary to provide basic public security in those all-important first hundred days.[36] Dag Hammarskjöld once famously observed: "Peacekeeping is not a job for soldiers, but only soldiers can do it."[37] Moreover, in most modern peace operations there is no clear demarcation between military activities and public security in the postconflict phase. One cannot neatly divide threats as requiring either a military response or police action; rather, some combination of the two is necessary. For example, even four years after the bombing stopped in Kosovo, North Atlantic Treaty Organization (NATO) troops, in a typical day, were under fire from insurgent groups, removed landmines, fought organized criminal gangs engaged in smuggling goods and trafficking women, and tried to stop grenades and mortars from being launched at minority ethnic enclaves.

Looting and revenge are usually widespread in the aftermath of conflict, and can threaten rule of law programming, as well as the entire peacekeeping and statebuilding undertaking. Street justice sets a tone of lawlessness, allows criminal networks to form, and makes it harder, later, to insist on equal treatment before the law. The looting and summary justice carried out by the Kosovo Liberation Army after the NATO bombing campaign in 1999 immensely complicated subsequent efforts to build the rule of law; UNMIK still reels from the consequences of this lax attitude. In Iraq, the extensive looting and other criminal activity by organized gangs in March–May 2003 were entirely predictable, largely avoidable, and deeply counterproductive for all subsequent rule of law initiatives. Mistakes made in the early days tend to have a long-term impact and are magnified many times over.

Rule of law and civilian police. Another common problem is the degree to which the existing police force is able to carry out the innumerable responsibilities in public security in the aftermath of war. Insight gained in recent peace operations warns that relying solely on the existing police in states as brutal and repressive as Iraq, Afghanistan, Liberia, Haiti, Kosovo, and Guatemala undermines rule of law efforts. Changing the color of their uniforms or their name, from "police force" to "police service," will not suffice. The

United States tried this in 1994–1995 in Haiti, and the population ran their former oppressors out of town.

Many states will need a new police force, comprised largely of new recruits because the old force is so tainted. Yet it takes time to create a new police force. Vetting the old police to weed out human rights abusers requires months, not weeks. Pressure will build to give the new recruits crash courses and deploy them quickly. Yet most will be rookies requiring oversight by more experienced police. In Kosovo, Bosnia-Herzegovina, East Timor, and Haiti, UN civilian police, recruited from a variety of countries, provided such mentoring. Yet it took months to get these experienced internationals in place. Finding the right mix of skills, experience, and temperament to ensure effective mentoring is also vital to the success of early policing efforts.

Rule of law and local actors. Peacekeepers have learned that picking the right local partners—genuine representatives who want to change a corrupt, venal system—is a high-order priority. State and nonstate actors should be involved in a meaningful way in all elements of rule of law programming, including analysis, design, implementation, and evaluation. This requires superb judgment and diplomatic finesse on the part of all peacekeepers. Likewise, insisting that the "old ways" must be jettisoned while introducing law-based police, courts, and public administration upsets local power-brokers, yet peacekeepers cannot compromise on fundamental principles. Peacekeepers should seek a balanced view that combines respect for local opinion and practices with a healthy understanding of the causes of conflict and human rights abuses.[38]

Rule of law practitioners must have a realistic understanding of what is possible. Putting too much responsibility in local hands too early can undermine rule of law efforts. In Kosovo, some officials working in UNMIK insisted that local courts should try war crimes cases. Even though all the judges and prosecutors were ethnic Albanian and the defendants in these cases were ethnic Serbs or Roma, UNMIK believed it was preferable to have local trials and no international involvement. It took several cases of severe miscarriages of justice, and death threats against judges, witnesses, and defense lawyers, before UNMIK realized what some had tried to tell mission administrators all along: that it was impossible to ensure fair trials for Serb defendants just yet. UNMIK belatedly agreed to enlist foreign judges and prosecutors for especially sensitive cases.[39] The challenge, then, is to determine how best to combine the experience, knowledge, resources, and skills on offer from international rule of law experts, with the needs, priorities, and skills of national counterparts in a way that builds on their strengths and knowledge of their own societies (see Chapter 7).

No single group of local entities has a more vital role in rule of law reform than NGOs. No reform—justice, police, corrections, military, or administrative—will take root and lead to real change without the support and understanding of civil society. Peacekeepers must consult, early and often, the population whom these institutions should serve and protect. And the consultations must not be mere window-dressing but meaningful opportunities for those concerned with justice and human rights, including for women, children, the mentally ill, the elderly, the disabled, and other marginalized and vulnerable groups, to have their say and contribute to analysis, planning, implementation, and evaluation of rule of law reform initiatives.

Rule of law and nonstate actors. Nonstate parties, paramilitaries, or rebel groups pose particular challenges for rule of law initiatives in peacekeeping operations. They are difficult to reach, lack international recognition, are seen as "bandits" or worse by the state, and often have shaky command of their troops.

Disarmament, demobilization, and reintegration programs have the greatest likelihood of incorporating nonstate actors into rule of law projects. Merging different warring factions into new armies or police forces is difficult and sometimes unavoidable. Vetting all applicants to assess their suitability for employment in police, military, or other public functions is now an important part of the immediate postconflict landscape. The UN missions in Kosovo, Haiti, Liberia, and the Democratic Republic of Congo have reviewed the records of both former military and police, and members of insurgent groups, to determine whether they are eligible to join new or reconstituted corps.

In case of rejection, the International Organization for Migration and other bodies have conducted job-training programs to offer alternative employment to people who often know only how to use a gun to earn a living. While these programs are obviously necessary to obviate the situation where suddenly unemployed people accustomed to violence wreak mayhem in a very fragile environment (El Salvador, Guatemala, and Liberia being recent examples), often no jobs exist for them at the end of the training. The World Bank, the International Monetary Fund, regional banks, and bilateral donors must do more to pump the economy with jobs, even short-term ones, to avoid blowing oxygen on a fire that is still smoldering.

Building the Capacity of Rule of Law Institutions

UN peace operations have devoted much time, energy, and resources to training local counterparts in the rule of law sector. These training efforts begin in the earliest days of a peace operation. In many places, rule of law professionals have had little opportunity to gain, let alone enhance, skills and learning essential to their professions. For example, many judges in Haiti do not even have law degrees, not to mention any specialized training on how to be a judge. The same situation prevailed for police in Afghanistan, Sierra Leone, Cambodia, and Angola. In Bosnia-Herzegovina, Kosovo, Georgia, Guatemala, and Burundi, the problem was that the police had received training that privileged security and order over respect for human rights. So those police had to "unlearn" what they had been taught and learn a new style of policing that would respect rights and foster a new policing ethos to serve the public rather than act as an occupying force.

Local nongovernmental organizations working on human rights or rule of law issues also need and receive large doses of training from the international actors in a peace operation. These NGOs can act as crucial counterweights if the state starts to overstep its authority or violate basic rule of law principles and human rights. In Rwanda, the UN's Human Rights Field Operation (HRFOR) had an entire department devoted to training local NGOs, teacher's organizations, women's groups, journalists, and others on human rights standards, rights of detainees and prisoners, children's rights, and fair trials.[40] The goal is to enhance the "demand" side in the justice equation: build the strength of local actors to demand justice and accountability from the government.

While training is a necessary part of reform, it is not sufficient. Training is not a panacea and must support other capacity-building activities. As one East Timorese colleague has noted, "Training is needed, but it is also important to create a 'human rights and rule of law culture,' which incorporates social mobilization, fundamental institutional change and vigorous watch-dog advocacy."[41]

Previously, any type of legal reform, prison administration, or concern about police practices was the work of the High Commissioner for Human Rights, the UNDP, or UNICEF in the course of their normal programming work; this usually meant a state at peace with functioning institutions needing some "fine-tuning." The UN departments and agencies, with minor variations, approached the work in a highly technical way, with great attention devoted to drafting constitutions or laws and ensuring that these were consistent with international standards. Training and workshops, often very short and conducted by foreigners who "parachuted in" from the outside, constituted what passed for "capacity building." Assessments of the impact of all this training on actual performance were rare.[42] No UN agency developed experience or expertise in how to build adequate capacity for functional and effective rule of law institutions. To do so would require a transformation in the way the United Nations, across the board, has conducted business in this area.

UN efforts should place legal reform and training within a broader strategy of transforming the core rule of law entities into functioning, effective, ethical, accountable, and transparent institutions. In particular, the United Nations has not identified or implemented projects that address the root causes of rule of law weaknesses in postconflict states. Tinkering with penal codes, conducting a three-day workshop for judges on the International Covenant on Civil and Political Rights, and training a few select prosecutors does not adequately address the causes of the rot in state institutions; neither do those causes spring solely or even primarily from a lack of legal knowledge.

Rule of law experience shows that an intimate connection exists between monitoring and institution building/reform. While those responsible for monitoring human rights, the administration of justice, police behavior, prison conditions, and corruption in public administration must investigate and verify whether violations have occurred, the primary purpose of this monitoring is not to amass evidence for reports to publicly denounce the perpetrators. Sound monitoring reveals strengths and weaknesses and permits a diagnosis so that reform projects can start from a thorough understanding of actual practice. Rule of law reform will fail unless the peace operation knows whether the minister of justice controls all judicial appointments and understands the root causes of corruption, and whether the police have disciplined their officers. Such knowledge only comes from intense, ongoing observation and interaction by peacekeepers in the field.

One successful approach to rule of law institution building has emphasized open competition for judicial posts based on objective criteria. When people don't owe their jobs to someone, they are much more likely to be independent and decide cases on the merits, not on their assessment of who has more power. A study by MINUGUA in Guatemala showed that those judges who were selected through competition under the new Judicial Career Law showed more commitment to their jobs, were more likely to use legal reasoning in their decisions, and demonstrated greater independence than judges employed under the old system. A sweeping change in the judicial personnel in the Special Brcko District in Bosnia-Herzegovina yielded a marked increase in quality and integrity. Hiring was done entirely on a rigorous and objective basis looking at education, experience, and behavior during the war.

As has been noted, "Perhaps the most important lesson from the field mission experience is the complementarity between human rights monitoring and institution building. Monitoring gave missions the ability to identify the sources and scope of human rights problems throughout the country. This information could then be used to design reform measures and training programs. Finally, field monitoring provided direct feedback on the effectiveness of reform strategies or programs as they were implemented."[43] This "virtuous circle" of analysis, diagnosis, planning, implementation, review, and assessment has proven the best approach to rule of law reform in postconflict countries.

The United Nations needs to devote more attention, effort, and resources toward strengthening the sinews of rule of law institutions. In particular, the DPKO, the OHCHR, and the UNDP should create effective management structures, transparent operational procedures, and sound financial management systems to ensure the optimal use of always-scarce resources. Otherwise, even the best-trained individuals will soon revert to coping strategies in their weak, opaque, and corrupt institutions. The effort and money devoted to training, however excellent, will be wasted, thus further demoralizing the public, donors, and perhaps most of all, the police, judges, and others who completed UN training programs.

UN development experts should work with peacekeepers to establish incentives and sanctions to reward integrity and competence while punishing misconduct. Transparency in all hiring and firing decisions destroys discriminatory practices that marginalize many people who felt that the police, military, and courts did not belong to them. Creating accountability mechanisms for personnel and the budget and installing modern methods of administration and management are more important to lasting rule of law reform than any training program.

Policy Recommendations

Based on the still-evolving policy and practice of the United Nations in peace operations, peacekeepers have identified a number of lessons for improving the implementation of rule of law programs in the aftermath of conflict. Clearly, many of the recommendations below are now well accepted by those working on the rule of law at headquarters and in the field. The greatest challenge, then, is to take the steps necessary to adopt them.

Rule of Law Strategy

The United Nations, bilateral donors, and the host government must agree on an overall rule of law strategy from the outset, specifying priorities, sequencing, benchmarks, indicators, evaluation mechanisms, responsibilities, and deadlines. Follow-up is as essential as planning and coordination. The failure to agree to an overall strategy dooms the effort to piecemeal, ad hoc initiatives that often result in waste and duplication.

Coherent, Unified Approach to Reform

The United Nations should adopt a unified approach across the rule of law spectrum. Judicial, police, and prison reforms must proceed together. While this has received rhetorical support, it is seldom put into practice, largely because various UN departments and agencies want to protect their "turf," budgets, and programs, and may be jealous of sharing credit. Moreover, police reform consistently tends to outpace all other reform efforts, thus creating problems of prison overcrowding and release of detainees who may well be dangerous. This subverts police morale and can lead to increased crime rates and the danger of "street justice" being applied by a population fed up with violence or by frustrated police officers themselves. It is therefore important to ensure the proper allocation of resources to the judiciary and corrections to decrease the time lag and increase the synchronization of reform.[44]

One positive example is Rwanda, where the authorities seized the initiative and presented their strategy to the donors, who in turn agreed to divide the labor based on their own expertise and resources. The government clearly ran the process and held donors and itself accountable for measurable progress in each of the core areas: police, judiciary, military, and corrections. Good donor coordination resulted.[45] This shows that some lessons had been learned, because the opposite situation prevailed just a year earlier in Haiti, where the government had no plan and the donors haggled over turf and priorities. No benchmarks were set, no one was accountable, and the result was a waste of millions of dollars and several years of effort, and a deeply suspicious and cynical attitude in the population toward the rule of law.

Resources

To accomplish the challenges inherent in rule of law work, the Security Council needs to allocate adequate resources to peace operations. As was stated in the 2000 Brahimi Report and reconfirmed in the 2002 final report of the ECPS task force, the staffing tables and funding for the various types of experts who are needed to work on rule of law issues must reflect the centrality of the rule of law to the success of the operation. The United Nations must recruit and deploy experts faster, improve logistical support, and dedicate funding for programs designed to yield quick and visible impacts to reassure the population and build momentum for change quickly.

Strategic Planning

Any reformed judiciary or police force will need help in strategic planning—how to budget, allocate resources, anticipate training and deployment needs, identify specialized needs (forensics, crime labs, domestic violence intervention and counseling, tackling organized crime, trafficking in humans and drugs, etc.). UN departments and agencies, especially the DPKO, the UNDP, and the DPA, should ensure that their rule of law teams include planning specialists and experts in administration and management, including personnel and finance.

Transparency and Accountability

The United Nations should address, early on, the need for transparency and accountability in public administration (vehicle registration, building permits, trash removal, public health inspectors, banking regulations, tax collection, etc.), since a large share of the population has contact with these agencies and their past histories of discriminatory practices and corruption. Any continuing bad practices by these agencies can quickly deepen "lawlessness" and the perception (real or not) that things are out of control or have not changed. Accountability is also critical for the police, judiciary, corrections, and other rule of law institutions. Judicial inspection units or internal disciplinary bodies must have adequate resources and total independence, and judicial misbehavior must be punished quickly and fairly; otherwise the public will lose faith in the enterprise, concluding quite reasonably that nothing has changed. Judges, prosecutors, and lawyers in general must be held to the highest standards of professional conduct and integrity. Internal and external police accountability mechanisms are likewise a first-order priority, as they help ensure police discipline and secure public trust.

Involvement of Local Actors

Early and meaningful involvement of local experts, both inside and outside government, is a prerequisite of success. When possible, UN missions should hire local experts to conduct periodic "reality tests" and to increase the chances that programs will continue after the UN's departure. UN operations in Haiti, East Timor, and Sierra Leone used local experts, while the Organization for Security and Cooperation in Europe (OSCE) in Bosnia-Herzegovina, Kosovo, and Macedonia has developed excellent models to draw on local lawyers' and judges' knowledge in designing and implementing programs in all the major rule of law areas. In Bosnia-Herzegovina and Macedonia, these national lawyers have completely taken over international lawyers' work on complex property law claims. The most technically sound, substantively perfect rule of law initiative will not succeed unless it includes meaningful local participation and support. The United Nations needs to consider developing more flexible employment guidelines to take advantage of the pool of local knowledge.

Access to Justice

Enhancing access to justice to people historically marginalized and left unprotected by the law should be a first-order priority. The lower courts should not be overlooked at the expense of the higher-profile cases and tribunals. Most people's contacts with the judiciary are at the lowest-level courts, and it is there that they must see that changes are occurring, and quickly.

In Sierra Leone, the UN peace operation, with substantial support from the United Kingdom's Department for International Development, has made reopening, staffing, and equipping lower-level magistrate courts in provincial capitals a top priority. For example, the court in Makeni, which previously had been the "capital" of the Revolutionary United Front rebels, was completely restored and stocked with law books, and a magistrate deployed to work with two assistants. The magistrate "rides the circuit" in the district, holding hearings in even smaller towns and villages on a rotating basis. The UN Observer Mission in Sierra Leone (UNOMSIL), on the advice of Sierra Leonean judges and lawyers, understood how crucial it was to "bring the courts" to the traditionally neglected countryside, which had suffered more than its share of violence during the war.

Public Outreach

Public understanding and acceptance of the reasons for rule of law reform is critical for the credibility and legitimacy of the reforms. Some people stand to lose if reform occurs, and power relations will change. Those who benefited from the previous regime will see reform as a threat. Therefore, the Security Council and the SRSG must publicly support those working on rule of law matters. If successful, reforming the courts and police, holding all government officials accountable, and giving the formerly excluded a voice in how they are governed will constitute a major transformation in postconflict states.

To this end, all UN rule of law efforts should emphasize public information campaigns. Explaining to the public their role in strengthening state institutions is essential to overall success. The United Nations has often learned this lesson the hard way. In Haiti, for example, a crowd threatened to kill a judge because he had ordered the release of an alleged gang leader. The crowd believed that the leader had bribed his way out of jail, a perfectly reasonable assumption in Haiti and many other places. Yet the judge had only done his job, reviewing the evidence within forty-eight hours of arrest as required by the constitution and concluding that there were insufficient grounds to justify detaining the suspect. Once this was explained to the population, they calmed down.

Program Monitoring and Evaluation

The United Nations should perform more systematic and rigorous evaluation of rule of law programs. "You can't improve what you can't measure" comes from professional business managers, and UN rule of law personnel should take this dictum to heart. Security Council resolutions or the peace operation's terms of reference should include a monitoring mechanism so that the United Nations can track any progress in the administration of justice, law enforcement, and related rule of law activities. Measures or benchmarks for the judiciary and police, for example, should include ethnic, racial, and gender diversity of key staff, financial resources (percentage of the national budget dedicated to the courts), objective appointment and promotion criteria, transparency in decisionmaking, accountability and applicability of professional codes of ethics, and protections from external interference.

An energetic inspector general of the new Haitian national police in 1994–1995 created trust with the population by disciplining, suspending, and handing over for prosecution misbehaving and abusive police officers. This sent a clear signal to both the police and the population: impunity is over; you can lose your job and even go to jail if you violate the law or police code of ethics. A Haitian official noted: "One police officer disciplined for misconduct is worth 100 training sessions on human rights."[46]

Similarly in Kosovo, UNMIK, through the OSCE, has created an internal oversight body that is highly effective in rooting out and punishing any misbehavior. As a result, according to a recent public opinion survey, the population's confidence in the Kosovo national police was the highest among all public institutions.[47]

Personnel Management

Successful police or judicial reform is as much about personnel management, career paths, and transparent disciplinary procedures as it is about human rights training and public awareness campaigns, improved crime-fighting equipment, or computerized case management systems. Yet the former set of issues has often been overlooked at the expense of the latter. Rule of law institutions do not operate in a vacuum, and it is often a national political ethos and system of incentives and punishments that need reforming. "The hardest part isn't cleaning it up, it's changing the mind-set of the people," said Major Chris Spohn, a US Army soldier working in Iraq but whose words speak for countless military and civilian peacekeepers everywhere.[48] The United Nations must recognize the broader governance challenges when it comes to rule of law reform.

In addition, as recommended by the ECPS task force, the United Nations should adopt more flexible hiring practices and easier rules to collaborate with relevant non-UN entities in order to accelerate the deployment of rule of law experts to peace operations.

Conclusion

The United Nations, though a predominant player in peace implementation, is but one actor among numerous others in this field. What, then, are some of the comparative advantages of the United Nations vis-à-vis other actors in implementing rule of law programs in peace operations?

The United Nations enjoys several advantages: its universal reach and the authority of its most powerful body, the Security Council; legitimacy and credibility; impartiality; a growing cadre of experts in the essential fields; access to the knowledge, expertise, and contacts of UN agencies with long experience in the rule of law sector; and its ability to implement rule of law programs that are increasingly comprehensive and mutually supporting, as planning and coordination become more streamlined.

However, this does not mean that powerful member states do not try to pursue their agendas through the United Nations, or that it is free from all taints of bias. The comparative advantages of other organizations include the following:

• Regional groups offer local knowledge and facility with local languages, and can help convince the host country that rule of law interventions are well-grounded in the region and compatible with regional goals and specificities. The European Union and the OSCE in Bosnia-Herzegovina and Macedonia, the African Union in Darfur, and the Organization of American States (OAS) in Haiti offer promising models for greater regional involvement.

• International financial institutions, including the World Bank and regional banks, offer comparatively vast resources—especially financial—which the United Nations usually lacks.

• Bilateral donors also have greater resources. However, they often have other agendas that can weaken the UN's claim of acting purely as an impartial actor. For example, in Haiti the dominant role of the United States in judicial reform undermined the entire enterprise for the United Nations, the OAS, and other bilateral donors.

By enhancing cooperation and coordination, then, the work of the United Nations and regional organizations, key member states, and international financial institutions as a whole can exceed the sum of the parts.

However, equally critical is the need for the United Nations to improve cooperation and coordination *within* the organization. The Secretary-General made a series of sound recommendations in Paragraph 65 of his August 23, 2004, report to the Security Council. These recommendations recognize something discovered by the ECPS task force two years earlier: the United Nations already has a wealth of experience on rule of law and transitional justice matters across agencies and departments. A spectrum of departments of agencies, including the UNDP, UNICEF, the UNHCR, the DPKO, the DPA, the OHCHR, the UN Development Fund for Women (UNIFEM), the Office of Legal Affairs (OLA), and Office for the Coordination of Humanitarian Affairs (OCHA), have something to contribute to postconflict reform efforts, whether it is a training manual for the police, a project on juvenile justice, oversight strategies for correctional facilities, or a public information campaign on access to justice. A major challenge for the UN family is to harness this expertise and keep refining and retooling it while responding more quickly to the precise demands of peace operations.

The Secretary-General's call for fundamental UN reform, as enunciated in his report *In Larger Freedom,* underscores the primacy of human rights, security, and development, all of which must be underpinned by the rule of law. It also implicitly recognizes that the rule of law is simply too important to be left to the various UN agencies and departments to pursue on their own based on their varying analyses and priorities. It is hoped that the Secretary-General's endorsement of the importance of the rule of law, coupled with the successes and failures of past peace operations, will catalyze the action needed to improve rule of law programming in postconflict situations.

Experience has shown that every dollar or hour spent on the rule of law reaps an immediate dividend for those the United Nations is meant to serve: the populations in war-torn societies who seek to put their lives back together. The challenge and opportunity for the United Nations is to devote greater resources and to deploy them more wisely and effectively.

Notes

1. This is also true for efforts to establish accountability for past violations of human rights. The exception proving this rule is Mozambique, but even here it is too early to make any final conclusions. Even in Spain, which used to be cited as an example of a state establishing the rule of law without addressing its past, nearly seventy years after the end of its civil war, descendants of those executed, tortured, and "disappeared" have begun to lobby parliament for a truth commission, reparations, and other relief. Some mass graves have been located and examined by forensic scientists in 2003–2004. For their descendants, "the justice they seek for their family members has been deferred for more than a half a century, and they are willing to wait no more." Geoff Pingree, "To Right Past Wrongs, Spaniards Seek Present Change," *Christian Science Monitor,* February 2, 2005, p. 1.

2. For a comprehensive list of all past and present UN peace operations, see http://www.un.org/depts/dpko/dpko.

3. Most experts date the first UN peacekeeping operation to 1956 and the Suez crisis. Canada's foreign minister at that time, Lester Pearson, is credited with inventing both the term and the concept of "peacekeeping" as a way to defuse a dangerous threat to world peace and security.

4. Some of the early Security Council resolutions on Bosnia-Herzegovina provided for the UN Protection Force (UNPROFOR) to secure the Sarajevo airport, to establish "safe areas," and to assist in the safe delivery of relief supplies, but the authorization to intervene to physically protect civilians at risk was absent.

5. UN Security Council Resolution 1296 (2000), para. 9.

6. See, respectively, the following UN resolutions: Security Council Resolution 693 (1991), General Assembly Resolution 47/20B (1993), and General Assembly Resolution 48/267 (1994). MICIVIH was a joint venture between the UN and the Organization of American States (OAS).

7. The Paris Peace Agreements on a Comprehensive Political Settlement of the Cambodian Conflict invited the UN Security Council to establish UNTAC's mandate as outlined in the agreements. The Secretary-General elaborated this mandate in his report to the Security Council: "Report of the Secretary-General on Cambodia*,"* UN Doc. S/23613 (February 19, 1992).

8. Dennis McNamara, "UN Human Rights Activities in Cambodia: An Evaluation," in *Honoring Human Rights and Keeping the Peace: Lessons from El Salvador, Cambodia, and Haiti,* edited by Alice Henkin (Washington, D.C.: Aspen Institute, 1995), p. 50.

9. These terms of reference of MICIVIH were agreed to by then-president Jean-Bertrand Aristide and the de facto prime minister, but were not published as a UN document. The government of Haiti later requested the United Nations to circulate the terms of reference, which it did as *The Situation of Democracy and Human Rights in Haiti,* UN Doc. A/48/944 (May 23, 1994).

10. This pertained particularly to the then-powerful chairman of the Senate Foreign Relations Committee, Jesse Helms, who considered judicial reform "nation building," a dirty term at the time in Washington, rather than "peacekeeping." The UN Mission in Bosnia and Herzegovina (UNMIB) had begged to keep the Judicial System Assessment Program. See International Crisis Group, *Bosnia: Reshaping the International Machinery* (Brussels, November 29, 2001), p. 6, n. 8.

11. For details on OHCHR technical cooperation programs, see http://www.ohchr.org/english/countries/coop/index.htm.

12. UN Interim Administration Mission in Kosovo, UN Security Council Resolution 1244 (1999).

13. UN Transitional Administration in East Timor, UN Security Council Resolution 1272 (1999).

14. United Nations, *Report of the Panel on United Nations Peace Operations* (Brahimi Report), UN Doc. A/55/305-S/2000/809, August 21, 2000.

15. United Nations/Organization of American States International Civilian Mission in Haiti, *Terms of Reference,* UN Doc. A/48/944 (May 23, 1994), para. 14.

16. "Haiti: On the Brink," *The Economist,* June 16, 2005.

17. UN Security Council Resolution 1536 (2004). This section relies on an internal memo produced by Stefano Varriale for the International Center for Transitional Justice, November 2004 (on file with author).

18. UN Security Council Resolution 1545 (2004).

19. UN Security Council Resolution 1493 (2003).

20. United Nations, *A Comprehensive Strategy to Eliminate Future Sexual Exploitation and Abuse in UN Peacekeeping Operations,* UN Doc. A/59/710 (March 24, 2005). This report, issued by the Secretary-General's adviser on sexual exploitation and abuse, Prince Zeid Al-Hussein, documented a serious problem plaguing some modern UN peace operations: the exploitation and sexual abuse of the local population, including children.

21. UN Security Council Resolution 866 (1993); UN Security Council Resolution 1020 (1995).

22. UN Security Council Resolution 1509 (2003).

23. United Nations, *The Rule of Law and Transitional Justice in Conflict and Post-Conflict Societies: Report of the Secretary-General,* UN Doc. S/2004/616 (August 23, 2004).

24. UN Secretary-General Office of the Spokesman, "Secretary-General's Address to the General Assembly," September 21, 2004.

25. See International Crisis Group, *Why Will No One Invest in Bosnia and Herzegovina?* Europe Report no. 64 (Brussels, April 21, 1999) for an analysis of the link between rule of law and investment/economic development. Admittedly, the relationship between rule of law, security, and economic development is complex, and some argue that development may occur without the "rule of law." See Chapters 2 and 3 in this volume.

26. "Wooing America," *Financial Times,* March 22, 2005.

27. United Nations, *In Larger Freedom: Towards Development, Security, and Human Rights for All—Report of the Secretary General,* UN Doc. A/59/2005 (March 21, 2005), para. 17.

28. United Nations, *Final Report of the Executive Committee on Peace and Security Task Force for Development of Comprehensive Rule of Law Strategies for Peace Operations* (August 15, 2002), approved by the Executive Committee on Peace and Security on September 30, 2002.

29. United Nations, *Fourth Report of the Secretary-General to the Security Council on the United Nations Operation in Burundi,* UN Doc. S/2005/328 (May 19, 2005).

30. UN Security Council Resolution 1528 (2004).

31. UNOCI, "Rule of Law Unit" (on file with author).

32. United Nations, *Report of the Panel on United Nations Peace Operations* (Brahimi Report), UN Doc. A/55/305-S/2000/809 (August 21, 2000), para. 37. According-ing to a study by the Henry Stimson Center, this particular recommendation on quick impact–projects has had a good record of implementation so far in many missions. See William Durch and Victoria Holt, *The Brahimi Report and the Future of UN Peace Operations* (Washington, D.C.: Henri Stimson Center, 2003), p. 118, tab. B-2: "Rating Implementation," http://www.stimson.org/pub.cfm?id=90.

33. "Presentation de l'Unite Rule of Law de l'ONUCI," February 24, 2005 (on file with author).

34. United Nations, *In Larger Freedom.*

35. Office of the High Commissioner for Human Rights, *The OHCHR Plan of Action: Protection and Empowerment* (May 21, 2005), pp. 2, 17, 20, 25, 29, and 31.

36. Simon Chesterman, "The Use of Force in UN Peace Operations," external study (New York: UN Department of Peacekeeping Operations, Peacekeeping Best Practices Unit, August 31, 2004), http://pbpu.unlb.org/pbpu/library/chesterman%20 (final%20final).pdf.

37. Quoted in *US Army Field Manual on Peace Operations,* Field Manual 100-23 Peace Operations (Headquarters, Department of the Army, December 1994), p. 1, http://www.dtic.mil/doctrine/jel/service_pubs/fm100_23.pdf.

38. For a discussion of the negative impact of showing too great a deference too soon to local actors and institutions, see William G. O'Neill, *Kosovo: An Unfinished Peace* (Boulder: Lynne Rienner, 2000).

39. Ibid., pp. 88–91; Gregory L. Naarden and Jeffrey B. Locke, "Peacekeeping and Prosecutorial Policy: Lessons from Kosovo," *American Journal of International Law* 98, no. 4 (2004): 727–743.

40. Ian Martin, "After Genocide: The UN Human Rights Field Operation in Rwanda" in *Honoring Human Rights: From Peace to Justice,* edited by Alice Henkin (Washington, D.C.: Aspen Institute, 1998), p. 281.

41. Author interview with anonymous UN official, May 2004.

42. Of the literally thousands of such trainings, I am aware of barely a handful of assessments of their effect on behavior and performance. See, for example, William G. O'Neill, "Gaining Compliance Without Force: Human Rights Field Operations," in *Civilians in War,* edited by Simon Chesterman (Boulder: Lynne Rienner, 2001), pp. 111–119.

43. Thomas Hammarberg and Patrick Gavigan, "Human Rights and Post-Conflict Institution Building," in Henkin, *Honoring Human Rights,* p. 183. See also William G. O'Neill, "Postscript," in Henkin, *Honoring Human Rights,* p. 188.

44. This was a major cause of lynching and other forms of summary execution in Haiti, which in turn fueled major political unrest throughout the late 1990s and up to President Aristide's forced departure in February 2004.

45. This is not to say that Rwanda is a rule of law paradise—far from it. Serious problems persist in the prisons, and freedoms of speech, association, and assembly are severely limited. But Rwanda does provide a positive example on the specific issue of securing donor coordination.

46. Author's interview with Haitian National Police Commissioner, Port-au-Prince, July 2004.

47. UNDP, "Public Opinion Survey of the Kosovo Police Service," (2004).

48. Bradley Graham, "A Sharp Shift from Killing to Kindness," *Washington Post,* December 4, 2004.

6

Model Codes:
Laying the Foundations
of the Rule of Law

Colette Rausch and Vivienne O'Connor

Reinstating the rule of law in a postconflict state is a work of gargantuan proportions. There is neither a quick fix nor a magic formula; rather, it is a lengthy, multilayered, and multileveled process. The UN Secretary-General's 2004 report *The Rule of Law and Transitional Justice in Conflict and Postconflict States* listed a number of postconflict tasks integral to the process of reinstating the rule of law: strengthening domestic law enforcement and justice institutions, coordinating international rule of law assistance, assisting in vetting and selection of police, judges, and prosecutors, establishing legal aid systems, and setting up legal training programs, to name but a few.[1] In addition to these tasks, it is important to ensure that "the law" is adequate. The Secretary-General's report points to the necessity of having an effective legal framework in the form of modern laws[2] that are consistent with international human rights norms and standards.[3]

The importance of having adequate laws cannot be overstated. They lay a solid foundation on which the rule of law can be built. As stated in the *Handbook on UN Multidimensional Peacekeeping Operations:* "A national legal framework or penal code, consonant with international human rights norms and standards, is the basis for establishing the rule of law and is the starting point for effective law enforcement and criminal justice."[4] The difficulty in the past has been that the criminal legislation in place in conflict and postconflict states has been found to be grossly inadequate, and thus in need of reform or revision.[5] It is a vital first step in filling the rule of law vacuum that is evident in many postconflict societies.

This chapter focuses on this law reform process as the starting point of overall efforts to construct or reconstruct the rule of law in conflict and postconflict societies, granting particular attention to the potential relevance and utility of a set of legal codes developed as part of the Model Codes for Post-Conflict Criminal Justice Project. The chapter begins with a historical overview of the challenges involved in the administration of justice in peace operations, exploring how these challenges have prompted significant advances in the field of rule of law and law reform. Despite such advances, significant gaps in current mechanisms for the administration of justice still exist. It is from these gaps that the impetus for the Model Codes Project arose. Next the chapter elaborates on the rationale and purpose of the project, detailing the development process of the model codes and addressing their implementation and utilization, and then discusses the potential challenges and problems in the application of the codes. Finally, the chapter highlights the promises and limitations of the model codes and offers policy recommendations for international actors.

UN Involvement in Justice Administration

The level of involvement of the United Nations in the administration of justice in conflict and postconflict states has increased significantly over time. In the early to middle 1990s, its role centered predominantly on policing: monitoring local police forces,[6] undertaking joint patrols with national police forces,[7] providing assistance in the reorganization and restructuring of police forces,[8] advising local governments on police practice and training,[9] or conducting police training.[10] The establishment of the UN Transitional Authority in Cambodia (UNTAC)[11] saw this role expand to one in which it was responsible "for direct control or supervision in the areas of maintenance of law and order, protection of human rights, law enforcement, and judicial processes."[12] It was in its missions in Kosovo and East Timor, however, that the United Nations received its baptism by fire in the realm of the administration of criminal justice and executive policing. Almost synchronistically, the UN Interim Administration Mission in Kosovo (UNMIK)[13] and the UN Transitional Administration in East Timor (UNTAET)[14] were mandated with rebuilding, restoring, and running the national criminal justice systems in these territories.[15] This enterprise was replete with what seemed like intractable challenges, such as an inadequate number of trained personnel, insufficient material and other resources, and damaged or limited infrastructure such as court buildings and prisons. In Kosovo, there were no typewriters, copying machines, standard court forms, windows on the courtrooms, or robes for the justices.[16] In East Timor, there were no records, court equipment, law books, or legal personnel.[17] The magnitude of this undertaking was amplified by the confusion and challenges surrounding the designation and application of the applicable law in both territories.[18] It was a task that the United Nations was not ready to confront, as the Secretary-General was prepared to admit. Speaking in relation to the mission in East Timor, he stated that "the last six months have also made clearer how daunting the task is that the United Nations has undertaken in East Timor. The organisation has never before attempted to build and manage a

State. Nor did it have the opportunity to prepare; the team in East Timor had to be assembled *ad hoc* and still lacks important expertise in a number of fields."[19]

In the wake of UNMIK and UNTAET, the United Nations was given cause to reflect on the adequacy of its responses in these and past missions in the 2000 *Report of the Panel on United Nations Peace Operations,* otherwise known as the Brahimi Report.[20] A section of this report concentrated specifically on the difficulties faced by UN missions in the reestablishment of law and order in Kosovo and East Timor.[21] The fact that the United Nations cast a spotlight on the administration of justice in postconflict settings was in itself a significant advance.

Since the Brahimi Report, the issue of the rule of law has remained at center stage in the contemporary discourse on peace operations. In 2003, the Security Council organized an open debate on the UN's role in justice and the rule of law.[22] It is apparent from these discussions that within the UN system, there is a growing realization of the need to reconceptualize the role the rule of law is ascribed in the planning and execution of peace operations. Once viewed as a mere "side-issue,"[23] the Security Council's recent proclamations cite the rule of law as lying "at the heart of [the UN's] work in rebuilding war-torn countries."[24] The correlation between addressing law and order issues in postconflict states, the sustainable resolution of conflict,[25] the rebuilding of societies,[26] and future economic development was acknowledged in that debate and in other forums.[27]

These statements have been given due recognition in the adoption of mission mandates. While there has not been a mission in which the United Nations played as much of a maximalist role in terms of responsibility for the administration of justice as it did in Kosovo or East Timor, rule of law components are consistently integrated into contemporary mandates, such as in the Democratic Republic of Congo,[28] Afghanistan,[29] Haiti,[30] and Liberia,[31] where its roles are more advisory or assistance-oriented in nature (see Chapter 5). As has long been recognized, in order to effectively address the administration of justice, attention should be focused beyond policing and look to the criminal justice system in its entirety.[32]

The Secretary-General was commissioned to draft a report for the Security Council as a follow-up to the September 2003 debates. The report was presented in August 2004 and discussed in October that year.[33] Just as the Brahimi Report had sought to provide "specific, concrete and practical recommendations"[34] to "assist the United Nations in conducting such activities better in the future,"[35] the Secretary-General's *Rule of Law* report aimed to ensure "that the lessons and experiences of the past could be learned and built upon."[36]

Amid the plethora of broader issues on peace operations addressed by the Brahimi Report, one key area of focus was the difficulties experienced in designating and implementing the applicable law in Kosovo and East Timor and the significant gaps in UN approaches.[37] The report noted that the difficulties encountered in curbing the enormous crime problems the missions faced in their early stages were exacerbated by the confusion surrounding the designation of a body of applicable law under which the law and legal systems prevailing prior to the conflict were questioned or rejected by key groups considered to be victims of the conflict.[38]

The Brahimi Report sought to posit a solution to this gap in UN responses and delivered a recommendation to the Secretary-General for potential implementation.[39] Rather than becoming entangled in the complex question of what the applicable law is, the panel, convened by the Secretary-General, proposed what it thought was a panacea. It recommended that the UN create a set of interim criminal codes that would be applied by international and national personnel in the field pending the reestablishment of the local rule of law and law enforcement capacity.[40] According to the panel, not only would this circumvent the prolonged gestation period in which the authorities scrambled to designate a body of law while crimes were committed unchecked, it would also mean that international personnel, pretrained on the interim codes, would not have to waste valuable time becoming acquainted with the local law before commencing work within the domestic justice system.[41] The recommendation contained in the Brahimi Report was based on the presupposition of the existence of an executive mission by which the United Nations is the legislative body in the state concerned—something that has not come to pass since Kosovo and East Timor.

Notwithstanding this, the idea of creating a set of model codes, as conceived in the Brahimi Report, was not redundant, and the discussion was taken up in the Secretary-General's *Rule of Law* report, albeit outside the context of executive missions in which the United Nations would simply use the codes as the applicable criminal law.[42] The report looked instead at the question of the applicable law as it pertains to assistance missions, where the United Nations is not the lawmaker per se, but is involved in an advisory capacity with the national legislature.

The *Rule of Law* report dealt with the issue of the applicable law not only with a different frame of reference, but also with a different focus from that of the Brahimi Report. At the heart of the discussion in that earlier report was the issue of political or popular opposition to preexisting criminal law as a bar to designating the applicable law.[43] Whereas this fact was acknowledged implicitly in the Secretary-General's report,[44] the crux of the discussion was the inadequacy of the criminal legislative framework rather than its objectionability on the above-mentioned grounds. The *Rule of Law* report, noting the state of lawlessness and disorder that is habitually found in postconflict settings, highlighted the fact that "legislative frameworks often show accumulated signs of neglect and political distortion, contain discriminatory elements and rarely reflect the requirements of international human rights and criminal law standards."[45] Advocating a comprehensive and integrated approach to the question of the reestablishment of the rule of law, the report emphasized the need to reform such laws.[46] Even if the preexisting criminal law in Kosovo and East Timor had been popularly and politically acceptable, its many inadequacies would have also necessitated considerable reform.[47] Thus, whether the law is objectionable or inadequate, or both, it is a significant impediment to the reestablishment of law and order and requires legislative initiatives and reform. The *Rule of Law* report points to the model codes, developed as part of the Model Codes for Post-Conflict Criminal Justice Project, as a useful tool for both local actors charged with amending the law, and international personnel providing technical assistance.

Responding to the Rule of Law Vacuum: The Role of the Model Codes

Rationale and Objective of the Model Codes

As explained above, the original impetus for the Model Codes for Post-Conflict Criminal Justice Project, at the time of its inception, came from the recommendation laid out the Brahimi Report that advocated the development of a set of interim criminal codes for use in future executive missions. Initially, the idea appeared to be to draft a set of skeletal codes that would provide "the basics of both law and procedure"[48] for the creation of an emergency legal system, staffed in part by international personnel. The Model Codes Project, spearheaded by the US Institute of Peace and the Irish Centre for Human Rights, in cooperation with the Office of the High Commissioner for Human Rights and the UN Office on Drugs and Crime, commenced in 2001 with this in mind.

However, what started as a set of skeletal codes became increasingly lengthy, comprehensive, and detailed. This change came about as a response to concerns expressed by experts from past and current peace operations that lacunae and a lack of specific guidelines in the codes would lead to a lack of clarity and confusion in the operationalization of the legal provisions and would thus greatly hamper their application. Forcing legal and law enforcement personnel to "fill in the blanks" would lead to a situation where the law was being applied in a different manner by each actor, if at all. In the past, the tendency of international personnel involved in maintaining law and order in peace operations has been to dispense with confusing or laconic laws and instead apply the laws of their home state. To forestall this eventuality, the drafters of the model codes were keen to ensure that their provisions were sufficiently prescriptive to enable understanding and application.

Toward this end, the model codes underwent a metamorphosis not only in their substance, but also in their perceived method of application. In the first instance, it appeared unlikely that another executive mission would be mandated in the near future, thus precluding the United Nations, as a legislative authority, from promulgating such a set of codes.[49] Second, experts were divided as to whether, executive mission or not, a set of interim codes should be deemed the applicable law in a postconflict territory, even just as a temporary stopgap. The majority held that they should not. An advisory note issued to the UN Panel on Peace Operations, which informed the Brahimi recommendation, had referenced one potential difficulty, stating that "it is evident that an attempt to impose an outside set of legal principles in a crisis of state legitimacy faces the immediate problem that the legitimacy of an outside system may itself be questioned."[50] Many of the international and national experts who were consulted on the Model Codes Project also raised this point.[51] Significantly, the UN Secretariat working group that the Secretary-General established to review the Brahimi recommendation voiced further concerns, primarily relating to the potential for the development of a set of codes meant to be applicable in all peace operations, given the diversity of country-specific legal traditions that would have to be taken into account.[52] Furthermore, it held that long-term reform efforts should be emphasized, centered on local judicial and legal communities and thus having a capacity-building function.[53]

This position was supported by many of the experts consulted. They also held that the national law should represent the starting point for discussions on the applicable law, and should thus be ameliorated rather than obliterated. This is also the contemporary wisdom of the United Nations, as was expressed in the Secretary-General's *Rule of Law* report: "We must learn as well to eschew one-size-fits-all formulas and the importation of foreign models, and, instead, base our support on national assessments, national needs and aspirations."[54] In his role as the Special Representative to the Secretary-General in Afghanistan, Lakhdar Brahimi advocated this approach in calling for the UN's adoption of a "light footprint" approach.[55] In this new paradigm, a set of model codes are more properly categorized as a tool for the assistance of national and international personnel engaged in the process of law reform. The need for such a tool is quite evident if one looks to the legal framework in place in most postconflict settings. It may be lacking in terms of the adequate protection of the rights of the citizen;[56] it may have fallen into a state of disrepair; or, having been neglected for years, definitions of crimes may be outdated or may not properly reflect the contemporary social reality it is confronted with.[57]

While a more substantial overhaul of criminal legislation will often be necessary, an initial "cleanup" of the law is also required. This process may be labeled "interim" or "transitional" law reform. Potentially, this could involve the revision and augmentation of preexisting codes or law, or indeed the drafting of a transitional law. For example, in Kosovo, despite the fact that a body of applicable law was designated,[58] transitional law reform efforts resulted in the promulgation of 391 separate regulations.[59] Some of these regulations were required to "fill the gaps" where either there was no preexisting legislation on an issue,[60] or the preexisting legislation was in violation of international standards.[61] In East Timor, over a four-year period, UNTAET drafted and promulgated 75 regulations, including an entirely new code of criminal procedure.[62] Notwithstanding the fact that the Indonesian criminal procedure code had initially been designated as the applicable law, it was later deemed to be "too complex to be applied in a devastated country"[63] and was substituted with a simplified procedural framework in the form of "UNTAET Regulation 2000/30 as amended by UNTAET Regulation 2001/25." Interim law reform was also undertaken in Afghanistan, with the promulgation of an interim criminal procedure code.[64] Given the fact that such temporary law reform efforts have been known to last up to thirteen years,[65] it is important to get them right. It is also imperative to act quickly to reform the law. It is with the intention of assisting, informing, and expediting this process that the model codes, as they stand in their current form, have been developed.

Development of the Model Codes

The conceptualization and drafting of the model codes began in late 2001. This process was conducted by a team of international experts, including practitioners from all sectors of the justice system (judges, police officers, prosecutors, and defense counsels), as well as academics, human rights advocates, and military personnel with experience in a broad range of legal disciplines, including domestic, comparative and international criminal law and procedure, international human rights law, international humanitarian law, military law, and policing law. Additionally, all members of the expert panel had served or were serving in UN peace operations in countries such as Cambodia, Haiti, Kosovo, Bosnia-Herzegovina, East Timor, Afghanistan, and Iraq. Experience had led many to the definite conclusion that the creation of tools in the form of model criminal and police codes was a matter of urgent necessity.

While the expert panel shared common field experience, their legal backgrounds were varied and diverse. This greatly informed the discussion on the codes and ensured that the sources of law utilized were wide-ranging. The consensus among the expert panel was that the codes should not be developed with one particular legal tradition in mind, such as common law or civil law. Rather, provisions were drawn from a variety of codes from various countries, or were drafted anew, and merged together to create a set of model codes that could potentially be universally applicable.[66] The aim was to create laws that are conducive to and workable in conflict or postconflict contexts. The experts sought to divorce themselves from any allegiances to their own domestic approaches to criminal and policing laws and to objectively consider the approach that would best suit conflict and postconflict settings. Due recognition was given to factors that are ever-present, such as lack of adequate resources or personnel. A central question when considering the inclusion of a particular provision was whether or not it could be practically implemented in the field. Another question considered at every juncture was whether the provisions drafted were fully compliant with international and regional human rights standards. A detailed study was conducted on these standards, both binding and nonbinding. Reference was made to the jurisprudence of human rights bodies and to secondary human rights sources.

On completion of a draft set of codes in June 2003, a process of widespread consultation and vetting began. This involved a significantly expanded expert group comprising nearly 300 international and national experts from across the globe who collectively, and on a voluntary basis, dedicated themselves to the Model Codes Project. The experts consulted hailed from all backgrounds and included both international and national personnel who worked or were working in peace operations: judges, prosecutors, defense counsels, military personnel, academics, corrections officials, police officers, and officials from nongovernmental, international, and regional organizations. The first consultation and vetting meeting was held in Geneva and gathered together rule of law experts from twenty-four countries representing legal traditions from the Middle East, Europe, North America, Africa, and Asia for a three-day line-by-line review of the substantive provisions of the codes. Individuals were divided into seven working groups and were requested to focus on specific areas of the codes based on their areas of expertise. In the months that followed the meeting, these experts continued to provide input on the codes, and additional experts were consulted individually. In February 2003, a further set of three meetings were held in Galway, Ireland, that focused, respectively, on policing, detention, and substantive and procedural criminal law. In June 2004, a meeting took place at the UN Office of the High Commissioner for Human Rights, where legal experts from the European Commission met with members of the drafting team to provide substantive input on the provisions of the model codes.

In June 2004, a series of meetings were convened to test the thesis that the model codes could, potentially, be universally applied. Again, a large number of national experts representing different regions of the world were consulted. This process commenced in Abuja, Nigeria, at a meeting bringing together experts from Botswana, Liberia, the Democratic Republic of Congo, Sierra Leone, Uganda, Nigeria, Zambia, Zimbabwe, Tanzania, Ghana, and Sudan. It was subsequently reconvened in London in September 2004 in partnership with the UN Association of the United States. This was followed by a meeting in July 2004 of experts from Islamic countries who examined the compatibility of the model codes with *sharia* law. This meeting, cohosted by the International Institute of High Studies in Criminal Sciences in Siracusa, Italy, garnered expertise from Morocco, Egypt, the United Arab Emirates, Syria, Libya, and Sudan. The final roundtable meeting was held in September 2004 in Bangkok, Thailand, in cooperation with the Judge Advocate General's Department of the Thai Military and the UN Association of the United States. Police, military officials, judges, and human rights advocates from Thailand, Sri Lanka, Nepal, Pakistan, China, Bangladesh, Fiji, the Philippines, New Zealand, and Malaysia examined the utility of the codes and their compatibility with Asian legal systems. Experts at each regional meeting ultimately drew the same conclusion as to the potential universality of the codes: that they represented a useful law reform tool in each context, subject of course to regional and local adaptation.

Structure and Content of the Model Codes

The model codes are a compendium of laws and procedure that seek to address each element of the criminal justice system in a cohesive and integrated manner. The model codes not only focus on criminal law, criminal investigation, and incarceration, but also address policing and public order laws that govern the power of the police outside the scope of criminal investigations. The package consists of four annotated bodies of work to be published in three volumes: Volume I, a draft penal code, the Model Criminal Code (MCC); Volume II, a draft procedure code, the Model Code of Criminal Procedure (MCCP); and Volume III, the Model Detention Act (MDA), a body of law that regulates procedural and substantive issues relating to pretrial detention and imprisonment, and the Model Police Powers Act (MPPA), a draft police act.

Specifically, the MCC contains general provisions on substantive law, as commonly found in national penal codes, such as criminal liability, grounds for defense, jurisdiction, and penalties. It also contains a list of the offenses most commonly found in conflict and postconflict environments, which are either frequently missing from national legislation or inadequately addressed (e.g., human trafficking, corruption, and organized crime). The definitions of such offenses are also contained in international and regional criminal law instruments, which a state that is party to the model codes treaty would be required to domestically implement. The MCCP consists of provisions on all aspects of criminal procedure, from investigation to appeal. It also contains provisions on issues such as juvenile justice, extradition and international cooperation, witness protection, and redress for victims. The MDA deals solely with detention, both pretrial and detention upon conviction. It contains a mix of both general principles and standard operating procedures applicable to the relevant detention authority. Finally, the MPPA is similar to the types of police acts found in many civil law systems: it focuses on the maintenance of public order as opposed to criminal investigation. Thus it contains provisions on issues such as public gatherings, road blocks, arrest and detention in situations other than in connection with a criminal offense, as well as the use of force and firearms, to name but a few.[67]

Not only do the codes provide substantive and procedural provisions on criminal and policing law and procedure, but they also contain lengthy commentaries that serve a number of purposes. They explain the choices of wording and approaches adopted by the expert panel, elaborate on the content of the legal provisions, articulate why these provisions are of particular consequence in conflict and postconflict environments, and provide practical information and insights based on previous experiences in applying similar provisions. These commentaries also explain what further legislative or institutional changes might be required to implement some of these provisions.

Each volume will also include a set of "guidelines for application" that explain the development and structure of the codes, a summary of their substantial provisions, recommendations for how they might be used in practice, and strategies on how one might approach criminal law reform.

Utilizing the Model Codes in the Transitional Law Reform Process

Before examining how the model codes could be of practical use to national and international rule of law practitioners in peace operations, a number of important points should be raised. First, while the codes have been labeled "model" codes, this is not to imply that they are a perfect model that "should" be adopted in all postconflict law reform processes. As with other "model" laws, such as the model laws on drugs created by the UN Office of Drugs and Crime to assist states in implementing drug legislation, or the US Model Penal Code, which served as the inspiration for many amendments to state legislation, the Model Codes for Post-Conflict Criminal Justice are a nonobligatory reform tool. It is common for those involved in domestic reform efforts to refer to external sources of law for inspiration. The model codes provide another source for inspiration and are in no way meant to be "imposed" on a postconflict state.

Second, the model codes are not intended to be used in whole or to be parachuted into a postconflict state as a quick-fix solution or as an emergency law. While, as outlined above, it was the original intent of the drafters to create such a skeletal emergency body of law, the model codes have moved beyond this. Parts of the codes may prove useful in developing emergency or transitional laws; however, given the fact that law is reflective of the society it governs and therefore must be adapted accordingly, it is clear that the model codes are unsuitable for wholesale transplantation into any postconflict state.

As noted above, each volume will include a set of application guidelines, some of which will address how the codes might be used in practice and offer strategies on approaching criminal law reform. There is no definitive "how to" in terms of code application or formulas for code reform. Still, there are general principles and best practices that have been distilled through years of code reform experience in both postconflict environments and the law and development sphere. Serious consideration, research, and consultations continue in order to develop these guidelines.

The basic premise is that the national law and the indigenous legal system are the starting points when addressing transitional law reform. Accordingly, those engaged in law reform should carefully look at the existing legal framework and determine its level of acceptability, in terms of both political relevance and substantive quality relating to international standards, as well as its ability to deal with current crime problems. In certain circumstances, the current law may be politically objectionable, so it may be more desirable to rely on laws that were in effect at an earlier time. For example, in Afghanistan a decision was made to use the 1974 law and reform it, rather than the law that was in effect when the Taliban fell in 2001.

Another principle is the importance of assessing the legal framework, diagnosing any gaps or inadequacies, engaging in strategic planning, and identifying short-term and long-term aims of law reform. For example, in the short term, depending on the situation, the aim may be to fill the gaps that can help efforts to curb, with immediate effect, serious criminal activities. In some postconflict environments, violence rooted in the tensions that drove a conflict itself (e.g., nationalism, ethnic or religious tensions, struggles for political power or control of resources) may continue despite the signing of a peace agreement or the establishment of a peace operation. In Kosovo, for instance, even after the Kosovo Force (KFOR) and UNMIK arrived, acts of violence on the part of Kosovo Serbs persisted. Additionally, criminal activity may result from conflict-related activities (e.g., profiteering, trafficking, and smuggling) that had been perpetrated during the armed conflict in order to help fund it or derive profit from it. Such activities do not always cease when the conflict ends. Laws addressing witness protection, organized crime, and trafficking may thus be part of an initial law reform strategy.[68] In the long term, the desired end-state is that of a fully functioning, domestically operated criminal justice system. This requires comprehensive and well-thought-out strategies on law reform and, more broadly, on issues such as institutional reform and training, for example.

Yet another principle in the law reform process is consultation. Just as the development of the model codes involved a drafting and vetting process, so should the process of developing new laws in a conflict or postconflict state. Dialogue between a wide array of actors in the criminal justice system should be encouraged, and should include members of civil society, both situations where local actors are leading the reform process and where local and international actors are working together in a cooperative effort. Failure to consult with local actors can ultimately lead to the outright rejection of the law, since the law is not an inanimate object but rather is reflective of the society it regulates. Conversely, engaging with civil society and actors in the criminal justice system to assess the popular legitimacy of the law enhances "ownership" and acceptance, in addition to providing a vital capacity-building function.[69] In Kosovo, when local actors became involved in the legal reform process, not only were the laws better accepted, but those engaged in the process also gained additional knowledge of law reform and developed solid legislative drafting experience. In contrast, when UNMIK promulgated regulations without adequately consulting or engaging the participation of local experts, not only were the regulations criticized and often unaccepted—and therefore not applied—but some even conflicted with local law as well.[70]

This brings us to the question of the utility of the model codes in the law reform process. There are a number of ways in which they could potentially be used, depending on the state of the criminal justice system and policing laws in a particular country (what follows is by no means an exhaustive set of illustrations).

Ensuring conformity to international human rights standards. In cases where certain aspects of the criminal law, criminal procedure law, or policing laws are contrary to international human rights standards, they may need to be repealed and new legal provisions may need to be added to ensure conformity to such standards. This may include isolated provisions, for example the right to challenge the lawfulness of arrest or detention, or more substantial additions to the law, such as the introduction of provisions that ensure that the law complies with international standards on juvenile justice. The model codes provide a useful yardstick of baseline human rights standards applicable within the criminal justice sphere. In the model codes, these provisions take the form of concrete and readily applicable legal provisions that incorporate these fundamental international standards. The role of the codes in ensuring adherence to such standards goes a long way in promoting a just and stable society, especially in postconflict countries where certain sectors of society may have been previously discriminated against by the criminal justice system.

Filling the gaps in preexisting law. The model codes could also prove useful in "filling in the blanks" in preexisting law. For example, criminal legislation and policing laws of postconflict states often are laconic, thereby giving actors in the criminal justice system little guidance and, frequently, too much discretion. If policing laws and procedures do not provide sufficient guidance for issues of fundamental importance such as the use of force or crowd control—two highly contentious issues particularly pertinent in a volatile postconflict context—the codes provide sample provisions that may be drawn on for guidance or inspiration. The same could be said for criminal procedures such as arrest, detention, interrogation, and search and seizure, to name but a few.

Updating existing law. Criminal and policing laws and procedures in postconflict states may also be outdated. Necessary reforms to tackle current crime problems, such as human trafficking and smuggling, cybercrime, drug trafficking, money laundering, and organized crime, may not have been undertaken. To effectively address these crimes, not only must the substantive crimes be added to the penal code, but further investigative tools may also be needed to supplement the existing criminal procedure code. For example, in the case of human trafficking, it is essential to ensure that the law provides for the protection of witnesses and victims of crime. Given the distinct nature of organized crime, covert or other means of surveillance may be required to gain sufficient evidence to allow prosecution. In reforming the laws of postconflict states, it may be necessary to add to the penal and procedure codes both the substantive crimes and the accompanying procedural provisions to properly investigate and prosecute these crimes.

Drafting a new code. In some situations, rather than reform and augment the preexisting laws and procedures, authorities may decide instead to start from scratch and create transitional laws, as was the case in East Timor,[71] Cambodia,[72] and Thailand.[73] In such cases, the model codes may provide valuable building blocks in the creation of a clear legal framework in which law enforcement officers, judicial actors, and the public know what the law is and what rights it protects. Legal certainty and transparency are essential elements of the rule of law;[74] without such a framework in place, together with the institutions to implement it, the local population often turns to self-help remedies and shadow security forces for protection.[75]

Prosecution based on complementarity under the Rome Statute.[76] With regard to the domestic implementation of international human rights standards, the model codes may also play a role in a postconflict state that is party to the Rome Statute of the International Criminal Court and that wishes to domestically prosecute crimes that occurred during the conflict. In order to ensure that the International Criminal Court does not usurp the state's jurisdiction under the complementarity regime set out in the Rome Statute, it must ensure that the relevant substantive and procedural laws comport with "general principles of due process recognized by international law."[77]

Use by special courts, chambers, or panels. The model codes would be equally useful in a situation in which special chambers, such as the organized crime, economic crime, and corruption divisions of Bosnia-Herzegovina's criminal and appellate court system, are established to deal with individual crimes or categories of crimes and new legislation governing such courts is required. Last, albeit not strictly related to the building of national criminal justice frameworks, another possible scenario for the use of the codes is in developing an accountability mechanism in a UN mission for personnel who have committed criminal offenses. In such situations, the provisions of the model codes may be used to draft relevant laws and procedures.

Application of the Model Codes: Identifying Challenges and Problems

As of the time of this writing, the model codes package is nearing its completion.[78] The next step in the process involves the practical use of the model codes, which may entail a number of challenges. An obvious initial challenge might be the question of how to widely disseminate and publicize the codes to potential users. However, given the lengthy and inclusive consultation process that has taken place since June 2003, this part of the implementation process has already been partially completed. Once available, the final codes will be disseminated directly to the many national and international experts who have been consulted over the years. At that point, the codes will also be made publicly available on the Internet, and distributed to international and local actors who are engaged in the reform process in current peace operations.

The next challenge will be how to track the use of the model codes. This step will rely significantly on word-of-mouth and informal networks. Contact will also be maintained with international and regional organizations that were involved in the drafting and that have indicated a desire to utilize the codes in their future law reform activities. It is hoped that the users of the codes will provide substantive input and feedback on the utility of the codes, and on any issues relating to the practical implementation of provisions of the codes that were adopted into national legislation and thus were "road-tested." The goal of the project sponsors would then be to evaluate the information received and determine at a suitable date whether the codes should be updated to take into consideration their use and the significant mission experience in law reform that will have accumulated by that time.

Another challenge for the future use of the model codes is the fact that law itself is not a rigid body of rules, but rather is constantly evolving in response to circumstantial, local, and global factors. For example, human rights jurisprudence may evolve to the extent that provisions of the codes may one day become outdated and need revision. This factor will have to be accounted for in order to ensure the sustainability of the codes beyond the immediate time frame after their publication.

There are other notable impediments to the use of the model codes that may have an impact both on their potential and on broader law reform issues. These factors include, first and foremost, the issue of resources. In all likelihood, there will be situations that lack qualified personnel and funding to undertake a comprehensive rule of law assessment prior to the reform process, or that lack personnel to provide technical assistance to domestic reform constituencies. Resources may also come into play in translating the model codes and their accompanying documentation into local language so that national experts and practitioners will be able to make full use of them. From a wider perspective, a lack of resources, such as a lack of physical infrastructure, basic supplies, or personnel, may also impact the ultimate operationalization of the newly drafted laws. As one participant at the African Roundtable consultation on the Model Codes Project pointed out: How can one enforce the procedures on registration of detained persons without pens and paper?

Finally, a significant potential impediment to the use of the model codes rests at the door of international donors and those international experts providing technical legal assistance in conflict or postconflict states. In the past, it has been noted that many such experts rarely step outside the "safe zone" of their own domestic legislation when proposing amendments to the law, thus imbuing law reform efforts with a national agenda. Explicit reference was made to this in a discussion paper emanating from the Best Practices Unit of the UN Department of Peacekeeping Operations, on lessons learned in Haiti: "In legal reform . . . the United States promoted structures modeled on the United States legal system while France attempted to use another paradigm. Since the United States model had no foundation in existing Haitian law, it was later abandoned."[79] This is merely one example of this practice. Such an approach, which sees international experts either intent on leaving the imprint of their own domestic legal system or simply resorting to the system most familiar to them, fails to take into account what should be of primary consideration: the best interests of the state and population concerned.

It is recognized that the model codes may not be ideal in all circumstances, and that national models have a valuable role to play in the law reform process in terms of presenting options for law reform to domestic constituencies. Experience has shown that many difficulties arise when using models from nonconflict states in a fledgling criminal justice system in a volatile postconflict environment. Given that the model codes are geared toward application in conflict or postconflict environments,[80] and do not adhere to a single legal tradition, they may provide a more suitable template for law reform efforts, and one that international experts should consider utilizing either in preference of or in conjunction with their own national legislation or that of other states.

A final significant hurdle was referred to in the Secretary-General's *Rule of Law* report under its section on "recognizing the political context."[81] The report emphasized that in conducting rule of law reform in conflict and postconflict states, due regard should be paid to issues beyond legal and institutional requirements. The report acknowledged the fact that, in some cases, "state authorities have been more concerned with the consolidation of power than with strengthening the rule of law."[82] In this regard, supporting reform efforts to ensure that government officials are just as accountable to the law as ordinary citizens would clearly be counterintuitive to such parties. The fact that law reform is necessary and that resources may be available to support this process is irrelevant. These efforts require the commitment and backing of the competent legislative authority in the conflict or postconflict state, which may not be readily forthcoming.

Policy Recommendations

As William Ellery Channing once said, difficulties are meant to rouse, not to discourage.[83] Despite the challenges that confront implementation of the model codes, they potentially have an important contributory role to play in future law reform efforts. They are not a "quick-fix" solution, but can be an integral part of broader processes of domestic law reform. Nor are they a "cure-all." As has been noted, there are many other components to reestablishing a society based on the rule of law. Even in the domain of law reform, working with penal codes, procedural codes, detention rules, and laws governing the police is only the beginning. Institutional reforms may be necessary, more detailed operating procedures may need to be drafted, and codes of conduct for judges, prosecutors, lawyers, and police may be required, along with items like standard forms, bench books for judges, and case management and tracking systems. If we use the analogy of building a house, the reform of the normative framework of a criminal justice system could be likened to laying its foundations.

Furthermore, just as the building of a house starts with an architect devising plans for the house, so too should the law reform process start out at this strategic level. It would be absurd for the builders of the house to show up on the first day and for each one to start on a different part of the house without reference to any sort of plans. Likewise, this would not be a wise course of action in the context of law reform. Rather, in a strategic approach to law reform, the issue of the applicable law should be considered by policymakers as an integral part of the preplanning phase of a peace operation and given due weight in terms of staffing and resources. Short-, medium-, and long-term strategies should be devised, as the many practical and political rule of law issues should be "war-gamed" by international and national experts. For example, short-term goals may include the designation of a body of applicable law and the establishment of a rudimentary justice system as an initial step. Attention at this stage should be given not only to criminal law, but also to the equally important areas of property law, civil law, and administrative law. At the planning stage, a premission assessment should take place in order to ascertain the current state of the justice system, along with the collection of the criminal laws in force in the state. This will provide the necessary input to assess what body of law could be deemed the applicable law and, furthermore, what sorts of reforms will be required in the near future to ensure that the applicable law is both compliant with international standards of due process and responsive to crime problems. The development of a strategy at this early stage will hopefully make for a coherent and coordinated effort rather than the sometimes ad hoc or piecemeal approach evidenced in the past. Equally important will be a cadre of qualified personnel to assist in the implementation of this strategy.

While the architect of a house may have a specific vision in mind, the big decisions ultimately rest with those who are to reside there. In the same way for law reform, the vision developed by international personnel should be presented to local experts, and more broadly to civil society, for their input, to assess its suitability and its political and popular legitimacy. The architect should refrain from setting his plans into action until this consultative process has been undertaken. The process itself may result in the architect being sent back to the drawing board to revise his or her strategic vision. Developing a suitable and agreeable strategy before the "legal house building" commences is all-important.

The development of a strategic vision and the laying of strong foundations will not, of themselves, make a house livable, even if the basic structure is in place. Nevertheless, as with laying the foundations of a house, providing the foundations for the rule of law in a conflict or postconflict state through the reform of inadequate laws—a process in which the model codes have the potential to play a significant role—is a necessary and valuable starting point in building or rebuilding the criminal justice system.

With this overview in mind, the following policy recommendations are offered in relation to legal reform in peace operations and, more specifically, the model codes:

• *Legal reform must be given priority in all missions.* Although rule of law strategies have received increased interest at least in the political discourse and in mission planning and organization, they often fail to receive priority status and continue to suffer from inadequate resources. The challenge for the future will be for the United Nations as a whole, in all its components, to continue to raise the profile of, and to give due attention to, rule of law issues.

• *Training modules should be developed.* Training should be offered both before and after deployment to rule of law–related missions. Training on code reform, code methodology, law reform, comparative law, and the codes themselves is vital to their proper use.

• *A cadre of experts should be assembled.* These personnel could be on call to provide assistance in legal reform and use of the codes. This cadre of experts should be developed as a rapid-reaction team. The process of reform is just as or more important than the product itself. The cadre of experts should be well versed in methodology, comparative law, and best practices in law reform in order to provide technical assistance to missions.

Notes

1. United Nations, *The Rule of Law and Transitional Justice in Conflict and Post-Conflict Societies: Report of the Secretary-General,* UN Doc. S/2004/616 (August 23, 2004), para. 12.

2. Ibid., para. 30.

3. Ibid., para. 6. The definition describes the requisite substantive quality of "the law" in order for there to be "rule of law."

4. United Nations, Peacekeeping Best Practices Unit, Department of Peacekeeping Operations, *Handbook on UN Multidimensional Peacekeeping Operations* (New York, December 2003), p. 95.

5. See United Nations, *The Rule of Law and Transitional Justice,* para. 27.

6. See UN Security Council Resolution 696 (1991), on Angola.

7. Ibid.

8. UN Security Council Resolution 897 (1994), on Somalia; UN Security Council Resolution 1181 (1998), on Sierra Leone.

9. UN Security Council Resolution 1181 (1998), on Sierra Leone.

10. UN Security Council Resolution 1144 (1997), on Bosnia-Herzegovina.

11. UNTAC was established pursuant to UN Security Council Resolution 745 (1992) to ensure the implementation of the Paris Peace Agreements on a Comprehensive Political Settlement of the Cambodia Conflict.

12. See arts. 6 and 16 of the *Agreement on a Comprehensive Political Settlement of the Cambodia Conflict; Agreement Concerning the Sovereignty, Independence, Territorial Integrity and Inviolability, Neutrality and National Unity of Cambodia; A Declaration of the Rehabilitation and Reconstruction of Cambodia and the Final Act of the Paris Conference on Cambodia;* and secs. B and E of annex 1 (available at http://www.usip.org/library/pa/cambodia/final_act_10231991.html). See also Chapter 5 in this volume.

13. UNMIK was established pursuant to UN Security Council Resolution 1244 (1999), tasking the mission, in para. 11(i), with "maintaining civil law and order, including establishing local police forces and meanwhile through the deployment of international police personnel to serve in Kosovo." In order to achieve this task, the Secretary-General appointed a Special Representative, Bernard Kouchner, who assumed executive and legislative authority in Kosovo. See UNMIK Regulation no. 1999/1, on the authority of the Interim Administration in Kosovo, para. 1.1: "All legislative and executive authority with respect to Kosovo, including the administration of the judiciary, is vested in UNMIK and is exercised by the Special Representative of the Secretary-General."

14. The mandate of UNTAET derived from UN Security Council Resolution 1272 (1999), which provided that the mission would "provide security and maintain law and order throughout the territory of East Timor," para. 2. The late Sergio De Mello, formerly UN High Commissioner for Human Rights, acting as the first transitional administrator, became both the executive and the legislature for East Timor pursuant to para. 1.1. of UNTAET Regulation no. 1999/1, on the authority of the Interim Administration in East Timor.

15. For an analysis of transitional administration in Kosovo, Afghanistan, and East Timor, see Simon Chesterman, *You, the People: The United Nations, Transitional Administration, and State Building* (Oxford: Oxford University Press, 2004). See also Ralph Wilde, "From Danzig to East Timor and Beyond: The Role of International Territorial Administration," *American Journal of International Law* 95, no. 3 (2001): 583.

16. See Organization for Security and Cooperation in Europe (OSCE), "Observation and Recommendations of the OSCE Legal System Monitoring Section: Report 1— Material Needs of the Emergency Judicial System" (OSCE Department of Rule of Law and Human Rights, 1999). Regarding the "vacuum of judicial experience" that UNMIK was confronted with in Kosovo, see Captain Alton L. Gwaltney III, "Law and Order in Kosovo: A Look at Criminal Justice During the First Year of Operation Joint Guardian," in *Lessons from Kosovo: The KFOR Experience,* edited by Larry Wentz, CCRP Publication Series (2002), p. 244, https://www.jagcnet.army.mil/jagcnetinternet/homepages/ac/clamo-public.nsf/0/85256a1c006ac77385256d1700643ff5?opendocument.

17. See Hansjörg Strohmeyer, "Collapse and Reconstruction of a Judicial System: The United Nations Mission in Kosovo and East Timor," *American Journal of International Law* 95, no. 1 (2001): 50. Strohmeyer writes: "The pre-existing judicial infrastructure in East Timor was virtually destroyed. Most court buildings had been torched and

looted and all court equipment, furniture, registers, records, archives. And—indispensable to legal practice—law books, case files, and other legal resources dislocated or burned." See also Nina Lahoud, "Rule of Law Strategies for Peace Operations," in *The Rule of Law on Peace Operations: Papers from the 'Challenges of Peace Operations' Project Conference,* edited by Jessica Howard and Bruce Oswald (New York: Kluwer Law International, 2003), pp. 130–131. In relation to a lack of personnel, see Wayne Hayde, "Ideals and Realities of the Rule of Law and Administration of Justice in Post-Conflict East Timor," *International Peacekeeping: The Yearbook of Peace Operations* 8 (2002): 73.

18. See Colette Rausch, "The Assumption of Authority in Kosovo and East Timor: Legal and Practical Implications," in *Executive Policing: Enforcing the Law in Peace Operations,* edited by Renate Dawn, SIPRI Research Report no. 16 (Oxford: Oxford University Press, 2002), p. 4, where Rausch discusses "the applicable law and legal anarchy" in Kosovo. On this issue in East Timor, see also Hansjörg Strohmeyer, "Making Multilateral Interventions Work: The U.N. and the Creation of Transitional Justice Systems in Kosovo and East Timor," *Fletcher Forum of World Affairs* 25, no. 2 (2001): 111–113.

19. See United Nations, *Report of the Secretary-General on the United Nations Transitional Administration in East Timor,* UN Doc. S/2000/53 (January 26, 2000), para. 68.

20. See United Nations, *Report of the Panel on United Nations Peace Operations* (Brahimi Report), UN Doc. A/55/305-S/2000/809 (August 21, 2000).

21. Ibid., paras. 76–83.

22. See United Nations, "Justice and the Rule of Law: The United Nations Role," in *Security Council Debates: Verbatim Records,* UN Doc. S/PV.4833 (September 24, 2003); United Nations, "Justice and the Rule of Law: The United Nations Role," in *Security Council Debates: Verbatim Records,* UN Doc. S/PV.4835 (September 30, 2004); United Nations, *Road Map Towards the Implementation of the United Nations Millennium Declaration: Report of the Secretary-General,* UN Doc. A/56/326 (September 6, 2001), para. 30, which recommends the incorporation of criminal justice concerns into UN peace operations.

23. See United Nations, "Justice and the Rule of Law: The United Nations Role," comments of Secretary-General Kofi Annan to the Security Council, in *Security Council Debates: Verbatim Records,* UN Doc. S/PV.4833 (September 24, 2003).

24. Ibid.

25. "The rule of law is a *sine qua non* for the sustainable resolution of conflict and the rebuilding of secure, orderly and humane societies." United Nations, "Justice and the Rule of Law: The United Nations Role," comments of Under-Secretary-General for Peace Operations Jean-Marie Guehenno to the Security Council, in *Security Council Debates: Verbatim Records,* UN Doc. S/PV.4835 (September 30, 2004), p. 3.

26. Ibid.

27. "Development agencies have increasingly recognized the importance of fair and effective criminal justice systems. Significant achievements in terms of development unfortunately have often been undermined by lawlessness and criminal behavior." United Nations, "Thematic Discussion on the Rule of Law and Development: The Contribution of Operational Activities in Crime Prevention and Criminal Justice," in *Note by the Secretary General,* Commission on Crime Prevention, 13th sess., Vienna, May 11–20, 2004, UN Doc. E/CN.15/2004/3 (April 20, 2004), para. 6.

28. UN Security Council Resolution 1493 (2003), para. 11.

29. UN Security Council Resolution 1401 (2002), endorsing the Agreement on Provisional Arrangements in Afghanistan Pending the Re-establishment of Permanent

Government Institutions, annex 2 (available at http://daccessdds.un.org/doc/undoc/gen/
n02/309/14/pdf/n0230914.pdf?OpenElement); United Nations, *Report of the Secretary-
General on the Situation in Afghanistan and its Implications for International Peace and
Security,* UN Doc. A/56/875-S/2002/278 (March 18, 2002), paras. 97(a), 103, setting out
the role of the UN Assistance Mission in Afghanistan (UNAMA) in relation to the rule
of law.

30. UN Security Council Resolution 1542 (2003), para. 7(1)(d).

31. UN Security Council Resolution 1509 (2003), para. 3.

32. "One of the key lessons learned by peacekeeping operations in this area is that,
in addition to the legislative system, three pillars of the criminal justice system—police, judiciary, and corrections institutions—are closely interconnected and should all
receive international attention and support." United Nations, Peacekeeping Best Practices Unit, Department of Peacekeeping Operations, *Handbook on UN Multidimensional Peacekeeping Operations,* p. 95.

33. See United Nations, "Justice and the Rule of Law: The United Nations Role,"
Security Council Debates: Verbatim Records, UN Doc. S/PV.4835 (October 6, 2004).

34. See United Nations, *Report of the Panel on United Nations Peace Operations:
Comprehensive Review of the Whole Question of Peacekeeping Operations in All Its
Aspects* (Brahimi Report), UN Doc. A/55/305-S/2000/809 (August 21, 2000), para. 2.

35. Despite "evident ambivalence" to the possibility that the United Nations may
ever again direct a transitional civil administration, in light of the fact that intrastate
conflicts continue and future instability is hard to predict, the Brahimi Report conjec-
tures that such missions may well be a possibility in the future. Thus the United Nations should prepare accordingly, rather than "do badly if it is once again flung into the
breach." See United Nations, *Report of the Panel on United Nations Peace Operations,*
para. 78.

36. United Nations, *The Rule of Law and Transitional Justice,* para. 1.

37. See United Nations, *Report of the Panel on United Nations Peace Operations,*
paras. 76–83.

38. Ibid., para. 79.

39. Ibid., para. 83.

40. Ibid.

41. Ibid., para. 80.

42. See United Nations, *Rule of Law and Transitional Justice,* paras. 27–30.

43. "Moreover, in both places, the law and legal systems prevailing prior to the
conflict were questioned or rejected by key groups considered to be the victims of the
conflicts." United Nations, *Report of the Panel on United Nations Peace Operations,*
para. 79.

44. United Nations, *The Rule of Law and Transitional Justice,* para. 27.

45. Ibid.

46. Ibid., para. 30.

47. For a discussion of the inadequacies of the law in place in East Timor, see
Megan A. Fairlie, "Affirming Brahimi: East Timor Makes the Case for a Model Criminal Code," *American University International Law Review* 18, no. 5 (2003): 1059. For
discussion on Kosovo, see Rausch, "The Assumption of Authority in Kosovo and East
Timor," p. 8.

48. See United Nations, *Report of the Panel on United Nations Peace Operations,*
para. 82.

49. Ibid., para. 78.

50. Christopher Lord, "Advisory Note for Stimson Center/United Nations Panel on Peace Operations," Prague Project on Emergency Criminal Justice Principles (Prague: Institute of International Relations, June 27, 2000).

51. For a comprehensive discussion of some of the difficulties associated with applying a Brahimi-style set of interim codes, see Bruce M. Oswald, "Model Codes for Criminal Justice and Peace Operations," *Journal of Conflict and Security Law* 9, no. 2 (2004): 1.

52. See United Nations, *Report of the Secretary-General on the Implementation of the Report of the Panel on United Nations Peace Operations,* UN Doc. A/55/502 (October 20, 2000), para. 31.

53. Ibid.

54. United Nations, *The Rule of Law and Transitional Justice,* "Summary."

55. See United Nations, *Secretary General Special Representative Brahimi Tells Security Council Rapid Disbursement of Funds Pledged Essential for Afghan Recovery,* Press Release no. SC/7925 (February 6, 2002), http://www.un.org/news/press/docs/2002/SC7295.doc.htm.

56. See also Martin Lau, *Afghanistan's Legal System and Its Compatibility with International Human Rights Standards* (Geneva: International Commission of Jurists, 2003), http://www.icj.org/news.php3?id_article=2736&lang=en.

57. This would include a situation where "newer" crimes, such as cybercrime, organized crime, and trafficking in persons, that were not being perpetrated at the time of drafting the penal code in force, have come to represent a huge threat to law and order in the state concerned. See, for example, Astrigildo Joao Pedro Culolo, "Combating Organised Crime in Angola" in *Organised Crime in Southern Africa: Assessing Legislation,* edited by Charles Goredema, Monograph no. 56 (Capetown, South Africa: Institute for Security Studies, June 2001), http://www.iss.co.za/pubs/monographs/no56/chap9.html.

58. Initially, in the same vein as in East Timor, UNMIK Regulation no. 1999/1 stipulated that the law to be applied in Kosovo was that which applied prior to March 24, 1999, insofar as it did not conflict with "internationally recognised human rights standards," the mandate given to UNMIK under UN Security Council Resolution 1244 or in subsequent regulations promulgated by UNMIK. Kosovo Albanians rejected this interpretation, as they associated these laws with the repressive Slobodan Milosevic regime, which in 1989 ended Kosovo's autonomy and held the Kosovo criminal code invalid. In the midst of public consternation at UNMIK Regulation no. 1999/1, coupled with judicial rejection of its applicability, it was subsequently revoked and replaced by UNMIK Regulation no. 1999/24, which set forth four sources of the applicable law in Kosovo: (1) the law as it existed on March 22, 1989 (prior to the ending of Kosovo's autonomy); (2) UNMIK regulations; (3) the law that was in force in Kosovo from March 22, 1989, to December 12, 1999, if it were more favorable to the accused or filled a gap where no law from March 1989 onward existed; and (4) international human rights law and standards.

59. See http://www.unmikonline.org.

60. For example, the applicable law in Kosovo, as set forth in UNMIK Regulation no. 1999/24, did not contain the criminal offense of organized crime; therefore, organized criminal gangs were in a position to operate with impunity. UNMIK Regulation no. 2001/21, on measures against organized crime, criminalized organized crime activities (sec. 1) and set out relevant penalties (secs. 2–3).

61. UNMIK Regulation no. 2001/28, on the rights of persons arrested by the law enforcement authorities. This regulation was promulgated to supplement the applicable

law to ensure that international and regional human rights standards, as they pertained to arrested persons, were integrated into Kosovo's domestic law.

62. See UNTAET Regulation no. 2000/30, "On Transitional Rules of Criminal Procedure" (September 25, 2000). This was amended by UNTAET Regulation no. 2001/25, "On the Amendment of UNTAET Regulation no. 2000/11 on the Organization of the Courts in East Timor" (September 14, 2001).

63. See Wayne Hayde, "Ideals and Realities."

64. See Laurel Miller and Robert Perito, "Establishing the Rule of Law in Afghanistan," Special Report no. 117 (Washington, D.C.: US Institute of Peace, March 2004).

65. Government of Cambodia, *Provisions Relating to the Judiciary and Criminal Law and Procedure Applicable in Cambodia During the Transitional Period* (September 10, 1992), http://www.icrc.org/ihl-nat.nsf/0/1eacfb8b87785c69c1256a3f0055cac3? opendocument. These provisions are still in force in Cambodia.

66. This thesis was tested at a set of regional consultative meetings that will be discussed later in the chapter.

67. A police act is a piece of legislation that would be more familiar to civil law police officers. Most civil law countries, in addition to the criminal code and procedure code, have promulgated such an act to regulate the organization and discipline of the national police force and police duties and powers outside the realm of criminal investigation. Issues addressed under such police acts include traffic control, use of firearms, identity checks, and search and detention other than in connection with criminal investigation and prosecution.

68. Colette Rausch, ed., *Combating Serious Crimes in Post-Conflict Societies* (Washington, D.C.: US Institute of Peace, 2006).

69. For an analysis of "ownership," see Chapter 7 in this present volume.

70. Colette Rausch, "Justice and Police Reforms in Kosovo," in *Constructing Justice and Security After Wars,* edited by Charles T. Call (Washington, D.C.: US Institute of Peace, 2007).

71. UNTAET Regulation no. 2000/30 on transitional rules of criminal procedure as amended by UNTAET Regulation no. 2001/25 on the amendment of UNTAET Regulation no. 2000/11 on the organization of the courts in East Timor and UNTAET Regulation no. 2000/30 on transitional rules of criminal procedure.

72. See Government of Cambodia, *Provisions Relating to the Judiciary and Criminal Law.*

73. On the UN Border Relief Operation in Thailand, see United Nations, *The Code of Justice and the Court System,* reprinted in *Cambodian Humanitarian Assistance and the United Nations (1979–1991)* (Office of the Special Representative of the Secretary-General of the United Nations for Coordination of Cambodian Humanitarian Assistance Programmes, 1992).

74. See the definition of the term "rule of law" as set out in United Nations, *The Rule of Law and Transitional Justice,* para. 6.

75. For example, in East Timor the National Council of Timorese Resistance (CNRT) and the armed forces for the National Liberation of East Timor (FALINTIL) moved into the vacuum of local authority, and in some places asserted a security role. See United Nations, *Report of the Secretary-General on the United Nations Transitional Administration in East Timor,* para. 3.

76. *Rome Statute of the International Criminal Court,* UN Doc. A/CONF.183/9 (July 17, 1998) (as corrected by the proces-verbaux of November 10, 1998, and July 12, 1999).

77. Ibid., art. 17(2).

78. The first of a three-volume set of monographs was published in September 2007. See Vivienne O'Connor and Colette Rausch, eds. *Model Codes for Post-Conflict Criminal Justice: Volume I—Model Criminal Code* (Washington, D.C.: United States Institute of Peace Press, 2007). The second and third volumes are expected to be published in early and mid-2008, respectively.

79. See Lama Khouri-Padova, "Haiti: Lessons Learned," discussion paper (New York: Peacekeeping Best Practices Unit, UN Department of Peacekeeping Operations, March 2004), http://www.smallwarsjournal.com/documents/haitilessonslearned.pdf.

80. This is not to say that the codes might not be useful in a nonconflict or non-postconflict context. While this was not the initial focus of the project, during the course of consultations on the codes a variety of participants from countries struggling with inadequate legal frameworks and fragile judicial systems saw the potential use of the codes in their own countries.

81. United Nations, *The Rule of Law and Transitional Justice,* para. 19.

82. Ibid.

83. William E. Channing, *The Works of William E. Channing* (Boston: James Munroe, 1843), p. 408.

7

"Ownership":
The Transfer of Authority in
Postconflict Operations

Simon Chesterman

n 1944, Judge Learned Hand spoke at a ceremony in Central Park, New York, to swear in 150,000 naturalized citizens. "Liberty lies in the hearts of men and women," he observed; "when it dies there, no constitution, no law, no court can save it; no constitution, no law, no court can even do much to help it."[1] Building or rebuilding faith in the idea of the state requires a similar transformation in mentality as much as it does in politics. Any effort to generate a rigid template for reconstructing the institutions of law and order in a post-conflict environment is therefore likely to fail. As Judge Hand recognized, the major transformation required is in the hearts of the general population; any foreign involvement must therefore be sensitive to the particularities of that population at the level of both form and substance.

Reconciling this need for sensitivity with the circumstances in which international actors have become responsible for rule of law issues in postconflict territories has led to difficulties. Two types of problems have arisen. First, the reason for international engagement is typically the malevolence or incapacity of existing governance structures: intervention is premised on the need to transform or build those structures, rather than to maintain them. Second, the limited time frame within which resources tend to be available to postconflict territories leads to problems in programming and sequencing. In the absence of ongoing strategic interest, such as the European Union's ties to the Balkans, the window of opportunity for sustained attention by international actors and large-scale reconstruction efforts appears to range from about one to two years. By the end of this period, control of the territory will have passed to national governments and the time for "sensitivity" may have elapsed.

How to use that window—and the significant leverage it gives the United Nations, its agencies, the international financial institutions, donors, and non-governmental organizations (NGOs)—is the subject of an increasingly voluminous literature.[2] In this chapter, the focus will be not on the specific programming

139

issues but on the location of political authority during the transition period. In particular, the chapter examines the relationship between actual political control and the transformation in mentality described by Judge Hand.

The language of "ownership" is commonly used in this context, but it is not clear that the term has either consistency or substance. It certainly does not have its literal meaning, in the sense of rights of possession either of property or a formal stake in an organization, such as shares in a corporation.[3] Instead, ownership tends to be used figuratively—much as "buy-in" in this context usually does not suggest an actual financial transaction—to refer in a more vague way to the relationship between stakeholders, with meanings ranging from a sense of attachment to a program or operation, to (rarely) actual controlling authority.

The chapter first sketches out the evolution of multidimensional peace operations, with particular emphasis on the emergence of a class of operations in which the United Nations has assumed responsibility not merely for rule of law issues but for the governance of postconflict territory. Such operations are far from the norm in the experience of the United Nations; they are used here to illustrate the logical extension of the influence and control of external actors in a wider set of circumstances. The chapter then turns to the parallel story of how ownership emerged as a shibboleth of the development community and how this affected policies where the United Nations exercised quasi-sovereign powers. This is followed by an examination of particular rule of law strategies—in theory and in practice—and an assessment of what works, what does not work, and what has yet to be tried.

The Role of Ownership in Governing Postconflict Territories

Multidimensional Peace Operations

Postconflict reconstruction through the 1990s saw an increasing trend toward rebuilding governance structures through assuming some or all governmental powers on a temporary basis. In early 1995, in the wake of a failed operation in Somalia, a failing operation in Bosnia-Herzegovina, and paralysis in the face of genocide in Rwanda, UN Secretary-General Boutros Boutros-Ghali released a supplement to his optimistic 1992 *Agenda for Peace*.[4] The more conservative supplement noted that a new breed of intrastate conflicts presented the United Nations with challenges not encountered since the Congo operation of the early 1960s. These intrastate conflicts were accompanied by the collapse of state institutions, especially the police and judiciary, meaning that international intervention had to extend beyond military and humanitarian tasks to include the "promotion of national reconciliation and the re-establishment of effective government." Nevertheless, Boutros-Ghali expressed caution against the United

Nations assuming responsibility for law and order, or attempting to impose state institutions on unwilling combatants.[5]

Despite his cautious words, by the end of 1995 the United Nations had assumed responsibility for policing in Bosnia under the Dayton Accords. The following January, a mission was established with temporary civil governance functions over the last Serb-held region of Croatia in Eastern Slavonia. In June 1999, the Security Council authorized an "interim" administration in Kosovo to govern part of what remained technically Serbian territory for an indefinite period; four months later a "transitional" administration was created with effective sovereignty over East Timor until independence. These expanding mandates continued a trend that began with the operations in Namibia in 1989 and Cambodia in 1993, where the United Nations exercised varying degrees of civilian authority in addition to supervising elections.

The expansion was part of a larger growth in activism by the Security Council through the 1990s, which showed itself willing to interpret internal armed conflicts, humanitarian crises, and even disruption to democracy as "threats to international peace and security" within the meaning of the UN Charter—and therefore warranting a military response under its auspices. However, the "new interventionism" was constrained by the inability of the United Nations to develop an independent military capacity; as a result, Council action was generally limited to circumstances that coincided with the national interests of a state or group of states that were prepared to lead.[6]

It is noteworthy that none of the major such operations took place in Africa, where the need is probably greatest. The primary barrier to establishing transitional administration-type operations in areas such as Somalia, Western Sahara, and the modern Democratic Republic of Congo has less to do with the difficulty of such operations than with the absence of political will to commit resources to undertake them. The "war on terror" has transformed this agenda, though triage is performed less according to need than in line with the strategic priorities of the dominant actors—most prominently (but not only) the United States.

The Contradictions of Transitional Administration

The transitional administration operations described above can be divided into two broad classes: those established where state institutions are divided, and those established where such institutions have collapsed. The first class encompasses situations where governance structures were the subject of dispute with different groups claiming power (as in Cambodia or Bosnia), or ethnic tensions within the structures themselves (such as Kosovo). The second class comprises circumstances where such structures simply did not exist (as in Namibia, East Timor, and Afghanistan). A possible third class is suggested by recent experience in Iraq, where regime change took place in a territory with far greater resources (human, institutional, and economic) than any comparable situation in which the United Nations or other actor had exercised civilian administration functions since World War II.[7]

It should be immediately apparent that contradictions arise between the stated end of transitional administration—legitimate and sustainable national governance—and the available means—benevolent autocracy under the rule of the UN Security Council or some other international actor. This approach to postconflict reconstruction embodies a blend of idealism and realism that runs through much of the work of the United Nations: the idealist project of saving a population from itself through education, economic incentives, and the space to develop mature political institutions—a project undergirded by the realist foundation of military occupation.

Of central interest here is how political power is managed up to the handover to local control. Analogies with military occupation and colonialism's *mission civilisatrice* are intellectually provocative but politically untouchable. At the establishment of the United Nations in 1945, 750 million people (approximately one-third of the world's population) lived in territories that were "non-self-governing." By the twenty-first century, fewer than 1 million people lived in such territories. The Trusteeship Council, established to oversee the transition of former colonies to independence, only concluded active business in 1994 with the independence of Palau. Though there are occasional murmurings about reviving the Trusteeship Council to oversee postconflict reconstruction efforts,[8] or to administer failed or failing states, the political barriers to doing this are insuperable.[9] The analogy with military occupation is no less provocative, though the explicit acceptance of that role by the United States and Britain in Iraq in 2003 suggests a possible rehabilitation of that body of law.[10]

In countering such implicit or explicit criticism, international actors tend to stress the temporary and benevolent nature of the international presence in the hope that these tensions will not boil over into open conflict. This is easiest where the political trajectory of the operation is clear and understood by all parties: Namibia's first elections, Eastern Slavonia's return to Croatian control, East Timor's transition to independence. Where that political trajectory is not clear—Bosnia's entities and armies, Kosovo's indeterminate political status—both the temporariness and the benevolence of the international presence have come to be questioned by local political forces.[11]

Given the important development component of all these operations, the appropriation of the language of "ownership" was perhaps inevitable. As we shall see, usage in the development context is itself a relatively recent phenomenon. But in the context of transitional administrations, the implications of such terms are at least questionable. As indicated earlier, such operations have tended to be undertaken precisely because of the malevolence or incapacity of existing governance structures. In such an environment it is at best disingenuous to suggest that local "ownership" should be asserted the moment that conflict ceases. If it was appropriate to undermine local ownership with the decision to send thousands of troops into a territory, the cessation of active hostilities does not indicate that the reasons for military intervention have dissipated. At worst, premature restoration of local control might lead to a return to the governing policies (or lack thereof) that led to intervention in the first place. Ownership is certainly the intended end of such operations, but almost by definition it is not the means.

The Origins of Ownership

Though some development actors had been using it far earlier,[12] the formal embrace of the language of "ownership" by the multilateral development community came in the policy document "Development Partnerships in the New Global Context," adopted by the Development and Assistance Committee (DAC) of the Organization for Economic Cooperation and Development (OECD) in May 1995: "For development to succeed, the people of the countries concerned must be the 'owners' of their development policies and programmes."[13] The next year, "local ownership" was a theme of the DAC's manifesto, "Shaping the 21st Century":

> Success will depend upon the broad acceptance of a comprehensive approach, drawing on the resources, energies and commitment of institutions and individuals in government at all levels, in the private sector, in nongovernmental organizations—in developing and industrialised countries and in international organisations. It will depend equally upon an individual approach that recognises diversity among countries and societies and that respects local ownership of the development process. We will need to change how we think and how we operate, in a far more coordinated effort than we have known until now.[14]

Operationally, it was never clear what this would mean. "Locally-owned" development strategies were said to emerge from an "open and collaborative dialogue by local authorities with civil society and with external partners, about their shared objectives and their respective contributions to the common enterprise."[15] How that dialogue would be managed and how these objectives would be determined were of course the central questions.

In 1999, World Bank president James Wolfensohn released his own proposal for a "comprehensive development framework." Writing of the need to develop a "holistic approach to the structural, social and human aspects of development," Wolfensohn put a strong case for the centrality of ownership:

> It is also clear to all of us that ownership is essential. Countries must be in the driver's seat and set the course. They must determine goals and the phasing, timing and sequencing of programs. Where there is not adequate capacity in the government to do this, we must support and help them to establish, own, and implement the strategy. And we must work to achieve the strategy

with our colleagues in the government, in the international development
community, the civil society, and the private sector. In some countries the
long and short term goals will be set by a process of public debate and consensus building led by the government with all sections of society. In other
countries, the establishment of goals will continue to be set more centrally.[16]

Here also, however, it was far from clear how "we" would help "them" to
"own" a given strategy.

The rise of "ownership" as a buzzword also ran directly against the simultaneous calls for greater accountability for the disbursement of funds, which
typically led to more conditionalities, less flexibility, and centralized management of the aid process.[17] As in postconflict reconstruction, however, ownership in the development field has frequently been of more rhetorical significance than anything else.[18] A great many aid programs are formulated around
the claim that recipients "own" the timetables and reform processes that have
been designed far away from their reality. Common sense suggests that sustainability is unlikely to be achieved unless the transformation under way includes a genuine commitment of local players. Common sense, however, cannot be assumed in this field.[19]

Even well-intentioned admonitions to take ownership seriously may point
to the essential contradiction in this view being enunciated by external actors.
The following statement is representative: "True ownership further entails (i)
the recognition that asymmetric relationships need to be addressed; (ii) the acceptance that capacity development is essential for development; and (iii) the
necessity to move the debate on ownership from rhetoric to reality (who owns
the idea)."[20] It is striking that all three action points suggest the need for action on the part of the donor community, rather than any specific action or assertion of agency or control by national actors.

And, here and there, one finds individuals questioning whether it would be
desirable for the rhetoric about ownership to be taken literally: "We are now in
a phase of talking about ownership, even if understanding varies widely on the
meaning of this word. By one definition, it is the exercise of control and command, from the idea to the process, from input to output, from ability to results.
Still, while a strong case can be made that ownership is a pre-condition for
commitment and capacity development, true transformation requires an important additional element: qualified leadership."[21]

This points to an issue that runs through the literature more generally: the
sobering assessment that statebuilding and development work best when a
population rallies behind a leader who is enlightened, but that very little at all
will work if they rally behind one who is not.[22]

Ownership is attractive as a concept also because of its implied connection with democracy. The 1990s saw the emergence of arguments that democ-

racy was not merely a form of political organization but a "right";[23] invocation of ownership both reinforced this right and lent support to the view that elections were both possible and desirable in certain postconflict environments. After the notable failure of elections in Angola (1992), Bosnia (1996 and onward), and Liberia (1997) to resolve conflicts in those countries, this enthusiasm came to be tempered. Successful multiparty elections may be evidence of the successful transition to postconflict stability, but they are only a small part of what is needed to achieve it.

Ownership and Postconflict Operations

In the context of peace and security, ownership has slightly different meanings. In peace negotiations, a common concern is that the various parties must "buy in" to the peace process to ensure the long-term viability of whatever settlement may emerge. The metaphor has a degree of accuracy, since, in addition to the need for parties to identify with the terms of any agreement, it is also important that actors see that their interests are represented in this agreement.

When we come to postconflict reconstruction and statebuilding, the meaning of ownership appears to fall somewhere between its development and peace negotiation meanings. In its most positive sense, it reflects a desire on the part of external actors to avoid undermining preexisting local processes that may be the most effective response to local political questions. Ownership may also be invoked defensively, asserted in order to avoid the appearance of paternalism or neocolonialism. (This reactive use at times mirrors the way in which the UN Secretariat and member states pass responsibility onto one another for the failings of the United Nations in the field.) Frequently, however, ownership is more aspirational than concrete,[24] only rarely being grounded in the blunt manner that Mark Malloch Brown has described it, with national ownership meaning that a given country must decide for itself how to allocate scarce resources: "choosing, for instance, whether girls' education should be a bigger budget priority than clean water."[25]

Following Ludwig Wittgenstein, however, the meaning is less important than how the term ownership is *used*. For present purposes, six distinct senses in which ownership has been used in the context of postconflict reconstruction will be distinguished. Ownership may refer to how a population comes to regard certain policies "as their own." Their involvement may be either passive (policies are designed to be responsive to local circumstances, culture, etc.) or active (policies are designed through consultation with local actors). Ownership may also refer to decisionmaking structures. Here it is necessary to distinguish between mechanisms to allow the participation of local actors (making representations to decisionmakers, participating in debates), mechanisms to allow local actors to hold international actors accountable (such as an ombudsperson, limitations on immunities of international staff), control by local authorities subject to being overridden by international structures (for example, to enforce a peace agreement or protect minority rights), and sovereignty (including, crucially, the power to demand the departure of international staff).

These six senses of "ownership"—responsiveness, consultation, participation, accountability, control, and sovereignty—are not intended to be exhaustive or definitive. For present purposes, they are simply intended to demonstrate that the term "ownership" embraces a range of possible meanings. Indeed, it oftentimes appears that that fuzziness is precisely the reason for the success of "ownership" as a buzzword.

International Strategies and Approaches

In response to a special Security Council session on the rule of law, Secretary-General Kofi Annan released a report in August 2004 attempting to draw lessons from the various roles played by the United Nations in conflict and post-conflict societies. "Too often," he wrote, "the emphasis has been on foreign experts, foreign models and foreign-conceived solutions to the detriment of durable improvements and sustainable capacity. Both national and international experts have a vital role to play, to be sure. But we have learned that effective and sustainable approaches begin with a thorough analysis of national needs and capacities, mobilizing to the extent possible expertise resident in the country."[26] Ultimately:

> No rule of law reform, justice reconstruction, or transitional justice initiative imposed from the outside can hope to be successful or sustainable. . . . [I]t is essential that these efforts be based upon meaningful public participation involving national legal professionals, Government, women, minorities, affected groups and civil society. . . . Most importantly, our programmes must identify, support and empower domestic reform constituencies. Thus, peace operations must better assist national stakeholders to develop their own reform vision, their own agenda, their own approaches to transitional justice and their own national plans and projects. The most important role we can play is to facilitate the processes through which various stakeholders debate and outline the elements of their country's plan to address the injustices of the past and to secure sustainable justice for the future, in accordance with international standards, domestic legal traditions and national aspirations. In doing so, we must learn better how to respect and support local ownership, local leadership and a local constituency for reform, while at the same time remaining faithful to United Nations norms and standards.[27]

Operationalizing these principles in territories targeted for intervention precisely because they either violate UN norms or fail UN standards has been difficult.

The Security Council resolution that established the UN Interim Administration Mission in Kosovo (UNMIK) authorized the Secretary-General to establish an international civilian presence to govern the territory.[28] In its first regulation, UNMIK asserted plenary powers: "All legislative and executive authority with respect to Kosovo, including the administration of the judiciary, is vested in UNMIK and is exercised by the Special Representative of the Secretary-General." The Special Representative was further empowered to appoint or remove any person, including judges, to positions within the civil administration. Beneath its brief text, UNMIK Regulation no. 1999/1 bore the signature "Dr Bernard Kouchner, Special Representative of the Secretary-General."[29]

The governance of postconflict territories by the United Nations embodies a central policy dilemma: how does one help a population prepare for democratic governance and the rule of law by imposing a form of benevolent autocracy? And to what extent should the transitional administration itself be bound by the principles that it seeks to encourage in the local population? The ombudsperson established by the Organization for Security and Cooperation in Europe (OSCE) to monitor, protect, and promote human rights in Kosovo published a damning report on UNMIK's record on both fronts three years into the mission: "UNMIK is not structured according to democratic principles, does not function in accordance with the rule of law, and does not respect important international human rights norms. The people of Kosovo are therefore deprived of protection of their basic rights and freedoms three years after the end of the conflict by the very entity set up to guarantee them."[30]

This section examines the practical involvement of local actors in decisionmaking processes, drawing on the different uses of "ownership" identified in the previous section. It focuses on three issues: selection of key international staff and policies, choice of transitional law, and appointment of judges. The operations to be considered are limited to five of the transitional administration operations referred to earlier: Bosnia, Eastern Slavonia, Kosovo, East Timor, and Afghanistan. The cases will not be treated exhaustively; the intention, instead, is to draw on them by way of illustration of recurrent issues that arise in the context of "ownership" in postconflict operations.

Selection of International Staff and Consultation
When authorizing the UN Transitional Administration for Eastern Slavonia (UNTAES, which included Baranja and Western Sirmium), the Security Council requested the Secretary-General to appoint a transitional administrator "in consultation with the parties and with the Security Council."[31] This was to be read in the context of the demand by Croatian president Franjo Tudjman that a US general be appointed head of the UN operation, and the importance of ensuring Tudjman's and Yugoslav president Slobodan Milosevic's commitment to the peaceful transfer of Eastern Slavonia from Serb to Croat control.[32] In Kosovo, consultation in the appointment of the Special Representative was only required with the Council itself.[33] In East Timor the Council merely welcomed the intention of the Secretary-General to appoint a Special Representative.[34] In Bosnia, which was not placed under UN control, other political constraints were

at work. In particular, there was an implicit agreement among the guarantors at Dayton that the High Representative would always be European, that one chief deputy was likely to be German and the other a US national, and that the OSCE head of mission would always be from the United States.[35]

Appointment of senior international staff is of course only one of a great many decisions that are made in the course of such an operation. Neither the mission in Eastern Slavonia nor that in Kosovo included in its mandate an obligation to consult more generally with local actors. This may be contrasted with the mandate for the UN Transitional Administration in East Timor (UNTAET), which stressed the need for the mission to "consult and cooperate closely with the East Timorese people."[36] Here it is noteworthy that senior UN staff in New York had a more restrictive view of the role of the early transitional administrations than they ultimately assumed. In particular, the UN legal counsel later lamented the fact that these bodies had become "legislative factories," assuming for themselves governing powers beyond the temporary caretaker function initially envisaged.[37]

Under the Dayton Accords, the High Representative in Bosnia was established to "facilitate" efforts by the parties and to mobilize and coordinate the activities of the many organizations and agencies involved in the civilian aspects of the peace settlement. The High Representative was also granted "final authority in theatre" to interpret the accords as they applied to the civilian implementation of the peace settlement.[38] After two years of ineffectual cohabitation, the Peace Implementation Council,[39] at a summit in Bonn, welcomed Carlos Westendorp's intention to use these powers "to facilitate the resolution of any difficulties" in implementing the mandate—in particular, his power to make "binding decisions" and to take "actions against persons holding public office or officials . . . who are found by the High Representative to be in violation of legal commitments made at Dayton or the terms for its implementation."[40] From March 1998 until December 2004, the different High Representatives dismissed, suspended, or banned from public office 115 elected officials at all levels of government—including a former prime minister of the Bosnian Federation (Edhem Bicakcic), a president of Republika Srpska (Nikola Poplasen), and a member of the Bosnian presidency (Ante Jelavic).[41]

The exercise of these "Bonn Powers" has been criticized both for particular incidents and for the broader message that it sends to local parties. The justification for Poplasen's dismissal, for example, was his refusal to accept as prime minister a moderate candidate who had majority support from the Republika Srpska National Assembly and was favored by Western powers.[42] More generally, the accretion of these powers marked a reversal of moves toward self-governance. This was driven by Western frustration at the slow pace of implementation on the political side and the fact that nationalist parties by late 1996 had consolidated their control both politically and demographically.[43] That this was only twelve months after an ethnic war that had lasted more than three years led some to argue that these deadlines had less to do with Bosnia than with the domestic concerns of the intervening powers.[44] By 2000, the situation was characterized by the International Crisis Group as a paradoxical combination of a flawed democracy and a semi-international protectorate, in which international actors often appeared reluctant to use their powers effectively.[45]

Lessons learned from Bosnia meant that Kosovo avoided a similar hydra-headed structure, but the territory was politically stillborn. Security Council Resolution 1244 (1999) authorized an international civil presence in Kosovo, but it was laced with compromise language necessary to achieve consensus in New York. In the end, the resolution stated that UNMIK was to provide "an interim administration for Kosovo under which the people of Kosovo can enjoy substantial autonomy within the Federal Republic of Yugoslavia, and which will provide transitional administration while establishing and overseeing the development of provisional democratic self-governing institutions to ensure conditions for a peaceful and normal life for all inhabitants of Kosovo."[46] This created a near impossible mandate on the ground. Some UN officials reported that Kouchner, head of the mission from July 1999 until January 2001, claimed to read the text of Resolution 1244 (1999) twice every morning and still have no idea what "substantial autonomy" meant.

A second lesson from Bosnia was avoiding a commitment to early elections. Instead, Kosovo was governed by UNMIK while structures were established through which Kosovar representatives could "advise" it. The only quasi-governmental body that included Kosovars was, for some time, the Kosovo Transitional Council. Intended to represent the main ethnic and political groups, it was designed to "provide [the Special Representative] with advice, be a sounding board for proposed decisions and help to elicit support for those decisions among all major political groups."[47] From February 2000, the Joint Interim Administrative Structure began to replace the parallel governance structures established by Kosovar Albanians that had for some years collected revenue and provided basic public services. The executive board of the new body was called the Interim Administrative Council, comprising the three Kosovar Albanian political leaders who were parties to the Rambouillet Accords of June 1999 (Rexhep Qosja, Ibrahim Rugova, and Hashim Thaçi), a Kosovar Serb observer (Rada Trajkovic), and four representatives of UNMIK. The council was empowered to make recommendations to the Special Representative, who could either accept these or advise in writing within seven days of "the reasons for his differing decision."[48]

No one was under the illusion that these bodies wielded any actual power. In the course of drafting the Constitutional Framework for Provisional Self-Government, adopted in May 2001, these tensions in the governance structures put UNMIK officials in the odd position of having to resist Albanian attempts to include reference to the "will of the people." Such a concept remained controversial in Kosovo precisely because the one thing that excited all parties—the final status of Kosovo—was the issue on which senior UN staff officially had to profess not to have an opinion. These problems continued to bedevil the "interim" administration: reporting back to the Secretary-General in 2004, Norwegian envoy Kai Eide noted that well-functioning institutions might well depend on a strong sense of local ownership, but that "such ownership cannot be achieved if the owners do not know what they own and what they are intended to govern."[49]

In contrast to the missions in Bosnia and Kosovo, East Timor had a uniquely clear political endpoint. The outcome of independence was never really questioned after UNTAET was established, but the timing and the manner in which power was to be exercised in the meantime soon became controversial. This manifested both in the different forms of consultation attempted in the first two years of the mission and the process through which a constitution was ultimately adopted prior to independence.[50]

The mandate of the UN Assistance Mission in Afghanistan (UNAMA) was interpreted as requiring the United Nations to facilitate rather than lead. In areas such as choice of laws, structure of the legal system, and appointment of judges, this was entirely appropriate. Such arguments were less persuasive in relation to basic questions of rebuilding courthouses, procuring legal texts and office equipment, and training judges. Instead, it appeared that rule of law was simply not a priority. Afghanistan may also serve as a cautionary tale against assumptions that local ownership will always enhance the effectiveness of rule of law strategies. In the forty-eight-page National Development Framework drafted by the Afghan Assistance Coordination Authority in April 2002, the justice system warranted only a single substantive sentence: "The judicial system will be revived through a sub-program that provides training, makes laws and precedents available, and rehabilitates the physical infrastructure of the judicial sector."[51] Similarly, although Italy agreed to serve as "lead donor" on the justice sector at the Tokyo pledging conference in January 2002, there was little evidence of activity in this area. The Afghan Interim Authority did appoint some new judges, including a number of women, but those courts that functioned at all continued to do so erratically. This was not helped by President Hamid Karzai's appointment of a septuagenarian chief justice who had never studied secular law.[52]

Choice of Transitional Law
The failure to establish political credibility from the outset of the mission compounded the internal contradictions of UNMIK's mandate. At Russian insistence, and consistent with the terms of Security Council Resolution 1244 (1999), the first UNMIK regulation established that the law in force prior to March 24, 1999 (the day on which the North Atlantic Treaty Organization [NATO] commenced its air campaign) would apply, provided that this law was

consistent with internationally recognized human rights standards and Resolution 1244.[53] The largely Albanian judiciary that was put in place by UNMIK rejected this, however, with some judges reportedly stating that they would not apply "Serbian" law in Kosovo. Though they accepted some federal laws, such as the federal code of criminal procedure, the judges insisted on applying the Kosovo criminal code and other provincial laws that had been in effect in March 1989, asserting that these had been illegally revoked by Belgrade. The judges nevertheless "borrowed" from the 1999 law to deal with cases involving crimes not covered in the 1989 code, such as drug trafficking and war crimes. In addition to lowering hopes that Serb judges would return to office, this dispute further undermined local respect for UNMIK—especially when it finally reversed its earlier decision in December 1999 and passed a regulation declaring that the law in effect on March 22, 1989, would be the applicable law in Kosovo.[54]

In East Timor, by contrast, choice of law was uncontroversial. UNTAET Regulation no. 1999/1 defined the applicable law as "the laws applied in East Timor prior to 25 October 1999."[55] This language—referring to "the laws applied," rather than "the applicable laws"—was chosen in order to avoid the retroactive legitimation of the Indonesian occupation of East Timor.[56] Curiously, however, these laws were never translated from Indonesian into English, greatly complicating the efforts of international judges to inform themselves of the laws governing the territory.

Appointment of Judges

UNMIK also had to reverse itself on the question of appointing international judges to oversee the legal system. Despite the resignation of Serb judges and concerns about ethnic bias and intimidation within the Albanian judiciary, UN officials were reluctant to introduce international judges.[57] A senior UN official reportedly responded to such a recommendation by stating: "This is not the Congo, you know." Instead, fifty-five local judges and prosecutors, operating under the Joint Advisory Council on Provisional Judicial Appointments, were proposed in the first months of the mission.[58] By February 2000, the rebellion of Albanian judges and a series of attacks against their few Serb counterparts led to a regulation allowing Special Representative of the Secretary-General Bernard Kouchner to appoint international judges to the district court in Mitrovica as an emergency measure. Within three months, this had been extended to every district court in Kosovo.[59]

Though East Timor presented fewer security and political problems than Kosovo, the lack of local capacity presented immense challenges. Under Indonesian rule, no East Timorese lawyers had been appointed as judges or prosecutors. The Transitional Judicial Service Commission was established, comprising three East Timorese and two international experts,[60] but the absence of a communications network meant that the search for qualified lawyers had to be conducted through leaflet drops by International Force in East Timor (INTERFET) planes. Within two months, sixty qualified East Timorese with law degrees had applied for positions, and on January 7, 2000, the first eight judges and two prosecutors were sworn in.[61]

As in Kosovo, the decision to rely on inexperienced local jurists came from a mix of politics and pragmatism. Politically, the appointment of the first Timorese legal officers was of enormous symbolic importance. At the same time, the emergency detentions during the Australian-led INTERFET operation required the early appointment of judges who understood the local civil law system and who would not require the same amount of translation services demanded by international judges. In addition, appointment of international judges would necessarily be an unsustainable temporary measure that would cause further dislocation when funds began to diminish.

In the end, UNTAET was more aggressive in Timorizing the management of judicial systems than the institutions working in political and civil affairs.[62] The trade-off, of course, was in formal qualifications and practical experience. Some of the appointees had worked in law firms and legal aid organizations in Indonesia, others as paralegals with Timorese human rights organizations and resistance groups.[63] None had ever served as judges or prosecutors. "Timorization" thus referred more to the identity of a particular official, rather than the establishment of support structures to ensure that individuals could fulfill their responsibilities. UNTAET developed a three-tier training approach, comprising a one-week "quick-impact" course prior to appointment, ongoing training, and a mentoring scheme. However, limited resources and difficulties in recruiting experienced mentors with a background in civil law posed serious obstacles to the training program, which UNTAET officials later acknowledged was grossly insufficient.

Assessment and Evaluation

Ownership in Theory and in Practice

Returning to the six-point definition of ownership elaborated earlier, it is clear that—regardless of what is said about moves toward local control—during a period of transitional administration the level of "ownership" at the general political level is typically very low indeed.

Efforts are made to ensure that international strategies are *responsive* to local needs, but even this has been routinely overridden—perhaps most explicitly in the promotion of women's involvement in political life. The decision to require high levels of female representation in elections for Kosovo's Provisional Institutions of Self-Government, for example, led to Kosovo having about 29 percent female representation (34 of 120 seats)—more than double the level of female representation in the US Congress or Senate. This is not to suggest that ownership requires cultural relativism: certainly, a higher representation of women might better reflect the desires and aspirations of women in a territory such as Kosovo. But it is clear that such decisions are being made not with a view simply to respond to local expectations. Indeed, moves to include significant numbers of women in the Kosovo Police Service were openly intended to lower the "testosterone level."[64] At the same time, it is far from clear that inclusion of women on the basis that they are more caring and community-oriented than men does more than reinforce gender stereotypes about the respective roles of each in society.[65]

Consultation has been a touchstone of many operations, but actually getting out and hearing what people want is both time-consuming and frustrating. The best example of this working is in the creation of the Commission on Reception, Truth, and Reconciliation in East Timor. An innovative variation on the South African Truth and Reconciliation Commission, the Timorese body linked the need for reconciliation to the need for reconstruction. The commission was empowered to establish nonprosecutorial "community reconciliation processes" (usually some form of community service) that barred future prosecution for criminal acts not amounting to serious crimes.[66] Through extensive consultations in its early planning stages with local actors across the country, the commission was able to garner endorsement from the highest ranks of the local political and religious leaderships. This contrasted with the controversy over the first significant civic education project in East Timor being abandoned after Timorese NGOs protested at inadequate consultation in the development of the project, and the fact that the vast majority of the US$8 million budget was earmarked for vehicles and the salaries of international staff.[67]

Participation in decisionmaking has been easiest at the political level when there is a clear role for nationals and internationals. Frequently it has depended on strong personal relations, as were developed over time in East Timor. At the judicial level, the failure of national judges adequately to fulfill functions thrust upon them meant that they were demoted from a position of "control" to one of, at most, participation.

There has been very little enthusiasm for actual *accountability* on the part of international staff. One of the more hypocritical examples of this is in consideration of corruption mechanisms. At various corruption conferences organized by donors, national leaders are enjoined to embrace accountability mechanisms for their emerging bureaucracies. These conferences tend, however, to ignore the manner in which internationals themselves undermine respect for the rule of law through toleration of prostitution (including the use of trafficked women and girls), failure to stand up to organized crime, and general consumption of pirated entertainment products that are manifestly violations of intellectual property laws. This trilogy of sex, drugs, and rock 'n' roll exacerbates the contradiction embodied in efforts to persuade nationals to abide by laws from which international staff are themselves immune.

While some individuals assume positions where they may fulfill the criteria of *control,* the Bosnian experience of transferring control and then removing it suggests the dangers of premature transfer of power. It is a depressing feature of Bosnia's political development that Brcko was, by 2003, the only municipality with significant minority returns and the beginnings of a functioning multiethnic police, judiciary, and town council. This was seen to be in significant part because Brcko (effectively a third entity in Bosnia) had an executive that was nominated and overseen by an internationally appointed supervisor; in the absence of local elections, the supervisor also appointed the twenty-nine-member Legislative Assembly. The autonomy of the supervisor was reportedly the subject of some envy on the part of other international agencies, including the Office of the High Representative.[68]

As for *sovereignty,* the downside of final authority was well understood by Timorese leaders who saw that once the United Nations ceased to be responsible for the territory, foreign assistance would start to disappear and the population would begin to target grievances in public administration toward them. For these reasons, some Timorese leaders advocated a slower rather than faster transfer of power. More recently, the test of nominal sovereignty continues to be played out in Iraq with the hypothetical possibility that an Iraqi government might ask US troops to leave its territory.

Tensions

Three sets of tensions run through the examples given in this chapter, pointing to problems with the use of the term "ownership," but more generally pointing to problems in the enterprise of transitional administration. First, invocation of a concept of ownership assumes that a "partner" has been located to whom some measure of responsibility can be transferred. As indicated earlier, since existing structures and political actors gave rise to a crisis of sufficient seriousness to warrant the deployment of international forces and civilians, it does not go without saying that former leaders should be reinstituted into positions of power. If former leaders are not reinstituted, how local partners are chosen may radically affect the future political development of a territory. For these reasons, transfer of power to local actors is rightly approached with caution. Typically, however, ownership is invoked in a far less specific way to refer to entire populations. This raises a different problem: the assumption that larger groups in what are typically deeply divided societies can be regarded as a single "partner" in anything more than an aspirational sense.

Second, even when partners can be identified, the relationship between international and national actors is always going to undermine the possibility of meaningful ownership. The international presence exists precisely in order to transform the polity in question. As the case of Bosnia demonstrates most clearly, premature transfer of power that must be withdrawn may undermine the broader political purpose of an operation. Without such a transfer, however, and while international staff operate with actual or effective immunity from local laws, there is an ongoing contradiction between how internationals behave and how nationals are told that they must act.

Third, the supply-driven nature of international assistance—military, financial, and political—undermines the possibility of meaningful transfer of power. Assistance is not merely more responsive to international than local need; the timeline on which it is available tends to reflect the fickle interests of donors rather than growing capacity on the ground. It is has become a cliché that absorptive capacity of a postconflict economy increases just as international interest wanes. This is a particular problem for rule of law issues, since the transformation of a society into one that respects the rule of law, implying subjugation to consistent and transparent principles under state institutions exercising a monopoly on the legitimate use of force, takes years.

This raises a related problem: how to measure success in rule of law activities. Donors frequently do this through quantifiable items such as numbers of judges trained, case files processed, or computers installed. These are important figures, but do not get to the heart of the problem: to whom people turn for solutions to problems that would normally be considered legal. Put bluntly, what would a woman do if her property were stolen—go to the police? Or what would a man do if his brother were murdered? This sociological aspect of the rule of law must be complemented by a political aspect: Is the head of government bound by the law also? Such qualitative measures are not adopted in part because of their imprecision, but in part also because they will typically take years or decades to change.

Policy Recommendations

At its simplest, a trope is a word used figuratively rather than literally: a metaphor. But its etymology is suggestive of a more complex set of meanings. Derived from the Greek word *tropos* (turn), a trope is a word whose meaning has turned away from its origins. In literature, a trope denotes a familiar repeated symbol that may characterize a genre. Through overuse, a trope becomes a cliché.

The figurative use of "ownership" embraces sensible policy objectives: ensuring that external assistance is responsive to local needs, is consistent with local capacities and priorities, and will be perceived as legitimate beyond the life of the international presence. This broadest use of the term is sometimes akin to "self-determination," a term that is notoriously hard to specify in its practical implications. At worst, both are so vague as to be widely accepted due their essential lack of content. But use of the term "ownership" also implies varying degrees of local control that are typically not realized.

A key lesson, then, is that managing expectations, as in every other aspect of postconflict transition, is vital. Recipients may have inflated expectations of what donors can and should do—expectations that are sometimes fostered by political leaders in both recipient and donor countries. Political ownership may well be the end of a transitional administration, but it is often not the means of achieving it. Local leadership may be desirable in development projects in general, but in a postconflict situation this must be tempered by those concerns that brought international administration to the country in the first place—at times creating a tension between the need to resolve conflict and respecting the political aspirations of the population. Nevertheless, structuring assistance around local needs as articulated by local actors may help to mitigate the supply-driven nature of aid. In addition, the transfer of funds directly to local hands is more likely to stimulate sustainable economic activity and reduce dependence on handouts.

A second lesson, frequently repeated in such contexts, is that the administration of justice should rank among the high priorities of a postconflict peace operation.[69] There is a tendency on the part of international actors to conflate armed conflict and criminal activity more generally. Drawing a clearer distinction and being firm on violations of the law increases both the credibility of the international presence and the chances of a peace agreement holding. This encompasses both the lawlessness that flourishes in conflict and postconflict environments and the vigilantism to settle scores. Swift efforts to reestablish respect for law may also help to lay a foundation for subsequent reconciliation processes. Failure to prioritize law enforcement and justice issues undermined the credibility of the international presence in Kosovo and led to missed opportunities in East Timor. In Afghanistan, rule of law simply did not feature on the agenda.

A third lesson is that, once the security environment allows the process of civil reconstruction to begin, sustainability generally should take precedence over temporary standards in the administration of basic law and order. Whether internationalized processes are appropriate for the most serious crimes should be determined through broad consultation with local actors. In some situations, such as those in which conflict is ongoing, this consultation will not be possible. In circumstances where there are concerns about bias undermining the impartiality of the judicial process, some form of mentoring or oversight may be required. In all cases, justice sector development must be undertaken with an eye to its coordination with policing and the penal system.

These themes are necessarily general. Indeed, the idea that one could map out a strict template for reconstructing the judicial system in a postconflict environment is wrongheaded. Nevertheless, developing practical and flexible management tools or guidelines to operationalize the various forms of "ownership" described in this chapter—and being clear about which form is applicable—may assist future peace operations. Some of these are basic, such as ensuring that all relevant material is available in local languages and that there is a functional medium to share information about the transition process (if necessary, this may involve establishing a radio network). Others relate to personnel policies, such as prioritizing individuals with relevant language backgrounds, training staff in the culture and history of the territory in which they are guests, and distinguishing between recruitment of foreign nationals to fulfill functions temporarily and recruitment of trainers to help nationals learn the skills to fulfill these functions themselves. A third set of tools operate at the political level, ranging from the nature and structure of local consultation bodies to the sequencing of security sector reform and demobilization, with the most important factor being clarity about who is in charge and who is going to be in charge.

As Judge Hand recognized, the key battleground lies in the hearts of the general population.[70] This is not to say that "ownership" requires that locals drive this process in all circumstances. On the contrary, international engagement will sometimes abrogate the most basic rights to self-governance on a temporary basis. But while the levels of foreign intervention may vary from a light footprint as in Afghanistan, to ambiguous sovereignty as in Kosovo, to benevolent autocracy as in East Timor, the guiding principle must be an appropriate balance of short-term measures to assert the reestablishment of the rule of law, and long-term institution building that will last beyond the life of the mission and the fickle interest of international actors.

Notes

1. Learned Hand, *The Spirit of Liberty,* 3rd ed. (Chicago: University of Chicago Press, 1960), p. 190.

2. See, for example, Chesterman, *You, the People: The United Nations, Transitional Administration, and State-Building* (Oxford: Oxford University Press, 2004); Francis Fukuyama, *State-Building: Governance and World Order in the 21st Century* (Ithaca: Cornell University Press, 2004); Roland Paris, *At War's End: Building Peace After Civil Conflict* (Cambridge: Cambridge University Press, 2004); Kimberly Marten Zisk, *Enforcing the Peace: Learning from the Imperial Past* (New York: Columbia University Press, 2004); Richard Caplan, *International Governance of War-Torn Territories: Rule and Reconstruction* (Oxford: Oxford University Press, 2005).

3. John Saxby, "Local Ownership and Development Co-operation: The Role of Northern Civil Society" (Ottawa: CCIC/CIDA, 2003), http://www.ccic.ca/e/docs/002_aid_the_role_of_northern_civil_society.pdf.

4. United Nations, *An Agenda for Peace: Preventive Diplomacy, Peacemaking, and Peacekeeping: Report of the Secretary-General,* UN Doc. A/47/277-S/24111 (June 17, 1992) (pursuant to the statement adopted by the Summit Meeting of the Security Council on January 31, 1992).

5. United Nations, *Supplement to An Agenda for Peace: Position Paper of the Secretary-General on the Occasion of the Fiftieth Anniversary of the United Nations,* UN Doc. A/50/60-S/1995/1 (January 3, 1995), http://www.un.org/docs/sg/agsupp.html, paras. 13–14.

6. See Simon Chesterman, *Just War or Just Peace? Humanitarian Intervention and International Law,* Oxford Monographs in International Law (Oxford: Oxford University Press, 2001), pp. 112–218.

7. See, generally, Chesterman, *You, the People.*

8. See, for example, International Development Research Centre, *The Responsibility to Protect: Report of the International Commission on Intervention and State Sovereignty* (Ottawa, 2001), paras. 5.22–5.24, http://www.iciss.gc.ca.

9. See, for example, United Nations, *A More Secure World: Our Shared Responsibility—Report of the Secretary General's High-Level Panel on Threats, Challenges, and Change,* UN Doc. A/59/565, December 1, 2004, para. 299, http://www.un.org/secureworld.

10. See Simon Chesterman, "Occupation as Liberation: International Humanitarian Law and Regime Change," *Ethics and International Affairs* 18, no. 3 (2004): 51–64.

11. See, for example, Office of the High Representative in Bosnia-Herzegovina, "Communiqué by the PIC Steering Board," Peace Implementation Council (Sarajevo, April 1, 2004), http://www.ohr.int/pic/default.asp?content_id=32163.

12. For example, the Swedish International Development Agency had been using comparable terms since the 1980s. See Jean Bossuyt and Geert Laporte, "Partnership in the 1990s: How to Make It Work Better," Policy Management Brief no. 3 (Maastricht: ECDPM, 1994), p. 2, http://www.srds.co.uk/partnerships/docs/bossuyt.rtf. Earlier language on "participation" also reflected similar trends within the discourse.

13. OECD, DAC, "Development Partnerships in the New Global Context" (Paris, May 1995), http://www.oecd.org/dataoecd/31/61/2755357.pdf.

14. OECD, DAC, "Shaping the 21st Century: The Contribution of Development Co-operation" (Paris, May 1996), p. 9, http://www.oecd.org/dataoecd/23/35/2508761.pdf.

15. Ibid., p. 14.

16. James Wolfensohn, "A Proposal for a Comprehensive Development Framework" (Washington, D.C.: World Bank, January 21, 1999), pp. 9–10, http://siteresources.worldbank.org/cdf/resources/cdf.pdf.

17. Bossuyt and Laporte, "Partnership in the 1990s," p. 2.

18. Neclâ Tschirgi, "Post-Conflict Peacebuilding Revisited: Achievements, Limitation, Challenges," prepared for the WSP International and IPA "Peacebuliding Forum" conference, New York, October 7, 2004, p. 16, http://www.ipacademy.org/pdfs/post_conflict_peacebuilding.pdf.

19. Rubens Ricupero, Preface to Carlos Lopes and Thomas Theisohn, *Ownership, Leadership, and Transformation: Can We Do Better for Capacity Development?* (New York: UN Development Programme, 2003), p. xiii.

20. Carlos Lopes, "Does the New Development Agenda Encapsulate Real Policy Dialogue?" in *Dialogue in Pursuit of Development,* edited by Jan Olsson (Stockholm: Almqvist and Wiksell International, 2003), p. 43.

21. Lopes and Theisohn, *Ownership, Leadership, and Transformation,* p. 2.

22. I. William Zartman, "Early and "Early Late" Prevention," in *Making States Work: State Failure and the Crisis of Governance,* edited by Simon Chesterman (Tokyo: UN University Press, 2005).

23. See Thomas M. Franck, "The Emerging Right to Democratic Governance," *American Journal of International Law* 86, no. 1 (1992): 46–91; Gregory H. Fox, "The Right to Political Participation in International Law," *Yale Journal of International Law* 17 (1992): 539–608; Gregory H. Fox and Brad R. Roth, eds., *Democratic Governance and International Law* (Cambridge: Cambridge University Press, 2000).

24. "The people of the war-torn society must own the reconstruction process. They must actively be involved in setting the agenda and leading the process, which is a highly political process complicated by the deep wounds of the conflict." Tschirgi, "Post-Conflict Peacebuilding Revisited," p. 9.

25. Mark Malloch Brown, foreword to Lopes and Theisohn, *Ownership, Leadership, and Transformation,* p. x.

26. United Nations, *The Rule of Law and Transitional Justice in Conflict and Post-Conflict Societies: Report of the Secretary-General,* UN Doc. S/2004/616 (August 23, 2004), para. 15.

27. Ibid., para. 17.

28. UN Security Council Resolution 1244 (1999), para. 10.

29. UNMIK Regulation no. 1999/1 (July 25, 1999), sec. 1.

30. Ombudsperson Institution in Kosovo, "Second Annual Report 2001–2002" (Prishtina, July 10, 2002), http://www.ombudspersonkosovo.org. See also David Marshall and Shelley Inglis, "The Disempowerment of Human Rights–Based Justice in the United Nations Mission in Kosovo," *Harvard Human Rights Journal* 16 (2003): 96.

31. UN Security Council Resolution 1037 (1996), para. 2.

32. Compare Richard Holbrooke, *To End a War* (New York: Random House, 1998), pp. 64–65, 236–239.

33. UN Security Council Resolution 1244 (1999), para. 6.

34. UN Security Council Resolution 1272 (1999), para. 6.

35. Elizabeth M. Cousens and Charles K. Cater, *Toward Peace in Bosnia: Implementing the Dayton Accords* (Boulder: Lynne Rienner, 2001), p. 46.

36. UN Security Council Resolution 1272 (1999), para. 8.

37. Author interview with Hans Corell, New York, December 3, 2002.

38. United Nations, *General Framework Agreement for Peace in Bosnia and Herzegovina* (Dayton Accords), UN Doc. S/1995/999 (December 14, 1995), annex 10, arts. 1(2), 5, http://www.yale.edu/lawweb/avalon/intdip/bosnia/daymenu.htm.

39. After the successful negotiations in Dayton in November 1995, a peace implementation conference was held in London on December 8–9, 1995, to mobilize international support for the Dayton Accords. The meeting resulted in the establishment of the Peace Implementation Council, comprising fifty-five countries and agencies that supported the peace process.

40. OSCE Mission to Bosnia and Herzegovina, "Conclusions of the Peace Implementation Conference" (Bonn: Peace Implementation Council, December 9–10, 1997), para. XI(2), http://www.oscebih.org.

41. Office of the High Representative in Bosnia, "High Representative's Decisions: Removals and Suspensions" (Sarajevo), http://www.ohr.int/decisions/removalss dec. By year, the number of persons removed or suspended were as follows: 1998, 7; 1999, 32; 2000, 28; 2001, 14; 2002, 21; 2003, 7; 2004, 6.

42. Office of the High Representative in Bosnia, "Decision Removing Mr. Nikola Poplasen from the Office of President of Republika Srpska" (Sarajevo, March 5, 1999), http://www.ohr.int/decisions/removalssdec.

43. Cousens and Cater, *Toward Peace in Bosnia,* pp. 129–130.

44. See, for example, David Chandler, *Bosnia: Faking Democracy After Dayton* (London: Pluto, 1999).

45. International Crisis Group, *Bosnia's November Elections: Dayton Stumbles,* Balkans Report no. 104 (Sarajevo, December 18, 2000), p. 17, http://www.crisisgroup.org/home/index.cfm?l=1&id=1569.

46. UN Security Council Resolution 1244 (1999), para. 10.

47. United Nations, *Report of the Secretary-General on the United Nations Interim Administration Mission in Kosovo,* UN Doc. S/1999/779 (July 12, 1999), para. 20.

48. UNMIK Regulation no. 2000/1 (January 14, 2000), on the Kosovo Joint Administrative Structure.

49. United Nations, *The Situation in Kosovo: Report to the Secretary-General of the United Nations,* statement delivered by Ambassador Kai Eide, UN Doc. S/2004/932, enclosure (August 6, 2004), para. 14.

50. See Chesterman, *You, the People.*

51. Afghan Assistance Coordination Authority, "National Development Framework," consultation draft (Kabul, April 2002), p. 47. See also Centre for Humanitarian Dialogue, *Assistance to Justice and the Rule of Law in Afghanistan* (Geneva, February 2004); Laurel Miller and Robert Perito, "Establishing the Rule of Law in Afghanistan," Special Report no. 117 (Washington, D.C.: US Institute of Peace, March 2004).

52. Hafizullah Gardish, "Chief Justice Under Scrutiny," Afghan Recovery Report no. 54 (Washington, D.C.: Institute for War and Peace Reporting, April 1, 2003).

53. UNMIK Regulation no. 1999/1 (July 25, 1999), secs. 2–3.

54. UNMIK Regulation no. 1999/24 (December 12, 1999), sec. 1.1.

55. UNTAET Regulation no. 1999/1 (November 27, 1999), sec. 3.1.

56. Hansjörg Strohmeyer, "Building a New Judiciary for East Timor: Challenges of a Fledgling Nation," *Criminal Law Forum* 11, no. 3 (2000): 267, n. 18.

57. See, for example, United Nations, *Report of the Secretary-General on the United Nations Interim Administration Mission in Kosovo,* UN Doc. S/1999/779 (July 12, 1999), para. 66: "There is an urgent need to build genuine rule of law in Kosovo, including through the immediate re-establishment of an independent, impartial and multi-ethnic judiciary."

58. UNMIK Emergency Decree no. 1999/1 (June 28, 1999) and UNMIK Emergency Decree no. 1999/2 (June 28, 1999) created the legal basis for the Joint Advisory Council and appointed its members (three internationals, and four locals: two Albanian, one Serb, and one Bosniak). This council was later succeeded by the Advisory Judicial Commission, under UNMIK Regulation no. 1999/7 (September 7, 1999).

59. UNMIK Regulation no. 2000/6 (February 15, 2000); UNMIK Regulation no. 2000/34 (May 27, 2000).

60. UNTAET Regulation no. 1999/3 (December 3, 1999), sec. 2.

61. Hansjörg Strohmeyer, "Collapse and Reconstruction of a Judicial System: The United Nations Missions in Kosovo and East Timor," *American Journal of International Law* 95, no. 1 (2001): 53–54.

62. See, for example, Joel C. Beauvais, "Benevolent Despotism: A Critique of UN State-Building in East Timor," *New York University Journal of International Law and Politics* 33 (2001): 1149.

63. Strohmeyer, "Collapse and Reconstruction," p. 54.

64. William G. O'Neill, *Kosovo: An Unfinished Peace* (Boulder: Lynne Rienner, 2002), pp. 112–113.

65. See, further, Cynthia H. Enloe, *Bananas, Beaches, and Bases: Making Feminist Sense of International Politics* (London: Pandora, 1989); Dyan E. Mazurana and Susan R. McKay, *Women and Peacebuilding* (Montreal: International Centre for Human Rights and Democratic Development, 1999); Barnett R. Rubin, *Blood on the Doorstep: The Politics of Preventive Action* (New York: Century Foundation, 2002), p. 180.

66. UNTAET Regulation no. 2001/10 (July 13, 2001). See Frederick Rawski, "Truth-Seeking and Local Histories in East Timor," *Asia-Pacific Journal on Human Rights and the Law* 1 (2002): 77–96.

67. See Chesterman, *You, the People,* p. 136.

68. See, for example, International Crisis Group, *Courting Disaster: The Misrule of Law in Bosnia and Herzegovina,* Balkans Report no. 127 (Sarajevo, March 25, 2002), p. 49, http://www.crisisgroup.org/home/index.cfm?l=1&id=1497; International Crisis Group, *Bosnia's Brcko: Getting In, Getting On, and Getting Out,* Balkans Report no. 144

(Sarajevo, 2 June 2003), http://www.crisisgroup.org/home/index.cfm?id=1475&=l=1; Mark Landler, "Rare Bosnia Success Story, Thanks to US Viceroy," *New York Times,* June 17, 2003.

69. See, for example, United Nations, *Report of the Panel on United Nations Peace Operations* (Brahimi Report), UN Doc. A/55/305-S/2000/809 (August 21, 2000), p. 8, http://www.un.org/peace/reports/peace_operations: "The Panel recommends a doctrinal shift in the use of civilian police, other rule of law elements and human rights experts in complex peace operations to reflect an increased focus on strengthening rule of law institutions and improving respect for human rights in post-conflict environments."

70. United Nations, *Report of the Panel on United Nations Peace Operations,* p. 8, n. 1.

8

Addressing the Past: Reparations for Gross Human Rights Abuses

Pablo de Greiff

While a great deal of attention has been paid to what countries that have undergone transitions to democracy, or at least out of conflict, have attempted to do against perpetrators of past abuses, much less has been paid to those countries' efforts to do something on behalf of the victims of such abuses. Clearly, both kinds of efforts, the penal and the reparative, can be considered elements of justice, yet an important dimension of the latter has not been sufficiently studied. There is a long history—and an extensive literature—on intrastate reparation in the aftermath of war, and a growing history—and accompanying literature—on judicial remedies, including compensation for relatively isolated cases of human rights violations. However, there is very little systematic information available on massive reparation programs. This is surprising, for most of the recent transitional processes have given some consideration to programs of reparations that seek to make up, in some way, for the harms endured by some members or sectors of society.

The focus of this chapter is therefore not the judicial resolution of sporadic cases of rights violations, but rather the types of programs that various transitional or postconflict countries have set in place in order to redress a large universe of victims. I begin by reviewing recent developments in the field of transitional justice. Next I focus on reparation processes, specifically the difficulties associated with the absence of a criterion of reparative justice for the massive cases, and then attempt to articulate an appropriate criterion and propose a taxonomy of reparation efforts. I also analyze some of the trade-offs that accompany the choices between different reparation measures, and address some important questions in relation to the financing of reparations. I conclude the chapter with some general policy recommendations.

Historical Overview

Emergence and Evolution of Transitional Justice Mechanisms

Transitional justice measures have been long utilized, and have gone through significant variations. These variations correspond roughly with historical periods, but are more properly thought of as developmental rather than temporal stages.

In the aftermath of World War II, under the influence of the Nuremberg trials and the guidance of the various international law instruments designed to prevent a repetition of the horrors of the Holocaust and the war itself, the international community adopted a retributivist position toward human rights abusers. The message seemed to be that there was no point in trying to escape, for perpetrators would be pursued, apprehended, tried, and punished. However, this approach required strong international cooperation, and alas the postwar consensus rapidly gave way to the Cold War, which undermined international cooperation on issues related to justice and human rights, making countries, especially the major powers, more prone to adopt "realist" positions in the international arena.

By the early 1980s, not surprisingly, a new approach to transitional justice on the part of the international community seemed to have taken hold, geared primarily toward regime stabilization—an objective that happened to dovetail nicely with Cold War politics as well as with the very real difficulties generated by the policy of trials and punishment. Thus the policy of pardon and oblivion gained some defenders. Granted, even its supporters—other than the perpetrators who stood to gain from it—understood that this was a compromise, acceptable only because of existing political constraints, including a balance of power between the various parties that was radically different from the situation in Germany after the war. However, foregoing not only criminal justice, but also the very possibility of investigating past misdeeds, was seen (briefly) as an admissible trade-off for the sake of stabilizing incipient democracies. The international community did not oppose, and in many ways supported, the policy of pardon and oblivion, such as the ample amnesty law in Brazil in 1979, which paved the way to the easy exit from power of the military in 1985; the Naval Club agreement in Uruguay in 1984, which reportedly included a decision not to press charges against violators of human rights abuses;[1] and the "due obedience" and the "Final Stop" decrees that put an end to the attempt to try the Argentinean military in 1986 and 1987.[2]

However, this is an incomplete account of developments in transitional justice, for it focuses on attitudes toward transitional justice on the part of the international community—that is, the community of nation-states that are subject to interpretations of state interest and highly susceptible to considerations of regime stability, balance of power, and sovereignty. Other actors, among which both national and international nongovernmental organizations (NGOs) were very important, rarely gave up the hope of seeing some form of justice done even if criminal justice could not be achieved. In this sense, the fact that criminal justice efforts stalled for a while may have acted as an incentive for NGOs to push for measures of justice other than criminal prosecutions. Be that as it may, the third identifiable approach to transitional justice issues is one that focused heavily on truth commissions.[3] Thus the experiences with truth commissions in Argentina, Chile, and El Salvador became crucial foundations of transitional justice, which led to the establishment of other such commissions in more than twenty countries around the world.[4]

Finally, the abiding promises of justice expressed in different post–World War II international law instruments helped usher in a fourth and more complex approach to transitional justice once the Cold War finished. The adoption of the Rome Statute of the International Criminal Court has given new wind to the prosecutorial component of transitional justice, especially at the national level. In this perspective, criminal justice is not the antagonist of transitional justice, but one of its components. Alongside criminal justice efforts, truth-telling efforts continue unabated, and, given cross-border learning experiences on the part of each successive truth commission, it is no wonder that their recommendations have become increasingly complex and comprehensive over time. Comparing the reports of the various truth commissions in the past twenty-five years, one cannot justifiably claim that there is a smooth, ascending curve, especially in terms of quality, yet a trend toward greater depth, breadth, and thoroughness can be identified. So it is now common for transitional justice measures to be thought of in terms of a range of measures that include, minimally, criminal justice, truth-telling, institutional reform, and reparations.

Recent interest in reparations emerged as a result of this trend toward increased complexity in transitional justice measures, with both negative and positive underlying incentives.[5] The remainder of this chapter focuses on reparations, paying almost exclusive attention to measures of material compensation, not for lack of interest in symbolic measures, but for reasons of space.[6] Before giving a brief overview of recent experiences with reparation efforts involving large numbers of beneficiaries—as opposed to reparation benefits stemming from the adjudication of relatively isolated cases—a few remarks about the history of the practice are in order. I distinguish between reparation *efforts* and reparation *programs* on the grounds that the latter term should be reserved to designate initiatives that are designed from the outset as a systematically interlinked set of reparation measures; most countries do not have reparation programs in this sense.[7]

A Short History of Reparations

The idea of providing reparations to the victims of various sorts of harms is of course not new. Aristotle, in the fifth book of *Nichomachean Ethics,* articulates what was surely not a novel view even at the time, according to which "recti-ficatory justice" requires the judge to "equalize by means of the penalty, tak-ing away from the gain of the assailant."[8]

However, the contemporary practice of providing reparations for victims of human rights violations has its more immediate roots both in national tort legislation—the idea of repairing harms is part and parcel of all established legal systems—and in interstate, postbellum reparations, which themselves have a long history. Grotius, in his 1625 work *On the Law of War and Peace*,[9] gives expression to a view of interstate reparations, without taking himself to be articulating a new obligation. In the domain of practice, not of mere texts, the Treaty of Westphalia of 1648 references reparations, in particular restitu-tion. The treaties that concluded the wars of 1830 and 1870, and, famously, World War I, included provisions for extensive reparations paid for by the de-feated parties.

But it is the reparations paid by Germany after the Holocaust that consti-tute a watershed in the history of reparations. Although they included elements of the interstate paradigm in the form of transfer of resources from one state (Germany) to another (Israel), these reparation measures also included novel elements:[10] first, they resulted from negotiations that included not only state actors, but also what would come to be known as nongovernmental organiza-tions; and crucially, it was understood that the provision of benefits to individ-ual victims was an essential aspect of the effort.[11]

Since then, in the wake of the different waves of "democratization" and of transition out of conflict, the obligation to provide reparations to victims has come to be understood also with respect to the victims of *intra*state conflicts and violence.

International Strategies and Approaches: Rationales and Objectives

Reparations and International Law

From the standpoint of international law, the right to reparations is one side of a more general right to a remedy—the other being the procedural right to crim-inal justice—contained in global and regional human rights treaties, as well as in humanitarian law instruments and in international criminal law.[12] This emerging consensus is grounded, in part, on the general principle that all vio-lations of international law, such as genocide, crimes against humanity, war crimes, torture, and extrajudicial executions, entail responsibility—that is, a secondary obligation to repair the violation of a primary obligation.[13]

International human rights instruments express this principle in many di-verse ways. Article 8 of the Universal Declaration of Human Rights talks about "effective remedies."[14] Article 10 of the American Convention on Human

Rights talks about "adequate compensation," Article 63 about "fair compensation," and Article 68 about "compensatory damages."[15] Article 9 of the International Covenant on Civil and Political Rights includes vocabulary about "an enforceable right to compensation";[16] Article 14 of the Convention Against Torture speaks about "fair and adequate compensation including the means for as full rehabilitation as possible";[17] and Article 50 of the European Convention on Human Rights talks about "just satisfaction to the victim."[18]

This, of course, does not fully settle the issue. What do the expressions "effective remedies," "fair and adequate compensation," and "just satisfaction" mean, precisely? The criterion of justice in reparations that underlies most national and international law instruments is *restitutio in integrum,* full restitution, the restoration of the status quo ante, or, when the harm is such that it is literally impossible to go back to the preharm situation, compensation in proportion to harm.

This criterion of reparatory justice is unimpeachable for relatively isolated cases of human rights violations. It is meant to neutralize the effects of the harm on the victim, and to prevent the perpetrator from enjoying the spoils of crime. The problem is that international practice suggests that it is virtually impossible to satisfy this criterion in massive cases of abuse. Most "really existing" reparation programs have failed to meet this criterion of justice. It would be too simplistic to conclude that therefore these programs have simply been "unfair," for even if true, this judgment would not help distinguish between earnest efforts to provide reparations to victims of human rights violations and those that have been a sham.

It is a significant fact that virtually all reparations programs have failed to satisfy the criterion of *restitutio in integrum,* for morality and law are not supposed to generate obligations that are impossible to fulfill. This could count in favor of revising the standard of justice for massive human rights abuses. The idea of articulating a standard of justice for the massive cases should not rest on the observation that the familiar criterion of justice in reparations has rarely been met. Judgments about the feasibility of paying certain costs are usually of the *ceteris paribus* type, and perhaps in transitional or postconflict situations it makes little sense for all other things to remain equal; absent a budget surplus, it will be impossible to engage in aggressive reparations for victims while leaving all other state expenditures untouched.[19]

However, the near impossibility of compensating victims in proportion to the harm they have suffered—and the blow to victims' expectations when they are led to believe that this is what they are entitled to but never receive—are not the only reasons to seek a criterion of justice suitable to massive cases. Ultimately, there is a difference between, on the one hand, awarding reparations within a basically operative legal system in relatively isolated cases of abuse, and on the other, awarding reparations in a system that in some fundamental ways needs to be reconstructed (or, as in some countries, built up for the very first time), precisely because it either condoned or made possible systematic abuses. In the former case it makes sense for the criterion of justice to be exhausted by the aim to make up for the *particular* harm suffered by the *particular* victim whose case is in front of the court. In cases of massive abuses, however, an interest in justice calls for more than an attempt to redress the particular harms suffered by particular individuals. Whatever criterion of justice is defended must be one that has an eye also on the preconditions of reconstructing the rule of law, an objective that carries a public, collective dimension.[20]

Goals of Reparation Programs

By examining in detail reparation programs and the history of their design, enactment, and implementation, one is able to reconstruct an account of how these aim at bringing some sort of justice. Here I do not attempt to derive an "ought" from an "is," to derive a normative account from observation. Ultimately, the move is reconstructive; it constitutes an effort to reconstruct the aims that actual reparation programs may be said to pursue. Arguably, these programs have pursued two goals that are intimately linked to justice. The first is to provide a measure of *recognition* to victims. The crucial point here is that the benefits provided by the program are not meant to solidify the status of victims *as victims,* but rather *as citizens,* as bearers of rights that are equal to those of other citizens. The benefits become a form of symbolic compensation for the fact that rights that were supposed to protect the basic integrity, possibilities, and interests of citizens were violated.

It is the violation of equal rights that triggers the provision of compensatory measures. And it is precisely because the benefits are given in recognition of the (violated) rights of citizens that this general aim of recognition is related to justice. Justice in a state governed by the rule of law is a relationship among citizens—that is, among the bearers of equal rights. The violation of this status is what generates the obligation to provide compensatory benefits. This is the first way in which reparations contribute to the achievement of justice: reparations are themselves a form of recognition of the status of individuals as citizens—that is, as bearers of rights. Reparations are, in a sense, a material form of recognition *owed* to fellow citizens whose fundamental rights have been violated. There is another way in which reparations contribute to justice. It is one aspect of the close relationship that binds the different elements of transitional justice together, and specifically, of the ways in which reparations complement other transitional justice processes. One can say that reparations contribute to justice not only because they complement transitional justice measures generally, but also because they do so in a particular way, namely by helping to keep those other measures from fading into irrelevance for most victims.

One important consequence that flows from this conception of reparations is that the proper metric for assessing the magnitude of the compensation owed, in fairness, to victims, stems directly from the very violation of rights held in common by the citizenry, and not from each individual's particular position prior to the violation. In other words, the fundamental obligation of a massive reparation scheme is not so much to return the individual to his or her status quo ante, but to provide a reliable indication of the fact that the successor regime is committed to respect the equality of rights of all citizens. This clearly involves both a retrospective and a prospective element. Retrospectively, the benefits must be sufficient in magnitude to constitute an adequate recognition of the perceived seriousness of the violation of the equal rights of fellow citizens. Prospectively, and by the same token, the magnitude of the benefits must be sufficient to signal the successor government's intentions to behave differently in the future.

The second important consequence that flows from this conception of the ends of reparations is that the design and implementation of reparation programs call for participation of those whom the program seeks to recognize. Recognition is not something that is simply bestowed, independently of whether the person on whom it is bestowed feels thereby adequately recognized. This is particularly true given that what is sought is to recognize beneficiaries as the bearers of equal rights. A paternalistic foisting of benefits without consultation or participation on the part of recipients is likely to undermine the goal to establish the beneficiaries in the eyes of others or in their own eyes as citizens with equal rights. Hence, civil society should be given an important role in the design and implementation of reparation programs. Accomplishing this is no easy task for several reasons, two of which are salient. First, in discussions about the mobilization of public resources, the voice of victims is of course important, but not solely determinative, given that investments in reparations compete against other perfectly legitimate state expenditures such as infrastructure, development, health, and education. Second, it is not uncommon in transitional and postconflict societies to find that victims and their representatives have concentrated on achieving other measures of justice, and therefore their expectations about reparations turn out to be as fluid and uninformed as those of other parties to the discussion. Thus participatory processes have to be designed in such a way that they contribute to the formation of reasonable expectations on everyone's part.

The other main goal that can be attributed to reparations programs—again, one related to justice—is to make a (modest) contribution to the fostering of trust among citizens, particularly between citizens and state institutions. Here the relevant sort of trust is not the thick kind that holds friends and relatives together, but rather the very general kind that can exist even among strangers and that stems from commitment to the same general norms and values. The point is that a well-crafted reparation program is one that provides an indication to victims and others that past abuses are taken seriously by the new government, and that it is determined to make a contribution to the quality of life of survivors. Implemented in isolation from other justice initiatives such as criminal prosecutions and, primarily, truth-telling, reparation benefits might be counterproductive and be perceived more like a payment in exchange for the silence or acquiescence of victims and their families. On the other hand, if integrated into a comprehensive transitional justice policy, reparations might provide beneficiaries with a reason to think that the institutions of the state take their well-being seriously, that they are trustworthy. To the extent that reparation programs may become part of a political agenda that enjoys broad and deep support, they might even have a positive impact not just on "vertical trust"—that is, trust between citizens and the institutions of the state—but also on "horizontal trust"—that is, trust among citizens.

Like recognition, trust is not something that it is merely desirable; it is also both a condition and a consequence of justice. Absent totalitarian supervision, legal systems cannot but rely on the trust of citizens at each level of their operation, starting with the trust that is necessary for citizens to report crime to the authorities. A well-functioning legal system is capable of catalyzing citizens' trust, and also, probably, the trust that citizens have for one another, not least because law stabilizes expectations, creates predictability, and lowers the risks of trusting others.

In sum, then, the claim is that reparations can play a role in fostering the rule of law in transitional and postconflict situations for two main reasons. First, reparations may provide recognition to victims, and, more to the point, recognition of their *rights*. Second, reparations can increase the level of civic trust, particularly trust in new institutions. This is of importance if the rule of law is going to take hold not merely as a set of ideas in texts, but as a set of ruling practices. However, the contribution of transitional or postconflict justice measures—including reparations—will always be modest. Changing social practices and relations is always a slow process, and no given measure can be expected to transform them on its own. Furthermore, the claim is obviously not predictive in character: whether or not reparation efforts do contribute is an empirical issue that depends on many factors.

Designing and Implementing Reparation Measures

Ongoing legal efforts to specify the obligation to provide reparations have led to a familiar classification of the different forms reparations can take under international law:

- *Restitution.* The goal of restitution is to reestablish the victim's status quo ante. Measures of restitution can include the reestablishment of rights, such as liberty and citizenship, and the return of property.
- *Compensation.* This is the essential and preferred component in reparations, especially at the international level. Compensation is usually thought to

involve providing an amount of money deemed to be equivalent to every quantifiable harm, including economic, mental, and moral injury.

• *Rehabilitation.* This includes measures such as necessary medical and psychological care, along with legal and social support services.

• *Satisfaction and guarantees of nonrecurrence.* These particularly broad categories include such dissimilar measures as the cessation of violations; verification of facts; official apologies and judicial rulings seeking to reestablish the dignity and reputation of the victims; full public disclosure of the truth; searching for, identifying, and turning over the remains of dead and disappeared persons; the application of judicial or administrative sanctions for perpetrators; as well as measures of institutional reform.[21]

In the design and implementation of massive programs, however, these main categories distinguish between material and symbolic benefits, and their individual or collective distribution. These two pairs of categories are not meant to substitute for the legal ones. The legal categories give expression to a wider understanding of the term "reparations"; by including judicial measures, truth-telling, and institutional reform, among others, the legal understanding of the term expresses the capacious notion of legal "remedies." While such a broad understanding of the term invites coordinating these various measures, in practice those who are entrusted with the responsibility to design massive reparation programs have tended to appeal to the narrower understanding, and have conceived of their role as that of crafting a program that provides benefits to victims directly, thereby distinguishing, in practice, reparations benefits from the reparatory effects of other measures.

Rather than summarizing the complex reparations efforts undertaken by various countries,[22] I concentrate below on the more useful attempt to provide a taxonomy of these efforts, one that in its basic categories presents some of the main challenges faced in undertaking reparation efforts.

Scope. Reparations efforts can have greater or lesser scope according to the total number of beneficiaries they cover. Using this as a classificatory criterion, one could order different reparations programs in the following way:[23]

> Brazil: 280 beneficiaries.[24]
> Chile: approximately 6,000 beneficiaries.[25]
> Argentina: 13,455 beneficiaries.[26]
> Japanese American reparations in the United States: more than 82,000 beneficiaries.[27]
> Germany: hundreds of thousands of beneficiaries.[28]

Understood in this manner, there is no inherent merit in a program having greater scope. The fact that one program provides reparations for a larger total number of people than another may simply be indicative of a very large universe of potential beneficiaries. In this respect, it is important to distinguish a program's scope from its "completeness."

Completeness. This refers to the ability of a program to cover, at the limit, the whole universe of potential beneficiaries. There is no existing program that satisfies this standard in full, not only due to the difficulties associated with determining, as a matter of principle, what constitutes the full set of *potential* beneficiaries of a program of reparations. Part of the issue here is the catalog of rights whose violation should lead to reparations, addressed below. There are two other considerations that impact a program's completeness. The first concerns evidentiary standards: if the evidentiary bar is set very high, the program will exclude many people who otherwise deserve to receive benefits. Various programs have had to grapple with this issue, including the German Holocaust reparations and various reparation efforts in Argentina. The second consideration that affects a program's completeness concerns structural issues, such as the outreach efforts undertaken to publicize the existence of the program and the procedural hurdles associated with accessing it, including narrow application deadlines, closed lists, personal application requirements, and others. Completeness is a desirable characteristic in a reparations program, and the mere availability of benefits will not guarantee it. Rather, strong commitment toward completeness is essential, particularly considering that a history of both marginalization and abuse might lead large numbers of potential beneficiaries, including entire groups, not to apply for the benefits available through a reparation program.

Comprehensiveness. A related category is the reparation program's comprehensiveness, which concerns the distinct types of crimes or harms it tries to redress. While there is growing consensus in international law about reparations, the boundaries of this obligation remain fuzzy. For instance, there seems to be an emerging agreement in international law about the obligation to provide reparations for disappearance and death. But there is a much weaker consensus on whether the obligation extends to forced displacement. The situation is still more complicated in practice. For instance, "really existing" reparation programs notoriously underrepresent the international law consensus on the obligation for reparations in cases of torture. Most bodies that have considered the possibility of providing reparations for torture have ended up refraining from doing so, on the basis of evidentiary difficulties. Programs tend to provide reparations for torture whenever the evidentiary questions can be sidestepped by folding torture into easier-to-prove categories such as illegal detention, or when the alleged torture has led to permanent injuries.[29]

In general, and perhaps not surprisingly, most reparations efforts have concentrated on a fairly limited (and traditional) catalog of civil and political rights, leaving the violation of other rights largely unrepaired. Obvious exclusions of various sorts impinge on the comprehensiveness of reparation efforts. In a context in which distinct forms of violence were perpetrated against multiple groups, excluding from benefits either some of the worst, or some of the most prevalent, forms of violence, or some of the targeted groups, automatically reduces the comprehensiveness and, as a consequence, the completeness of the reparation effort.

What follows is an attempt not to precisely rank past or current reparation programs along the axes of comprehensiveness, but rather to indicate the types of crimes that various reparation efforts have tried to redress, and to comment on classes of victims that they may have excluded.

- *Brazil.* To the extent that this effort was intended to provide reparations only to the victims of disappearance and death for "non-natural causes in police or similar premises"[30]—notwithstanding how expansively this last criterion was understood by the commission in charge of the program—the Brazilian effort left out important categories of victims, including victims of illegal detention, torture, and exile.
- *The United States: Japanese American internment.*[31] The 1988 US Civil Liberties Act, which gave rise to reparations for the surviving Japanese Americans interned during World War II, compensated them in an undifferentiated way for the internment.[32] This would place the act on the lower end of the spectrum of comprehensiveness, although, interestingly, given the nature of the phenomenon calling for redress—the forced internment of an entire ethnic group—as well as aggressive outreach efforts and years of mobilization on the part of civil society organizations, the efforts rank relatively high in terms of completeness: virtually all eligible beneficiaries, as defined by the act, were located and received their benefits. However, there were notable exclusions: the act targeted Japanese Americans who were US citizens or permanent residents at the time of the internment, which of course precluded many internees who were neither citizens nor permanent residents,[33] as well as those who were not of Japanese ancestry but were interned with their Japanese American spouses.[34]
- *Chile.*[35] Chile has engaged in a series of efforts to redress different types of crimes by means of individual legislative initiatives. Initially, a good part of the attention of these reparatory efforts was focused on the crimes covered by the mandate of the Truth and Reconciliation Commission, namely "human rights violations under the previous dictatorship that resulted in the death of the victims." This is to say that the relevant categories of crimes leading to reparations were deadly political violence, political executions, and disappearance while in detention.[36] Ancillary initiatives were taken in order to provide different forms of assistance—not reparations, strictly speaking—to returning exiles;[37] to the fewer than 400 political prisoners still in jail after the Augusto

Pinochet regime came to a close ("Cumplido Laws"); to those who had been dismissed from their jobs for political reasons;[38] and to those excluded from agrarian reform or those who had been expelled from their land.[39] One noteworthy effort undertaken by the Chilean government has been a comprehensive healthcare program for victims of political violence, which makes available to them medical services, including mental healthcare, through the national healthcare system, while waiving copayments and giving victims priority in the delivery of services.

For decades, the huge omission in Chile's reparation efforts was the exclusion of victims of the most prevalent forms of violations during the Pinochet regime: illegal detention and torture. Recently, this omission received attention from a commission appointed to examine precisely these crimes, which submitted at the end of 2004 a comprehensive report including recommendations on reparations. The recommendations, accepted by the government, will give victims of these crimes a monthly pension and other symbolic reparatory measures.

• *South Africa.* The Truth and Reconciliation Commission (TRC) made far-reaching recommendations for the reparation of the victims of apartheid. A "victim" was someone who had "suffered harm in the form of physical or mental injury, emotional suffering, pecuniary loss or substantial impairment of human rights, (i) as a result of a gross violation of human rights; or (ii) as a result of an act associated with a political objective for which amnesty has been granted." A gross violation of human rights, in turn, was defined as "(a) the killing, abduction, torture or severe ill-treatment of any person; or (b) any attempt, conspiracy, incitement, instigation, command or procurement to commit [killing, abduction, torture or severe ill-treatment]."[40] At least in part because of the nature of the apartheid system, a system that involved controlling fundamental aspects of the lives of the majority of South Africans for essentially repressive purposes, the point has been made repeatedly that the conception of "victims" was excessively narrow, and therefore that important categories of potential beneficiaries had been entirely left out of consideration.[41] Such a repressive system, which affected so many aspects of people's lives—including, of course, their standard of living—can rightly be said to have made victims of virtually all those subjected to it. While true, this is not particularly helpful from the standpoint of reparations. This general sense of victimhood is best addressed through distributive justice policies that lead to the redress of structural imbalances, something that reparation programs are not in a position to do. Arguably, the Truth and Reconciliation Commission failed to consider important categories of victims: combatants who died during military actions in situations that did not constitute clear violations of international humanitarian law; victims of the routine violence that accompanied the social engineering aspects of apartheid, such as people who died not in political demonstrations, but, for example, in forced removals; and people who were detained under state-of-emergency provisions. None of them were eligible for reparations as a class, and arguments can be made that they should have been.[42]

• *Argentina.*[43] There is no such thing in Argentina as a reparation program in any strict sense of the concept. Instead, there have been several initiatives, each stemming from a separate piece of legislation and covering a distinct category of victims. The main laws cover the following sets of crimes: disappearance,[44] arbitrary detention, and grave injuries and death while in detention.[45] A 2004 law redresses categories of victims who had been overlooked by the initial reparations laws,[46] namely persons who were born while their mothers were illegally detained; minors who remained in detention due to the detention or disappearance of their parents for political reasons; and those who remained in military areas. The 2004 law also redresses those who were the victims of "identity substitution," the term used in Argentina to refer to cases of children of disappeared parents who were registered as the legitimate children of other families, in many cases as the children of the military or security personnel who stole them from their biological parents.

• *Germany: Holocaust reparations.* The very broad categories used by the German reparation laws—harm to life, body, and health; harm to freedom; harm to possessions and assets; and harm to career and economic advancement—make Germany's Holocaust reparations the most comprehensive program in the sample presented here. However, and once again to emphasize the difference between comprehensiveness and completeness, while the very generality of the categories used by the German reparation laws cover a good number of the more narrowly defined crimes that have become common today and hence make the German efforts quite comprehensive, this does not mean that they were complete. Indeed, the obvious exclusion of important categories of claimants, such as those who did not fulfill the residency requirements of reparation law—meaning most people persecuted outside Germany who remained in their native countries—or the Roma, or forced laborers, among others, illustrates the incomplete nature of the effort and became one of the most frequently criticized aspects of these laws. Some of these groups have been redressed in later legislation.[47]

All things considered, comprehensiveness is a desirable characteristic. It is better, both morally and practically, to repair as many categories of crime as possible; leaving important categories of victims unaddressed virtually guarantees that the issue of reparations will continue to be on the political agenda, which means it will remain the target of legislative or bureaucratic give-and-take. This may undermine the stability and reliability of reparation agreements, as the Chilean case exemplifies.

Complexity. Whereas comprehensiveness relates to the types of crimes that reparation efforts seek to redress, complexity refers to the ways in which the efforts attempt to do so. Thus, rather than focusing on the motivating factors, complexity measures the character of the reactions themselves. A reparation program is more complex if it distributes benefits of more distinct types, and in more distinct ways, than its alternatives. Thus, at one end of the spectrum lie very simple programs that distribute, say, money, exclusively, and in one payment, as in Argentina.[48] Money and an apology, as in the case of US reparations for Japanese Americans, or money and some measure of truth-telling, as the Brazilian effort ended up providing, create greater complexity. Monetary compensation, healthcare services, educational support, business loans, and pension reform, as in Germany and Chile, increase the complexity of the reparation efforts even more. In general, since there are certain things that money cannot buy, complexity brings with it the possibility of targeting benefits flexibly so as to tailor them to victims' needs. All other things being equal, then, this is a desirable characteristic. Of course, in most cases not all things remain equal. There are some costs to increased complexity that may make it undesirable beyond a certain threshold.

Coherence. Reparation programs should ideally display a type of integrity that I call "coherence," which can be analyzed in two different dimensions, internal and external. *Internal* coherence refers to the relationship between the different types of benefits a reparation program distributes. Most reparation programs deliver more than one kind of benefit. These may include symbolic as well as material reparations, and each of these categories may include different measures and be distributed individually or collectively. Obviously, in order to reach the desired aims, it is important that benefits internally support one another. Thus, arguably, US reparations for Japanese Americans, which included an apology with the reparation payment, gave expression to an internally more coherent plan than Brazil's, which distributed money with no official acknowledgment of responsibility, and which acquired an important truth-telling function only incidentally, not as a matter of design.

External coherence expresses the requirement that the reparation efforts be designed in such a way as to bear a close relationship with other transitional mechanisms—that is, minimally, with criminal justice, truth-telling, and institutional reform. This requirement is important for both pragmatic and conceptual reasons. It will help ensure that each of these mechanisms will be perceived as successful (despite the inevitable limitations that accompany each of them), and, more important, that the transitional efforts, on the whole, will satisfy the expectations of citizens. But beyond this pragmatic advantage, it may be argued that the requirement flows from relations of complementarity between the different transitional justice mechanisms. It is not just that truth-telling, in the absence of reparation efforts, can be seen by victims as an empty gesture. The relation holds in the opposite direction as well, since efforts to repair in the absence of truth-telling could be seen by beneficiaries as the state's attempt to buy victims' and their families' silence or acquiescence. The same tight and bidirectional relationship may be observed between reparations and institutional reform, since a democratic reform that is not accompanied by any attempt to dignify citizens who were victimized can hardly be understood. By the same token, reparative benefits in the absence of reforms that diminish the probability of the repetition of violence are nothing more than payments whose utility and, furthermore, legitimacy are questionable. Finally, a bidirectional relationship also links criminal justice and reparations. In this sense, from the standpoint of victims, especially once a possible moment of satisfaction derived from the punishment of perpetrators has passed, the condemnation of a few perpetrators, without any effective effort to positively redress victims, could be easily seen by victims as a form of more or less inconsequential revanchism. Reparations without any effort to achieve criminal justice may seem to them as nothing more than blood money. These complex relations obtain not only between reparations and each of the other components of transitional justice, but also among all of them. In other words, parallel arguments may be constructed to describe the relation between criminal justice and truth-telling, and between each of these and institutional reform.

Needless to say, both internal and external coherence are easier to achieve if reparations are designed as a *program,* and if this program is part of a transitional justice policy. But this is rarely the case, hence the reference to the cases under review here as reparations "efforts" rather than "programs." Although the Argentinean and Chilean cases were developed in temporal proximity to other transitional mechanisms, and in the case of Chile as part of the political platform of the Concertación (the alliance of parties that have governed since the end of Pinochet's regime), none of the cases reviewed here were really designed programmatically, either in an internal sense—that is, in a way that coordinates benefits for distinct crimes in a systematic way—let alone in an external sense—that is, so as to coordinate the reparation effort with prosecutorial, truth-telling, and institutional reform policies.

Finality. By the "finality" of a reparation program I refer to whether it stipulates that receiving its benefits forecloses other avenues of civil redress. Not all reparation efforts are final in this sense. In particular, among the cases mentioned, the reparation efforts of Germany, the United States, and Argentina (in one of the latter's laws) are final, whereas Brazil's and Chile's are not. It is difficult to decide, in the abstract, whether it is desirable, in general, for reparation programs to be final. On the one hand, finality means that courts are made inaccessible to citizens. On the other, once a government has made a good faith effort to create an administrative system that facilitates access to benefits, for the reasons mentioned above, allowing beneficiaries to initiate civil litigation poses the danger of not just obtaining double benefits for the same harm, but also, and worse, jeopardizing the whole reparation program. While the first problem can be easily addressed by stipulating that no one can gain benefits twice for the same violation, the second problem is not so easy to avoid, for the benefits obtained through the courts typically surpass the benefits offered by a massive program. This can lead to a significant shift in expectations, and to a generalized sense of disappointment with the program's benefits. Moreover, the shift may be motivated by cases that probably are unrepresentative of the whole universe of victims, making civil litigation prone to entrenching prevalent social biases. Wealthier, more educated, urban victims usually have a higher chance of successfully pursuing reparation litigation in civil courts than do poorer, less educated, rural individuals, who may also happen to belong to less favored ethnic, racial, or religious groups.[49]

Munificence.[50] This is the characteristic of reparation programs that relates to the magnitude of their benefits from the individual beneficiary's perspective.[51] Clearly there is no absolutely reliable way to measure the absolute worth of the benefits, and the difficulties only increase if one aspires to do a cross-country analysis of their comparative worth. Nevertheless, abstracting from other complications, a simple comparison of the dollar value of material benefits directly distributed to victims by some recent reparations programs leads to the following rough ascending order of munificence: South Africa, which finally gave a onetime payment of less than US$4,000 to each victim, would lie on the lower side of the spectrum; next would be the United States, which gave each Japanese American victim a onetime US$20,000 payment; followed by Chile, Germany, and Brazil; and at the higher end of the spectrum would be Argentina, which gave to each family of a disappeared victim a bond payment valued at US$224,000.[52] As this ordering makes clear, munificence, by itself, is not a criterion of success in reparations. It would be difficult to argue that the Argentinean reparations, the most munificent in this list, have been significantly more successful than, say, the significantly less munificent US reparations for Japanese Americans.

Assessment and Evaluation

I concentrate here on two issues: the trade-offs implied in reparation choices, and the financing of reparation efforts.

Dealing with Trade-Offs

Although the final details of a reparation program for a particular country will depend on heeding many contextual features, the trade-offs between different measures can be clarified in very general terms. While theorists should not be in the business of designing blueprints for such programs—at least not in their capacity as mere theorists—there is a great deal of work that can be done in the clarification of the advantages and disadvantages that may accompany different design choices. The following scheme illustrates the basic orientation that should guide policymakers in the consideration of reparation measures:

Symbolic Measures
    Individual (personal letters of apology, copies of truth-commission reports, proper burial for the victims, etc.)
        Advantages:
- Show respect for individuals.
- Express recognition for the harm suffered.
- Low cost.

        Disadvantages:
- May be perceived as constituting, by themselves, sufficient reparations for victims.

    Collective (public acts of atonement, commemorative days, establishment of museums, changing of street names and other public places, etc.)
        Advantages:
- Promote the development of
    collective memory,
    social solidarity, and
    a critical stance toward, and oversight of, state institutions.

        Disadvantages:
- May be socially divisive.
- In societies or social sectors with a proclivity toward feeling victimized, this feeling may be heightened.
- May be perceived as constituting, by themselves, sufficient reparations for victims.

Service Packages
    Service packages may include medical, educational, housing, and other forms of assistance.
        Advantages:
- Satisfy real needs.
- May positively impact equal treatment.
- May be cost-effective if already-existing institutions are used.
- May stimulate the development of social institutions.

        Disadvantages:
- Do not maximize personal autonomy.
- May reflect paternalistic attitudes.
- Quality of benefits will depend on the services provided by current institutions.
- The more the program concentrates on a basic service package, the less force the reparations will have, as citizens will naturally

think that the benefits being distributed are ones they have a right to as citizens, not as victims.

Individual Grants
  Advantages:
  • Respect personal autonomy.
  • Satisfy perceived needs and preferences.
  • Promote the recognition of individuals.
  • May improve the quality of life of beneficiaries.
  • May be easier to administer than alternative distribution methods.
  Disadvantages:
  • If they are perceived solely as a way of quantifying the harm, they will always be viewed as unsatisfactory and inadequate.
  • If the payments fall under a certain level, they will not significantly affect the quality of life of victims.
  • This method of distributing benefits presupposes a certain institutional structure (the payments can satisfy needs only if institutions exist that "sell" the services that citizens wish to purchase).
  • If they are not made within a comprehensive framework of reparations, these measures may be viewed as a way to "buy" the silence and acquiescence of the victims.
  • Politically difficult to bring about, as the payments would compete with other urgently needed programs, may be costly, and may be controversial, given that they would probably include former combatants from both sides as beneficiaries.

It has been argued that reparations can also take the shape of development and social investment programs (I do not subscribe to this approach), to which the following scheme may apply:

Development and Social Investment
  Advantages:
  • Give the appearance that underlying causes of violence are being addressed.
  • Seem to allow due recognition of entire communities.
  • Give the impression that goals of justice as well as development can be achieved.
  • Politically attractive.
  Disadvantages:
  • Have very low reparative capacity, because
        development measures are too inclusive (are not directed specifically toward the victims), and

they are normally focused on basic and urgent needs, which make the beneficiaries perceive them as a matter of right and not as a response to their situation as victims.

- In places characterized by a fragmented citizenry, these measures do nothing to promote respect for individuals other than as members of marginal groups.
- Uncertain success: development programs are complex and long-term, which threatens the success of the institutions responsible for making recommendations regarding reparations, which may in turn lead the society to question the seriousness of the transitional measures in general.
- Development plans easily become victim to partisan politics.

In principle, there is no conflict at all between the distribution of symbolic and material reparations. In fact, ideally, these benefits can lend mutual support to each other, something that will be especially important in contexts characterized by scarce resources, where symbolic reparations will surely play a particularly visible role. Nor is there any conflict at all, in principle, between individual and collective measures. As long as there is a substantial individual component, the exact balance between the two kinds of measures should be established by considering, among other factors, the kind of violence to be redressed. In those places where the violence was predominantly collective, it makes sense to design a program that also places special emphasis on these kinds of methods.

However, I am skeptical of the effort to turn a reparation program into a development or social investment program, such as to solve structural problems of poverty and inequality; strictly speaking, a development program is not a reparation program. In fact, development programs have a very low reparative capacity, because, to reiterate the fundamental points outlined above, they do not target victims specifically, and because they try to satisfy basic and urgent needs, which means that their beneficiaries perceive them, correctly, as distributing goods to which they have rights as citizens, and not necessarily as victims.

Here it is worth returning to the distinction between reparations in their strict sense, and the reparative effects of other programs. Development, just as criminal justice, for example, may have reparative effects. Nevertheless, this does not make either of them part of the domain of responsibility of those who design reparation programs. Naturally, one may insist here that the latter cohere with other aspects of transitional policies. That is to say, the program must be internally and externally coherent, and it must avoid reproducing and perpetuating unjust social structures. A transitional government in a poor country will most likely propose a development plan, and ideally the reparation program should also cohere with that plan. But it is important to set boundaries of responsibilities between different policies, because, strictly speaking, the aims of a reparation program are not the same as those of a development or social investment program.

In contexts of deep poverty (accompanied, as is usually the case, by weak state institutions), it is likely that transitional governments will be particularly tempted to forego reparations in favor of development programs. The case is often made that when a society is missing even the most basic elements of a productive infrastructure or of the rule of law—not to mention the case of a welfare state—there is no point in trying to give reparations to victims. This position merits two responses, one from a normative and the other from a pragmatic perspective. Both of them start by acknowledging that, of course, context matters. The normative response, however, insists that if it is true that reparations to victims are a matter of obligation, contextual factors matter not in the sense that they can dissolve the obligation, but merely in the sense that they can "modulate" the way the obligation is met. Here the most important variables are munificence, the magnitude of awards given, and the timing of the program vis-à-vis other elements of the transition.[53] The pragmatic response consists of a reminder not just of the potential advantages to be had if the reparation program indeed contributes to the fostering of trust in state institutions, but also of the fact that, historically, claims to justice, including reparations, have not faded away, and sometimes have (re)emerged in socially divisive ways. Thus, all things considered, it may be that reparations, even under conditions of scarcity, constitute one of those issues in which morality and prudence converge.

Financing Reparations

I highlight here just two important points, based on a careful analysis of various experiences in different parts of the world.[54] First, despite the expectations of many postconflict or transitional societies, the international community rarely provides significant resources to finance reparation initiatives. The main reason for this reluctance results from the fact that reparation benefits should not simply be the equivalent of a crime-insurance scheme, but rather should always involve a dimension of acknowledged responsibility, and thus the international community has often argued that reparations should be primarily a local initiative.[55] As well, given that implementing reparation programs always involves sensitive political decisions, the international community has little incentive to get involved in a potentially divisive arena.

Low socioeconomic development, and a large universe of potential beneficiaries, place great constraints on the ability of a local government to implement a reparation program. To illustrate the point with examples from the Americas: Guatemala, El Salvador, and Haiti, for instance, have not implemented reparations plans, whereas Chile, Argentina, and Brazil have. This correlation between socioeconomic development and reparations is more complex than it seems, however. While it appears that some minimum threshold of economic development is needed for implementing reparations, once that threshold is reached, countries in similar economic situations often take quite different paths on the issue, as shown most clearly in the cases of Chile and Argentina. As well, and perhaps more important, in the example countries where reparation programs have not been implemented, the political constraints to implementing them have been perhaps as significant as the economic constraints. What clearly emerges from an analysis of failed efforts at implementing reparations is that in the absence of strong and broad coalitions in favor of reparations, no programs at all, or very modest programs at best, are implemented, even if the country could have afforded to do better, South Africa being a good example.

A second point in the financing of reparations concerns the two main models utilized: creating special trust funds, and introducing dedicated reparations into the national budget. Countries that have experimented with the first model have fared significantly worse than countries that have used the second. Part of the reason may relate to political commitment. Nothing illustrates commitment more clearly than the willingness to create a budget for it. The expectation that it will be possible to find alternative sources of funding (recovery of illegal wealth, donations, special taxes, debt swaps, etc.) for purposes of reparations underlying the creation of trust funds may either demonstrate, or actually give rise to, weak political commitments—emphasizing yet again that although socioeconomic development is important, it should not cloud the crucial significance of political factors.

Policy Recommendations

In crafting a reparation program, it is important to consider the following:

- Ideally, the class of beneficiaries of the program should be complete, coinciding with the class of victims of abuse or conflict. Special care should be taken in implementing effective outreach measures to publicize the existence of the programs. More important, great attention should be paid to the way in which the categories of crimes that give rise to benefits are selected. Frequently, such categories have been selected in a way that excludes from benefits those who have been traditionally marginalized, including women and some minority groups. To compensate all victims, of course, does not mean that all of them have to be compensated equally, that they must receive the same benefits.

- The possibility of achieving completeness, of providing benefits to all the victims of abuse or conflict, is related to the program's comprehensiveness. Focusing on a very narrow set of crime categories means that the program will exclude large numbers of victims, which not only is unfair, but also increases the likelihood that those victims' claims will remain on the political agenda for a long time to come.

• In order to make it feasible to provide benefits to all victims of all relevant crime categories, it is important that the reparation program distribute a variety of material and symbolic benefits, and do so in a coherent way.

• In addition to coordinating the benefits it distributes, a reparation program should itself operate in coordination with other justice measures, because otherwise the program may easily become the target of justified criticism. Reparation programs that function in the absence of other justice measures invite the interpretation that the benefits they distribute constitute blood money, with the state trying to buy the silence or acquiescence of victims and their families. Hence it is important to ensure that reparation efforts cohere with other justice initiatives, including criminal prosecutions, truth-telling, and institutional reform.

• If two of the critical aims of a reparation program are to provide recognition to victims, in their status not just as victims but also as citizens, as bearers of equal human rights, and to promote their trust in the institutions of the state, it is important to involve victims in the process of designing and implementing the reparation program through open, deliberative, and participatory processes.

• States should not expect to receive substantial financial assistance from the international community for purposes of repairing victims. This means that those agents who favor reparations should prepare themselves for protracted political struggles of the sort that are always necessary to mobilize large amounts of resources.

• There are still plenty of roles for the international community to play in the domain of reparations. The international community could (1) rethink, at least in some cases, particularly in those cases in which international actors have played an important role in a conflict, its reluctance to provide material support to reparations efforts; (2) provide technical assistance in the design and implementation of reparation programs; (3) pressure multilateral institutions to foster conditions under which postconflict economies can afford to pay due attention to the victims of conflict (comparable to the international attention and assistance that former combatants often receive); and (4) pressure local governments to establish meaningful reparations for victims.

Notes

This chapter draws from my chapter "Justice and Reparations," in my edited volume *The Handbook of Reparations* (Oxford: Oxford University Press, 2006); and from my chapter "Reparations Efforts in International Perspective: What Compensation Contributes to the Achievement of Imperfect Justice," in *To Repair the Irreparable: Reparations and Reconstruction in South Africa,* edited by Erik Doxtader (Cape Town: David Phillips, 2004). *The Handbook of Reparations* is the result of the massive research project on reparations undertaken by the International Center for Transitional Justice. It contains eleven case studies, ten thematic papers, and basic documents on reparations efforts in different parts of the world.

1. For an account of these two cases, see Lawrence Weschler, *A Miracle, A Universe: Settling Accounts with Torturers* (New York: Pantheon, 1990). See also Alexandra Barahona de Brito, *Human Rights and Democratization in Latin America: Uruguay and Chile* (Oxford: Oxford University Press, 1997).

2. See, for example, Paula Speck, "The Trial of the Argentine Junta: Responsibilities and Realities," *University of Miami Inter-American Law Review* 18 (1987): 491–534; Alejandro Garro and Henry Dahl, "Legal Accountability for Human Rights in Argentina: One Step Forward and Two Steps Backward," *Human Rights Law Journal* 8 (1987): 283–344; Carlos S. Nino, "The Duty to Punish Abuses of Human Rights Put Into Context: The Case of Argentina," *Yale Law Journal* 100, no. 8 (1991): 2619–2640.

3. Compare Aryeh Neier, "Rethinking Truth, Justice, and Guilt After Bosnia and Rwanda," in *Human Rights in Political Transitions: Gettysburg to Bosnia,* edited by Carla Hesse (London: Zone, 1999).

4. These three commissions were established in contexts in which, predictably, criminal prosecutions were not going to make great strides. However, it is a mistake to think that they constituted the beginning of an explicit trade-off between truth and justice; none of them offered amnesty in exchange for truth. The first commission to do this was the South African Truth and Reconciliation Commission (TRC). Even here it is not entirely fair to say that the South African model assumed the truth versus justice dilemma wholesale. The decision to grant an amnesty to a particular perpetrator was made by a different committee than that which took the testimony, and the amnesty could be denied if the testimony was incomplete or inaccurate, or if it related to incidents that bore either no relationship to a political cause or no proportionality to the causes sought. Indeed, of the 7,116 amnesty petitions received by the TRC, only 1,167 were granted. Those denied amnesty are liable to prosecutions. However, the prosecutorial efforts continue to be slow and not particularly successful. See Martin Coetzee, "An Overview of the TRC Amnesty Process," in *The Provocations of Amnesty: Memory, Justice, and Impunity,* edited by Charles Villa-Vicencio (Trenton, N.J.: Africa World, 2003), p. 193.

5. John Torpey argues persuasively that the recent emphasis on reparations has also been aided by the "death of politics." In an age in which claims to distributive justice have lost virtually all their political track, some claims to redistribution are made in the vocabulary of reparations for victims. See his insightful article "'Making Whole What Has Been Smashed': Reflections on Reparations," *Journal of Modern History* 73, no. 1 (2001): 333–358.

6. As I argue later, the complexity and integrity of reparations measures are crucially important factors.

7. Reparations benefits are most often the result of relatively isolated initiatives that come about incrementally, rather than from a deliberately designed plan.

8. Compare Aristotle, *Nichomachean Ethics,* translated by David Ross, revised by J. L. Ackrill and J. O. Urmson (Oxford: Oxford University Press, 1998), 5.2–5.4.

9. Ibid., 17.10.

10. The fact that the recipient state (Israel) came into existence only *after the conflict* makes the case novel even from the perspective of interstate reparations.

11. See Ariel Colonomos and Andrea Armstrong, "German Reparations to the Jews After World War Two: A Turning Point in the History of Reparations," in de Greiff, *The Handbook of Reparations.*

12. For a fuller treatment of the issues discussed in this section, see de Greiff, "Justice and Reparations"; de Greiff, "Reparations Efforts in International Perspective."

13. In the Chorzow Factory case, the Permanent Court of International Justice (PCIJ) declared that "it is a principle of international law that the breach of an engagement involves an obligation to make reparation in an adequate form." Chorzow Factory (Jurisdiction), 1927 PCIJ, Ser. A, no. 9, at 21 (July 26). For a fuller treatment of the international law on remedies, see Dinah Shelton, *Remedies in International Human Rights Law* (Oxford: Oxford University Press, 1999); Dinah Shelton, "The United Nations Principles and Guidelines on Reparations: Context and Contents," in *Out of the Ashes: Reparation for Victims of Gross and Systematic Human Rights Violations,* edited by M. Bossuyt, P. Lemmens, K. De Feyter, and S. Parmentier (Brussels: Intersentia, 2006).

14. United Nations, *Universal Declaration of Human Rights,* UN Doc. A/RES/217A (III) (December 10, 1948).

15. Organization of American States (OAS), *American Convention on Human Rights,* OAS Treaty Series no. 36, 1144 UNTS 123; entered into force on July 18, 1978; reprinted in *Basic Documents Pertaining to Human Rights in the Inter-American System,* OEA/Ser.L.V/II.82, doc. 6, rev. 1, at 25 (1992).

16. United Nations, *International Covenant on Civil and Political Rights,* UN Doc. A/RES/2200A (XXI) (December 16, 1966).

17. United Nations, *Convention Against Torture and Other Cruel, Inhuman, or Degrading Treatment or Punishment,* UN Doc. A/RES/39/46 (December 10, 1984).

18. Council of Europe, *The Convention for the Protection of Human Rights and Fundamental Freedoms* (November 4, 1950).

19. A good illustration of this point comes from South Africa, where the government, at the same time that it was refusing to implement the recommendations on reparations made by the TRC, arguing that to do so would be too expensive, was buying two submarines for its navy. See Brandon Hamber and K. Rasmussen, "Financing a Reparations Scheme for Victims of Political Violence," in *From Rhetoric to Responsibility: Making Reparations to the Survivors of Past Political Violence in South Africa,* edited by Brandon Hamber (Johannesburg: Centre for the Study of Violence and Reconciliation, 2000), pp. 52–59. The Peruvian government seems to be following the same lead. More than a year after its own truth commission made comprehensive recommendations on reparations, which so far remain largely unheeded, the government is considering an expansion of its navy.

20. *Justice and Reparations,* a forthcoming book that I have authored, spells out the reasons why the procedure that would have to be implemented in order to satisfy the criterion of full restitution may end up underserving the notion of justice that is called for in the latter type of situation. The problem related to the fact that in the effort to repair *each individual* in proportion to the harm she or he has suffered, the procedure ends up "disaggregating" both the victims and the reparation efforts. In the process, a dangerous inegalitarian message might be sent, namely that violation of the rights of the affluent is a more serious offense than violation of the rights of the less well-off. See also Pablo de Greiff and Marieke Wierda, "The Trust Fund for Victims of the International Criminal Court: Between Possibilities and Constraints," in Bossuyt et al., *Out of the Ashes.*

21. See, for example, Theo van Boven (Special Rapporteur of the United Nations), *Study Concerning the Right to Restitution, Compensation, and Rehabilitation*

for Victims of Gross Violations of Human Rights and Fundamental Freedoms, final report, UN Doc. E/CN. 4/Sub.2/1993/8 (July 2, 1993). On April 13, 2005, the UN Human Rights Committee finally adopted the principles, without changing these categories substantially. See *Basic Principles and Guidelines on the Right to a Remedy and Reparation for Victims of Gross Violations of International Human Rights Law and Serious Violations of International Humanitarian Law,* UN Doc. A/RES/60/147, March 21, 2006.

22. See the very detailed case studies of twelve countries in de Greiff, *The Handbook of Reparations;* and de Greiff "Reparations Efforts in International Perspective."

23. The numbers of beneficiaries, of course, need not correspond to the number of victims of human rights abuses in any given case.

24. See Ignacio Cano and Patricia Ferreira, "The Reparations Program in Brazil," in de Greiff, *The Handbook of Reparations.*

25. This figure includes only the beneficiaries of the pension program started in 1991 by the Corporación Nacional de Reparación y Reconciliación, and represents the program's highest number, at its inception, since some of the benefits terminated when children of the victims turned twenty-five or finished university education. By the end of 2001 the number of beneficiaries had declined to 3,210. The 6,000 figure therefore does not include the many thousands of beneficiaries of the health program, or beneficiaries of pensions for the politically dismissed, and the like. Nor does it include the tens of thousands of persons who will become the beneficiaries of the effort suggested by the recent Commission on Illegal Detention and Torture. See Elizabeth Lira, "The Reparations Policy for Human Rights Violations in Chile," in de Greiff, *The Handbook of Reparations.*

26. This figure includes 7,800 beneficiaries under Law no. 24.043 (on illegal detention, death, and grave injury), and 5,655 under Law no. 24.411 (on disappearance and death). It is therefore an upper limit, for Law no. 24.043 gave benefits for cases other than loss of life. See María José Guembe, "The Argentinean Experience with Economic Reparations for Serious Human Rights Violations," in de Greiff, *The Handbook of Reparations.*

27. See Eric Yamamoto and Liann Ebesugawa, "Report on Redress: The Japanese American Internment," in de Greiff, *The Handbook of Reparations.*

28. As reported above, Germany's individual reparations efforts have benefited more than 2 million persons. But this figure includes recipients of the various benefits. As of December 2001, Germany had spent US$3.5 billion on loss-of-life compensation. But I have no precise figures on the number of beneficiaries. See Ariel Colonomos and Andrea Armstrong, "German Reparations to the Jews After World War Two: A Turning Point in the History of Reparations," in de Greiff, *The Handbook of Reparations.*

29. Argentina provided reparations for "grave injuries" caused during illegal detention, starting with Decree no. 70/90 (1990) and continuing with Law no. 24.043 (1991). Perhaps the most expedient, but not the most accurate, way of dealing with the problem of evidence is that adopted by the Chilean Commission on Torture and Illegal Detention, which, after investigating the modus operandi of certain detention centers, asserted that it could safely be assumed that anyone who had been detained in those centers had, indeed, been tortured. See Government of Chile, *Reporte de la Comisión Nacional Sobre Prisión Política y Tortura* (Santiago, 2004).

30. Government of Brazil, Law no. 9,140/95, art. 1. See also Cano and Ferreira, "The Reparations Program in Brazil."·

31. See Yamamoto and Ebesugawa, "Report on Redress."

32. This lack of differentiation contrasts with the very precise definition of the crimes the victims suffered in the *Hori* class-action suit, filed in 1983, which charged

the government with twenty-one separate legal injuries, and demanded the payment of US$10,000 to each victim for each of these violations. The suit was dismissed on statute-of-limitations grounds, but nevertheless served to galvanize the movement in favor of reparations for Japanese-Americans. See Yamamoto and Ebesugawa, "Report on Redress."

33. This included 2,260 Latin Americans of Japanese ancestry whom the United States helped to kidnap and placed in the internment camps for possible hostage exchanges with Japan. A June 1998 class-action suit, *Mochizuki et al. v. United States,* led to an official apology by the US government and redress payments of US$5,000 to each eligible Japanese Latin American. Some victims continued the legal struggle to gain the same benefits offered to US citizens or permanent residents by the 1988 Civil Liberties Act, namely US$20,000.

34. This problem was addressed by a 1992 amendment to the 1988 act.

35. See Lira, "The Reparations Policy."

36. Government of Chile, Law no. 19.123 (1992).

37. Government of Chile, Law no. 18.994 (1990), Law no. 19.074 (1991), Law no. 19.128 (1992).

38. Government of Chile, Law no. 19.234 (1993), Law no. 19.582 (1998).

39. The government of President Eduardo Frei Ruiz-Tagle used Law no. 18.056 (1981), authorizing grace pensions to deal with this particular set of beneficiaries.

40. Government of South Africa, *Promotion of National Unity and Reconciliation Act no. 34 of 1995,* sec. 1(1)(xix)(a), 1(1)(ix).

41. See, for example, Mahmood Mamdani, "Reconciliation Without Justice," *Southern African Review of Books* 46 (November–December 1996): 3–5.

42. I am grateful to Paul van Zyl at the International Center for Transitional Justice for conversation about these issues.

43. See Guembe, "The Argentinean Experience."

44. Government of Argentina, Law no. 23.466 (1986), Law no. 24.411 (1994).

45. Government of Argentina, Decree no. 70 (1991), Law no. 24.043 (1991).

46. Government of Argentina, Law no. 25.914 (2004).

47. See John Authers, "Making Good Again: Compensation for Nazi Concentration Camp Inmates," in de Greiff, *The Handbook of Reparations.*

48. This, of course, simplifies reality. It abstracts from the complexities introduced by the fact that the payments were made in bonds, and from other features of the general context like the vagaries of the prosecutorial efforts, the significant amount of information about the past that became available through "truth trials" and other means, and the institutional reforms that were taking place in Argentina as the reparation laws were being enacted and implemented. See Guembe, "The Argentinean Experience."

49. For a contrasting perspective on this issue, see Jaime Malamud Goti and Lucas Grossman, "Reparations and Civil Litigation," in de Greiff, *The Handbook of Reparations.* Regardless of one's position on the merits of finality, it is important to acknowledge the very significant catalytic role played by litigation in different instances. In the Latin American context, cases before the Inter-American Human Rights Commission and Court have prodded different governments to establish massive reparations programs.

50. I have chosen this old-fashioned term because I do not want to talk about the "generosity" of reparations programs. I see reparations as a matter of right, not generosity. Nevertheless, it is clear that even if one considers this an issue of right, a large range of options exists concerning what it takes to satisfy that right.

51. The caveat is important, for in the aggregate, if the number of victims is significant, programs may end up distributing large amounts of money—with each victim

receiving a small amount, of course. US reparations for Japanese Americans is a case in point.

52. I emphasize the roughness of the ordering. Part of it is due to the fact that some of the programs gave benefits in lump sums (the United States, Brazil, Argentina), and two of them in the form of pensions (Chile and Germany). In any case, establishing the total value of a pension is always a difficult exercise.

53. Thus, one of the great advantages of conceptualizing reparations in terms of recognition and civic trust is that it clearly accommodates contextual factors more easily than a less flexible criterion such as *restitutio in integrum.*

54. See Alexander Segovia's original contribution to this area: "Financing Programs of Reparation: Reflections from International Experience," in de Greiff, *The Handbook of Reparations.*

55. This, of course, would count in favor of international support for reparations in those (various) cases in which parts of the international community have contributed to fueling internal conflicts!

PART 3

Linking Security, Development, and Human Rights

9

Beyond Restitution: Housing, Land, Property, and the Rule of Law

Agnès Hurwitz

The relation between land and conflict is anything but new. From the Old Testament's account of the conquest of Canaan to the Plantation of Ulster and the current situation in Darfur, land-related conflicts have been a common feature of human history. Yet policy-oriented research has only recently rediscovered the importance of housing, land, and property policies for poverty alleviation, economic growth, and conflict prevention.

Housing, land, and property (HLP) pose great challenges to policymakers and practitioners in many different respects. First, the topic is both highly technical and potentially explosive in political terms. Second, it will in most cases require immediate attention as well as long-term support. Most fundamental, global processes can significantly affect domestic policy options on housing, land, and property. Economic deregulation and commodity markets are likely to impact the outcomes of propoor policies; tensions between human rights, security, and development concerns can also be particularly difficult to resolve in postconflict contexts.

This chapter evaluates current rule of law policies on housing, land, and property and identifies a number of policy options that can be used by international agencies with a view to ensuring tenure security, access, and restitution. In particular it highlights the importance for the United Nations to go beyond strict restitution concerns to address HLP concerns more comprehensively; integrate rule of law policies related to housing, land, and property at an earlier stage in peace mission work; and adopt conflict-sensitive approaches in HLP-related programming.

I begin with an overview of the interaction between HLP and conflict, and then analyze HLP policies, actors, and programmatic approaches. Next I analyze the outcomes of current policies and identify specific policy challenges and ensuing recommendations for international actors, specifically the United Nations.

Overview

Housing, Land, and Property: Broadening the Perspective

I rely in this chapter on basic concepts of legal anthropological scholarship, a discipline that provides important insights into law as a "dimension of social organisation"[1] and into the significance of property for human relations. Legal anthropologists have long studied "property relationships," defined as the "relationships between societies' constituents with respect to material or immaterial objects that are regarded as having value."[2] They have also developed the concept of "legal pluralism" to describe legal systems that recognize "different positions of socio-political authority that give a different content to the rights of the incumbents of socio-political authority as well as to the rights of the community's members in general."[3] Legal pluralism is particularly relevant to understand many of the conflicts that revolve around housing, land, and property in the developing world insofar as it provides an important conceptual framework for the analysis of nonstate law—for example, customary or religious law—as it relates to state law.

Most important, anthropologists have long concluded that the concept of property carries multiple functions. In order to be fully understood, the institution of property must be considered not only in legal terms, but also in its economic, social, political, and religious dimensions. From an economic perspective, property constitutes a key asset and effectively operates as a social safety net.[4] According to development economists, HLP policies, ranging from support to sales and rental markets to titling and redistribution, have the potential, if adequately designed, to create a propitious investment climate and reduce poverty through increases in agricultural production, credit access, and financial market development. But aside from their role as essential sources of livelihood, land and property are also crucial components of kinship and social relationships, as they ensure the survival of future generations.[5] Finally, land and property are also important in political terms, as a source of reputation and power, or in religious terms, as a link with spiritual forces and ancestors.

While land and property have traditionally been examined in conjunction, human rights advocates have recently made a compelling case for a broader conceptualization of livelihood and residential issues, one that would also include housing and in this way consider the needs of the huge number of homeless people.[6] Thus the inclusion of housing is justified to bring to light the fact that international programs should address the rights of all people, including tenants, cooperative dwellers, dwellers without secure tenure, and the like. Additional arguments point to the fact that the concept of property may be narrowly defined in some domestic legal systems, denying legal protection to holders of housing and land-related rights.[7]

Housing, Land, Property, and Conflict

Due to their multifunctional nature, it is not surprising that conflicts often crystallize over housing, land, and property.[8] While it would be an oversimplification to state that HLP disputes are a direct cause of internal strife, numerous studies have demonstrated that they may in certain circumstances constitute a determining or aggravating factor in the outbreak of violent conflict.[9]

The causes of HLP disputes are extremely varied and range from increased demographic pressure, resource scarcity, agricultural transformation, and the exploitation of valuable natural resources, to tenure insecurity, inequalities in the (re)distribution of land and property, in particular along ethnic, religious, or other cleavages, and intergenerational tensions over landownership and use.[10] HLP issues are also used as proxy to advance other agendas, and by political entrepreneurs seeking economic advantages.[11] Finally, HLP disputes are often a legacy from discriminatory policies of a former regime, such as in South Africa, Zimbabwe, and Namibia.[12]

El Salvador, Rwanda, Sierra Leone, and Sudan offer illuminating examples of the pervasiveness of HLP issues in conflicts that are, by any other measure, diametrically different. In El Salvador, severe inequalities in land distribution and landlessness that resulted from the development of commercial farming provided the breeding ground for the creation of the Farabundo Martí National Liberation Front, which led the rebellion against the government until the 1992 peace agreements.[13] In Rwanda, while ethnic rivalry was primarily urban, it was land scarcity in the countryside that allegedly brought the conflict to full-scale genocide.[14] In Sierra Leone, young men were drawn to join the Revolutionary United Front due to the traditional land tenure system, which conferred power over land to elder men, enabling them to marry multiple wives. A young man found to have had an affair with an elder's wife would be heavily fined and become a de facto slave laborer. The defeat of the rebellion has now forced demobilized fighters back into a *lumpen* agrarian class, raising concerns about the perpetuation of rural conflict.[15] Finally, in Darfur, the relative symbiosis that traditionally existed between farmers and nomads was fundamentally disrupted by ecological change and agricultural transformation that started in the 1980s, contributing, along with misadministration and regional interferences, to the current outbreak of violence.[16]

HLP disputes may also proliferate in postconflict contexts. Situations characterized by large-scale displacement, abandoned land and property, illegal occupation, overlapping claims, reduced housing stock, lack of documentary evidence, and gender discrimination in access to land and property assets are extremely frequent, predictably creating the potential for social conflict and renewed violence.[17] East Timor, Bosnia-Herzegovina, and Cambodia provide well-known cases of the types of problems encountered by international actors in dealing with the devastating impact of violent conflict on housing, land, and property. In many countries, the problem is compounded by multiple layers of property and land contestation, making a resolution of the land situation even more complex. In the Kivu region of eastern Congo, for instance, the impact of the recent regional conflict was characterized by the emergence of a war economy around the exploitation of mineral resources, compounded by the socioeconomic effects of cattle-ranching activities. These had led to land-grabbing by the political elite during the Mobutu regime, and existed alongside older tensions related to the colonial creation of "ethnic homelands,"[18] which had petrified formerly fluid understandings of customary rules.

Relevance of Housing, Land, and Property for Rule of Law Programming

The frequency and potentially destabilizing impact of HLP disputes justifies that these be considered within comprehensive rule of law strategies.[19] Yet HLP relations have been relatively neglected by rule of law practitioners in peacekeeping and peacebuilding contexts. This might be due to the fact that rule of law programming tends to be based on "*ad hoc* laundry lists of institutions to reform" such as a "well-functioning judiciary" or "an effective law-enforcement apparatus."[20] If, on the other hand, one were to focus on the ends pursued by rule of law programs, one could readily see the relevance of including housing, land, and property issues in these strategies.

According to Rachel Kleinfeld Belton, five distinct end-goals of rule of law programs are identifiable: making the state abide by law, ensuring equality before the law, supplying law and order, providing efficient and impartial justice, and upholding human rights.[21] Because HLP policies affect people's basic livelihoods, respect for these principles will be particularly important for preserving peaceful community relations and promoting sustainable development. As sadly illustrated by the Zimbabwean government's decision to evict over 700,000 urban dwellers among the poorest strands of the population, governmental policies on housing, land, and property will often be arbitrarily decided with a view to discriminating against vulnerable groups and advantaging political or corporate clients.

In this perspective the principles of equality before the law and of nondiscrimination are paramount, for severe inequalities in housing, land, and property relations can have damaging socioeconomic and political consequences. Effective and fair judicial and alternative dispute settlement mechanisms are also essential for ensuring greater predictability in HLP policies and protecting tenure security.[22] As well, both restitution and tenure security are increasingly recognized as relevant principles of international human rights law.[23]

In other words, rule of law institutions have a fundamental role to play in alleviating HLP-related conflicts and in promoting social and economic development through adequate legislation and adjudication on housing, land, and property. Flawed dispute resolution mechanisms can indeed contribute to ethnic cleavages; rigid approaches to titling may not conform to flexible land uses; and plural legal frameworks may lead to competing claims.[24] In postconflict contexts, questions related to the applicable law (e.g., validity of abandonment laws, arbitrary legislation from the former regime), the validity of precolonial, colonial, and postcolonial titles, and lack of documentation on property and tenancy rights must be addressed as part of restitution or HLP reforms.

Finally, HLP issues may be linked to wider legal questions, such as citizenship rights,[25] personal status (e.g., marital status, inheritance rights), and group status (e.g., for indigenous and minority populations). Thus, in Côte d'Ivoire, a toxic cocktail of land and citizenship disputes created the conditions for the ongoing conflict, which many observers fear could still deflagrate into further and unprecedented violence.[26] These disputes can be traced to the policy, under the regime of Felix Houphouët-Boigny, that "the land belongs to the one who farms it," which led to the migration of farmers from the northern regions and from neighboring countries. At that point, less than 2 percent of Côte d'Ivoire's land was formally registered. The 1998 Ivorian land law sought to provide tenure security through the transformation of customary rights into registered titles, but also stipulated that pre-1998 titles could not be transferred to non-Ivorian heirs. Taken in conjunction with the broader political question of the definition of "autochthonous Ivorian" or *Ivoirité,* the law effectively exacerbated the land conflict by excluding rural migrants from its benefits.[27]

Plural Legal Frameworks and Customary Law

The legal systems of most developing countries reflect in their complexity and plurality a history of invasion, occupation, and colonization.[28] For these reasons, the existence of plural legal frameworks and the application of customary laws deserve specific attention when examining housing, land, and property questions.[29]

Customary legal systems are in many developing countries one of the main sources of law, and in Africa, for instance, less than 1 percent of the land area has been subjected to a cadastral survey.[30] It is therefore not surprising that rule of law experts have recently focused their attention on these systems, based on the consideration that they should be better understood and utilized by international actors as part of rule of law reforms.[31] While it is no doubt true that, in many contexts, customary systems are of great significance and should be integrated as part of rule of law strategies, legal anthropologists have warned that customary law, as any other legal system, is based on power relationships,[32] and may in particular discriminate against disadvantaged groups. In addition to gender discrimination, analyzed in greater detail below, custom may disenfranchise certain tribes or groups who have settled in the last generation, contributing thereby to ethnic violence, like in Côte d'Ivoire.[33] Another example is Afghanistan, where customary systems have been "manipulated" to favor local leaders, dramatically restricting access to land assets.[34] Many experts seem to prefer the concept of informal, grassroots "communitization" processes—"a move from customarily-based to community-based rights and administration."[35]

Also, customary systems are extremely complex and varied, and analogies to Western legal traditions tend to distort their very nature.[36] For instance, the concept of common or communal property has either been regarded as *terra nullius,*[37] or been compared to if not assimilated into the concept of public property, a simplification carried out by colonial powers and well-intentioned Western economists and environmentalists alike.[38] This analogy has had major consequences, in particular with respect to the exploitation of subterranean or forest resources. In reality the category of "commons" or communal property comprises a broad range of property complexes, including grazing or forest land, land reserves for agricultural use, and lineage estate property complexes that are held by descent groups or tribal segments.[39] Thus, unlike public property, common property complexes comprise a mix of individual rights and smaller or larger social units.

Finally, customary systems are not static and "immemorial." They are, as any legal system, and perhaps even more so than state law, adjustable to changing political and economic circumstances.[40] For this reason, the very notion of "customary title" may be misleading as a rigid Western construct, resulting from an awkward attempt to acknowledge the existence of nonstate law.

International Human Rights Standards on Housing, Land, and Property

Three distinct categories of rights are relevant to HLP policies: the right to return as well as prohibitions related to forced displacement and deportation existing under international humanitarian and human rights law; procedural standards, namely the right to an effective remedy; and certain economic and social rights, in particular the right to adequate housing. Other provisions frequently mentioned are the prohibition of discrimination, the right to privacy, the right to freedom of movement, and the right to peaceful enjoyment of possessions.[41]

Several internal armed conflicts in the past two decades have led to gross violations of the HLP rights of civilians, such as individual and mass forced transfers and deportations, forced movements of civilians, and other forms of forced displacement.[42] These breaches of international law have been condemned by the international community in numerous instances,[43] and have logically led to calls for reparations, including through restitution processes. The right of return has also reinforced legal arguments for restitution claims.[44] Originally framed as the return to one's country,[45] the right of return, which is reaffirmed in many international human rights and refugee law instruments, has been construed as an individual right to return to one's home.[46] The provisions of the Dayton Accords (Annex 7) and the implementation of property restitution policies in the Balkans have provided some support for this progressive interpretation.[47]

These legal developments have also opened the way to the emergence of a right to property restitution that would derive from the fundamental right to an effective remedy.[48] The principle of restitution has been granted particular importance in postconflict settings,[49] as evidenced by UN Security Council resolutions on Kosovo, Georgia, Croatia, and Cyprus. Several repatriation agreements have also recognized this principle.[50] Scott Leckie thus concluded that "while it may still be difficult to argue that all persons who have ever been displaced have a universally applicable codified right to housing and property restitution under international human rights law in all circumstances, or that all people with this right will actually be capable of exercising it, the emergence of this principle as a core human rights issue for refugees and internally displaced persons (IDPs) is now abundantly clear."[51] The link between displacement, return, and effective remedies was reinforced when the UN's Commission on Human Rights appointed a special rapporteur on housing and property restitution, in the context of refugees and other displaced persons, who recently submitted principles and guidelines on the subject that were adopted by the Subcommission on the Promotion and Protection of Human Rights.[52]

There have also been significant advances in the elaboration of international human rights standards on housing.[53] The right to adequate housing, first formulated in the Universal Declaration of Human Rights (art. 25.1), has been reaffirmed in the International Covenant on Economic, Social, and Cultural Rights (art. 11.1); the International Convention on the Elimination of All Forms of Racial Discrimination (art. 5[e][iii]); and the Convention on the Elimination of All Forms of Discrimination Against Women (art. 14, para. 2[h]). It has been cited in instruments protecting the rights of migrant workers, refugees, disabled persons, the elderly, and indigenous people,[54] as well as further reaffirmed in various international declarations and resolutions.[55] Two general comments on this topic were adopted by the Committee on Economic, Social, and Cultural Rights.[56]

The formulation of a prohibition on forced, arbitrary, or illegal evictions and the principle of tenure security have given much greater relevance to the right to adequate housing.[57] The committee's General Comment no. 7 regarded tenure security as key to upholding the right to adequate housing and preventing forced evictions, including forced population transfers, internal displacement, forced relocations, and mass exoduses. The committee had also found that the right to adequate housing is justiciable, for instance, through legal appeals aimed at preventing planned evictions and demolitions, and through compensation following illegal eviction, illegal actions by landlords or their agents, and discrimination in the allocation or availability of housing.[58] Housing rights are now commonly relied on in postconflict contexts, and the UN High Commissioner for Refugees (UNHCR) has recognized the importance of the linkage between the right to return to one's home and the right to adequate housing.[59]

International Strategies and Approaches

Housing, Land, and Property Policies

Among the wide range of existing HLP policies, one may roughly distinguish those that are part of mainstream developmental policies from those that are specific to transitional and postconflict contexts. Policies under the first category are generally seen to encompass registration and titling, land taxation, regulatory frameworks related to land and property sales and rentals, and policies dealing with the (re)distribution of housing, land, and property.[60]

The debate in this field has traditionally been characterized by an ideological standoff between free-market positions on the one hand, and redistribution policies on the other. In recent years, however, there has been increased support for middle-ground approaches that mix market-oriented reforms with propoor strategies.[61] The 2003 policy research report of the World Bank provides a telling illustration of this "third way," stating that there is no single solution to achieve poverty reduction and economic growth.[62] The document therefore proposes a range of policy options that include both market and non-market mechanisms. For instance, both the World Bank and the US Agency for International Development (USAID) put greater emphasis than before on the improvement of land rental markets,[63] and on the allocation of state-owned land.[64]

Most revealing is the fact that the World Bank now recognizes the value of redistributive land reform where the land situation is characterized by extreme inequality in distribution, underutilized land, and serious rural poverty.[65] Redistributive approaches have been adopted recently in southern Africa to redress the discriminatory policies of apartheid regimes. While such policies have been particularly destructive in Zimbabwe, in contrast South Africa and Namibia's "soft" redistributive approach, based on market transactions ("willing buyer, willing seller"), has been far less damaging, but still not particularly effective.[66]

Titling—that is, the provision of formal property titles—has long been regarded as the bread and butter of land policy and administration programs, and has also been undertaken on a smaller scale by the UNHCR in postconflict contexts.[67] Yet there is little evidence from recent development research that titling programs significantly improve the livelihoods of poor farmers.[68] Registration programs in Africa have apparently failed to reduce the number of land-related disputes, and have not provided the majority poor with increased opportunities to benefit from the system.[69] The success and effectiveness of titling programs will in fact depend to a great extent on other conditions, in particular the existence of adequate institutional capacity.[70] The World Bank now advocates a case-by-case and pragmatic approach toward formal registration.[71] Innovative approaches include customary title registration short of conversion to freehold or leasehold tenure, and the assimilation of common property to private group-owned property.[72] Experts also point to the political ramifications of titling programs, which have too often been regarded as purely technical exercises, and the potentially violent consequences of poorly designed registration programs.[73]

Other approaches, which relate more squarely with "mainstream" rule of law programs, have focused on legal reform, dispute settlement mechanisms, and legal empowerment.[74] African countries have undertaken important land reforms in the past decade. For instance, Mali, Guinea, and Mauritania have adopted pastoral codes that regulate the use of land between farmers and pastoralists, an issue that has often been at the root of conflict in the rural areas of these countries.[75] Effective dispute resolution mechanisms are now also found to be crucial for preventing open-ended conflicts.[76] Improved legal disputes settlement can be achieved through the strengthening of the main court system, through the creation of specialized land courts, or through alternative resolution processes, in particular mediation and arbitration, community-based, and customary mechanisms for conflict resolution.[77]

While land policies have always been a hallmark of development strategies, their linkage with violent conflict has only been recently underscored. Three important policy documents that address this topic have been published in the past few years.[78] The World Bank's 2003 policy document, mentioned earlier, includes a separate section on land-related conflicts.[79] A study by the Organization for Economic Cooperation and Development (OECD) on land, violent conflict, and development formulates a set of preliminary proposals on conflict-sensitive land policies.[80] And USAID recently published a toolkit that provides a brief account of the relation between land and conflict and identifies a set of lessons learned for development practitioners.[81]

Postconflict or transitional situations may call for additional measures, primarily related to the mass restitution and compensation of HLP claims. Restitution has featured prominently in recent peace operations, specifically in Bosnia-Herzegovina and Kosovo.[82] Restitution processes have also been established during political transitions to redress discriminatory policies of the previous regime. In South Africa, the Land Claims Court, established in accordance with the constitution, settled 74,417 out of 80,000 claims lodged between 1996 and 2007.[83] In Iraq, a property claims commission was established in accordance with the transitional administrative law to settle property claims arising from the former regime's "ethnic redistribution" policies, in particular its "Arabization" policy in Kurdistan.[84]

The most basic prerequisites for the success of restitution processes are an adequate legal framework, a sound public information strategy, easily accessible processing centers, and the provision of adequate assistance to potential claimants. Adjudicating institutions should also be given the power to ensure the enforcement of their decisions. Leckie nevertheless recognizes that political discretion will apply in determining, for instance, temporal or personal status limitations to the right to lodge a claim, the possibility of appealing a decision on restitution, and the choice of settlement mechanism.[85]

Most large-scale restitution processes will entail the establishment of property or claims commissions. These institutions are seen as having distinct advantages: they are able to undertake essential data collection and process a large number of restitution and compensation claims, while facilitating dialogue on these delicate issues.[86] Bosnia-Herzegovina and Kosovo constitute the best-known examples of large-scale claims settlement in postconflict settings. Both the Commission on Real Property Claims of Displaced Persons and Refugees established under the Dayton Accords in the case of Bosnia-Herzegovina, and the Housing and Property Directorate and Claims Commission established by the UN Interim Mission in Kosovo (UNMIK),[87] were created to process a large number of claims resulting from mass displacement.[88] The systems relied on decentralized offices that were in charge of claims collection based on detailed interview forms and documentary evidence. The procedures were entirely written, with no hearing provided in most cases, and the decisions were final and binding.[89] The procedure in Kosovo provided first for a mediation phase, followed in case of failure by a quasi-judicial decision. However, both institutions have been faced with serious problems of implementation. In Bosnia-Herzegovina, the Commission on Real Property Claims received insufficient financial backing, and the Office of the High Representative eventually drove the political process, leading to the adoption of a Property Legislation Implementation Plan, which relied on local authorities to undertake restitution. The OSCE's human rights monitoring tasks under the Dayton Accords also played a crucial role in settling property restitution claims at the local level.[90] In Kosovo, eviction processes proved particularly difficult for UNMIK police.[91]

Thus far, large-scale restitution processes have generally taken place in legal environments characterized by the existence of private property based on registered titles, or through legal occupation in socialist regimes. In these cases, restitution is not only possible but also desirable from the standpoint of the protection of the rule of law. Consequently, abandonment laws should not be applicable to returnees, on the grounds that they were forced to leave their land or property.[92]

In most cases, restitution will necessarily entail the eviction of secondary occupants. This definitely applies where secondary occupation results from a concerted policy to deny the rights of original owners, such as in Guatemala, where the army provided "abandoned" land for its supporters. In Bosnia-Herzegovina, abandoned property legislation was adopted by all parties to the conflict, in order to formalize the ethnic cleansing and confiscation policies that occurred during the war.[93]

However, there are many situations where secondary occupation occurs in good faith and simply results from years of war and lawlessness. In these instances, conflicting claims of former owners and secondary occupants will be much more difficult to resolve, and a rigid application of restitution standards may not always be the best approach, unless the rights of secondary occupants and their protection against homelessness is addressed.[94] For instance, the fate of "Arabization Arabs," who were relocated to northern Iraq, has not been addressed yet, and there is great concern that the complete reversal program advocated by the Kurdish leadership will lead to further conflict and human rights violations.[95] In East Timor, policymakers elaborated the principle of "competing equities," consisting of "balancing the interests of returning owners with those seeking temporary use of abandoned properties."[96] Finally, in situations where customary laws are of primary application, restitution may prove far more complex. Because ownership may be based on long-term occupation of land, "original" and secondary occupants may have equally valid claims.[97]

Additional obstacles to the implementation of restitution principles include economic and structural factors, such as lack of available arable land or property,[98] and lack of funding for restitution mechanisms.[99] Corruption will also significantly affect the long-term effects of restitution processes. In Cambodia, the UNHCR recognized that, in many cases, land was eventually taken away from returnees with the complicity of local authorities, and that longer term follow-up by international agencies should have been provided for.[100]

It is only in cases where restitution is not feasible that compensation should be considered.[101] It may consist of financial compensation or compensation in kind, through the provision of equivalent property, which took place in Guatemala. In Bosnia-Herzegovina, compensation was not provided for but happened de facto, through the sale of restituted property by owners who were reluctant to return to areas dominated by another ethnic group.[102]

The Actors

Compared to other organizations, the UN's approaches to housing, land, and property have been fragmented and inadequate from a peacebuilding perspective. The World Bank, as explained earlier, has changed its approach considerably in recent years. Since the publication of its 2003 policy report, the World Bank's lending portfolio has expanded significantly: during the 1990–1994 financial period, only three standalone land projects were approved, but this number increased to nineteen (US$0.7 billion commitment) and twenty-five (US$1 billion commitment) in the 1995–1999 and 2000–2004 periods, respectively.[103]

Other financial institutions, such as the Inter-American Development Bank, have also financed land-related projects, including land titling and administration.[104] Regional organizations as well, such as the Organization of American States in Guatemala, have supported land programs, with a focus on peaceful dispute resolution.[105]

In terms of bilateral aid, USAID had until recently adopted an orthodox market-oriented approach strongly influenced by Hernando De Soto's theories,[106] and funded a large number of projects on titling, law reform, institution and capacity building of land and property agencies, and dispute settlement mechanisms. The recent land and conflict toolkit mentioned earlier still favors "market-assisted" initiatives, but insists that they be "community-managed."[107] The German Development Agency's land management project provides advice, training, and education with a view to reducing poverty and conflicts,[108] including advice on rule of law programs, such as those concerning constitutional reform and human rights, judicial reform, mediation, and support for implementation and enforcement, which it has undertaken in Cambodia for instance. The project grants special attention to marginalized groups, in particular refugees in postconflict countries and women.

A large number of nongovernmental organizations (NGOs) are also involved in land-related programs. Oxfam has designed programs to demarcate and title customary common property in Angola and Mozambique,[109] and has now adopted key principles for its work on land in Africa, based on equity, justice, poverty alleviation, secure access and tenure, community support, decentralization, gender-sensitiveness, and support to pastoralists. It also puts strong emphasis on the need to regulate market forces and foreign investment. The Centre on Housing Rights and Evictions, in Geneva, has built its niche in housing rights advocacy at the international and national levels, and has greatly contributed to the development of international standards on housing and property restitution and gender-sensitive policies. It also provides legal assistance and supports numerous nationally based housing rights initiatives.[110] NGOs are particularly well equipped for legal empowerment programs, and a large number of international and grassroots organizations have developed expertise in this area.[111]

Compared to the approaches of these international actors, the UN's seem disjointed and "a-strategic." Two organizations have core expertise on housing, land, and property within the UN system. First, the Food and Agriculture Organization (FAO) has long-standing experience in rural development and food security. Its Sustainable Development Department provides assistance for restructuring rural institutions and designing land tenure and institution building for food security and sustainable rural development projects, as well as access to land programs, in particular for disadvantaged groups. The FAO has also established policy guidelines and legislative mechanisms for conflict resolution to improve access of the landless to land, using various land reform approaches in a manner that is gender-responsive and environmentally sustainable.[112] In El Salvador, for instance, the FAO supported programs designed to facilitate community decisionmaking and dispute resolution around land titling, delineation, and registration. Secondly, UN-Habitat has strong expertise in housing issues and has developed advocacy campaigns for tenure security. It has done significant work in Afghanistan, where it designed programs for housing reconstruction,[113] and in Kosovo, where it provided legal and technical assistance on property issues to UNMIK, as an implementing partner of the Housing and Property Directorate and Claims Commission.[114]

The Office of the High Commissioner for Human Rights (OHCHR), aside from its standard-setting work briefly reviewed above, has been involved with the UN Development Programme (UNDP) in the latter's Human Rights Strengthening Programme, a joint effort established to monitor and support the UNDP's human rights mainstreaming process. The program is involved in numerous propoor activities, but only one current project, on indigenous peoples, seems to touch on the question of ownership and use of land and natural resources.[115] The OHCHR has also partnered with UN-Habitat to create the UN Housing Rights Programme (UNHRP), in order to monitor and evaluate progress in the realization of housing rights, research and analyze issues related to housing rights, and build capacity and support training for the monitoring and implementation of housing rights.[116]

The only UN agency that, due to the very nature of its mandate, has granted specific attention to housing, land, and property issues in conflict settings is the UNHCR. The refugee agency has long been developing and expanding its HLP activities, as part of its repatriation operations.[117] Its approach has been context-specific and rights-based, and has consisted of using the various policy tools identified above to support the safe and sustainable return of refugee populations. It recently recommended to its field offices the adoption of strategic action plans on HLP restitution.[118]

Programmatic Issues

Strategic planning and sequencing. One of the more relevant recent policy research findings on housing, land, and property in their relation to conflict is the importance of addressing these issues at an early stage in postconflict contexts.[119] The recently issued USAID toolkit states that "the importance of land issues to post-conflict development is often not recognized early enough" and that "property registration issues can be an obstacle to peace and, therefore, should receive more attention from policy makers and donors during the immediate post conflict period."[120] Similar conclusions can be found in the OECD study.[121]

Strategic planning is particularly crucial for the success of HLP policies due to their complexity and long time span. Planning should include thorough conflict analysis that defines the boundaries of intervention, followed by a needs assessment that encompasses essential data on land, housing, emergency housing needs, tenure security, market productivity, regulatory frameworks, applicable laws, and profiles and needs of targeted groups.[122] Pilot projects should also be envisaged to test different approaches and open up the policy dialogue.[123] USAID's toolkit includes a summarized appraisal guide on conflict-sensitive approaches to land issues to be used by development practitioners.[124]

The immediate postconflict phase should focus on temporary housing and land allocation, the protection of existing land and property records, the establishment of a basic deed registration system, the establishment and strengthening of dispute resolution mechanisms, and the initiation of legal reforms on the basis of public consultations with key stakeholders and reform constituencies.[125] Depending on existing provisions in peace agreements, and repatriation arrangements, restitution processes may have to be put into place. At the institutional level, the creation of a special land task force or the inclusion of housing, land, and property in an existing rule of law task force created within the national government are also recommended.[126]

In the longer term, programmatic approaches should focus on the implementation of restitution legislation and the processing of restitution claims; institution and capacity building to ensure the implementation of HLP policies; and policies designed to enhance tenure security for the general population, in particular the most disadvantaged groups.[127]

Participation and capacity building. As often is the case with "ownership,"[128] rhetorical commitments have not been matched by genuine participation in the planning, design, and implementation of HLP policies. Many land development experts nonetheless consider consultations with and participation of local stakeholders in the design of HLP policies as essential to avoiding errors and irregularities in land demarcation and registration, preventing future contestation, building consensus, and opening up genuine policy dialogue.[129] The danger, however, is participation processes that operate as mere "window-dressing" and do not involve all groups of land and property users.[130] As indicated above, NGOs have developed substantial expertise in supporting grassroots initiatives, such as propoor land titling.[131] An interesting case is Mozambique, where conflicts arising from the return process were mediated and resolved by local institutions, and where the adoption of a land law was preceded by consultations with over 200 NGOs and 50,000 individuals.[132]

However, support for participatory approaches and consultation processes may have to be qualified in some postconflict settings. The case of Bosnia-Herzegovina reveals the fundamental ambivalence and incredible complexity of tackling housing, land, and property issues in these contexts. On the one hand, experts agree that restitution processes in the Balkans would not have taken place if the process had exclusively depended on the goodwill of local constituencies. At the same time, however, it is the involvement of these same

local communities—as a result of international pressures—that made completion of this process possible, rather than the specialized international institution established by international negotiators. Second, popular decisionmaking
may contradict international agencies' obligations to uphold international standards. In those cases, the only solution is to try to build reform constituencies
or "progressive coalitions."[133]

Differences also abound in terms of programmatic approaches to HLP
management. Genuine decentralization is regarded by many as the most effective way to ensure accountability, transparency, access, and effective land management; moreover, decentralized approaches are simpler, cheaper, and more
self-sufficient than centralized approaches.[134] Others consider that local politics
may actually favor the powerful, and that reforms also have to be "linked up-
ward," to ensure adequate legal and administrative reforms at state level.[135]
One essential condition to effective decentralized administration, which tends
to be overlooked, is the availability of local revenue sources. Land taxation provides the ideal source of revenue for local administrations and will avoid the
need for financial transfers from the central government.[136]

Addressing discrimination.   There is now wide agreement on the importance
of addressing the specific problems faced by disadvantaged groups in accessing housing, land, and property.[137] Important advances have been made by international actors at the normative and operational levels to ensure fairer HLP
policies toward two specific groups: indigenous communities and women.

Land rights are a particularly crucial and sensitive issue for indigenous
groups, not least because of the religious significance of land in indigenous
cultures. Article 13 of the International Labour Organization's Convention no.
169 highlights the "special importance for the cultures and spiritual values of
the peoples concerned of their relationship with the lands or territories, or both
as applicable, which they occupy or otherwise use, and in particular the collective aspects of this relationship."[138]

Many countries, mostly in Latin America, have included in their constitutions specific provisions on the status and rights of indigenous groups, but the
enforcement of these principles is still lagging, and conflicts revolving around
the exploitation of natural resources (timber, minerals, oil) on indigenous land
are still frequent.[139] For instance, the right of consultation that is recognized to
indigenous groups has been constantly violated in Ecuador, where several of
these groups have opposed mining and oil projects.[140]

One of the more pervasive grounds of discrimination over access to HLP
is gender.[141] In many countries, women's property rights are "secondary," in
the sense that they derive from marriage or kinship.[142] Societal changes such
as the increase in the number of women-headed households as a result of war
or the HIV/AIDS epidemic may clash with customary rules that do not recognize women's right to inherit, leading to increased land-related disputes. The

Convention on the Elimination of All Forms of Discrimination Against Women provides only limited recognition of women's HLP-related rights, and the convention has been complemented by the adoption of various resolutions by the UN Commission on Human Rights.[143] In the field, the UNHCR has designed programs that provide legal assistance to women in Guatemala, Liberia, and Rwanda.[144] Titling programs also had to be reviewed in order to ensure that property that was customarily held by a couple would be formalized through joint titling, and not through the provision of the title to the male household head, which would lead to greater disempowerment of women.[145] However, the strengthening of gender-sensitive rule of law strategies can have only a limited impact on cultural practices in the short term. In this perspective, rule of law programs need to be part of a broader educational and capacity-building strategy aimed at greater tenure security and access to land and property for women.

Coordination. One of the problems identified in the USAID toolkit lies in the cross-sectoral nature of HLP policies, which are relevant to democracy and governance (under which the rule of law is subsumed in USAID's structure), economic growth, agriculture, and environmental issues.[146] The document calls for intra-institutional coordination as a first step toward coherent and comprehensive strategies.[147] The OECD study, on the other hand, calls for improved interinstitutional coordination and goes as far as suggesting institutional integration in conflict-prone settings.[148]

Improved coordination and integration of HLP policies into peacekeeping and peacebuilding structures is perhaps the single most significant improvement that the United Nations could make at this stage. Though solid expertise exists in its various agencies, the UN approach is fragmented and not adequately tailored to address conflict management objectives. As early as 1998, a UNHCR working paper called for the strengthening of coordination on access to land and ownership through the creation of a working group that would bring together the UNDP, the FAO, the World Food Programme, the World Bank, and the International Labour Organization to devise a global approach with common objectives.[149] But overall, there has been limited involvement of peace operations in HLP issues. Apart from Bosnia-Herzegovina, East Timor, Kosovo, and Tajikistan, where efforts were made to tackle HLP concerns, in most cases these have been regarded as secondary issues.[150] In a recent UNDP document on access to justice, property rights are only briefly mentioned as a potential "entry point" for the UNDP's longer-term postconflict support.[151] In Kosovo, UN-Habitat was the implementing partner of the Housing and Property Directorate and Claims Commission, but this solution could not be easily accommodated with the rigid pillar structure of UNMIK, which led to prolonged institutional and funding deficiencies. In the end, a memorandum of understanding was concluded between UN-Habitat and UNMIK, granting the Property Directorate independent status.[152] Some UN agencies are definitely conscious of the need to tackle the problem in a more proactive manner. The UNHCR and UN-Habitat convened an interinstitutional workshop in November 2004 in which participants representing other UN agencies and programs supported the proposal to appoint an HLP expert within the Department of Peacekeeping Operations, with the responsibility of raising HLP issues during the early phases of peace missions, and overseeing the planning, design, and implementation of the resultant HLP policies.[153]

Assessment and Evaluation

Impact and Outcomes

The outcomes of housing, land, and property policies in conflict-prone countries, and in particular their impact on the prevention of violent conflicts, are difficult to assess. There are nevertheless some encouraging findings: according to a study conducted by Canada's International Development Research Centre and the World Bank Institute, conflict over natural resources can become collaborative rather than openly confrontational, through the adoption of a policy framework that includes the strengthening of local governance, enhanced coordination with local authorities, inclusive consultations with stakeholders, and dispute settlement mechanisms based on customary law or informal processes.[154]

There indeed seems to be empirical evidence that strengthened dispute settlement mechanisms can serve as crucial conflict prevention tools that avoid "institution shopping" and conflict of jurisdictions.[155] While formal titling programs have not been consistently effective, alternative approaches, such as the use of conditional titling (where a title's validity may be challenged through the provision of contrary evidence), adverse possession, and the admission of oral evidence of property rights, are now favored, particularly in situations characterized by multiple layers of property titles.[156] Deed registration systems in which registered transactions are prioritized over nonregistered ones are less overwhelming to implement than title registration, while enabling authorities to assert rapid control of housing and land markets.[157] In the immediate postconflict phase, temporary housing allocation, which was used in East Timor and Kosovo, provides a record of occupation and a source of public revenue, but its success depends on the adoption and implementation of adequate legislation on restitution and long-term security tenure.[158]

Normative approaches, such as the inclusion of HLP-related rights in constitutional arrangements, peace accords, and repatriation agreements, have also become commonplace.[159] As mentioned above, the Dayton Accords affirmed the right of refugees and displaced persons to return freely to their homes of origin and to have property restored or compensated through the establishment of the Commission on Real Property Claims. An earlier example of UN practice in this area is the peace process in Guatemala,[160] which included three agreements dealing with land and property. The Agreement on Resettlement of the Population Groups Uprooted by the Armed Conflict recognized a right to voluntary, secure, and dignified return for refugees and IDPs and established a right of restitution and/or compensation.[161] The Agreement on Identity and Rights of Indigenous Peoples provided for the establishment of administrative and legal mechanisms that would award "title, protection, restitution, compensation, recognition and recovery of communal, collective and individual tenure rights."[162] Finally, the Agreement on Socioeconomic Aspects and the Agrarian Situation stipulated that "the modification of the system for ownership and use of land must strive to include the rural population in the economic, social and political development."[163]

However, the mere inclusion of HLP issues in peace accords is no guarantee that the rights of returnees will be effectively upheld.[164] Despite the agreements listed above, the land situation in Guatemala has not really improved, compensation and restitution programs have not been implemented for IDPs due to the absence of an adequate land policy in the rural areas,[165] and there are now new concerns about land-related violence.[166]

Nor have restitution processes, such as in Bosnia-Herzegovina and Kosovo, fully achieved their original objectives. Redress has been provided for the victims of mass displacement and ethnic wars, but their actual contribution to reconciliation is thus far not convincing. They have not yet led to the effective return of a majority of displaced persons and to the reversal of the ethnic divisions that occurred as a consequence of the war.[167] As noted by Charles Philpott, "Access to property was not the only, or in many cases, the main barrier to return. Security and discrimination concerns, lack of education opportunities and employment prospects, and the elapse of time . . . have all negatively impacted upon the willingness of IDPs and refugees to return." Philpott concludes that "it was much easier to concentrate on an issue that was obviously central to the issue of return, for which the pressure points—e.g., state institutions—were easily identified, and of which progress was easily measured, namely, property restitution. 'Real' or sustainable return was much harder to plan for and achieve, almost impossible to measure, and would, inevitably, be significantly lower in absolute numbers."[168]

What has been consistently missing is the adoption of more comprehensive approaches to HLP issues that would reach out to the whole population.[169] Comprehensive policies are advocated by human rights advocates,[170] but also by practitioners who were confronted with major HLP challenges in postconflict contexts. As noted by Leckie, "There is . . . growing realization that viewing, conceiving and executing restitution programs not only as tools promoting justice and the return of displaced persons to their homes, but also as part of a larger process of development, will contribute greatly to the rule of law and overall stability."[171]

East Timor provides a dramatic example of the consequences of ad hoc approaches on long-term HLP issues.[172] According to Daniel Fitzpatrick, "There was virtually no planned policy response to the relatively predictable effects on housing of widespread property destruction, mass population return, and the rapid influx of well-remunerated international personnel."[173] While immediate measures to temporarily allocate public and abandoned properties were adopted,[174] the absence of a property or land claims commission led to legal uncertainty around temporary allocation, and opened the way for the multiplication of competing claims and to social unrest.[175] In Afghanistan, which is also plagued with land and housing problems, in particular landlessness and conflict around grazing and pasture lands, piecemeal approaches have proved utterly insufficient. A land disputes court was created, but its limited remedies make it constitutionally questionable, and it has focused thus far on claims by affluent returnees or claimants.[176] Fitzpatrick therefore recommends that policymakers and planners better address the linkages among refugee return, housing, and land administration; that they elaborate template strategies for land and housing policies in peacebuilding contexts; and that they develop enhanced institutional coordination among international actors.[177]

Strategic Challenges

Not only do the planning, design, and implementation of HLP rule of law programs require specific technical expertise, but programmatic success will also depend on a thorough understanding of the "politics of land."[178] There are far too many cases of HLP programs that were successful in the short term, but that did not prevent the resurgence of conflict because they overlooked the political dimension of land and property reform and management.[179]

Developing successful strategies on HLP issues is also particularly challenging because these will often require both immediate attention as well as sustained support over the long term. As noted in the OECD study, "The deleterious effects of interrupting land mediation processes initiated by donors, especially in tense situations, cannot be overemphasized. It is essential that projects be funded until they are completed, otherwise populations skeptical of the co-operative process may contribute to sharpening antagonisms by providing justification to those who, in each group, foster violent action."[180] In other words, funding for HLP programs should ideally be provided by contributions devoted to peacekeeping as well as longer-term peacebuilding activities.[181] HLP programs are in this sense particularly vulnerable to the current flaws that affect funding mechanisms for peacebuilding.[182] It is hoped that the establishment of a standing fund for peacebuilding and of the Peacebuilding Commission—which will in particular assist in planning the transition between conflict and post-conflict peacebuilding—will eventually prompt the adoption of a comprehensive UN framework on housing, land, and property.[183] Also deserving of further attention is the inclusion of HLP issues in rule of law work both at headquarters and in the field.

Global Trends, Local Concerns

HLP policies entail choices that may clash with some of the stated objectives of the international discourse on the rule of law. At the normative level, the growing recognition of restitution principles may appear at odds with peace-making and peacebuilding processes.[184] In 1998 the UNHCR was still advocating a case-by-case approach to restitution, based on political, economic, as well as legal specificities, with a view to making it supportive of national reconciliation.[185] It also considered that "the objective should be to adapt the demand to local possibilities, and not necessarily make freedom of choice of place of return an inviolable principle. In other words, return reintegration must necessarily be combined with constraints related to national reconciliation and the reconstruction and development of the country."[186]

The emergence of stricter international standards that have now been integrated into the approaches of international agencies may seem to considerably restrain the margin of maneuver of international negotiators, policymakers, and practitioners.[187] Peacemaking experts would argue that certain contexts require "creative" solutions rather than compliance with rigid principles. The Annan Plan, which was eventually rejected by the Greek Cypriot population, adopted a two-pronged approach, based on restitution and territorial adjustments, but international negotiators admitted that full restitution and return would not be possible in each individual case.[188] The resolution of the refugee question in the Israeli-Palestinian conflict will likely test the strength of the international standards that have emerged in the past decade.[189] However, this apparent contradiction must be qualified by the consideration that international human rights law—except as far as nonderogable rights such as the prohibitions against torture and slavery are concerned—allows exceptions to many of its principles on grounds of national security, public order, or public health or morals. In other words, the need to balance individual rights with collective interests has long been recognized as a fundamental concern in the interpretation and implementation of international human rights law by scholars, policymakers, and adjudicators.

There are in fact far more ominous global processes that will challenge the effectiveness of HLP rule of law strategies. As shown above, most of the current good practices emphasize community-based, gender-sensitive, and propoor approaches. However, even if it were hypothetically possible to devise an ideal HLP strategic model, its outcomes would still likely be affected by the dominance of deregulatory trends in macroeconomic policies,[190] as well as by the current imbalances in international trade. Even though there now is great awareness about the importance of policy coherence in development circles,[191] the views of development agencies are still marginalized in the current debate on trade and economic globalization.

Policy Recommendations

Significant improvements could be made to current rule of law approaches to housing, land, and property at the United Nations.

Objectives

Specific objectives need to be identified for rule of law policies to be coherent and for their effectiveness to be measurable:

• HLP policies should primarily seek to alleviate poverty and reduce the likelihood of violent conflict, through the adoption of propoor, rights-based approaches.

• With these broad objectives in mind, HLP policies should specifically pursue the following goals: access to housing, land, and property; tenure security; and restitution as a result of forced displacement.

Strategies

Strategic planning will be critical to the success of HLP rule of law policies, due to their relevance throughout the "rule of law continuum":

• Conflict-sensitive approaches to HLP rule of law policies should be mainstreamed into current UN programs.

• In postconflict contexts, the United Nations should adopt comprehensive approaches on HLP and agree on the adoption of a strategic policy framework that goes beyond narrowly framed restitution policies; the other two objectives, access to HLP and tenure security, merit additional attention.

• Successful comprehensive approaches require rigorous planning, including thorough conflict analyses, methodologically sound needs assessments, and effective designs based on these preparatory procedures.

• HLP rule of law policies should be more systematically integrated into the work of UN peace operations; they should be seen as a crucial component of disarmament, demobilization, reintegration, repatriation, and reconciliation processes.

Policies

• Community-based decentralized processes of land reform and management should, where possible, be preferred to top-down approaches. Reliance on customary systems should not be overemphasized, as they might deny access to specific groups, and may therefore not be conducive to conflict prevention and poverty alleviation.

• Conditional titling should be preferred in conflict-prone countries, in order to diminish the risk of multiple layers of competing claims.

• Redistribution may be envisaged where there is widespread inequality in land and property access; compensation for legal expropriation should in all cases be provided.

• Restitution processes must be accompanied by measures that address housing and land shortages and the situation of secondary occupants, as well as by long-term plans toward tenure security for the whole population.

• Clear legislative HLP frameworks, alternative dispute resolution mechanisms, and specialized land and property courts can help prevent HLP disputes from degenerating into violent conflict.

• Specific policies may have to be considered to address the specific difficulties of disadvantaged groups, in particular women and indigenous groups, in terms of access to HLP, tenure security, and restitution.

Next Steps

• *In the short term.* Raise housing, land, and property as issues of particular importance in the follow-up process to the Secretary-General's report on the rule of law and transitional justice in conflict and postconflict societies,[192] after assessing the outcomes of the UN reform process in relation to the Peacebuilding Support Office and the newly created Rule of Law Coordination and Resource Group.

• *In the middle term.* Address flagrant resource and institutional shortages in current UN housing, land, and property policies, including their integration into UN peacebuilding strategies.

• *In the long term.* Support greater interinstitutional integration of HLP policies into peacebuilding, and further research on the linkages between HLP and violent conflict.

Notes

This chapter partly draws on the findings of the international workshop "Land, Property, and Conflict: Identifying Policy Options for Rule of Law Programming," which was convened by the International Peace Academy's Security-Development Nexus Program on December 2–3, 2004, in New York and led to the publication of a policy report in October 2005 (available at http://www.ipacademy.org/publications/policy papers). I thank all the participants of the workshop for lending their invaluable expertise to this project. I am grateful to Reyko Huang, Gordon Peake, and Kaysie Studdard for their useful comments on earlier drafts of this chapter. All errors are my sole responsibility. The views expressed herein are those of the author and do not necessarily represent the views of the United Nations or of the International Criminal Tribunal for the former Yugoslavia.

1. Franz von Benda-Beckmann, "Who Is Afraid of Legal Pluralism?" *Journal of Legal Pluralism* 47 (2002): 37, 48.
2. Franz von Benda-Beckmann, *Property in Social Continuity* (The Hague: Nijhoff, 1979), p. 42.
3. Ibid.
4. See Klaus Deininger, *Land Policies for Growth and Poverty Reduction* (Washington, D.C.: World Bank and Oxford University Press, 2003), pp. xvii–xviii.
5. von Benda-Beckmann, *Property in Social Continuity,* p. 39.
6. In Afghanistan, for instance, many refugees have no land to return to, and landlessness is prevalent among the rural population. See Liz Alden Wiley, "Land Rights in Crisis: Restoring Tenure Security in Afghanistan," Issue Paper Series (Kabul: Afghanistan Research and Evaluation Unit, March 2003), p. 2.
7. Scott Leckie, "United Nations Peace Operations and Housing, Land, and Property Rights in Post-Conflict Societies: A Proposed UN Integral Policy Framework," background paper submitted for the "Expert Meeting on Housing, Land, and Property Rights in Post-Conflict Societies: Proposals for Their Integration into UN Policy and Operational Frameworks," Geneva, March 2005, p. 9. Housing has in fact received wider attention in international human rights law than property. See Scott Leckie, "New Directions in Housing and Property Restitution," in *Returning Home: Housing and Property Restitution Rights of Refugees and Displaced Persons,* edited by Scott Leckie (Ardsley, N.Y.: Transnational, 2003), p. 3; UN High Commissioner for Refugees (UNHCR), Executive Committee, "Legal Safety Issues in the Context of Voluntary Repatriation of Refugees," Conclusion no. 101 (LV), UN Doc. EC/54/SC/CRP.12 (June 7, 2004), paras. c, h–j.
8. Land- or property-related violent conflict may be defined as "personal injury or death and/or physical property damage in a land/property dispute." See Nicholas Pons-Vignon and Henri-Bernard Solignac Lecomte, "Land, Violent Conflict, and Development," Working Paper no. 233 (Paris: Organization for Economic Cooperation and Development, 2004), p. 18; Deininger, *Land Policies,* p. 18.
9. Stephen Baranyi, Carmen Diana Deere, and Manuel Morales, *Land and Development in Latin America: Openings for Policy Research* (Ottawa: North-South Institute and International Development Research Centre, 2004), p. 55.
10. Pons-Vignon and Solignace Lecomte, "Land, Violent Conflict, and Development," p. 18; Deininger, *Land Policies,* pp. 161–162; Indra de Soysa, "The Resource Curse: Are Civil Wars Driven by Rapacity or Paucity," in *Greed and Grievance: Economic Agendas in Civil Wars,* edited by Mats Berdal and David M. Malone (Boulder: Lynne Rienner, 2000), pp. 113, 125.
11. See Mats Berdal and David M. Malone, Introduction to *Greed and Grievance,* p. 4.
12. Pons-Vignon and Solignace Lecomte, "Land, Violent Conflict, and Development," p. 35.
13. In Central America, land has traditionally been concentrated into the hands of large landowners or large agroindustrial companies, depriving small farmers of their means of subsistence. See UNHCR, *The Problem of Access to Land and Ownership in Repatriation Operations,* Inspection and Evaluation Service, UN Doc. EVAL/03/98 (May 1998), p. 8; see also paras. 93–94.
14. Pons-Vignon and Solignace Lecomte, "Land, Violent Conflict, and Development," p. 22.
15. Ibid., p. 27; International Crisis Group, *Liberia and Sierra Leone: Rebuilding Failed States,* Africa Report no. 87 (Brussels, December 8, 2004), p. 13.

16. Alex de Waal, "Counter-Insurgency on the Cheap," *London Review of Books* 26, no. 15 (August 2004), http://www.lrb.co.uk/v26/n15/waal01_.html; Liz Alden Wiley, "Land and the Constitution," Policy brief, Kabul: Afghanistan Research and Evaluation Unit, September 2003, p. 3.

17. See US Agency for International Development (USAID), *Land and Conflict: A Toolkit for Intervention* (Washington, D.C., 2004), p. 6; Scott Leckie, "New Directions," pp. 11–17; UNHCR, *The Problem of Access,* p. 2, para. 7.

18. See Stephan Jackson, "Land and Conflict in the Kivus, DR Congo," paper presented at the International Peace Academy (IPA) workshop "Land, Property, and Conflict Management: Identifying Policy Options for Rule of Law Programming," New York, December 2–3, 2004. See also P. Mathieu, S. Mugangu Matabaro, and A. Mafikiri Tsongo, "Enjeux fonciers et violences en Afrique: la prévention des conflits en se servant du cas du Nord-Kivu (1940–1994)" (Rome: September 1999), http://www.fao.org/sd/frdirect/ltan0034.htm.

19. See United Nations, *The Rule of Law and Transitional Justice in Conflict and Post-Conflict Societies: Report of the Secretary-General,* UN Doc. S/2004/616 (August 23, 2004).

20. Rachel Kleinfeld Belton, "Competing Definitions of the Rule of Law: Implications for Practitioners," in Democracy and Rule of Law Project, Rule of Law Series, No. 55, Carnegie Endowment for International Peace, 2005, www.carnegieendowment.org/files/CP55.Belton.Final.pdf.

21. Ibid., p. 7. See also Chapter 2 of this volume.

22. Kleinfeld Belton, "Competing Definitions," p. 12.

23. United Nations, *Housing and Property Restitution in the Context of the Return of Refugees and Internally Displaced Persons*, Final Report of the Special Rapporteur, Paulo Sérgio Pinheiro, UN Doc. E/CN.4/Sub.2/2005/17, June 28, 2005, see spec. paras. 3–4, 6–7, 8.

24. Deininger, *Land Policies,* p. 162.

25. See Leckie, "New Directions," p. 54.

26. Richard Crook, "Civil War in Côte d'Ivoire: Behind the Headlines" (Sussex: Institute of Development Studies, University of Sussex, January 25, 2005), http://www.ids.ac.uk/ids/govern/pdfs/cdicivilwarlongv.pdf.

27. See International Crisis Group, *Côte d'Ivoire: No Peace in Sight,* Africa Report no. 82 (Brussels, July 12, 2004).

28. von Benda-Beckmann, *Property in Social Continuity,* p. 44.

29. Deininger, *Land Policies,* p. 35.

30. See Liz Alden Wiley, "Formalizing the Informal: Is There a Way to Safely Secure Majority Rural Land Rights?" Paper presented to EGDI-WIDER conference "Unlocking Human Potential: Linking the Informal and Formal Sectors," Helsinki, September 17–18, 2004, p. 2.

31. See, for example, UN Development Programme (UNDP), *Access to Justice: Practice Note* (New York, September 2004), p. 9; Tracy Dexter and Philippe Ntahombaye, *The Role of Informal Justice Systems in Fostering the Rule of Law in Post-Conflict Situations: The Case of Burundi* (Geneva: Centre for Humanitarian Dialogue, July 2005); Andre Le Sage, *Stateless Justice in Somalia: Formal and Informal Rule of Law Initiatives* (Geneva: Centre for Humanitarian Dialogue, July 2005).

32. "Regardless of the nature of tenure systems (customary or 'modern'), land associated with promising economic opportunities tends to be privately appropriated." See Pons-Vignon and Solignace Lecomte, "Land, Violent Conflict, and Development," p. 38.

33. Alden Wiley, "Formalizing the Informal," p. 13; Crook, "Civil War in Côte d'Ivoire." The International Crisis Group, in *Liberia and Sierra Leone,* p. 14, reports that the DfID supported the reestablishment of systems of chieftaincy, which easily fell into despotism, with disastrous results.

34. Pons-Vignon and Solignace Lecomte, "Land, Violent Conflict, and Development," p. 29.

35. Alden Wiley, "Formalizing the Informal," p. 14.

36. Franz von Benda-Beckmann, "Relative Publics and Property Rights: A Cross-Cultural Perspective," in *Property and Values: Alternatives to Public and Private Ownership,* edited by Charles Geisler and Gail Daneker (Washington, D.C.: Island, 2000), p. 151.

37. Alden Wiley, "Formalizing the Informal," p. 12.

38. Von Benda-Beckmann, "Relative Publics and Property Rights," p. 152.

39. Ibid., p. 157.

40. In Mali, flexible customary land tenure and management are necessary to adapt to modified locations of productive land that occur as a result of climatic changes. Pons-Vignon and Solignace Lecomte, "Land, Violent Conflict, and Development," p. 38.

41. United Nations, *Housing and Property Restitution in the Context of the Return of Refugees and Internally Displaced Persons,* Final Report of the Special Rapporteur, Paulo Sérgio Pinheiro, UN Doc. E/CN.4/Sub.2/2005/17, June 28, 2005, see spec. paras. 3–4, 6–7, 8.

42. United Nations, *Geneva Convention (IV) Relative to the Protection of Civilian Persons in Time of War* (August 12, 1949), art. 49; United Nations, *Protocol Additional to the Geneva Conventions of 12 August 1949, and Relating to the Protection of Victims of Non-International Armed Conflicts (Protocol II)* (June 8, 1977), art. 17.

43. United Nations, *International Covenant on Civil and Political Rights,* art. 12; United Nations, *Universal Declaration of Human Rights,* art. 13.2.

44. See, for example, UNHCR Executive Committee Conclusion no. 101 (LV) of 2004, on legal safety issues in the context of voluntary repatriation of refugees, paras. h–i.

45. United Nations, *Universal Declaration of Human Rights,* art.13.2; United Nations, *International Covenant on Civil and Political Rights,* art. 12.4. For a complete list of relevant human rights instruments, see Leckie, "New Directions," p. 28; UNHCR Executive Committee Conclusion no. 101 (LV) of 2004, para. c.

46. See United Nations, Commission on Human Rights, *Commentary on the Draft Principles on Housing and Property Restitution for Refugees and Displaced Persons,* UN Doc. E/CN.4/Sub.2/2004/22/Add.1 (June 8, 2004), p. 7, para. 27. See also UN General Assembly Resolution 35/124 (1980), on international intervention to avert new flows of refugees.

47. Marcus Cox and Madeline Garlick, "Musical Chairs: Property Repossession and Return Strategies in Bosnia and Herzegovina," in Leckie, *Returning Home,* pp. 65, 69.

48. United Nations, *Universal Declaration of Human Rights,* art. 8; United Nations, *International Covenant on Civil and Political Rights,* art. 2.3; United Nations, Commission on Human Rights, *Draft of Basic Principles and Guidelines on the Right to a Remedy and Reparation for Victims of Violations of Human Rights and International Humanitarian Law,* UN Doc. E/CN.4/2000/62 (January 18, 2000), which recognized a broad right to restitution. The specific right to property restitution was mentioned in United Nations, Committee on the Elimination of Racial Discrimination, General Recommendation no. 22, *Article 5 and Refugees and Displaced Persons,* UN Doc. A/51/18 (August 24, 1996).

49. See United Nations, Commission on Human Rights, *Draft of Basic Principles and Guidelines.*

50. Leckie, "New Directions," pp. 3, 12.

51. Ibid., p. 4.

52. See United Nations, Commission on Human Rights Decision no. 2003/109, UN Doc. E/CN.4/DEC/2003/109 (April 24, 2003); United Nations, *Housing and Property Restitution in the Context of Refugees and Other Displaced Persons,* UN Doc. E/CN.4/Sub.2/2005/17, June 28, 2005.

53. Leckie, "New Directions," pp. 31–32.

54. United Nations, *International Convention on the Protection of the Rights of All Migrant Workers and Members of Their Families,* UN Doc. A/RES/45/158 (December 18, 1990), art. 43.1.

55. United Nations, *Declaration on Social Progress and Development,* UN Doc. A/RES/2542 (December 11, 1969); United Nations, *Declaration of the Rights of the Child,* UN Doc. A/RES/1386 (November 20, 1959); UN Human Settlements Programme, *Vancouver Declaration on Human Settlement,* final document of "Habitat: United Nations Conference on Human Settlements," Vancouver, May 31–June 11, 1976; United Nations, *Declaration on Race and Racial Prejudice,* adopted and proclaimed by the General Conference of the UN Educational, Scientific, and Cultural Organization at its twentieth session (October 27, 1978); United Nations, *Declaration on the Right to Development,* UN Doc. A/RES/41/128 (December 14, 1986). For a comprehensive list of resolutions on the right to adequate housing, see Fact Sheet no. 21, "The Human Right to Adequate Housing," http://www.ohchr.org/english/about/publications/docs/fs21.htm (last accessed November 15, 2007).

56. See United Nations, Committee on Economic, Social, and Cultural Rights, *The Right to Adequate Housing,* General Comment no. 4, UN Doc. E/1991/23 (December 13, 1991), and *The Right to Adequate Housing,* General Comment no. 7, UN Doc. E/1998/22 (May 20 1997), annex IV.

57. Leckie, "New Directions," p. 34.

58. United Nations, Committee on Economic, Social, and Cultural Rights, *The Right to Adequate Housing,* para. 16; according to the committee, "Tenure takes a variety of forms, including rental (public and private) accommodation, cooperative housing, lease, owner-occupation, emergency housing and informal settlements, including occupation of land or property. Notwithstanding the type of tenure, all persons should possess a degree of security of tenure which guarantees legal protection against forced eviction, harassment and other threats" (para. 8). See also United Nations, *Forced Evictions: Analytical Report Compiled by the Secretary General Pursuant to Commission Resolution 1993/77,* UN Doc. E/CN.4/1994/20 (December 7, 1993), paras. 153–158, http://www.unhchr.ch/huridocda/huridoca.nsf/(symbol)/e.cn.4.1994.20.en?opendocument.

59. UNHCR, *The Problem of Access;* UNHCR Executive Committee, "Legal Safety Issues in the Context of Voluntary Repatriation," UN Doc. EC/54/SC/CRP.12 (June 7, 2004), para. 16; UNHCR Executive Committee Conclusion no. 101 (LV) of 2004, paras. h–j; Leckie, "New Directions," pp. 29–31.

60. Pons-Vignon and Solignace Lecomte, "Land, Violent Conflict, and Development," p. 30.

61. Deininger, *Land Policies,* p. 186. Alden Wiley considers, however, that propoor and livelihood objectives are still regarded as "an adjunct" of overtly market-oriented mechanisms. See Liz Alden Wiley, "Formalizing the Informal," p. 2.

62. Deininger, *Land Policies,* p. 6.

63. "For this scheme to work, rental contracts must be sufficiently equitable and of long enough duration to motivate investment in and conservation of the rental property." See USAID, *Land and Conflict,* p. 9; Deininger, *Land Policies,* pp. 74, 115.

64. USAID, *Land and Conflict,* p. 9.

65. Deininger, *Land Policies,* pp. 150–151.

66. Ruth Hall, "Redistributive Land Reforms in Southern Africa," paper presented at IPA workshop "Land, Property, and Conflict Management."

67. UNHCR, *The Problem of Access,* para. 76 on Cambodia, para. 105 on El Salvador and Guatemala.

68. Baranyi, Deere, and Morales, *Land and Policy Development,* p. 38.

69. Alden Wiley, "Formalizing the Informal," p. 2.

70. USAID, *Land and Conflict,* p. 10; Alden Wiley, "Formalizing the Informal," p. 10; Deininger, *Land Policies,* p. 179.

71. Deininger, *Land Policies,* pp. 30, 75.

72. Alden Wiley, "Formalizing the Informal," p. 11.

73. Pons-Vignon and Solignace Lecomte, "Land, Violent Conflict, and Development," p. 18; Deininger, *Land Policies,* pp. 36–37.

74. On legal empowerment, see Stephan Golub, "Beyond Rule of Law Orthodoxy: The Legal Empowerment Alternative," Democracy and Rule of Law Project, Rule of Law Series no. 41 (Washington, D.C.: Carnegie Endowment for International Peace, 2003), p. 25, http://www.carnegieendowment.org/files/wp41.pdf.

75. Alden Wiley, "Formalizing the Informal," p. 4.

76. A study on Uganda found that unresolved disputes can lead reduced output by more than 30 percent. Deininger, *Land Policies,* pp. 160, 162.

77. USAID, *Land and Conflict,* pp. 10–11; Alden Wiley "Formalizing the Informal," p. 7; Deininger, *Land Policies,* p. 35.

78. The North-South Institute and the International Development Research Centre also published a report that examines the relation between land and conflict. See Baranyi, Deere, and Morales, *Land and Policy Development,* pp. 54–58.

79. Deininger, *Land Policies,* p. 157.

80. Pons-Vignon and Solignace Lecomte, "Land, Violent Conflict, and Development," p. 38.

81. USAID, *Land and Conflict,* p. 18.

82. Leopold von Carlowitz, "Settling Property Issues in Complex Peace Operations: The CRPC in Bosnia and Herzegovina and the HPD/CC in Kosovo," *Leiden Journal of International Law* 17, no. 3 (2004): 599–600; Charles Philpott, "Though the Dog Is Dead, the Pig Must Be Killed: Finishing with Property Restitution in Bosnia-Herzegovina's IDPs and Refugees," *Journal of Refugee Studies* 18, no. 1 (2005): 1.

83. Hall, "Redistributive Land Reforms."

84. See Human Rights Watch, "Claims in Conflict: Reversing Ethnic Cleansing in Northern Iraq" (August 3, 2004), http://hrw.org/reports/2004/iraq0804.

85. Leckie, "New Directions," p. 38.

86. Pons-Vignon and Solignace Lecomte, "Land, Violent Conflict, and Development," p. 41.

87. See *General Framework Agreements for Peace in Bosnia-Herzegovina* (1995), annex 7, chap. 2, art. VII; Cox and Garlick, "Musical Chairs," pp. 65, 73. On Kosovo, see UNMIK Regulation no. 1999/23 (November 15, 1999), on the establishment of the Housing and Property Directorate and the Housing and Property Claims Commission; Alan Dodson and Veijo Heiskanen, "Housing and Property Restitution in Kosovo," in Leckie, *Returning Home,* pp. 225, 231.

88. The war in Bosnia-Herzegovina led to approximately 1.3 million refugees fleeing across the borders and 1.3 million internally displaced persons within the territory, for a total population of 4.3 million. During the intervention in Kosovo, around 860,000 Kosovars fled to neighboring states, while 230,000 Serbs and Roma from

Kosovo fled possible reprisals at the end of the crisis. See von Carlowitz, "Settling Property Issues," pp. 601, 606.

89. Note that in the case of the Commission on Real Property Claims, "reconsideration" of the decision was provided for where a party was able to present new evidence challenging the commission's decision. See Cox and Garlick, "Musical Chairs," p. 73.

90. von Carlowitz, "Settling Property Issues," pp. 603–605; Cox and Garlick, "Musical Chairs," pp. 75–76; Philpott, "Though the Dog Is Dead," pp. 5–7, 11.

91. von Carlowitz, "Settling Property Issues," p. 612.

92. UNHCR, *The Problem of Access,* para. 44; Leckie, "New Directions," p. 45; von Carlowitz, "Settling Property Issues," p. 603.

93. Von Carlowitz, "Settling Property Issues," p. 603; Philpott, "Though the Dog Is Dead," p. 3.

94. UNHCR, *The Problem of Access,* para. 48; Leckie, "New Directions," p. 47.

95. Human Rights Watch, "Claims in Conflict."

96. Daniel Fitzpatrick, "Land Policy in Post-Conflict Circumstances: Some Lessons from East Timor," working paper (UN High Commissioner for Refugees, February 2002), p. 13.

97. UNHCR, *The Problem of Access,* paras. 49–51.

98. Ibid., para. 53.

99. Leckie, "New Directions," p. 55.

100. UNHCR, *The Problem of Access,* para. 79.

101. Leckie, "New Directions," p. 38; UNHCR, *The Problem of Access,* paras. 45, 71. Most of the land originally provided to returnees was found to be heavily mined or in frontline areas that were still insecure. Much of the land was also used by secondary occupants, following the government's privatization policy.

102. von Carlowitz, "Settling Property Issues," p. 605. Note that compensation was not provided for in Kosovo either (ibid., p. 612). Compensation should in principle be provided in Iraq; see Human Rights Watch, "Claims in Conflict."

103. See World Bank, "Land Policy and Administration," http://lnweb18.world bank.org/essd/ardext.nsf/11bydocname/topicslandpolicyandadministration (last accessed on November 15, 2007).

104. Baranyi, Deere, and Morales, *Land and Policy Development,* p. 28.

105. USAID, *Land and Conflict,* p. 17.

106. Hernando De Soto, *The Mystery of Capital* (New York: Basic, 2000).

107. USAID, *Land and Conflict,* p. 9.

108. German Development Agency, "Project Land Management," http://www.gtz .de/en/praxis/2202.htm (last accessed on November 15, 2007).

109. Oxfam, "Land Rights in Africa," http://www.oxfam.org.uk/what_we_do/ issues/livelihoods/landrights/index.htm (last accessed on November 15, 2007).

110. Centre on Housing Rights and Evictions, *Protecting Housing Rights, Preventing Evictions: Activity Report 2000–2002* (Geneva, 2003), pp. 14–18, 29–54.

111. See http://landcoalition.org for information on International Land Coalition Network activities, including capacity building, legal support, and conflict resolution.

112. Food and Agriculture Organization, "Land Tenure," http://www.fao.org/sd/ in1_en.htm (last accessed on November 15, 2007).

113. UN Human Settlements Programme, http://www.unhabitat.org.

114. von Carlowitz, "Settling Property Issues," p. 609.

115. See UNDP, "Human Rights Strengthening Programme (HURIST)," http:// www.undp.org/cso/areas/human.html. The Centre on Housing Rights and Evictions was also asked by Human Rights Strengthening Programme to collaborate on a num-

ber of land rights issues and to prepare a draft land rights and development policy for UNDP offices throughout the world. See Centre on Housing Rights and Evictions, *Protecting Housing Rights,* p. 21.

116. UN Human Settlements Programme, "United Nations Housing Rights Programme," http://www.unchs.org/programmes/housingrights (last accessed on November 15, 2007). See also the report of Special Rapporteur Miloon Kothari on adequate housing as a component of the right to an adequate standard of living and to nondiscrimination: UN Doc. E/CN.4/2003/5 (March 3, 2003).

117. UNHCR, *The Problem of Access;* UNHCR Executive Committee, *Legal Safety Issues,* para. 16; Leckie, "New Directions," p. 27. For a recent example of the UNHCR's work, see UNHCR, "Potential Returnees Ask: Will We Still Have a Home in Liberia?" (September 30, 2004). In Liberia, the UNHCR has established housing and property committees to serve as mediators on restitution as a result of the return of over 800,000 civilian internally displaced persons and refugees.

118. Leckie, "New Directions," pp. 29–30.

119. Ibid., p. 21, para. 30.

120. USAID, *Land and Conflict,* pp. 7–10.

121. Pons-Vignon and Solignace Lecomte, "Land, Violent Conflict, and Development," p. 41.

122. Leckie "New Directions," pp. 21–22, paras. 33–34, and p. 33, para. 78. See also Deininger, *Land Policies,* p. 183; USAID, *Land and Conflict,* pp. 9–10.

123. Alden Wiley, "Land and the Constitution," p. 6; Deininger, *Land Policies,* p. 181.

124. USAID, *Land and Conflict,* p. 18.

125. Pons-Vignon and Solignace Lecomte, "Land, Violent Conflict, and Development," p. 40.

126. Alden Wiley, "Land and the Constitution," p. 5. On the establishment of a rule of law task force, see Centre for Humanitarian Dialogue, *Assistance to Justice and the Rule of Law in Afghanistan* (Geneva, February 2004).

127. Leckie, "New Directions," p. 35.

128. On ownership, see Chapter 7.

129. Deininger, *Land Policies,* pp. 56, 184.

130. Pons-Vignon and Solignace Lecomte, "Land, Violent Conflict, and Development," p. 44.

131. Baranyi, Deere, and Morales, *Land and Policy Development,* p. 47. The authors mention the example of the SUBIR project in Ecuador, which brought together Indigenous and Afro-Ecuadorian communities to ensure the provision of land titles to their communities.

132. Deininger, *Land Policies,* p. 159.

133. Pons-Vignon and Solignace Lecomte, "Land, Violent Conflict, and Development," p. 46.

134. Alden Wiley, "Formalizing the Informal," p. 10.

135. Baranyi, Deere, and Morales, *Land and Policy Development,* p. 57; Pons-Vignon and Solignace Lecomte, "Land, Violent Conflict, and Development," pp. 33–34.

136. Deininger, *Land Policies,* p. 165.

137. Ibid., p. 186; specifically: on women, see pp. 32, 57–58; on indigenous groups, see p. 66.

138. International Labour Organization, *Convention Concerning Indigenous and Tribal Peoples in Independent Countries* (Convention no. 169) (June 27, 1989). Article 14 deals with the recognition of indigenous territory by state authorities. See also United Nations, Committee on the Elimination of Racial Discrimination, *Rights of In-*

digenous Peoples, General Recommendation no. 23, UN Doc. A/52/18 (1997); United Nations, *Declaration on the Rights of Persons Belonging to National or Ethnic, Religious, and Linguistic Minorities,* UN Doc. A/RES/47/135 (December 18, 1992).

139. Organization of American States, Inter-American Commission on Human Rights, *The Kichwa People of the Sarayako Community and Its members vs. Ecuador,* Report no. 64/04, Petition no. 176/03 (Admissibility) (October 13, 2004), http://www.cidh.oas.org/annualrep/2004eng/ecuador.167.03eng.htm.

140. Baranyi, Deere, and Morales, *Land and Policy Development,* p. 53.

141. Deininger, *Land Policies,* p. 57; Eve Crowley, "Women's Rights to Land and Natural Resources: Some Implications for a Rights-Based Approach" (Rome: Food and Agriculture Organization, June 1999), http://www.fao.org/sd/ltdirect/ltan0025.htm.

142. Deininger, *Land Policies,* p. 58.

143. United Nations, Commission on Human Rights, *Women's Equal Ownership of, Access to, and Control over Land and the Equal Rights to Own Property and to Adequate Housing,* Commission on Human Rights Resolution 2001/34 (April 23, 2001).

144. UNHCR, *The Problem of Access,* para. 62; UNHCR Executive Committee Conclusion no. 101 (LV) of 2004, para. i.

145. Baranyi, Deere, and Morales, *Land and Policy Development,* p. 50.

146. Ibid., p. 8.

147. USAID, *Land and Conflict,* p. 9.

148. Pons-Vignon and Solignace Lecomte, "Land, Violent Conflict, and Development," p. 47.

149. UNHCR, *The Problem of Access,* p. 6.

150. Leckie, "New Directions," p. 18. In Rwanda and Cambodia, for instance, civil and political rights were prioritized.

151. UNDP, *Access to Justice,* p. 26.

152. von Carlowitz, "Settling Property Issues," p. 611.

153. UNHCR, *Housing, Land and Property Rights in Post-Conflict Societies: Proposals for Their Integration into UN Policy and Operational Frameworks. Main Issues Discussed and Summary Conclusions (Geneva Expert Meeting, 10–11 November 2004)* (Geneva: February 2005), http://www.unhcr.org/cgi-bin/texis/vtx/refworld/rwmain?docid=425690684.

154. Daniel Buckles, *Cultivating Peace: Conflict and Collaboration in Natural Resources Management* (Washington, D.C.: World Bank Institute, 1999).

155. Deininger, *Land Policies,* p. 164.

156. Ibid., p. 171. Adverse possession is the equivalent of the concept of "prescription acquisitive" in civil law systems.

157. Fitzpatrick, "Land Policy," p. 25.

158. Ibid., p. 24; von Carlowitz "Settling Property Issues," p. 609.

159. Summary conclusions of the Geneva Expert Meeting, November 10–11, 2004, p. 7; Leckie, "New Directions," p. 30. See also United Nations, Commission on Human Rights, *Commentary on the Draft Principles,* p. 11, paras. 47–48.

160. The 1992 Comprehensive Peace Agreement in Mozambique also guarantees "restitution of property owned by [refugees] which is still in existence and the right to take legal action to secure the return of such property from individuals in possession of it." See Leckie, "New Directions," p. 17.

161. For the full text of the agreement, see http://www.usip.org/library/pa/guatemala/guat_940617.html.

162. Cecilia Baillet, "Property Restitution in Guatemala: A Transnational Dilemma," in Leckie, *Returning Home,* p. 173. For the full text of the agreement, see http://www.usip.org/library/pa/guatemala/guat_950331.html.

163. Baillet, "Property Restitution in Guatemala," in Leckie, *Returning Home*, p. 172. For the full text of the agreement, see http://www.usip.org/library/pa/guatemala/guat_960506.html.

164. Baillet, "Property Restitution in Guatemala," in Leckie, *Returning Home,* pp. 165, 169.

165. Ibid., pp. 167–168.

166. Ibid., p. 197.

167. Philpott, "Though the Dog Is Dead," p. 14. Marcus Cox and Madeline Garlick defend the relative success of restitution in terms of the reconciliation process. See Cox and Garlick, "Musical Chairs," p. 66.

168. Philpott, "Though the Dog Is Dead," pp. 17–18.

169. On Bosnia-Herzegovina, see Cox and Garlick, "Musical Chairs," p. 74. To be fair, there have been instances where property claims bodies have been granted additional competencies, such as the Housing and Property Directorate in Kosovo, which supervised housing allocation by municipal bodies. See von Carlowitz, "Settling Property Issues," p. 607.

170. Leckie, "New Directions," p. 6.

171. Ibid., p. 39.

172. See also Jean du Plessis, "Slow Start on a Long Journey: Land Restitution Issues in East Timor, 1999–2001," in Leckie, *Returning Home,* pp. 143–144.

173. Fitzpatrick, "Land Policy," p. 12.

174. Ibid., p. 7.

175. According to Daniel Fitzpatrick, "The whole question of property ownership has been left to the future democratically elected government of East Timor. . . . [T]here is thus still in East Timor: no functioning land registry, no system to record or verify private land transactions, no effective regime to govern and legalize foreign interests in land, and no framework to determine competing claims to land." See Fitzpatrick, "Land Policy," p. 15. Jean du Plessis, in "Slow Start," pp. 150–152, 157, indicates that plans were drawn up in East Timor to address long-term housing, land, and property, and were included in the joint assessment mission, but were never adopted by the cabinet.

176. Alden Wiley, "Land and the Constitution," p. 2.

177. Fitzpatrick, "Land Policy," p. 23.

178. Pons-Vignon and Solignace Lecomte, "Land, Violent Conflict, and Development," p. 41.

179. Ibid., p. 42.

180. Ibid., p. 41.

181. See also a similar analysis in the summary conclusions of the Geneva Expert Meeting, November 10–11, 2004, p. 4.

182. The inadequacy of funding structures severely affected the beginning work of the Housing and Property Directorate and Claims Commission in Kosovo, because these bodies were not formally part of UNMIK and had to rely on voluntary contributions, despite the fact that their peacekeeping role had been recognized. See von Carlowitz, "Settling Property Issues," p. 610. See also International Peace Academy and WSP International, "Building Effective Partnerships: Improving the Relationship Between Internal and External Actors in Post-Conflict Countries," Peacebuilding Forum conference report, New York, October 2004, recommendation 1, pp. 5–6.

183. See United Nations, *A More Secure World: Our Shared Responsibility—Report of the Secretary General's High-level Panel on Threats, Challenges, and Change,* UN Doc. A/59/565 (December 1, 2004).

184. UNHCR, *The Problem of Access,* para. 14.

185. Ibid., para. 5.

186. Ibid., para. 81.

187. The UNHCR has since espoused the views of human rights advocates on restitution. See Executive Committee Conclusion no. 101 (LV) of 2004, paras. c, h–j; UNHCR Inter-Office Memorandum no. 104/2001 (November 28, 2001), which is reproduced in Leckie, "New Directions," p. 29.

188. Didier Pfirter, "Property, Land, and Return in the Comprehensive Settlement Plan of the UN Secretary General for Cyprus (Annan Plan)," paper presented at the IPA workshop "Land, Property, and Conflict Management."

189. See Rex Brynen, "Palestinian Refugees and Final Status: Key Issues," February 1996, http://www.arts.mcgill.ca/mepp/new_prrn/background/background_resolving .htm.

190. Deininger, *Land Policies,* p. 155.

191. Pons-Vignon and Solignace Lecomte, "Land, Violent Conflict, and Development," p. 29.

192. United Nations, *The Rule of Law and Transitional Justice.*

10

Corruption:
A Rule of Law Agenda?

Madalene O'Donnell

*The rule of law bakes no bread, it is unable to distribute loaves or fishes
(it has none), and it cannot protect itself against external assault, but it
remains the most civilized and least burdensome conception of a state yet
to be devised.*

—*Michael Oakeshott*[1]

*People could make it against flood and pestilence, but not against the laws;
they went under.*

—*Jorge Amado*[2]

International financial institutions have identified corruption as one of the
greatest obstacles to development. More recently, corruption has emerged as
a first-order concern in many postconflict transitions as well. Whether corruption is indeed a priority will always be a case-by-case determination. But in
several cases the determination has been that worrying about corruption
"later" is a luxury that countries emerging from conflict cannot afford.

Corruption is a broad term that covers a range of behaviors, including
"petty" or "administrative" corruption such as bribery or asset-stripping, as
well as "grand" corruption such as illicit influence over legislation or policy.
When it becomes endemic, corruption can derail political and economic transitions, undermine state capacity and legitimacy, exacerbate poverty, and inflame
grievances linked to conflict. Because the proximate causes and patterns of corruption can vary widely across and within countries, explicit efforts to analyze
and "unpack" corruption are critical, and innovative methods exist to do so.

Tactics to address corruption have focused, at various points, on law enforcement and investigation techniques to prosecute corruption, administrative
reforms to help "prevent" corruption, and external advocacy and watchdog activities to spur reform and raise awareness. More recent efforts have focused
not only on lower-level administrative corruption, but also on less visible forms

of grand corruption, involving political and economic elites and transnational actors. These various approaches constitute a menu of options to address corruption that must be tailored to differing needs and opportunities on the ground. There is no "silver bullet" to address corruption, the popularity of freestanding anticorruption commissions notwithstanding. Efforts to address corruption must be coordinated with efforts to address other closely related problems, such as weak rule of law, physical and economic insecurity, and weak political accountability.

Corruption is not just a long-term "drag" or "tax" on development, but has real and immediate political salience often poorly understood by outsiders. For this reason, it has quickly become a first-order priority in some postconflict transitions despite the fact that national capacities are often stretched thin by urgent demands on the ground and the avalanche of international aid and conditionality. Interesting and varied approaches are emerging in Afghanistan, Liberia, the Democratic Republic of Congo (DRC), and elsewhere to respond to growing problems of corruption.

This chapter summarizes the literature on corruption, emphasizing the close links between corruption, the rule of law, statebuilding, and peacebuilding. It also reviews the evolution of international anticorruption policy and practice, and examines the applicability of general practice to postconflict settings.

Corruption, Rule of Law, and Statebuilding

Within the international community, there is a renewed acknowledgment of the importance of building or rebuilding states—not only to improve the well-being of citizens living under them, but also to reduce the negative spillover effects of state failure for global stability and security. States that can govern well, it is now argued, are the key to long-term development, to combating terrorism, and to preventing conflict and the resurgence of conflict in postconflict transitions. Renewed emphasis on efforts to strengthen the rule of law is in large part propelled by this new consensus on the importance of statebuilding and governance.

But the degree of corruption within the state can fundamentally alter whether laws lift people up or, as described by Jorge Amado in one of the epigraphs that opens this chapter, pull them under. Although Montesquieu argued that "law should be like death, which spares no one," corruption is the system by which those who pay are spared, enriching public officials in the bargain. Therefore, efforts to control corruption are critical to ensuring access to justice and equal treatment before the law. Efforts to strengthen the rule of law, by challenging an environment of impunity, are also critical to controlling corruption.

While there is a new consensus on the importance of statebuilding, there is no consensus yet on how to incorporate the prevention of corruption into it.

This is in part because many international actors have framed the problem as one of state fragility (i.e., lack of power) rather than state predation (i.e., abuse of power). To outsiders, many states do appear weak, fragile, overstretched, and underresourced. To citizens living under them, however, they appear often far more powerful than any other actor in society. The United Kingdom's Department for International Development (DfID) tries to encompass both dimensions in its study of "difficult environments" in which the state is either unwilling or unable to perform.[3] While these two realities often coexist, they are distinct problems that have distinct policy implications.

In countries at critical junctures, such as postconflict transitions, perceptions of corruption can help to shape whether, in the eyes of much of society, the state is the solution or the problem.[4] Corruption undermines both state effectiveness (the ability to govern) and state legitimacy (the recognition of the right to govern). While effectiveness may matter over time, legitimacy is essential for sustaining fragile states that are not yet effective. While corruption hampers development in the long run, it also has real and immediate political salience. As one Brazilian activist put it, "People have no idea how directly proportional the existence of corruption is to the misery of our people."[5] International actors and national leaders ignore it at their peril.

In the international policy arena, after decades of efforts to support development and achieve security despite corruption, a growing number of actors are trying to understand and address corruption itself. The single greatest challenge they face is intense opposition from political and economic elites who benefit tremendously from corruption. As Peter Evans points out, "For predatory states 'low-level equilibrium traps' are not something to be escaped; they are something to be cherished."[6] The problem of corrupt elites is analogous to references in peace implementation literature to the "spoilers problem."[7] As the rule of law and statebuilding move increasingly to the center of postconflict efforts, then "governance spoilers" must be identified and strategies developed to address them. An obvious question is whether the peace spoilers and the governance spoilers are one and the same. If so, can they be brought into the peace process without being brought into the state? In practical terms, what can be done to address corruption by reformers within society or within the state, and what is the role of international actors?

The obstacles are tremendous, particularly in postconflict environments where institutional tools may be weak and the objectives of short-term stabilization and long-term governance may be at odds. However, the objective should not be viewed in terms of eliminating corruption, but rather in terms of ensuring that the state is seen to be making a credible effort to address it. Research and practice in the anticorruption field have evolved significantly, as described below, but relatively little of this learning has filtered into adjacent but specialized fields of the rule of law and postconflict reconstruction.

Corruption: Defining the Problem

Corruption, in contrast to the rule of law, distributes "loaves and fishes" valued at around US$1 trillion per year, or approximately 3 percent of world income today.[8] It exists in all countries at all times, although this chapter focuses on how corruption affects developing countries, including international and national factors that drive it. It exists across all sectors—public, private, civil society—but public sector corruption remains the more serious problem given the state's role in regulating the private sector and civil society.

The most common definition of corruption is "the abuse of public office for private gain."[9] It covers a range of actions including bribery, extortion, asset-stripping, and illicit influence. This definition suggests that gains may accrue to individuals or to groups, and that what is considered "abuse" may vary according to situations and settings regardless of whether it is legal or illegal. Several issues that are closely linked to corruption but distinct from it are clientelism and patrimonialism,[10] rent-seeking,[11] and organized crime.

Corruption is a loaded term. For governments and outsiders, it implies a degree of judgment or even crusading zeal they find inflammatory or unhelpful. But anticorruption advocates are "loathe to separate the element of moral disapproval from the word itself."[12] Euphemisms in international discourse, such as "lack of transparency" or "poor governance," may make people more comfortable, but cast a technical glaze over issues that, within their respective societies, do have a normative dimension.

An important drawback of the term *corruption* is that it encompasses many behaviors with distinct causes and solutions. It is essential to unpack corruption and, in particular, to distinguish between "administrative" corruption (i.e., corruption among low- and mid-level bureaucrats) and "grand" corruption (i.e., corruption among political and economic elites). Administrative corruption may be addressed through institutional reforms designed to improve accountability and transparency, in conjunction with state and societal actors. Grand corruption, however, requires a focus on the incentives of political elites and key economic interests seeking to influence them or "capture" the state.[13]

Under very broad definitions, corruption and the rule of law may be considered two sides of the same coin; the rule of law is a set of *formal* rules partially regulating behavior, while corruption is a set of *informal* rules and practices partially regulating behavior. The rule of law is founded on impersonal trust in laws and institutions; corruption has been associated with higher levels of "particularized trust" between individuals. For that reason, rotating public officials among offices can reduce some forms of corruption.[14] The rule of law is typically the goal; corruption is sometimes the prevailing practice.

In broad terms, therefore, corruption and the rule of law are closely linked and there is good reason to believe that efforts to reduce corruption and strengthen the rule of law are mutually reinforcing. Corruption and rule of law measures are highly correlated,[15] and are often described as two dimensions within a broader concept of governance.[16] Both are dependent on reformers at the highest level and shaped by broader societal and market dynamics.

Approaches to addressing corruption and building the rule of law, however, do not overlap so neatly. Anticorruption efforts typically focus on corruption across all agencies and branches of government, while rule of law programs usually focus on a more narrow set of public actors in the justice and security sectors,[17] though both deal with a number of societal actors outside the state. Looking at various areas of law, rule of law specialists typically focus on constitutional and criminal law in postconflict countries (and civil and commercial law in developing countries), while anticorruption specialists might be more likely to focus on administrative law (or public law). Administrative law governs all agencies typically operating under the executive and charged with "the day-to-day minutiae of governing."[18] Regulating the transparency and accountability of these agencies is critical not only for corruption, but also for building a rule of law culture in the executive branch, the "public face" of the state most visible to citizens.

Economic, Political, and Social Consequences of Corruption

Corruption may have paradoxical effects. For example, one study on Morocco found that corruption in land reform was functional for the survival of the regime and dysfunctional for the economy.[19] But over time, the onus of scholarship has shifted decisively away from arguments in the 1950s and 1960s about the utility of corruption,[20] to mounting evidence in the 1980s and 1990s of the costs of corruption.[21] Contributing factors included the spread of democratic regimes (in which the costs of corruption were quite significant),[22] as well as new tools to measure corruption and quantify some of its impact.[23]

As Cartier-Bresson recently argued,

> Theoretical and empirical analyses of the causes and consequences of, as well as the means of fighting against, corruption have reached a certain level of maturity. The functionalist currents, which viewed corruption as a system that lubricates the cogs of the bureaucratic machine, have disappeared. Economists have reached a consensus on the very negative effects of the phenomenon. . . . Unfortunately, this maturity has still not paved the way for a meaningful advance in the improvement of governance, for the political barriers erected by the losers of such reforms are formidable.[24]

Corruption slows economic growth primarily by reducing investment,[25] but also by reducing the quantity and effectiveness of international aid and the quality of infrastructure, and is associated with weak rule of law, insecure property rights, and declining government effectiveness, which are also detrimental to investment and growth.[26]

The political consequences of corruption are more difficult to quantify. It is generally accepted that growing perceptions of corruption diminish trust in public institutions.[27] Only recently, however, have scholars identified the perception of corruption as one of the key determinants of legitimacy and regime support in multicountry analyses.[28] State corruption has buttressed support for military governments in Pakistan, Uganda, Nigeria, and elsewhere, undermining demilitarization. In many cases, citizens are willing to tolerate some loss of freedoms in exchange for less corruption. In Afghanistan, this was a large part of the Taliban's initial appeal. Democracy appears, therefore, to undermine corruption, and corruption appears to undermine aspects of democracy. Michael Bratton argues that "Africa's prospects for democracy depend critically on whether state elites can establish a reputation for probity and honesty in the eyes of ordinary people."[29]

Until recently, the social costs of corruption received little attention in policy discussions. Studies now show that corruption is associated with lower health and education outcomes,[30] and with lower levels of education spending.[31] Corruption exacerbates inequalities; women, the poor, and rural areas are disproportionately affected.[32] Studies of public expenditures at the local level indicate that better-off communities experience less "leakage" in education funding, resulting in de facto social spending that is even more regressive than de jure allocations.[33]

Corruption and Conflict

Sorting through the links between corruption and conflict is very complex, with causality flowing in both directions. The 2004 report of the UN Secretary-General's High-Level Panel on Threats, Challenges, and Change notes that "corruption, illicit trade and money-laundering contribute to State weakness, impede economic growth and undermine democracy. These activities thus create a permissive environment for civil conflict."[34] Clearly, corruption undermines the state and its capacity to manage and prevent conflict. It exacerbates grievances and inequalities. Massive corruption at times of national emergency, described by Michael Johnston as "crisis corruption," can be particularly explosive.[35] For example, after decades of repression under the Somoza regime in Nicaragua, it was the massive corruption in his handling of emergency relief for earthquake victims that finally began to seriously erode his national and international support, eventually leading to the collapse of the regime.[36]

But the conflict field, given its emphasis on stability, is one of the few areas where some of the functionalist arguments for corruption retain a foothold.[37] When corruption networks exacerbate existing societal or ethnic fault lines, the outcome can be explosive.[38] If corruption networks bridge these divisions among elites, however, they might have some mitigating effects. Shared economic interests of elites, it is argued, may lead them to temporarily set aside differences in order to get rich together—albeit at the expense of others. Some argue that this was the case, for a certain time, in both Rwanda and Macedonia. Philippe Le Billon also argues that anticorruption reforms can be destabilizing. International anticorruption efforts and pressure to comply with international standards in public finance and good governance may, he maintains, serve as an external shock, leading either to new openings for reform or to new possibilities of instability and conflict.[39]

Conflict feeds corruption as well. Even the risk of conflict and perceptions of growing insecurity can undermine accountability and create a permissive environment for state impunity—for both human rights abuses and corruption. There is a large literature on wartime economies and their association with rising corruption.[40] In wartime, the state can act as a protection racket, demanding increasingly greater bribes in return for security provision.[41]

Finally, only recently has there been a growing emphasis on the costs of corruption not only for developing countries themselves, but also for international security. The head of Interpol, four weeks after September 11, 2001, noted that the most sophisticated security systems could be sidestepped by a simple bribe.[42] The 2002 US National Security Strategy identifies corruption as creating an enabling environment for terrorism, organized crime, and trafficking in persons.[43] The international security lens tends to focus particularly on corruption in police and border agencies.

Unintended Consequences of Anticorruption

Pressure on the part of donors and the public to address corruption can have unintended effects on the rule of law and other objectives. Military officers may feel emboldened to step in and "clean up" government. The executive itself may respond with a "crackdown" on corruption involving draconian law and order approaches and violations of due process. International and popular pressure may prompt cabinet reshufflings that may provide a cover for eliminating rivals. Trumped-up charges may be lodged against anticorruption reformers themselves.[44] International agencies and public opinion are usually not in a position to distinguish scapegoating from well-intentioned efforts, undercutting their ability to protest.

Exposing corruption can be economically destabilizing, as evidenced by the explosion of unregulated pyramid schemes and their subsequent collapse in Albania in 1997, and recent bank failures in the Dominican Republic linked to revelations of corruption. It can also be politically destabilizing, fed by excessive expectations on the part of both voters and international actors. In some cases, anticorruption campaign promises can become the "third rail" of politics—limiting patronage, antagonizing key "clients," but failing to provide a political payoff at the polls. International actors often seek strong, up-front commitments from political leaders to address corruption and pursue comprehensive reforms. Meanwhile, anticorruption assistance programs ramp up slowly, well into the middle of the leader's term in office, undermining efforts to deliver results before the next elections. Attention must be paid to how international actors can work with committed governments in a timely way to help them show results. A "throw the bums out" mentality may be just what some countries need, but it often leads to a high rate of turnover. As one voter said after the Hamas landslide in the 2005 Gaza municipal elections: "I voted for [Hamas] because we haven't tried them out before. We've tried all the others, and they only brought us corruption."[45]

Determinants of Corruption

There is no clear answer to the causes of corruption. Corruption and various dimensions of governance, such as the rule of law, accountability, stability, and regulatory effectiveness, are so closely intertwined that separating cause from effect is very difficult.[46] Economic factors linked to lower corruption include more developed economies, higher imports, and more variable inflation. Political factors linked to lower corruption include a higher degree of female participation in public life,[47] larger electoral districts,[48] and nonfederal systems.[49] Democracy appears to influence corruption only over the long-term. Social factors associated with lower corruption include countries with Protestant traditions, histories of British rule, and higher levels of trust.[50] Michael Johnston combines many of these factors, arguing that the *relative* pace of political and economic opening overlaid onto an institutional and social context generates discrete "corruption syndromes."[51] It is very likely that all of these factors play a role, resulting in patterns of corruption that vary in both degree and kind across countries.

Measuring Corruption Across and Within Countries

International surveys of firms, as summarized by Daniel Kaufmann, suggest that, at the global level, aggregate levels of corruption have not changed significantly in recent years. But this masks important regional differences, including deterioration in South Asia, Latin America, Africa, and the former Soviet Union, while other regions have shown improvement or no measurable change. Patterns vary within regions as well. The same study notes that, within Africa, a survey of businesses detected improvements in Mauritius and Botswana in sharp contrast to Zimbabwe and Nigeria. Other countries perceived to have growing patterns of corruption include Venezuela, Guatemala, Paraguay, Ukraine, Romania, Indonesia, Bangladesh, and Germany.[52]

Among postconflict countries, levels of corruption are high (i.e., control of corruption is low), although the variation across countries is significant. As shown in Figure 10.1, many countries have higher levels of corruption than countries with comparable income levels (although margins of error are large).

**Figure 10.1   Perceptions of Corruption in Selected
Postconflict Countries, 2006**

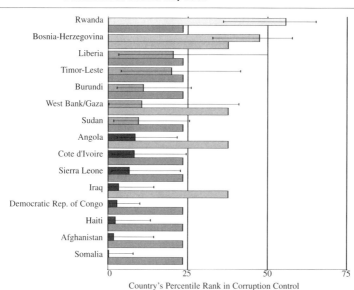

Country's Percentile Rank in Corruption Control

Source: Daniel Kaufmann, Art Kraay, and Massimo Mastruzzi, "Governance Matters VI: Governance Indicators for 1996–2006," (Washington, D.C.: World Bank, 2007).

Note: Lower bar shows comparison with income category average. The governance indicators presented here aggregate the views on the quality of governance according to a large number of enterprise, citizen, and expert survey respondents in industrial and developing countries.

⊢————————⊣ (thin horizontal bars) = 95 percent confidence interval.

While levels of corruption may be a rough but useful initial indicator of the relative importance of corruption across countries, they are of little assistance in developing specific policy responses. Corruption may be organized and driven from the top, as in Palestine,[53] or more anarchic and chaotic, as in Liberia. Institutional tools to address corruption will therefore vary tremendously. Although Haiti and Iraq have comparable levels of corruption, Haiti is a very weak state, while Iraq, until recently, was a "fully institutionalized autocratic system" with low legitimacy but considerable strength.[54] The approaches will have to vary considerably, reflecting historical, social, institutional, political, and economic factors on the ground.

Within countries, anticorruption assessments and surveys can be helpful in determining the importance of corruption relative to other problems (see Figure 10.2) or aggregating perceptions of corruption across institutions (see Table 10.1).

Figure 10.2   Perceptions of the Most Serious Problem in Cambodia, 2000

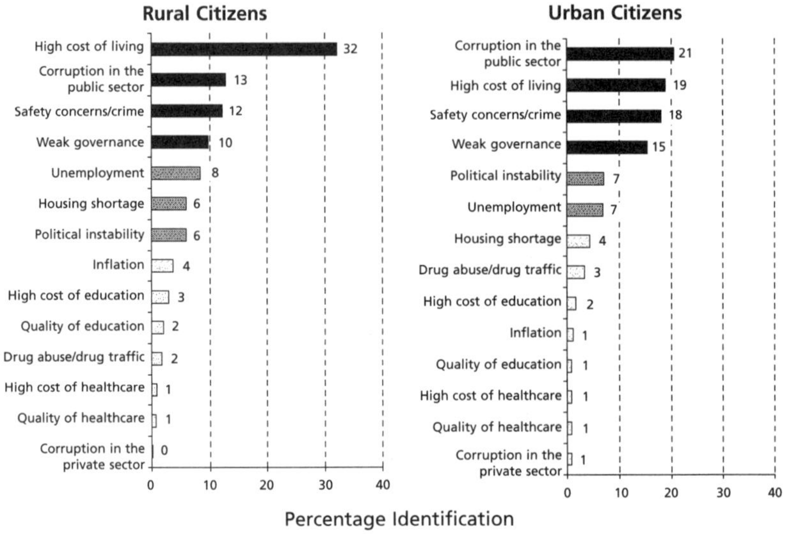

Rural Citizens

High cost of living	32
Corruption in the public sector	13
Safety concerns/crime	12
Weak governance	10
Unemployment	8
Housing shortage	6
Political instability	6
Inflation	4
High cost of education	3
Quality of education	2
Drug abuse/drug traffic	2
High cost of healthcare	1
Quality of healthcare	1
Corruption in the private sector	0

Urban Citizens

Corruption in the public sector	21
High cost of living	19
Safety concerns/crime	18
Weak governance	15
Political instability	7
Unemployment	7
Housing shortage	4
Drug abuse/drug traffic	3
High cost of education	2
Inflation	1
Quality of education	1
High cost of healthcare	1
Quality of healthcare	1
Corruption in the private sector	1

Percentage Identification

Source: World Bank, *Cambodia Governance and Corruption Diagnostic: Evidence from Citizen, Enterprise, and Public Official Surveys* (Washington, D.C., May 2000).

International Strategies and Approaches: Three Phases

Though the anticorruption field is new, it is evolving rapidly. Serious efforts to address corruption through international diplomacy and technical assistance began only in the 1980s. Since that time, international knowledge and practice can be characterized as having passed through three broad stages: law enforcement, prevention, and a more recent focus on elite and international corruption. These three approaches are not mutually exclusive, and all have been employed at different times. But it is fair to say that an initial emphasis on law enforcement has gradually been supplemented by an emphasis on administrative reforms to prevent corruption. Even more recent is the emphasis on grand corruption and prescriptions to address it.

Law Enforcement

Many of the pioneers of international anticorruption efforts were law enforcement officials, who in 1983 began to organize regional and international conferences to raise awareness and exchange experiences across countries.[55] At the regional level, work began on a series of international and regional conventions, and has continued through to the present. The emphasis on criminalization of corruption in earlier conventions gradually gave way to emphasis on prevention in latter ones:

Table 10.1 Perceptions of Public Corruption in Kosovo, 2003

Institution	Percentage Who Believe That Corruption Is High or Very High
Power Corporation	78.2
Businesspeople	57.0
Telecommunications Company	55.2
Customs	54.9
Hospitals	45.6
Lawyers	43.3
Political party leaders	33.7
Tax offices	31.8
UNMIK administration	31.0
Municipal government	28.2
Judiciary	27.7
Prosecutors	25.2
UNMIK police	24.5
Universities/schools	23.0
Municipal administration	22.6
Kosovo Trust Agency	16.5
Presidency	16.4
Parliament	15.6
Media	15.5
Journalists	15.0
Kosovo government	14.3
KFOR	13.3
Nongovernmental organizations	11.9
Kosovo Police Service	9.4
Teachers	8.6
Kosovo Banking Authority	8.4
Statistical Institute	7.3
Kosovo Defense Body	5.9

Source: Bertram I. Spector, Svetlana Winbourne, and Laurence D. Beck, "Corruption in Kosovo: Observations and Implications for USAID" (Washington, D.C.: Management Systems International, July 2003).

- The European Union has adopted multiple legal instruments since 1995, aiming to protect the European Community's financial interests by criminalizing fraudulent conduct.[56]
- The Inter-American Convention Against Corruption, of the Organization of American States, which entered into force in 1997, was the first regional convention.[57]
- The Organization for Economic Cooperation and Development adopted the Convention on Combating Bribery of Foreign Public Officials in International Business Transactions in 1997, which entered into force in 1999.[58]

- The Council of Europe adopted the Criminal Law Convention on Corruption and the Civil Law Convention on Corruption in 1999.[59]
- The UN's Convention Against Transnational Organized Crime, which included measures to criminalize corruption, was adopted in 2000 and entered into force in 2003.[60]
- The African Union approved a regional anticorruption convention in 2003.[61]
- Most recently adopted, in 2003, was the UN's Convention Against Corruption,[62] which entered into force in December 2005.[63]

Within developing countries, many governments faced growing domestic pressure to address corruption. Expanding press freedoms and civil society activism exposed an increasing number of corruption scandals. Some governments turned to international agencies for assistance in prosecutions and investigation.

International actors worked to improve legal frameworks, including through the development of "model" anticorruption laws, conflict of interest provisions, asset declaration requirements for public officials, clauses criminalizing various forms of corruption, and the like.[64] The UN's Global Programme Against Corruption,[65] as well as justice and finance ministry officials from donor countries, trained police and prosecutors in the new laws and investigation techniques.

As it became clear, however, that many of the investigating police, prosecutors, and judges were themselves corrupt, efforts were made to establish specialized anticorruption units. Anticorruption commissions became de rigueur among donors and governments alike. Many were inspired by the highly successful Hong Kong commission established in 1974, but few ever replicated its success.[66] Conventional wisdom held that it was essential to "fry a few big fish," but governments were often careful not to vest commissions with sufficient resources or authority to do so. More worrisome, local and international pressure for prosecutions in these weak rule of law environments had led in some cases to scapegoating and politically targeted investigations.

A World Bank report on Pakistan expresses some of the typical frustrations associated with an emphasis on law enforcement and anticorruption agencies:

> Corruption is a pervasive, deep-seated problem in Pakistan, affecting the civil service as well as most other institutions. There are twelve laws to deal with corruption, apart from the disabling provisions in the Constitution. The number of agencies to deal with corruption cases has expanded in recent years as politicians have made public commitments to stem it and bring corrupt employees to justice. Yet the record is bleak. Very few corrupt officials are convicted. With little or no power to investigate and prosecute, new institutions such as the Ehtesab [Accountability] Commission established to fight corruption have in effect added other non-functioning layers to the bureau-

cracy. . . . Anti-corruption commissions, by themselves, can accomplish little in the absence of other fundamental accompanying actions (e.g. regulatory procedures, strengthening judicial institutions) and broader efforts to improve civil servants' accountability to the public.[67]

Administrative Reforms to Prevent Corruption

Comprehensive efforts to prevent rather than prosecute corruption gained momentum for several reasons. In 1996, then–World Bank president James Wolfensohn argued that corruption was not a political issue but a development one,[68] and many donors and foundations, including the World Bank, the UN Development Programme (UNDP), the US Agency for International Development (USAID), the DfID, the Open Society Institute (OSI), and others, became increasingly active in this area.[69] The emphasis on institutional reform, rather than police investigations, played to their strengths, and many hoped that a preventive approach would be not only more effective but also less divisive and threatening to high-level government officials.

Prevention, in essence, consisted of working with civil society, the media, and the private sector to mobilize *demand* for reform, and working with governments to increase its *supply*. Getting the public to care about corruption was often fairly straightforward. But channeling this displeasure toward constructive change and holding governments accountable is like trying to grab a slippery bar of soap.

At the national and local level, at least in southeastern European countries, public education efforts did appear to have some impact on attitudes, generating more public pressure and reducing tolerance for corruption through radio segments and publicity campaigns.[70] Training programs in investigative journalism may have helped to expand coverage of corruption issues. Despite assassinations, disappearances, and imprisonment, journalists around the world continue to report on government corruption.[71]

Civil society groups generally began to shift from general education to watchdog activities targeting specific forms of corruption. For example, several chapters of Transparency International (TI), a major nongovernmental organization (NGO) dedicated to fighting corruption, focused on procurement-related corruption. TI introduced the concept of "integrity pacts"—a process whereby bidders and government officials pledge neither to offer nor to accept kickbacks, while the national TI chapter in that country monitors the bidding process closely. TI's Argentina chapter monitored the award of a tender for garbage collection for the city of Morón, resulting in an award costing the city US$13 million less than the previous contract. Monitoring in Nepal led to a new practice of posting information at construction sites, including project cost, its financing, and where to report irregularities on-site.[72]

A number of research institutes in developing countries began focusing on transparency in the budget process, providing independent analyses of national budgets and helping, such as in the case of Fundar in Mexico, to identify and expose presidential "slush funds."[73] The Public Affairs Center in Bangalore, India, pioneered the use of citizen report cards that track satisfaction with municipal services and problems of bribes for services.[74]

In general, progress on the "demand" side has been striking. At the global level, Transparency International, which began as a small Berlin-based NGO in 1993, has affiliated chapters in almost a hundred countries today, defining its mission as "prevention and reforming systems."[75] In 1995, Moíses Naím called attention to the "corruption eruption" asking: "From India to Italy, from Japan to Brazil—why have societies which have traditionally tolerated corruption at the highest levels in government and the private sector suddenly lost their patience, their citizens willing to take to the streets to topple high officials accused of wrongdoing?"[76] Corruption became a galvanizing issue for broad-based democracy movements in Mexico, Georgia, and Ukraine; it sparked efforts to uphold constitutional term limits for Daniel Arap Moi in Kenya, and for Frederick Chiluba in Zambia. David Ignatius observed in early 2001 that "the most interesting political movement in the world today doesn't have a name, and it doesn't even have a clear ideology. It is the global rebellion against corruption."[77]

Despite the growing demand to address corruption, working with states to increase the "supply" of such reforms has been more difficult. One initial high-profile approach was to appoint a commission to develop a national anticorruption strategy or action plan, an approach supported by the World Bank, USAID, and other donors in Eastern Europe, Central Asia, and Latin America. These "omnibus" programs were often announced with great fanfare at national public workshops following months of preparation. Most strategies were comprehensive to a fault, containing over a hundred measures to reform the civil service, public financial management, taxation and customs, public procurement, auditing, court administration, business regulation, whistleblower protection, hotlines, and the like.[78] Where governments were committed to advancing some reforms, as in the Slovak Republic and Latvia, these processes were useful. But they were also supported in environments of little or no political will and, after an initial spurt of press, these efforts quickly stalled.[79] Anticorruption strategies are very important but need to be done well. In order to be useful, they must be adequately resourced, and locally owned rather than donor-driven; they must also identify clear priorities for both near-term gains (to establish credibility) and long-term strategic objectives (to ensure durable impact).[80]

In addition to omnibus programs, international donors worked with governments to advance "good governance reforms." These were public management reforms that combined (or replaced) the traditional objectives of downsizing and capacity building with a focus on accountability.[81] Which administrative reforms matter most to preventing corruption? The short answer is that "it depends"—on where corruption is most pervasive, where leadership exists to address it, whether priority should be given to types of corruption that more directly impact the security, economic, or political objectives at hand, and other factors. These will always be context-specific decisions. Often, in monetary terms, the biggest fraud lies in the area of public procurement. For the investment climate, corruption in the courts and legal system, undermining contract enforcement and property rights, is of particular concern. From the perspective of political legitimacy, the reputation and trustworthiness of the head of state matter, as well as corruption in the agency most visible to the public—the police (especially traffic police). Corruption in border agencies (border police, customs, immigration) is often of concern to international security and trade specialists, but it also undercuts public revenues. Citizens may not pay much attention to whether corruption is predictable or arbitrary, but this is tremendously important to firms. For example, Suharto's Indonesia was a highly corrupt but fairly predictable and stable environment. As the system then began to break down, there was not necessarily more corruption, but it became more chaotic, more rapacious, less stable, and far more damaging for investment and growth.

What should administrative reforms look like? The initial instinct is almost always to turn to public salaries and working conditions. Providing a basic dignified wage to public employees is essential, but there is little evidence that, once corruption is pervasive, simply providing raises to everyone will solve the problem. World Bank studies find that creating a climate of "meritocracy" appears to have a larger effect on corruption than wage levels. Rafael Di Tella and Ernesto Schargrodsky have looked at experiences in Argentina to support the "Becker-Stigler" hypothesis that adequate wages, combined with regular auditing and monitoring, is far more effective than either one on its own (citing Juan Domingo Perón's observation: "People are good. But if you monitor them, they are better").[82]

Therefore, administrative reforms ideally combine a carrot and stick approach—improving basic conditions but also monitoring performance closely. Improved financial management and treasury systems, clear and enforceable procurement rules, internal auditing capacity, and external auditing bodies are all important. Taxation and customs administrations are usually an early target for reform, since, if effective, these reforms yield additional revenues to fund government operations.

Measuring the impact that such reforms may have had on corruption is more difficult. Public-expenditure-tracking surveys in Uganda determined that in 1995 78 percent of non-wage funds for schools were "leaking," according to a 2003 World Bank paper. Due to improved oversight by the central government, local newspapers, and parents, capture had been reduced, on average, to 18 percent in 2001.[83] Many administrative and management reforms have focused on strengthening not only the executive but also the judiciary, parliament, and independent audit agencies—applying many of the same techniques described above. For example, comprehensive, incentive-based reforms were incorporated into several rule of law assistance programs.[84] Court and case management reforms were emphasized. This included introducing clearer laws and sentencing guidelines, publication of reasoned decisions and random assignment of cases, guaranteed minimal appropriations from the executive, separate courtroom entrances for judges, tamper-proof software for entering evidence in courts and prosecutors' offices, and improved processes for investigating complaints against judges, including the use of judicial inspection panels.

In general, it is extremely difficult to politely dislodge an ingrained culture of corruption at the highest levels of the judiciary. Early efforts that emphasized elite training seminars for judges, better working conditions, and better pay have now been combined with tentative efforts to press not only for more independence but also for greater accountability and performance. Judges (particularly chief justices) resisted reforms such as changes in appointment, promotion, and dismissal procedures, which they correctly saw as undercutting their authority and discretion. The executive often joined the public and media in condemning corruption in the judiciary, feeding calls to "clean house."

In these environments, international advisers were uncertain how to press for change in the judiciary without undermining judicial independence. In Georgia and Albania, however, onetime competency tests of all sitting judges resulted in substantial turnover without politicizing the courts. Some Latin American countries have turned to judicial councils, composed of a mix of judges, justice ministry officials, and civil society representatives to improve judicial accountability within the bounds of judicial independence. One study concluded that judicial councils in Latin America had not made a clear contribution to judicial governance, and often fell prey to corruption and cronyism themselves.[85] But combining judicial councils with vigorous civil society oversight did seem to improve the appointment process for judges in Argentina. The Transparency International chapter there, Poder Ciudadano, closely monitored the work of the councils, analyzing and publishing the qualifications of all proposed nominees. This effort has been replicated in Peru and Bolivia.

Parliaments would appear to be the last refuge of scoundrels. They are a potentially important source of oversight, but are perceived in many country surveys as among the most corrupt institutions. More than elections are needed to hold them accountable; financial and legal accountability are also critical but rarely examined. Recorded votes and open hearings are valuable, but also more attention should be focused on the sweeping immunities that parliaments grant themselves, including, in some cases, immunity for crimes committed before taking office.[86] Transparency in operating budgets for parliaments is almost never discussed. A recent exception is the ad hoc committee established to investigate administrative and financial malpractices within the Liberian parliament, which in 2005 led to the suspension of its speaker on corruption grounds.

There is now a rich array of innovative tools to prevent corruption. But the single greatest obstacle has been the lack of political will to allow these efforts to take root. Efforts to address corruption have tremendous distributional impacts. What makes them valuable makes them extremely difficult to enact. In Kenya, for example, President Mwai Kibaki launched one of the most high-profile corruption crusades. Expectations were high and donors responded with many of the programs cited above. But in February 2005 these efforts appeared to hit a wall. The highly respected anticorruption adviser, John Githongo, resigned due to obstruction of his work at the highest levels. The United States suspended its anticorruption assistance. Great Britain announced a new policy of refusing visas for Kenyan officials or businessmen suspected of corruption.[87] Administrative reforms were now being coupled with diplomatic instruments targeting elites. Efforts to prevent corruption initially focused on reshaping and reforming institutional environments that were "corrupting" individuals but, as in Kenya, attention had finally begun to shift to how powerful individuals were "corrupting" institutions.

Targeting Grand Corruption

Administrative corruption and grand corruption are overlapping problems, but require very different solutions. In 2000 the World Bank issued a report distinguishing between "administrative corruption" and "state capture," rated all transition countries as high, medium, or low in each category, and recommended differentiated approaches for addressing each one.[88] This helped to open discussions on low-level versus high-level corruption. Political and corporate governance scandals in the United States and Europe also revived interest in high-level political corruption and corporate fraud in developed countries.

Efforts to curb grand corruption are still relatively recent and not yet well defined. They require a focus on the incentives driving political and economic elites, including international and transnational elites operating in the country. Initially, it was argued that political and economic liberalization would expose politicians and firms to competition, squeezing out corruption and creating incentives to improve the performance of each. However, many economies and regimes that have liberalized have not become less corrupt, for a few reasons. First, many of the reforms were hijacked by elites and became instruments of corruption, as was the case of "crony privatizations."[89] Second, entrenched but uncompetitive firms have more incentive than ever to purchase state influence. Third, politicians who have to face elections have more incentive than ever to collect rents to finance their campaigns and distribute resources to supporters. Grand corruption, rather than being squeezed out, has adapted well. Regulating economic competition is particularly difficult when the rule of law is weak and many firms are international. Some studies indicate that foreign firms are not any less likely than local firms to bribe public officials, and that they provide by far the largest payments.[90]

Methods of Addressing Grand Corruption

Aid conditionality. Craig Burnside and David Dollar argued influentially in the late 1990s that aid was less effective in environments of high corruption (as well as bad policies and weak institutions).[91] This left policymakers struggling with the dilemma of how to design aid programs to address corruption if corruption itself undermined the effectiveness of aid. The result was a heavy emphasis on conditionality and "selectivity" that would create incentives for states to reduce corruption and improve governance. The Monterrey Consensus, adopted in 2002 at the UN's International Conference on Financing for Development, was a "grand bargain" in which donors promised more aid in exchange for better governance. The US Millennium Challenge Corporation seeks to offer supplemental aid for "good performers," and it is not a coincidence that the program singles out corruption as the initial performance indicator. The World Bank has beefed up governance criteria in its country allocation formulas. The primary objective is to make its own aid more effective, but the hope is that these financial "carrots" will also make good governance a more attractive and financially viable option for leaders. In postconflict environments, however, conditionality is particularly problematic. Where international actors often have large forces deployed on the ground, "walking away" is not an option and could destabilize the transition.

Sanctions. As is well known by the human rights community, smart sanctions can send an important signal to high-level officials who are not held accountable by their own courts. In 2002 the US State Department announced a new policy of denying visas to Latin American public officials involved in corruption or money laundering, "just as we deny entry to war criminals or narcotics traffickers."[92] The first denial was to a Nicaraguan official who had been implicated but never charged in any corruption case.

Abuse of immunities. Limited immunities for parliamentarians, heads of state, and judges and magistrates are appropriate to prevent harassment and intimidation. But many enjoy sweeping immunities. In Italy, legislation passed in 2003 granted immunity to the prime minister and other high-level officials even for those crimes committed before their terms of office began. Legislation passed in Guatemala in 2002 gave Congress unlimited time to decide whether to lift the immunities of political officials but set a two-month deadline for judges.[93]

Electoral reforms and party finance. Political party finance "has arrived," as evidenced by the publication of several handbooks and toolkits by international donors and NGOs in 2004.[94] The next step is to test out new approaches on the ground, taking care to tailor approaches carefully. Other dimensions of electoral reform, such as open versus closed list systems, also have implications for transparency and political corruption. At the local level, the ability to field independent candidates against nationally registered parties may improve the quality of candidates and governance overall.

Tracking stolen assets. The UN's 2002 Global Convention Against Corruption was considered weaker than some earlier regional conventions, with one exception: the inclusion of provisions to assist in tracking and recovery of stolen assets moved overseas. Some progress has been made in identification and reporting on bank accounts held by "politically exposed persons" as well as officials, but more emphasis on preventing initial transfers overseas is important.

Industry-specific approaches. Some of the most interesting initiatives, propelled by joint international human rights, environmental, and anticorruption advocacy groups, have taken an industry-by-industry approach. Industrywide approaches help to address private sector concerns regarding a level playing field.[95] The past few years have seen an explosion of vigorous advocacy, research, and eventually diplomacy on extractive industry management and revenues and their implications for corruption, conflict, growth, poverty, and the environment. Transparency in revenues is essential in order to track downstream expenditures. Focusing just on bribes generated by various sectors (rather than total revenues diverted), Transparency International's Bribe Payers Index identifies the arms and construction industries as generating more bribes in developing countries than oil, gas, and mining, yet relatively few industrywide initiatives have emerged within the construction and arms industries.[96]

The OECD Anti-Bribery Convention. International conventions matter little if the rule of law is extremely weak. It is often presumed that they matter quite a lot in countries that belong to the Organization for Economic Cooperation and Development (OECD), but effective enforcement is still not automatic by any means. If enforced, such conventions can be vital to addressing the international "supply" side of grand corruption. One of the most remarkable examples of leadership in international anticorruption efforts was the passage and approval of the 1977 Foreign Corrupt Practices Act. This US law prohibited bribery to "foreign officials," including members of government and political parties, and to political candidates by US firms, and arguably placed US firms at a disadvantage in highly corrupt environments. Even with the US government and business community lobbying strongly, it took twenty years for the other OECD countries to follow suit. The OECD's Anti-Bribery Convention took effect in 1999 and included a well-defined peer-monitoring process. Unfortunately, monitoring of the convention is perennially underfunded.[97]

Evaluating International Anticorruption Assistance

The three categories of approaches described above—law enforcement, prevention, and efforts to address grand corruption—all have a role to play in curbing corruption. Many good resources now exist that summarize some of the lessons that have been learned.[98] There is a tendency to favor new ideas over old ones, but in reality the lack of systematic, long-term evaluation makes it difficult to prioritize investments to address corruption. Surveys of development practitioners conducted by the OECD's Development and Assistance Committee (DAC), the DfID and the Utstein Group, USAID, the OSI, and the World Bank help to analyze trends, practices, and emerging lessons.[99]

Targeted and short-term studies, several of which have been referenced above, suggest that anticorruption commissions, omnibus programs, and international conventions have not demonstrated their effectiveness, and that, within institutional reform, a focus on creating a meritocracy, rather than building capacity, may have more impact on fighting corruption. Furthermore, combining decent pay with regular monitoring may be far more effective than either measure on its own. Researchers at the European Bank for Reconstruction and Development analyzed three types of anticorruption activities—omnibus anticorruption programs, legal reforms, and adherence to international anticorruption conventions—in twenty-four transition countries implemented in 1999–2002.[100] They found no discernible effect of omnibus programs or membership in international conventions on corruption, but did find that new or amended laws were associated with lower levels of petty or administrative corruption—a reminder that administrative and grand corruption are closely related but distinct problems requiring different solutions.

Perhaps the most persistent weakness in international efforts to address corruption is that international actors are particularly ill-suited to identify politically feasible strategies and, as Ivan Krastev has argued, rarely even try.[101] The difficulty for any government is that efforts to address grand corruption will quickly alienate powerful elites, and that efforts to address administrative corruption will take time. Anticorruption commissions are popular with reluctant governments because they send an immediate signal that someone is "on the job," but they rarely have the financial or institutional independence to escape their political masters.

Corruption in Postconflict Transitions

Measures designed to address corruption have rarely, if ever, been incorporated into peace agreements. Yet corruption by the state is often a root cause of conflict. Failure to build in controls against corruption can also undermine implementation of political, economic, and security objectives, such as restoring state authority and delivering services to such key beneficiary groups as demobilized combatants, returning refugees, and war-ravaged communities.

But how applicable to postconflict settings are the broader anticorruption approaches reviewed above? Countries emerging from conflict frequently have very high or endemic corruption, low state legitimacy,[102] low state capacity,[103] weak rule of law, and high levels of physical insecurity and residual violence. Economic legacies of civil wars involve concentrations of wealth flowing from illegal or unregulated trade and unofficial "taxes" collected by soldiers, rebel factions, and the like.[104] Where postconflict countries vary considerably is in the quality of emerging leadership. In other words, some postconflict countries are unable to control corruption, while others are unwilling to do so. Afghanistan and East Timor are examples of countries where credible leadership does exist. In other countries, such as Iraq, Liberia, and Sudan, leaders may be associated with corrupt patterns of governance, and fear of opposing factions often prevents followers from throwing off "strong" leaders in search of more accountable and transparent ones.

It is typically more difficult, therefore, to address corruption in postconflict settings than in other developing countries. Poor legal conditions mean that prosecutions in local courts are rarely advisable. Security conditions rarely exist to enforce compliance with laws. The tremendous uncertainty in these environments may lead to hand-over-fist corruption as soldiers and rebels grasp for rents before they are disarmed,[105] and economic elites search for friends in emerging power structures. Second-tier controls, such as freestanding anticorruption commissions, may be premature before first-tier legal, administrative, and financial controls are designed, established, and staffed.

But in other ways, these environments provide unusual opportunities to address corruption. Because political and economic environments are largely fluid, shifting alliances may create opportunities to sideline elites who would be highly entrenched in more stable countries. International actors tend to have a larger influence in these settings due to high troop deployments or massive infusions of aid. Finally, in their own large assistance programs, aid agencies have the opportunity to set an example of transparent and accountable practices. Unfortunately, these agencies answer first and foremost to their bosses back home; as a result, in-country transparency and accountability are often quite weak.

Is it realistic to address corruption in postconflict countries? After all, many of these states cannot even provide minimal public order, so how can they be expected to control corruption? An important critique of international postconflict efforts is that international actors are already trying to do too many things at once, overwhelming absorptive capacity and failing to set priorities with national counterparts.[106] Is corruption one of those second-order priorities that can wait? Shouldn't the basic institutions be created before they are cleaned up? Shouldn't the emphasis be on disbursing state and international funds quickly rather than carefully?

The challenge in postconflict environments is to target the types of corruption that, if not addressed, can derail the entire transition, but to do so in ways that do not create large additional demands on already overwhelmed reformers within and outside fragile state structures. Some recent examples from postconflict situations today might help to illustrate how practitioners are trying to thread this needle.

Liberia

The security situation in Liberia has improved since the signing of the peace agreement and the deployment of UN peacekeepers there in 2003. However, this has led one news report to conclude, "corruption has now replaced the AK-47 rifle as the preferred method of illicit enrichment."[107] Massive corruption was undermining state legitimacy and citizens' hopes for the future. It was also undermining the effectiveness of large aid flows into Liberia. Massive looting continued unabated under the nose of international forces in the freeport of Monrovia. Per the initial peace terms, the port was still under the control of rebel factions in 2004, denying the new government a key source of revenue and choking economic recovery.

In 2005, national reformers and international actors took several steps. An ad hoc committee, led by parliamentary speaker and former rebel leader George Dweh, opened an investigation of corruption. In March 2005, UN forces stepped up security at parliament and called for calm among Dweh's supporters as parliamentarians called a special session and suspended him. In April 2005, UN forces seized control of the port while the World Bank began preparations to award a contract for its external management. In May 2005, corruption topped the list of international priorities emphasized at an international donor conference with Liberian government officials. In September 2005, the National Transitional Government of Liberia and Liberia's international partners signed a Governance and Economic Management Assistance Programme (GEMAP) for Liberia. GEMAP was, in turn, welcomed in a UN Security Council resolution on September 19, 2005. Among other aspects, the program calls for deployment of internationally recruited experts with co-signing authority to key government offices.[108]

These measures may or may not have a critical impact on Liberia's transition. Some have argued that nothing short of sustained international engagement for fifteen to twenty-five years will create the conditions for new, less corrupt political forces to develop.[109] But they do indicate an acknowledgment that something more than procurement and financial management reformers was called for, and some action was taken to marginalize potential "spoilers" in parliament and the port even at the risk of antagonizing supporters of Liberians United for Reconciliation and Democracy (LURD) and other factions. Liberia's experience illustrates the links between security and anticorruption in postconflict settings. Without a strong security presence, there would have been very little space to move against flagrant corruption within the capital city itself.

Afghanistan

Afghanistan is an example of how initial efforts to bring potential spoilers into the peace processes and into the state may have long-term costs for a country. In this case, three closely linked problems—warlords, drug trafficking, and corruption—threaten to overwhelm nationally led and internationally supported statebuilding and development efforts. International troop deployments were never sufficient to secure the entire country and, as a result, warlords controlling local militias were invited into the transitional government in a power-sharing arrangement. Continuing US military cooperation with warlords on efforts to root out Al-Qaida and Taliban fighters further strengthened their hand. Finally, when opium production exploded in the post-Taliban period, warlords quickly moved to control lucrative drug-trafficking networks, reasserting control at the local level. For many Afghans, these steps signaled that their hopes for a clean and honest public administration would again not be met. As one Afghan put it, "We were so anxious to escape the warlords that many even supported the harsh measures of the Taliban and now, after hiding up in the hills, these warlords are invited back to Kabul and put in charge of ministries."[110]

Gradually, however, a recognition began to emerge that things were moving in the wrong direction. The US ambassador admitted that, "rather than getting better, [the situation has] gotten worse. There is a potential for drugs overwhelming the institutions—a sort of a narco-state."[111] Observers noted that corruption had actually increased since the end of the conflict and appeared to be driven from the top. President Hamid Karzai's last-minute change of running mate for the 2004 presidential elections and the cabinet he compiled afterward suggest important steps in this direction. It remains unclear, however, given the uncertain security environment and the slow pace of disarmament, how much space there is for maneuver. Massive rents from drug trafficking now ensure that warlords have an independent financial power base that they can use to buy state influence even after they no longer directly control state ministries. The drug trade represents more than half of Afghanistan's formal gross domestic product, constituting a tremendous risk of state capture unless additional steps are taken quickly.[112]

Democratic Republic of Congo

The Democratic Republic of Congo is a massive country with endemic levels of grand and administrative corruption. The DRC's transition from war toward the 2005 elections began in 2003. But fighting continues in the east, and signatories to the Sun City agreement continue their scramble for resources at the center, exerting weak control over their respective political and military forces at the periphery. An independent analysis in March 2005 concluded that neither the UN Organization Mission in the DRC (MONUC) "nor the wider international community has shown the ability or the will to address the Congo's crises. While donors finance over half the country's budget, they have been unable or unwilling to take serious action against the spoilers in the transitional government, who work against unification of the army and administration. Some members of the government have been suspended for corruption but none have faced criminal charges."[113]

In the midst of this environment, one interesting initiative focused on local-level efforts to mobilize against corruption along the Congo River.[114] An international NGO, Innovative Resources Management (IRM), began a program financed by USAID to address the *tracassaries,* or illegal taxation, of river traders in Western Congo, where 80 percent of commercial produce travels by water. The massive illegal taxation by unsalaried civil servants stationed at ports throughout the interior had effectively dried up river-based commerce, devastating the rural economy, which had served as a bread basket for the capital and contributing to food scarcities in Kinshasa.[115] The project began with a recognition that these bribery points were an "epiphenomenon" of patterns of corruption and natural resource exploitation dating back to the 1970s and 1980s and driven from Kinshasa. It produced a report that, for the first time, measured and documented the problem along the Congo. It found that 92 percent of traders' operating costs were accounted for by illegal taxes and fees imposed by unauthorized civil servants for trumped-up or fictional services ("loading rights," "docking permission," etc.). Only 8 percent of fees were authorized; even less actually accrued to the state. During one trip to Kinshasa, a river transporter had to pay off an average of 24 government services at 9 different ports of call, for a total of 216 payments and a delay of 24 hours at each port.[116]

The IRM obtained copies of legislation specifying that only four agencies were authorized to collect fees in ports, and determined that 90 percent of the unofficial payments were obtained by agents linked to the Ministry of Interior.[117] The IRM conducted a series of meetings with officials in Kinshasa and secured the backing of the interior minister to bring these payments in line with the law, arguing that fewer payments would increase river traffic and legal government revenues. Associations of transporters and communities were formed along the river to share information on *tracassaries,* and high-frequency radios were distributed to communities, allowing them to report illegal payment points directly to the Ministry of Interior. After several months, a "critical mass" of community oversight and state monitoring began to change practices in the first province, and efforts also began to build momentum in two additional provinces. The IRM argues that opening dialogue with territorial administrators was central. An organized "convoy" containing representatives of the provincial and national governments, the private sector, and donor organizations "offered a forum to civil society . . . *for the first time* to publicly, in a transparent manner, express itself concerning abuses and corrupt government agency practices."[118] The effort built new patterns of cooperation among communities, transporters, and the state, and helped to begin, however slowly, a revival of commerce along the Western Congo. These types of approaches are sometimes called "islands of integrity"; while they cannot substitute for political will at the highest levels of government, they can achieve real gains in discrete areas, such as revival of regional commerce and livelihoods—an example of the "quick wins" so vigorously sought in postconflict transitions.

Postconflict Lessons

There are many examples of bad ideas that the international community should not support in many postconflict environments. The Afghan constitution, for example, calls for the creation of a commission to investigate acts of corruption. In 2004 the presidency requested international assistance to train and equip this anticorruption commission. Meanwhile, several line ministries did not even have chief financial officers in place. Primary systems should be in place before secondary bodies, like anticorruption commissions, look to see whether those systems are working.

The continued pattern of early elections leads political parties to scramble for supporters, offering whatever inducements they can, accumulating whatever resources they can. In order to reduce pressures on parties to turn to these tactics, donors in Mozambique took the unusual step of creating a trust fund for political parties. Today, through this special trust fund, Mozambique remains one of the few countries that permits international financing of political parties.

Another temptation is for international actors to step in and take over. Steps toward "shared sovereignty" are receiving increased attention.[119] Sometimes this may be necessary, as is the case in Liberia. Unfortunately, failures would appear to outnumber successes in this area. One frequent example is international administration of customs agencies. In Pakistan, a Swiss firm, Société Générale de Surveillance (together with its subsidiary Cotecna Inspection SA), was hired by the government to conduct preinspection customs clearances, but admitted that in December 1997 it itself had paid a "substantial commission" in 1992 to obtain the original contract.[120] Mozambique, in contrast, appears to offer a relative success; crown agents took over customs operations in 1997, financed by the DfID, and transferred responsibility to the government in 2003, but continued to provide technical assistance and to work closely with state officials throughout. Among the lessons learned are that increasing revenues is far easier than reducing corruption, and that reforms require substantial purges of the entire customs work force and selective rehiring.[121]

One of the best approaches may be for international actors to finance vigorous and professional monitoring efforts. An emphasis on monitoring does not sideline the state but instead provides an incentive for it to improve its performance while diagnosing key problems. Publication of all monitoring efforts can increase democratic accountability. These same monitoring efforts could also be directed toward international aid agencies, increasing accountability of both national and international actors. Ideally, these concurrent and random audits would be undertaken by national offices of donor countries on a rotating basis. But it is precisely because executives of donor countries do not control their own auditing bodies that they may resist efforts to bring them in.

Given the incentives at play, donor agencies are clearly far more concerned about insulating their own programs from corruption than focusing on how corruption in the use of public resources undermines state structures. The tendency, in highly corrupt environments, is to travel around the state in order to deliver services, build highways, and construct schools rather than building state capacity to do so. That leads to a focus on avoiding, rather than reducing, public sector corruption. An emphasis on closely monitoring state performance rather than substituting for it would help to better align these objectives. Afghanistan's trust fund, operated by the World Bank, channels international resources toward government-identified priorities. Such an approach addresses international fiduciary concerns without undercutting states that are making credible efforts to improve their effectiveness over time.

In postconflict settings, it is even more important than usual for international agencies to make extraordinary efforts to operate in a transparent manner with high public accountability, constantly providing information on their programs, procurements, and impacts. Donors are quick to call press conferences to announce massive "pledges," and citizens are slow to see the direct impact on their well-being, opening them up to believe all accusations of corruption and mismanagement that they read and hear about.

Conclusion

A survey of the anticorruption literature and practice yields some general lessons. The academic literature has evolved from viewing corruption as functional, to benign, to one of the greatest obstacles to development. It has shed light on the links between corruption and the rule of law, conflict, inequality, democratization, and economic development. International anticorruption practice, at various times, has emphasized law enforcement and administrative reforms, and more recently a focus on grand corruption; all three have a role to play. Both experience and research emphasize the importance of distinguishing between administrative and grand corruption. As discussed in this chapter, a variety of tools exist to monitor and address specific forms of corruption (procurement fraud, budget leakages, bribes, etc.) in specific types of organizations (judiciary, police, health, education, customs, etc.). Experience suggests that there are risks to addressing corruption, such as scapegoating and character assassination, that must be managed carefully. In addition, international actors need to work with national reformers to identify strategies that are politically feasible for leaders operating in democratic or partially democratic environments.

All of these lessons need to be carefully tailored to postconflict environments, where security may not exist, political authority may be contested, and
institutional capacity may be constrained. Aid bonanzas in these environments
create opportunities to assist in the development of legal, financial, and political accountability structures that are essential to controlling corruption, but
they also create risks of corruption bonanzas.

"Most wars," Wesley Clark argued, "are much more about money than
they are about ideology. . . . We should have been looking at bank accounts instead of military targets before we went into some of these countries."[122] International actors need better information and analysis to understand the links
between corruption, conflict, and the viability of new states. In broader efforts
to address corruption in developing countries as a whole, international actors
are simultaneously criticized for both overemphasizing and underemphasizing
corruption. In fact, international efforts too often combine strong public rhetoric with very limited resources, diplomatic leverage, or staying power, and
ask the equivalent of political suicide for leaders and parties standing for internationally mandated elections. Efforts to address corruption need to draw
from law enforcement approaches as well as efforts to address both administrative and grand corruption—depending on prevailing patterns in the country.
Up against serious and entrenched corruption, halfhearted efforts to "do something" are rarely commensurate with the size of the problem itself, make it
more difficult for governments to take international rhetoric seriously, and
may therefore be worse than no efforts at all.

Increasingly, however, international actors are recognizing that addressing
corruption requires not only rhetoric but also a willingness to walk away, to
apply muscle, and to understand local dynamics. It requires a comprehensive
focus not only on narrow financial accountability but also on legal and political accountability. Recent lessons from Liberia, Afghanistan, and the Democratic Republic of Congo suggest that, even in postconflict settings, addressing
corruption is emerging as a fundamental and early priority that is strongly supported by local populations. Despite tremendous challenges, openings may
exist in these settings, given political and economic fluidity. The window to address corruption in some transitions may be short-lived, and action is necessary,
where feasible, to prevent a slide toward entrenched "low-level equilibrium
traps" through which the state becomes more the problem and less the solution.

Notes

1. Cited in Rachel Kleinfeld Belton, "Competing Definitions of the Rule of Law:
Implications for Practitioners," Democracy and Rule of Law Project, Rule of Law Series no. 55 (Washington, D.C.: Carnegie Endowment for International Peace, January
2005), p. 5.

2. Cited in Gloria Steinem, Introduction to *North Carolina Journal of International Law and Commercial Regulation* 24, no. 2 (Winter 1999): 225.

3. Magüi Moreno Torres and Michael Anderson, "Fragile States: Defining Difficult Environments for Poverty Reduction," Poverty Reduction in Difficult Environments Team, Working Paper no. 1 (London: Department for International Development, August 2004). This DfID paper argues that one source of state failure is "clientelist politics" in which "the political logic of the system diverts state authority from the stated policy goals to the pursuit of private wealth and power," p. 6.

4. Jean Cartier-Bresson, "From the State of the Question to the Question of the State" (Copenhagen: Copenhagen Consensus Opponent Notes on Poor Governance and Corruption, April 2004).

5. Luis Roberto Mesquita, a Brazilian businessman awarded an Integrity Award by Transparency International in 2002 for leading efforts that resulted in the removal of the local mayor and council members, quoted at http://www.transparency.org/news_room/award/integrity_awards/integrity_award_winners/winners_2002. For experiences and views of the poor regarding state institutions and corruption in some fifty developing countries, see Deepa Naranyan with Raj Patel, Kai Schafft, Anne Rademacher, and Sarah Koch-Shulte, *Voices of the Poor: Can Anyone Hear Us?* (New York: Oxford University Press, 2000), chap. 3.

6. Peter Evans, *Embedded Autonomy: States and Industrial Transformation* (Princeton: Princeton University Press, 1995), p. 248.

7. Stephen John Stedman, "Spoiler Problems in Peace Processes," *International Security* 22, no. 2 (Fall 1997): 5–53.

8. World Bank, "High-Level Political Signing Conference for the United Nations Convention Against Corruption," press release (Merida, Mexico, 2003), http://www.worldbank.org/wbi/governance/events/merida.html.

9. This simpler version is increasingly used in place of Joseph Nye's 1967 definition of corruption as "behaviour which deviates from the formal duties of a public role because of private-regarding (personal, close family, private clique) pecuniary or status gains; or violates rules against the exercise of certain types of private-regarding influence." See Joseph Nye, "Corruption and Political Development: A Cost-Benefit Analysis," *American Political Science Review* 61 (June 1967): 419.

10. Susan Rose-Ackerman offers the following distinction: in patrimonial systems, public officials are the patrons and private interests the clients, while in clientelistic states, private interests are dominant and control the state. See Susan Rose-Ackerman, *Corruption and Government: Causes, Consequences, and Reform* (Cambridge: Cambridge University Press, 1999.) See also Derek W. Brinkerhoff and Arthur A. Goldsmith, "Clientelism, Patrimonialism and Democratic Governance: An Overview and Framework for Assessment and Programming," paper prepared for USAID Office of Democracy and Governance (Cambridge, Mass.: Abt Associates, December 2002), http://www.abtassociates.com/reports/2002601089183_30950.pdf.

11. For a discussion of the distinction between rent-seeking and corruption, see Paolo Mauro, "Why Worry About Corruption?" *Economic Issues*, no. 6 (Washington, D.C.: International Monetary Fund, February 1997), p. 2.

12. Graeme C. Moodie, cited in Michael Johnston, "The Political Consequences of Corruption: A Reassessment," *Comparative Politics* 18, no. 4 (1986): 461.

13. Joel Hellman, Geraint Jones, and Daniel Kaufmann, "Seize the State, Seize the Day: State Capture, Corruption, and Influence in Transition," Working Paper no. 2444 (Washington, D.C.: World Bank, September 2000).

14. "Generalized trust" is associated with lower levels of corruption, and "particularized trust"—between individuals—is associated with higher levels of corruption. See Vartuhi Tonoyan, "The Bright and Dark Sides of Trust: Corruption and Entrepreneur-

ship," in *Trust and Entrepreneurship: A West-East Perspective,* edited by H. Hoehmann (Cheltenham: Elgar, 2003).

15. Jack A. Goldstone et al., *State Failure Task Force Report: Phase III Findings* (McLean, Va.: Science Applications International, September 30, 2000).

16. The authors of the World Bank "Governance Matters" dataset identify six dimensions of governance: rule of law, control of corruption, voice and accountability, government effectiveness, regulatory quality, and political stability/absence of violence. They argue that control of corruption and rule of law, taken together, "summarize in broad terms the respect of citizens and the state for the institutions which govern their interactions." See Daniel Kaufmann, Art Kraay, and Massimo Mastruzzi, "Governance Matters IV: Governance Indicators for 1996–2004" (Washington, D.C.: World Bank, May 2005), p. 130.

17. For example, the Secretary-General's report on the rule of law and conflict defines the rule of law to include broader "supremacy of law" and "fairness in the application of law" by all public authorities, but focuses primarily on a specific subset of institutions and processes. "Corruption" is not mentioned in the report. See United Nations, *The Rule of Law and Transitional Justice in Conflict and Post-Conflict Societies: Report of the Secretary-General,* UN Doc. S/2004/616 (August 23, 2004).

18. William F. Fox, *Understanding Administrative Law,* 4th ed. (Newark: Matthew Bender, 2000), p. 6.

19. John Waterbury, cited in Johnston, "The Political Consequences of Corruption," *Comparative Politics.*

20. Particularly influential were Edward Banfield's study of how elites used corruption to bind citizens to them and construct clientelist systems, and Samuel Huntington's argument that corruption facilitated economic exchange under rigid, authoritarian regimes. See Edward Banfield, *The Moral Basis of a Backward Society* (Chicago: Free Press, 1958); Samuel Huntington, *Political Order in Changing Societies* (New Haven: Yale University Press, 1968).

21. See, for example, Susan Rose-Ackerman, *Corruption: A Study in Political Economy* (New York: Academic Press, 1978). See also Robert Klitgaard, *Controlling Corruption* (Berkeley: University of California Press, 1988); Rose-Ackerman, *Corruption and Government.*

22. See, for example, Christopher J. Anderson and Yuliya V. Tverdova, "Corruption, Political Allegiances, and Attitudes Toward Government in Contemporary Democracies," *American Journal of Political Science* 47, no. 1 (January 2003): 91–109.

23. The most important include the World Bank's Control of Corruption measure and Transparency International's Corruption Perceptions Index. Both are aggregate indexes drawn from many of the same sources and are highly correlated. They indirectly measure corruption through perceptions and have significant margins of error. The Transparency International index covers more years, while the World Bank index covers more countries.

24. Cartier-Bresson, "From the State of the Question to the Question of the State," p. 2.

25. Mauro, "Why Worry About Corruption?"

26. Kaufmann, Kraay, and Mastruzzi, "Governance Matters IV."

27. See Susan Rose-Ackerman, "Trust, Honesty, and Corruption: Reflection on the State-Building Process," *Archives of European Sociology* 42, no. 3 (2001): 526–570. See also Eric Uslaner, "Trust and Corruption," in *Global Corruption Report 2005* (London: Pluto, 2005). Eric Uslaner qualified this, finding that trust in institutions has a greater impact on corruption than corruption has on trust.

28. Mitchell Seligson, "The Impact of Corruption on Regime Legitimacy: A Comparative Study of Four Latin American Countries," *Journal of Politics* 64, no. 2 (2002): 408–443; Anderson and Tverdova, "Corruption, Political Allegiances, and Attitudes"; Michael Bratton, Robert Mattes, and E. Gyimah-Boadi, *Public Opinion, Democracy, and Market Reform in Africa* (Cambridge: Cambridge University Press, 2004).

29. Michael Bratton, "Statebuilding and Democratization in Sub-Saharan Africa: Forwards, Backwards, or Together?" Working Paper no. 43, *Afrobarometer,* September 2004, p. 22.

30. See Sanjeev Gupta, Hamid Davoodi, and Rosa Alonso-Terme, "Does Corruption Affect Income Inequality and Poverty?" Working Paper no. 98/76 (Washington, D.C.: International Monetary Fund, 1998). See also Omar Azfar, "Corruption and the Delivery of Health and Education Services," in *Fighting Corruption in Developing Countries: Strategies and Analysis,* edited by Bertram I. Spector (Bloomington: Kumarian, 2005).

31. Mauro, "Why Worry About Corruption?" David Chapman has argued that, within the education sector, "The most direct, and in some ways the most inconsequential, cost of corruption is the waste of the financial resources. . . . The more serious costs are incurred when . . . a generation of children come to believe that personal effort and merit do not count." See David Chapman, "Education," in Spector, *Fighting Corruption in Developing Countries,* p. 68.

32. See Gupta et al, "Does Corruption Affect Income Inequality and Poverty?" and Azfar, "Corruption and the Delivery of Health and Education Services," in Spector, *Fighting Corruption in Developing Countries.*

33. See Ritva Reinikka and Jakob Svensson, "Local Capture: Evidence from a Central Government Transfer Program in Uganda," *Quarterly Journal of Economics* 119, no. 2 (2004): 679–705.

34. United Nations, *A More Secure World: Our Shared Responsibility: Report of the Secretary General's High-level Panel on Threats, Challenges, and Change,* UN Doc. A/59/565 (December 1, 2004), p. 15, http://www.un.org/secureworld.

35. Michael Johnston, "The Political Consequences of Corruption."

36. Paul Reynolds, "The Politics of Earthquakes," *BBC News,* December 30, 2003.

37. Philippe Le Billon, "Buying Peace or Fueling War: The Role of Corruption in Armed Conflicts," *Journal of International Development* 15, no. 4 (2003): 413–426.

38. Michael Johnston, "The Political Consequences of Corruption."

39. Le Billon, "Buying Peace or Fueling War."

40. Summarized in David M. Malone and Heiko Nitzschke, "Economic Agendas of Civil Wars: What We Know, What We Need to Know," Discussion Paper no. 2005/07 (Helsinki: UNU-WIDER, April 2005).

41. William Stanley, *The Protection Racket State: Elite Politics, Military Extortion, and Civil War in El Salvador* (Philadelphia: Temple University Press, 1996).

42. Remarks of Ronald Noble, Plenary Session on "Accountability of Political Leaders," Tenth International Anti-Corruption Conference, Prague, October 8, 2001.

43. US Department of State, *U.S. National Security Strategy* (Washington, D.C., September 2002), http://www.state.gov/r/pa/ei/wh/c7889.htm.

44. In Aceh, the Indonesian government charged the head of a national anticorruption NGO with stealing tsunami emergency aid. The arrest took place one week after publication of the NGO's report on government corruption and manipulation of aid figures.

45. Laila El-Haddad, "Gazans Vote in Municipal Polls," *Al-Jazeera,* January 27, 2005, http://english.aljazeera.net/English/archive/archive?ArchiveId=9170.

46. Kaufmann, Kraay, and Mastruzzi, "Governance Matters IV."

47. David Dollar, Raymond Fisman, and Roberta Gatti, "Are Women Really the 'Fairer' Sex? Corruption and Women in Government" (Washington, D.C.: World Bank, 2001). See also Anand Swamy, Stephen Knack, Young Lee, and Omar Azfar, "Gender and Corruption," *Journal of Development Economics* 64 (2001): 25–55.

48. Torsten Persson, Guido Tabellini, and Francesco Trebbi, "Electoral Rules and Corruption," *Journal of the European Economic Association* 1, no. 4 (2003): 958–989.

49. Daniel Treisman, "The Causes of Corruption: A Cross-National Study," *Journal of Public Economics* 76, no. 3 (2000): 399–457.

50. See Eric Uslaner, "Trust and Corruption," in *Global Corruption Report 2005;* Margit Tavits, "Causes of Corruption: Testing Competing Hypotheses," Working Paper in Politics no. 2005-W3 (Oxford: Nuffield College, March 23, 2005). Margit Tavits draws on social theory to challenge the impact of trust on corruption.

51. Michael Johnston, *Syndromes of Corruption: Wealth, Power, and Democracy* (New York: Cambridge University Press, 2005).

52. Global Competitiveness Report, Executive Opinion Surveys (1997–2002), as discussed in Daniel Kaufmann, "Rethinking Governance: Empirical Lessons Challenge Orthodoxy" (March 2003), pp. 13–14, http://ssrn.com/abstract=386904.

53. "Arafat doesn't allow the building of strong institutions," says Khalil Shikaki, head of the Palestinian Center for Policy and Survey Research in Ramallah. "Instead, he has people who are loyal to him, and the institutions are irrelevant." See Khaled Abu Toameh and Larry Derfner, "A State of Corruption: Palestinians Desire Nationhood, but Is This the Kind of Nation They Want?" *US News and World Report,* July 1, 2002, p. 18.

54. Goldstone et al., *State Failure Task Force Report.*

55. The idea for the first international anticorruption conference came from a number of anticorruption law enforcement agencies, including Hong Kong's Independent Commission Against Corruption, the Inspector General for the District of Columbia, and the New York City Department of Investigation.

56. See the European Anti-Fraud Office website: http://europa.eu.int/scadplus/leg/en/lvb/l34008.htm.

57. Organization of American States, *Inter-American Convention Against Corruption,* http://www.oas.org/juridico/english/treaties/b-58.html.

58. Organization for Economic Cooperation and Development, *Convention on Combating Bribery of Foreign Officials in International Business Transactions,* http://www.oecd.org/document/21/0,2340,en_2649_34859_2017813_1_1_1_1,00.html.

59. Council of Europe, *Criminal Law Convention on Corruption,* http://conventions.coe.int/treaty/en/treaties/html/173.htm; Council of Europe, *Civil Law Convention on Corruption,* http://conventions.coe.int/treaty/en/treaties/html/174.htm.

60. United Nations, *Convention Against Transnational Organized Crime,* http://www.unodc.org/unodc/en/crime_cicp_convention.html.

61. African Union, *Convention on Preventing and Combating Corruption,* http://www.africa-union.org/official_documents/treaties_%20conventions_%20protocols/convention%20on%20combating%20corruption.pdf.

62. United Nations, *United Nations Convention Against Corruption,* http://www.unodc.org/pdf/crime/convention_corruption/signing/convention-e.pdf. The convention's first chapter is on national-level prevention as a signal of its importance.

63. See http://www.unodc.org/unodc/en/crime_signatures_corruption.html.

64. Internationals tried to strike a balance between facilitating prosecution and adhering to standards of due process. One measure they frowned on was illicit enrichment provisions developed in Mexico and elsewhere that shifted the burden of proof onto public officials to prove that their declared assets were acquired legally. Lack of central

registries in developing countries makes it very difficult for states to meet this burden of proof.

65. The UN Centre for International Crime Prevention, Office for Drug Control and Crime Prevention, and the UN Interregional Crime and Justice Research Institute collaborate in the Global Programme Against Corruption.

66. The Hong Kong Commission benefited from incorporation of police officers from the United Kingdom, dedicated and very well-paid staff, a strong legal framework, and a mandate that included not only investigation of cases but also efforts to prevent corruption through public education and recommendations for administrative reforms. For a discussion of experiences with anticorruption commissions, see Chapter 11, "Independent Anti-Corruption Agencies," in Jeremy Pope, *Confronting Corruption: The Elements of a National Integrity System* (Berlin: Transparency International, 2000).

67. World Bank, *Pakistan: A Framework for Civil Service Reform in Pakistan,* vol. 1 (Washington, D.C., December 15, 1998), p. 25.

68. Opening Address by the President of World Bank Group, James D. Wolfensohn, *Summary Proceedings of the Fifty-First Annual Meeting of the Board of Governors* (Washington, D.C.: IMF), October 1–3, 1996.

69. The US, UK, Dutch, and Norwegian aid agencies were particularly active. The Utstein Group, including the United Kingdom, the Netherlands, Norway, and Germany, collaborates on anticorruption issues and maintains an extensive online resource; see the website of the U4 Anti-Corruption Resource Centre: http://www.u4.no.

70. However, some efforts might have been more effective if they had been linked to specific actions and reforms or less donor-driven. See Martin Tisné and Daniel Smilov, "From the Ground Up: Assessing the Record of Anticorruption Assistance in Southeastern Europe," CPS Policy Studies Series (Budapest: Central European University, July 2004).

71. Reporting on government corruption is one of the most frequent reasons cited for the murder or imprisonment of journalists. See Committee to Protect Journalists, *Attacks on the Press in 2004* (New York), March 14, 2005, http://www.cpj.org/attacks04/pages/attacks04index.html.

72. Transparency International, *The Integrity Pact: The Concept, the Model and the Present Applications* (Berlin, December 2002).

73. International Budget Project, *A Taste of Success: Examples of the Budget Work of NGOs* (Washington, D.C., October 2000).

74. A "Citizen Report Card Learning Toolkit" is available at http://www.citizenreportcard.com.

75. See http://www.transparency.org/about_ti/index.html.

76. Moíses Naím, "The Corruption Eruption," *Brown Journal of World Affairs* 2 (1995): p. 245.

77. David Ignatius, "Crusaders Against Corruption," *Washington Post,* March 4, 2001, p. B07.

78. For a discussion of problems in the Albania experience, see World Bank, *Anti-Corruption in Transition: A Contribution to the Policy Debate* (Washington, D.C., November 2000), p. 65.

79. Less successful efforts were launched under Leonid Kuchma in Ukraine, Hun Sen in Cambodia, Eduard Shevardnadze in Georgia, and Alfonso Portillo in Guatemala.

80. See, for example, OECD Development Co-operation Directorate, "Synthesis of Lessons Learned of Donor Practices in Fighting Corruption," DCD/DAC/GOVNET(2003)1 (Paris, June 23, 2003), http://www.oecd.org/dataoecd/14/44/19936969.pdf.

81. See, for example, World Bank, *Civil Service Reform: A Review of World Bank Assistance,* Report no. 19599 (Washington, D.C.: World Bank, Operations Evaluation Department, 1999).

82. Rafael Di Tella and Ernesto Schargrodsky, "The Role of Wages and Auditing During a Crackdown on Corruption in the City of Buenos Aires," *Journal of Law and Economics* 46, no. 1 (April 2003): p. 269.

83. Ritva Reinikka and Jakob Svensson, "Survey Techniques to Measure and Explain Corruption," World Bank, April 15, 2003, p. 8, http://siteresources.worldbank .org/INTPEAM/Resources/PETS2.pdf.

84. Mary Noel Pepys, "Corruption in the Justice System, Sectoral Perspectives on Corruption," in *Pervasive Corruption: Strategies for Prevention in Developing and Transitional Countries,* edited by Bertram Spector (Bloomfield: Kumarian, 2004).

85. Linn Hammergren, "Do Judicial Councils Further Judicial Reform? Lessons from Latin America," Democracy and Rule of Law Project, Rule of Law Series no. 28 (Washington, D.C.: Carnegie Endowment for International Peace, 2002).

86. It became clear that the Russian Duma had become a magnet for organized crime figures precisely because of the immunity it offered for prior crimes. Several Honduran mayors facing corruption charges acquired immunity once their parties placed them on "safe" slates in the next legislative elections.

87. Gray Phombeah, "Corruption Haunts Kenya's Leader," *BBC News,* February 23, 2005.

88. Some long-term strategies to address state capture may include economic diversification, competition and antitrust, and political finance reforms. See World Bank, *Anti-Corruption in Transition.* Short-term measures might include internationally monitored procurements and privatizations, disclosure of contract terms, and management contracts for utilities.

89. Jorge Martinez-Vazquez, "Corruption, Fiscal Policy, and Fiscal Management" (Washington, D.C.: US Agency for International Development, 2004).

90. Joel Hellman, Geraint Jones, and Daniel Kaufmann, "Far From Home: Do Foreign Investors Import Higher Standards of Governance in Transition Economies?" draft (August 2002).

91. See Craig Burnside and David Dollar, "Aid, Policies, and Growth," *American Economic Review* 90, no. 4 (September 2000): 847–868; William Easterly, Ross Levine, and David Roodman, "Aid, Policies, and Growth: Comment," *American Economic Review* 94, no. 3 (June 2004): 774–780.

92. "US Planning to Keep Corrupt Latin American Officials Out," *Miami Herald,* March 10, 2002, p. 8A.

93. Transparency International, *Global Corruption Report 2004* (London: Pluto, 2004).

94. US Agency for International Development, *Money in Politics Handbook: A Guide to Increasing Transparency in Emerging Democracies* (Washington, D.C., 2003). See also International Institute for Democracy and Electoral Assistance, *Handbook on Funding of Political Parties and Electoral Campaigns* (Stockholm, 2003); Transparency International, *Global Corruption Report 2004.*

95. Examples include the Kimberly Process, on diamonds, and the Wolfsberg Principles, on money laundering.

96. Transparency International, *Bribe Payers Index 2002,* May 14, 2002, http:// www.transparency.org/policy_research/surveys_indices/bpi. Individual reports on Halliburton and other contracting firms focus efforts on the firm level rather than on industrywide proposals to change the rules of the game and its players. See Transparency In-

ternational, *Global Corruption Report 2004,* for a focus on corruption in the construction industry.

97. Evaluating the impact of these measures on the behavior of OECD firms is very difficult. Prosecutions under the Foreign Corrupt Practices Act, long dormant, have recently been stepped up. The first cases of prosecutions under the OECD Anti-Bribery Convention are just now reaching the courts in Europe and elsewhere. Some argue that the Foreign Corrupt Practices Act significantly changed the behavior of US firms overseas, but others claim US firms simply shifted to widespread use of "brokers" to arrange and pay bribes on their behalf. Transparency International's 2002 Bribe Payers Index ranked US firms as having a higher "propensity to bribe" compared to firms in Belgium, Spain, and France. US experts strongly disputed the 2002 index, claiming it did not correct for the frequency of contact with the more numerous US firms. See Transparency International, *Bribe Payers Index 2002.*

98. See, for example, *Confronting Corruption;* OSCE, *Best Practices in Combating Corruption* (Vienna: Office for the Co-ordinator for Economic and Environmental Activities, 2004); UN Office on Drugs and Crime, *The UN Anti-Corruption Toolkit* (Vienna, September 2004).

99. See, for example, OECD Development Co-operation Directorate, "Synthesis of Lessons Learned of Donor Practices in Fighting Corruption," DCD/DAC/GOVNET(2003)1 (Paris, June 23, 2003); World Bank, *Reforming Public Institutions and Strengthening Governance: A World Bank Strategy—Implementation Update* (Washington, D.C., April 2002); US Agency for International Development, *Field Perspectives: A Report on the Field Mission Anti-Corruption Survey* (Washington, D.C., 2003).

100. Franklin Steves and Alan Rousso, "Anti-Corruption Programmes in Post-Communist Transition Countries and Changes in the Business Environment, 1999–2002," Working Paper no. 85 (London: European Bank for Reconstruction and Development, December 2003).

101. Ivan Krastev, *Shifting Obsessions: Three Essays on the Politics of Anti-Corruption* (New York: Central European University Press, 2004).

102. Exceptions are states emerging from independence, and liberation movements like in East Timor and Eritrea, which often enjoy high legitimacy.

103. Iraq is a notable exception; it was considered to be an illegitimate but relatively strong state until being forcibly overthrown.

104. See Malone and Nitzschke, "Economic Agendas in Civil Wars," for recent discussion.

105. In Sierra Leone and Liberia, the phenomenon of "sobels" emerged. Soldiers during the day worked with rebels at night to extort and steal—a classic example of the ability of corruption to encourage some groups to work "cooperatively," but to the clear detriment of the rest of society.

106. Marina Ottaway describes how the postconflict reconstruction model has expanded significantly to encompass new goals, activities, and international partners, overwhelming the capacity of local counterparts to absorb or monitor—let alone direct—assistance. See Marina Ottaway, "The Post-War 'Democratic Reconstruction Model': Why It Can't Work," paper presented to the US Institute of Peace, Washington, D.C., 2002.

107. "Port Boost for Peace," *BBC News,* April 26, 2005, http://news.bbc.co.uk/2/hi/africa/4485545.stm.

108. For background on establishment of this initiative, see Renata Dwan and Laura Bailey, "Liberia's Governance and Economic Management Assistance Pro-

gramme (GEMAP): A Joint Review by the Peacekeeping Operations' Peacekeeping Best Practices Section and the World Bank's Fragile States Group," May 2006.

109. International Crisis Group, *Liberia and Sierra Leone: Rebuilding Failed States,* Africa Report no. 87 (Brussels, December 8, 2004).

110. Author interview with an anonymous Afghan doctor and aid worker, Kabul, June 2004.

111. Barnett R. Rubin, "Road to Ruin: Afghanistan's Booming Opium Industry" (New York: Center for International Cooperation, October 2004), p. 1, http://www.cic.nyu.edu/archive/pdf/RoadtoRuin.pdf.

112. By comparison, the drug trade is less than 5 percent of formal gross domestic product in Colombia and Bolivia. Barnett Rubin recommends several measures, including targeted sanctions against warlords/traffickers, greater security and reconstruction aid, international cooperation in Afghan counternarcotics efforts, support for improved rule of law, and less emphasis on crop eradication. See Rubin, "Road to Ruin."

113. International Crisis Group. *The Congo's Transition Is Failing: Crisis in the Kivus,* Africa Report no. 91 (Brussels, March 30, 2005), p. ii.

114. Michael Brown, Phillipe Ngwala, Albert Songo, and Leonard Wande, "Combating Low-Level Corruption on Waterways in the Democratic Republic of Congo: Approaches from Bandundu and Equateur Provinces," Public Law Research Paper no. 116 (Washington, D.C.: George Washington University Law School, October 1, 2004).

115. Edward B. Rackley, "Predatory Governance in the DRC: Civilian Impact and Humanitarian Response," *Humanitarian Exchange Magazine,* no. 29 (London: Humanitarian Practice Network), March 2005, http://www.odihpn.org/report.asp?id=2653.

116. Brown et al., "Combating Low-Level Corruption."

117. Ibid.

118. Ibid, p. 14.

119. Stephen Krasner, "Shared Sovereignty," *Journal of Democracy* 16, no. 1 (2005): 69–83.

120. "Pakistan Success Fee Admitted," *Financial Times,* December 17, 1997.

121. Michael Hubbard, "Changing Customs: Lessons from Mozambique," presentation to the Christian Michelsen Institute, Bergen, Norway, February 17, 2005.

122. Wesley Clark, presentation to the US Institute of Peace, Washington, D.C., March 23, 2005. Video available at http://www.usip.org/events/2005/0323_reconstructing.html.

11

Counterterrorism and the Rule of Law

Reyko Huang

The current flurry of activity within the United Nations on the issue of terrorism is a recent phenomenon, instigated by the attacks on the United States on September 11, 2001, and goaded on by related events of the ensuing years. The UN's member states did successfully conclude a dozen international conventions on terrorism over the preceding decades; yet, confounded by the complexity of the problem and the politics of dealing with it, member states remained unable to forge a coherent strategy or even agree on a common definition of terrorism. The tragedy of September 11 was thus as much a wake-up call to the United Nations as it was for the United States. With acts of terrorism surging in many parts of the world and often enmeshed in local and regional conflict, the United Nations could not eschew the problem as irrelevant to its operational work on international peace and security.

The context in which this awakening occurred is significant. For a decade prior, the United Nations had been becoming involved in an increasing number of peace operations following the outbreak of intrastate conflicts of the post–Cold War era. Paralleling these efforts in the field were major developments at headquarters on the normative, institutional, and policy approaches to conflict management that reflected the UN's growing recognition of the links between security, development, and human rights.[1] Emphasis on the rule of law, justice, and accountability emerged as part of this post–Cold War discourse on peace and security. The 2000 Brahimi Report, which reviewed UN peace operations, and the 2004 report of the Secretary-General on the rule of law and transitional justice, are milestones in this trajectory. By September 2001, the United Nations had made notable progress not only in conceptualizing and operationalizing conflict management and postconflict peacebuilding, but also in dissecting and better understanding their component parts—including security, development, human rights, and the rule of law, the intersections of which have become highly relevant in the post–September 11 era.

This chapter discusses post–September 11 counterterrorism efforts led primarily by the United Nations but also with mention of other international bodies.[2] Following a brief discussion of the links between counterterrorism and the rule of law, it provides an overview of international approaches to counterterrorism over the past few decades. The chapter then examines and analyzes post–September 11 initiatives, focusing particularly on the interplay between international counterterrorism agendas and the domestic priorities of developing countries. I argue that the United Nations has made important achievements in laying the basis for an international normative and legal framework for counterterrorism. However, implementation of counterterrorism policies has been problematic and, arguably, potentially deleterious, as many developing countries have viewed such initiatives as constituting yet another "Western agenda" that has little to do with their actual domestic concerns. I argue for more cautious approaches that would make better use of the UN's track record in dealing with the multiple facets—political, economic, and social—of peace and security. Moreover, such approaches should ensure that competing domestic and international agendas do not override possibilities for progress on both fronts.

Terrorism and the Rule of Law

Before detailing international counterterrorism efforts, a brief discussion on why counterterrorism should be examined in conjunction with the rule of law is in order. How are they conceptually related, and why is it important to recognize such relationships? Some answers can be gleaned by noting the disconnect between the rhetoric and practice of counterterrorism.

The rhetoric since September 11 has emphasized the positive relationship between counterterrorism and the rule of law. The prevailing argument has been that bolstering the institutions needed for law and order would stymie potential terrorist activity and weaken terrorist organizations and networks. The mobilization of law enforcement agencies across the globe as the foremost bulwark against terrorism demonstrates the (mostly Western) consensus that strengthening rule of law institutions—in particular the police and the criminal justice system—is vital for successful counterterrorism. Beyond law enforcement, this law and order argument has also been advanced by security and development institutions and experts alike, through claims that efforts aimed at statebuilding and "good governance" would help prevent terrorism (just as they have made the contrary claim—that, for instance, it was the failure to strengthen the Afghan state after the anti-Soviet war of the 1980s that led to the rise of the Taliban).[3] As shown below, the United Nations has also focused on a rule of law approach to counterterrorism, both through the work of the Security Council's Counter-Terrorism Committee (CTC) and Counter-Terrorism Executive Directorate (CTED) to strengthen the rule of law domestically within member states, and through the introduction of a series of conventions against acts of terrorism aimed at strengthening, so to speak, the international rule of law.

In practice, the law enforcement approach, even as it aimed to enforce adherence to the law, has in most cases expanded law enforcement and intelligence capabilities without ensuring sufficient safeguards to prevent abuse.[4] Thus, while the objective was to make the environment more difficult for terrorists to operate in, the concomitant result was that the environment became one in which it was easier for state officials to disregard the rule of law in the process. In the United States, new security measures introduced after the attacks of September 11, such as the detention of over 1,200 people in late 2001 mostly on the basis of breaches of immigration law, many without due process protections, has been labeled by critics as a "detachment from the rule of law as a whole."[5] In the Israeli-Palestinian conflict, as in the Sri Lankan civil war, acts described as terrorism and counterterrorism have sometimes been indistinguishable—an indication that the rule of law is in serious peril. As a number of scholars and observers have argued, terrorism can be effectively combated within the means provided under law; international law recognizes and accommodates states' need to restrict certain rights in times of public emergency (though at the same time, it seeks to limit the extent of such derogations while specifying certain rights as nonderogable).[6] Perhaps more important, these scholars and experts argue that disregard for such fundamental principles as civil liberties and the rule of law are likely to be at best ineffective and at worst detrimental to counterterrorism in the long term, as they may fuel further resentment against the government and increase the popularity of extremist groups.[7]

In short, the relationship between the rule of law and counterterrorism has been a complex one. The rule of law, primarily through strengthened law enforcement, is said to be necessary for counterterrorism, and yet counterterrorism activities have themselves been criticized for undermining the rule of law and hurting efforts to improve national and international security.

Overview of International Counterterrorism

Terrorism had been an issue on the international agenda long before September 11, 2001. During the Cold War decades, terrorist attacks increased in frequency, scope, complexity, and visibility, while a number of terrorist organizations took on an increasingly transnational nature.[8] However, international organizations' approaches to combating terrorism remained largely piecemeal and reactive, with new initiatives trailing behind the occurrence of major terrorist attacks.

The United Nations

Owing primarily to the state of global politics, until the late 1990s the United Nations hesitated to take an active stance on the question of terrorism. For decades the Security Council remained deadlocked in its efforts to come to an agreement on what constituted terrorism and how to respond to its manifestations. This problem was acutely demonstrated two years after the Security Council adopted its first resolution on terrorism, when a string of hijackings, bombings, and hostage-taking culminated in the killing of Israeli athletes at the Munich Olympics in 1972. With draft resolutions failing to even mention terrorism or the Munich massacre, in the end the Council was unable to articulate a satisfactory response despite days of internal wrangling.[9] Debates over the next decade were largely stagnant, the major sticking point being disagreements over what constituted terrorism as opposed to legitimate armed struggle. Such stonewalling led terrorism scholar Paul Wilkinson to declare in 1986 that "the United Nations has proved a broken reed on the whole subject of terrorism. It has proved as useless in countering terrorism as the League of Nations before it."[10] That these developments were taking place within the context of the Cold War, and particularly over issues related to the Middle East, explains a large part of the underlying tensions within the United Nations, and is characteristic of the broader impasse that defined much of the organization's efforts during those decades.

The end of the Cold War introduced opportunities for more decisive action. In 1992 the Security Council invoked Chapter VII of the UN Charter to impose targeted sanctions on Libya,[11] marking the first time that the Council used its coercive powers under Chapter VII against a state accused of sponsoring terrorism. The Council imposed sanctions based on Chapter VII in two other situations during the 1990s, the first against Sudan in 1996 in response to Khartoum's failure to turn over suspects of an assassination attempt against the Egyptian president,[12] and the second in 1999 against the Taliban in Afghanistan.[13] On the general issue of terrorism, in 1999 the Security Council recognized acts of terrorism as a threat to international peace and security and called on member states to enhance cooperative measures to deny terrorists safe havens and suppress their financing.[14] It should be mentioned that Russia and the United States were lead advocates of these Security Council measures. While major governments around the world also increasingly recognized the need for a coordinated response to terrorism, Libya's vocal rejection of the UN's sanctions as illegitimate was heard and shared by a number of developing countries, especially those in the Arab world.[15]

During the Security Council's stalemate years, it was up to the General Assembly, particularly (and tellingly) the Sixth Committee—the arm of the Assembly that deals with legal issues—to take more proactive measures on terrorism.[16] In the aftermath of the Munich killings, for instance, it was on the General Assembly that then–Secretary-General Kurt Waldheim called to issue a statement after debates in the Security Council foundered.[17] The General Assembly also passed a series of resolutions in the 1980s and 1990s condemning acts of terrorism as criminal and urging member states to take measures to prevent and combat the problem.[18]

Perhaps the most significant work of the General Assembly, together with specialized agencies of the United Nations and other international organizations, was the successful conclusion of twelve international conventions that composed the global counterterrorism framework before September 2001. While the Assembly remained unable to define terrorism, these instruments criminalized specific *acts* of terror, usually with deliberate omission of the undefined term. The aim of this growing agglomeration of conventions was to strengthen the basis for a norm of universal jurisdiction over acts of terrorism. Each convention brought additional terrorist crimes under this legal regime. Beginning with the 1963 Convention on Offenses and Certain Other Acts Committed on Board Aircraft, the conventions deal with seizure of aircraft, civil aviation, protection of diplomats, hostage-taking, protection of nuclear material, maritime navigation, plastic explosives, bombings, and terrorism financing, among other issues.[19] Significantly, only the last two conventions prior to September 11 (on terrorist bombings and financing of terrorism) actually refer to "terrorism" in their titles. The Ad Hoc Committee on Terrorism, established by the General Assembly in 1996, was instrumental to the success of these two conventions.[20]

However, the momentum of the Ad Hoc Committee stalled when it moved on to drafting a comprehensive convention on international terrorism—an initiative, introduced by India, that sought to provide a comprehensive legal regime prohibiting all forms of terrorist activity. Member states mainly disagreed over three issues: the legal definition of terrorism; the relationship of the comprehensive convention to the existing twelve antiterrorism treaties and to any such future treaties; and the convention's treatment of the right to self-determination and to struggles against foreign occupation.[21]

Disagreement over the definition of terrorism in fact has been, and still remains, an intractable problem that has impeded progress in strengthening the international legal framework against it. For some, member states' inability to draw a consensus on this issue reflects not only the complexity of dealing with terrorism, but also the diversity of political and moral positions espoused. Others view the stalemate as a deliberate strategy by those member states that do not wish to have the comprehensive convention see the light of day. With persisting differences of opinion on the scope of the draft convention, prolonging the quagmire over the definition, as some saw it, was a convenient way for certain member states to avoid the convention idea altogether.

Earlier General Assembly resolutions reflect the degree of ambivalence and confusion over these predicaments. For example, Resolution 3034 (1972) expressed "deep concern over increasing acts of violence" and urged "States to devote their immediate attention to finding just and peaceful solutions to the underlying causes which give rise to such acts of violence." However, the resolution went on to reaffirm "the inalienable right to self-determination and independence of all peoples under colonial and racist regimes and other forms of alien domination and upholds the legitimacy of their struggle, in particular the struggle of national liberation movements."[22] The General Assembly adopted similar resolutions both exhorting states to find the causes of (terrorist) violence and reaffirming the right to self-determination in four subsequent instances, possibly suggesting that the resort to terrorism may be justified in the struggle for self-determination.[23]

Despite the obstacles created by these discords over the definition, UN counterterrorism efforts prior to September 11 made headway in forging a nascent international norm against acts of terrorism. Though limited in many ways, collectively the resolutions and international conventions were beginning to allow counterterrorism to be rooted in international law.[24] Aside from the development of international norms, however, the United Nations as a forum played a reluctant role in counterterrorism prior to September 11. It drew no consensus on the use of violence for self-determination struggles, left terrorism undefined, appeared to prove itself ill-suited to deal with nonstate actors, and was, in spite of itself, generally loath to confront states that harbored terrorists.

Other International Bodies

Partly owing to the UN's limited involvement, other international organizations sought their own modes of cooperation against terrorism. In 1971, the Organization of American States became the first regional body to respond to the terrorist threat with a convention to prevent and punish acts of terrorism.[25] The Council of Europe followed with its 1977 European Convention on the Suppression of Terrorism, though even within Western Europe accession of all states proved difficult to come by.[26] The South Asian Association for Regional Cooperation, however, succeeded in getting all seven members of the association to become parties to its 1987 Regional Convention on Suppression of Terrorism. In addition to these, four other regional instruments were established prior to September 2001—by the League of Arab States, the Commonwealth of Independent States, the Organization of the Islamic Conference, and the Organization of African Unity.[27]

Terrorism was also discussed at multilateral economic summits and within Western institutions such as the North Atlantic Treaty Organization, as well as on a bilateral level.[28] UN resolutions and international conventions against terrorist acts no doubt influenced these regional efforts. However, many terrorism experts and policymakers felt that, at least until the end of the Cold War, UN responses to terrorism had minimal impact and that the organization generally was not best placed to take a lead in counterterrorism.[29]

International Counterterrorism Strategies and Approaches Since September 11

United Nations

In a definitive break with their characteristic dissension over the issue of terrorism, UN member states demonstrated a swift and decisive response to the events of September 11, 2001. On September 12 the Security Council unanimously adopted Resolution 1368, which recognized the "inherent right of individual or collective self-defense in accordance with the Charter," condemned the terrorist attacks, and expressed readiness "to take all steps necessary" in response.[30]

On September 28 the Security Council unanimously adopted Resolution 1373, which invoked Chapter VII of the Charter to impose sweeping legal obligations on member states. In clear contrast to the twelve international conventions that bound only state parties, this resolution introduced binding obligations on all member states to, among other things, prevent, suppress, and criminalize the financing of terrorism; freeze terrorists' financial assets; refrain from supporting or providing safe havens to terrorists; and cooperate with other governments in sharing information and prosecuting criminals.[31] As noted by the Policy Working Group on the United Nations and Terrorism, the Security Council "for the first time imposed measures not against a State, its leaders, nationals or commodities, but against acts of terrorism throughout the world and the terrorists themselves" in what became "one of the most expansive resolutions in the history of the Council."[32]

Demonstrating the Council's resolve to ensure member states' compliance, Resolution 1373 went further to establish what has come to be called the Counter-Terrorism Committee to monitor the implementation of the resolution. The CTC, consisting of all fifteen members of the Security Council, is now widely regarded as the main operational arm of UN efforts against terrorism.

In the words of its first chairman, Jeremy Greenstock, the CTC is aimed at "upgrading the capacity of each nation's legislation and executive machinery to fight terrorism."[33] Similar to UN sanctions regimes, which are usually accompanied by monitoring committees, every member state is required to report regularly to the CTC on the steps taken to implement the far-reaching obligations of Resolution 1373. In addition, the CTC is to be "proactive, transparent, cooperative and even-handed in this task,"[34] meaning that the committee's monitoring process, unlike sanctions, would involve no coercion or censure on states that fail to meet its standards. Furthermore, rather than targeting a particular group, area, or state as a sanction would, the scope of Resolution 1373 is broader and does not specify such targets. Some have pointed out that it is such features as these that have helped make the CTC acceptable to the UN's broad membership—that the resolution "has no teeth," and thus no real obligations.

Since numerous observations have been made on the CTC since its inception, it suffices to comment on its key achievements and limitations to date. In the remarkable atmosphere of international cooperation and resolve to combat the terrorist threat in the immediate weeks and months after September 11, UN member states' response to the requirements of Resolution 1373 was as unprecedented as the resolution itself. In the first round of required reporting, all

191 member states submitted reports to the CTC—the greatest compliance ever achieved by a Security Council mandate.[35] After the committee responded with requests of additional information or clarification, it received at least 161 reports in the second round.[36]

However, by the fourth round only 26 states were submitting reports. With each report followed by requests for further information from the CTC, representatives of some developing countries began to express a "reporting fatigue."[37] By the end of 2003, there was general consensus within the CTC that the committee needed a "revitalization."[38] The reformed CTC would be more engaged in assessing states' needs and improving coordination among international, regional, and subregional organizations in order to facilitate the delivery of technical assistance to countries that requested it. In March 2004 the Security Council thus created the Counter-Terrorism Executive Directorate as a special political mission,[39] expanding the CTC's staffing to boost its capacity to respond to states seeking to fulfill their counterterrorism requirements. Spain's ambassador to the United States, Javier Rupérez, became the first CTED executive director in June 2004, and subsequently met with a number of international organizations to enhance cooperation. A key feature of this "second phase" of the CTC was the country visits led by the CTED, aimed at assessing how member states were actually implementing Resolution 1373—a response to the limited utility of written reports.[40]

To sum, from its reserved and restrained efforts focused on international norm building, the United Nations has since September 2001 demonstrated full recognition of the need to play a greater and more urgent role in combating terrorism. This has been manifested in the form of a new emphasis on building state capacity to prevent and suppress acts of terrorism. Meanwhile, the United Nations has continued to strengthen the norm-building front through persistent antiterrorism rhetoric. Along with the Security Council, for instance, the General Assembly and the Secretary-General have also vocally condemned terrorism and exhorted states to cooperate in the fight against it. Whether they represented a sufficient response from the world body, or were effective in contributing to counterterrorism, will be reserved for the discussion below.

Sufficiency and effectiveness aside, by 2004 it was clear that the environment and enthusiasm for collective counterterrorism had become a far cry from what it had been in the wake of the September 11 attacks. Despite the CTC's "revitalization" and a bold Security Council resolution in October stating that "criminal acts [that constitute acts of terrorism] are under no circumstances justifiable,"[41] the global schism created by the US invasion of Iraq and the conflation of that war with the "war on terror" seemed to overshadow any such efforts by the United Nations.

It was at such a time that the Secretary-General's High-Level Panel on Threats, Challenges, and Change proposed a definition of terrorism as part of its December 2004 report on the UN's future role in collective security. The panel's report defined terrorism as

> any action, in addition to actions already specified by the existing conventions on aspects of terrorism, the Geneva Conventions and Security Council resolution 1566 (2004), that is intended to cause death or serious bodily harm to civilians or non-combatants, when the purpose of such an act, by its nature or context, is to intimidate a population, or to compel a Government or an international organization to do or to abstain from doing any act.[42]

The report also noted that states' use of armed forces against civilians is already governed by international law and therefore does not need to be incorporated into the definition.

The Secretary-General readily endorsed the High-Level Panel's definition in his report of March 2005, at the same time urging member states to conclude a comprehensive convention on terrorism before the historic UN summit in September 2005.[43] Momentum seemed to be gaining: in April 2005 the General Assembly adopted the Nuclear Terrorism Convention after seven years of negotiation, making it the first antiterrorism convention to be adopted after the September 11 attacks and bringing to thirteen the number of conventions against terrorism.[44]

Despite these developments, the issue remained highly politicized and divisive throughout the months leading up to the summit. At the meeting of the Ad Hoc Committee on Terrorism in March–April 2005, member states expressed at best only lukewarm appreciation for the High-Level Panel's definition, with many claiming that it simply reignited controversy over issues that had already been resolved by years of negotiation by the Ad Hoc Committee.[45] The deliberate focus on the definition also raises questions regarding the overall utility of an international definition vis-à-vis the threat of terrorism. For example, while strengthening the antiterrorism framework remains an important task for the United Nations, the debate over the definition risks detracting attention from efforts to actualize the "global strategy for fighting terrorism" that the Secretary-General introduced in March 2005. This "comprehensive approach" consists of five principles (known as the "five Ds"): "first, to dissuade disaffected groups from choosing terrorism as a tactic . . . ; second, to deny terrorists the means to carry out their attacks; third, to deter States from supporting terrorists; fourth, to develop State capacity to prevent terrorism; and fifth, to defend human rights in the struggle against terrorism."[46]

The outcomes of the much anticipated September 2005 World Summit, so far as it concerned the issue of terrorism, disappointed many, surprised no one, and remained open-ended. Member states failed to endorse the definition of terrorism put forth by the High-Level Panel and the Secretary-General, not least due to the continued insistence by some states that it should exclude "legitimate" struggles for liberation and self-determination. Member states did, however, issue a clear, unqualified condemnation of terrorism "in all its forms and manifestations, committed by whomever, wherever and for whatever purpose."[47] They also agreed to work toward a comprehensive convention against terrorism within a year.[48] With the ongoing conflict in the Middle East and its political implications for Islamic countries, however, drawing a consensus remains an immense challenge.

Brief mention should be made of the counterterrorism initiatives of other bodies of the United Nations. Important among these is the close collaboration of the CTC with the UN Office on Drugs and Crime (UNODC) in strengthening states' legislative capacities against terrorism.[49] While the CTC/CTED comments on states' reports on the implementation of Resolution 1373 and facilitates the provision of technical assistance, the UNODC delivers such assistance by reviewing domestic legislation and advising on the drafting of new laws, providing training on the new legislation, and providing assistance on the implementation of new legislation.[50] At the time of this writing, the UNODC has so far provided legislative assistance to over fifty countries and trained over 600 lawmakers, law enforcement officials, and other officials on the requirements of Resolution 1373.[51]

Although successive UN High Commissioners for Human Rights have spoken up on the importance of protecting human rights while fighting terrorism, as an institution the Office of the High Commissioner for Human Rights (OHCHR) has so far assumed a restrained role, in particular compared to the CTC and the UNODC. It "examines" the human rights implications of counterterrorism, "makes general recommendations" on the issue, and assists states on request in this general area.[52] In mid-2005 the Commission on Human Rights appointed a "special rapporteur on the protection and promotion of human rights while countering terrorism" to make recommendations, promote best practices and the exchange of information within the UN system, and provide technical assistance and advisory services on the protection of human rights in counterterrorism.[53]

Other International Bodies

In response to the strong emphasis Resolution 1373 placed on curbing terrorist financing, the Organization for Economic Cooperation and Development (OECD), through its Financial Action Task Force (FATF), an international organization that had until then been devoted to anti–money laundering, added to its mandate an anti–terrorist financing component in October 2001. The result was the issuing of new standards on combating the financing of terrorism, known as the eight "special recommendations," aimed at denying terrorists access to the international financial system. Members of the FATF, comprising over thirty states, including all of the industrialized countries, are required to make self-assessments of their implementation of the eight recommendations.[54] The FATF works in close collaboration with institutions such as the

World Bank and the International Monetary Fund to deliver technical assistance to countries seeking to strengthen financial and regulatory frameworks against terrorist financing.

For their part, regional organizations each renewed their commitment to fighting terrorism in their various declarations, action plans, and frameworks after the September 11 attacks. While they express support for the international legal counterterrorism regime established by the United Nations and share more similarities than differences in condemning terrorist acts and urging states to take action, they also include predictable regional nuances. For example, at a meeting of the Association of Southeast Asian Nations (ASEAN) on terrorism in May 2002, delegates did not fail to recognize "that the sovereignty, territorial integrity and domestic laws of each ASEAN member country shall be respected and upheld in undertaking the fight against terrorism"— the expected line on national sovereignty.[55] The Organization of the Islamic Conference has continued to emphasize that its Convention on Combating International Terrorism defines terrorism in a way that safeguards the rights of people who struggle against foreign occupation.[56]

The traditional "regional nuance" of the Organization for Security Cooperation in Europe (OSCE) is noteworthy in its contrast to the focus on legal codification, domestic legislative capacity building, and international norm building that lie at the heart of all of the above initiatives. Indicative of its unique approach, in the OSCE the Coordinator on Anti-Terrorism is situated within the Office for Democratic Institutions and Human Rights. As with other regional organizations, member states reaffirmed their commitment to implement the obligations of Security Council Resolution 1373; at the same time, states also reaffirmed that "respect for human rights and fundamental freedoms, democracy and the rule of law is at the core of the OSCE's comprehensive concept of security" in what the organization calls its "human dimension commitments."[57] In addition to providing member states with legislative technical assistance to comply with Resolution 1373, it monitors "counter-terrorism practice to ensure . . . conformity of anti-terrorism measures with international law."[58] The OSCE has thus adopted a two-pronged approach, one focusing on building states' capacities, much as other organizations have done, and the other on "promoting 'co-operative security' through democracy, the rule of law, good governance and protection of human rights."[59]

Assessment and Evaluation

Taking a step back from the minutiae of international counterterrorism programs, discourses, and debates, what has been the overall effect of these initiatives, taking into account the context of the US-led "war on terror"? This section examines the impact on state behavior of the international normative framework, rhetoric, and activities on counterterrorism, highlights the main achievements as well as deficiencies of current international approaches to counterterrorism, and then pits current international counterterrorism activities against three programmatic issues that are now widely regarded as critical for successful international efforts to strengthen the rule of law:[60] the participation of regional, national, and local partners in decisionmaking; the need to build local and national capacity; and coordination among the actors involved.

Achievements and Deficiencies

International counterterrorism led by the United Nations has achieved important progress on several fronts. First, through successive conventions, resolutions, and declarations, the United Nations and regional organizations have laid out a solid international legal and normative framework against terrorism. With the criminalization of acts of terrorism and the necessity of a coordinated global response codified in international law, it has become difficult for any group or state to justify terrorist acts on any grounds.

Second, the international efforts have tightened regulatory mechanisms—at least in the formal sector—to make terrorist activity more difficult. UN and regional efforts, together with state policies, have promoted more rigorous law enforcement, border security, and intelligence, as well as tighter regulation of flows of money and people. In numerous reported instances since September 2001, these efforts helped enable counterterrorism operations to successfully foil terrorist plots, raid terrorist cells, gather valuable intelligence, and arrest and prosecute terrorist suspects.

Third, recognizing that only states are capable of such tactical operations, international and regional organizations have placed the focus squarely on building the capacity of member states to fight their own fight against terrorism. For the United Nations, because it is ill equipped to deal with nonstate actors and cannot be directly involved in counterterrorism "on the ground," building states' capacities to fight and suppress terrorism through the CTC and its institutional partners was a much needed initiative.

Nevertheless, there remain significant deficiencies in the international approach, which become particularly palpable when placed in the contextual reality of the US-led "war on terror." While measuring success in combating terrorism continues to baffle those who attempt to do so, examining states' responses to the call to join the fight against terrorism provides some sense of the reach and effectiveness of international conventions, norms, discourses, and programs. The findings below are neither new nor comprehensive, but help uncover some major limitations of the UN approach thus far.

Overall, counterterrorism efforts since September 11 have had readily perceivable negative impacts on the security situation of many countries and regions. First, responding to post–September 11 "obligations," a number of states turned to their internal problems and newly branded them as terrorist threats, thus seeking to justify drastic measures against their citizens as part of the global counterterrorism effort. According to a Human Rights Watch report, in China this came in the form of intensified repression of its Muslim Uighurs, as the government claimed that the minority group harbored terrorists with links to Al-Qaida and treated the region's so-called separatists, peaceful or otherwise, as terrorists.[61] In several countries, according to the same report, the government listed in its report to the CTC the domestic laws that it employs as tools of repression as examples of legislation fulfilling the requirements of Resolution 1373. The Malaysian government, for example, presented in its first report to the CTC its Internal Security Act, long known internationally as a measure used by the government to indefinitely detain individuals without charge or trial. Similarly, the Uzbekistan government, in its report to the CTC, pointed to articles of its criminal code that it uses to suppress nonviolent independent Muslims—a tactic the government has used since the mid-1990s but that it has justified as counterterrorism since September 11.[62] The list goes on, and includes the United States, which passed legislation to curtail certain civil liberties at home while violating human rights and humanitarian law in known and unknown detention centers in Iraq, Guantanamo Bay, and elsewhere.

A related problem is that a number of countries have conflated their long-running conflicts—be they at the national, regional, or international level—with the "war on terror" in an attempt to secure the attention, legitimacy, backing, and resources they need to pursue their national interests. Thus, Russia turned to labeling Chechnya as its own front in the global "war on terror," while India did the same with Kashmir, despite the fact that both of these conflicts long predate September 11. In Somalia, faction leaders declared their support for the global antiterrorism campaign while labeling opponents as members of "extremist" groups.[63] Mirko Sossai argues that in Colombia, Resolution 1373 became a useful tool for President Alvaro Uribe as he recast the country's ongoing internal conflict as an "antiterrorist fight," relabeled Revolutionary Armed Forces of Colombia (FARC) guerrillas as terrorists, and strengthened the military and police forces.[64]

In addition, as part of the overhaul of national priorities in the aftermath of the September 11 attacks, the United States, United Kingdom, and other developed countries began to boost their foreign assistance to regimes they had hitherto chastised for their tolerance of human rights violations and disregard for international law. Critics feared that such aid would be used for unintended and undesirable purposes to the detriment of global security.[65] Nevertheless, Pakistan—a nuclear power led by a self-appointed president whose climb to the helm via a coup had resulted in economic sanctions from the United States—found itself a newfound US ally in the wake of the September 11 attacks. Despite the persistence of the nuclear problem, the United States promptly lifted a series of sanctions and showered the government with generous offers of economic and military aid.[66] The United States also quickly warmed its relations with Indonesia, a majority Muslim country of strategic importance in the "war on terror." By February 2005 Washington had taken major steps toward restoring full military relations with Jakarta for the first time since 1992, despite the fact that the conditions for such a move, including accountability for those responsible for human rights violations and reforms to strengthen civilian control of the military, remained unfulfilled.[67]

As for the countries that have been on the receiving end of exhortations, programs, and aid, many states that have been criticized for their repressive policies since the onset of the "war on terror" argue that it is international pressure—with UN resolutions and rhetoric undoubtedly included—that left these governments no choice but to take action against their own "terrorists" to win international approval. For instance, according to Amnesty International, Yemeni authorities admitted that their own state policies since September 11 breached international human rights law and domestic laws, but also stated that this was because they had "no option" but to fight terrorism and thereby prevent a possible US military action against Yemen.[68] Laurent Bonnefoy and Renaud Detalle argue that such external pressure on Yemen after September 11, and the inevitable decision by the government to cooperate in combating terrorism in order to avoid the consequences, have been a source of internal instability.[69]

Seen in this light, UN counterterrorism initiatives appear important, yet far from sufficient and potentially deleterious because of the associated risks to human rights and security. While developed and developing countries alike pursue policies that threaten human rights and appear to contradict the overarching goal to strengthen security, the United Nations as a forum exerts its energy getting those same states to ratify antiterrorist treaties and drafting new ones. While states usurp the "war on terror" to advance particular national interests, often at the cost of increased insecurity, the CTED has focused on building these same states' capacities to suppress the terrorist threat. The contradictions between the rhetoric and the practice of a comprehensive strategy as outlined in the Secretary-General's "five Ds" approach are palpable. In terms of the effect on the rule of law, these outcomes essentially amount to a promotion of the formal rule of law domestically (through counterterrorism legislation) and internationally (through treaties), while a blind eye is turned to actual state behavior that contravenes international norms—a highly problematic outcome from a maximalist perspective (see Chapter 2).

Certainly, it is important to be realistic about what the United Nations as an organization is and isn't meant to do, and what tasks are best left to governments. The United Nations is not an enforcement agency, but it does have the ability to define international norms and to urge states to act in conformity with them. That, in fact, is where its comparative advantage as an international organization with near universal membership lies, and the organization itself has recognized this in laying out for its member states a "comprehensive strategy" that goes beyond rule-making to promoting, and adhering to, the rule of law.

Participatory Approaches and Consultation

For the kinds of international counterterrorism initiatives discussed, there are two sides to the issue of participation and consultation. On the one hand, the UN leadership in most of these efforts—certainly in strengthening international legal norms but also in setting the basis for regional programs through resolutions such as Resolution 1373—bestows the initiatives with a great amount of legitimacy, because of the involvement of the UN's diverse membership of states in the decisionmaking process. Secretary-General Kofi Annan stated as much in his report on the rule of law and transitional justice: "United Nations norms and standards have been developed and adopted by countries across the globe. . . . As such, these norms and standards bring a legitimacy that cannot be said to attach to exported national models."[70]

On the other hand, the UN's participatory approach has generally been limited to consultation with certain select states only (and this is part and parcel of the anachronistic composition of the Security Council—itself an intractable issue of debate among member states). Take the CTC/CTED for instance: although its obligations are binding on all member states, it is composed only of the fifteen members of the Security Council. As seen above, for most of the countries of the developing world the exorbitant pressure from the United Nations and Western powers to be on the "right" side of the "war on terror" left no option but to respond to the antiterrorism agenda despite more urgent, entrenched, and debilitating domestic problems. For such states, heeding to Western demands to cooperate in the "war on terror" guaranteed diplomatic and financial support, while ignoring such demands guaranteed castigation or worse. As far as these countries were concerned, there was little distinction between pressures from the United States to join the "war on terror" and the requirements of Resolution 1373 to take counterterrorism measures and meet regular deadlines for reporting to the CTC/CTED: such efforts were all well removed from their immediate priorities, not to mention beyond the technical capacity of many states. A seminar report on African security poses a question that strikes at the heart of the participation dilemma: "Africa must cooperate . . . or else it will lose valuable aid. African leaders have signed up to this war on terrorism, but are they speaking for most of their populations?"[71] Indonesia, in contrast, by 2005 appeared to have moved past its earlier attempts to appease external pressures. In the wake of the second set of terrorist attacks on Bali in two years, and in the face of renewed Australian efforts to strengthen Indonesia's counterterrorism laws, the foreign minister declared that Jakarta welcomed Australia's "initiative to share their experience, but we do not feel obliged" to follow Australia's advice.[72] Similarly, Indonesian parliamentarians stated in defiance that "by sending a team of experts like that, the impression we get is that they are lecturing us," and that Australia's approach was "insulting."[73]

There is a need for international actors to be more sensitive to countries' domestic political contexts, to appreciate the dilemmas and political constraints that governments face in choosing to comply with international counterterrorism obligations. Even countries such as Indonesia and Yemen, both of which have witnessed a series of terrorist attacks on their own soil after September 11, fear further radicalizing segments of their populations if they too readily throw their weight behind the "war on terror."[74] At the same time, these states are keen to maintain positive ties with the United States, which is possible only if they demonstrate a high level of support for the antiterrorist campaign. Treading a fine political line, their participation in counterterrorism has therefore been visible yet cautious. The overshadowing imperative of fighting terrorism has also raised questions on these states' capacity to simultaneously address other—often more pressing—concerns. For instance, the International Crisis Group contends that in Yemen, "an exclusive focus on terrorism—and on combating it almost exclusively through military means— . . . could obscure, and therefore leave unaddressed, the domestic roots of the many problems that confront Yemen," such as the increasingly unequal distribution of wealth and other social inequalities.[75] Many countries face similar political predicaments over domestic priorities and international pressures. The CTC's "revitalization" effort, aimed at enhancing dialogue with states, is an improvement in the effort to better understand domestic needs and contexts, but its focus on technical assistance and capacity building overlooks the political dimensions of such efforts. Overall, then, current approaches continue to lend insufficient attention to the issues at stake domestically, raising the question as to how long developing countries can continue the juggling act before it becomes unsustainable.

An obvious caveat here is that paying heed to domestic contexts is entirely distinct from abandoning obligations under international law. The (mis)use of "counterterrorism" or "antiterrorism" agendas and terminologies for politically expedient purposes, as in the examples mentioned earlier, is counterproductive. Clearly, the call for more engaged and nationally appropriate counterterrorism approaches should be firmly grounded in the need to respect international norms and standards established by the United Nations and its member states.

Capacity Building

Related to the issue of participation, the critical question is not whether national and local capacity building have been achieved, but rather what kinds of capacity have been built. As discussed, capacity building in the form of technical assistance—for drafting and reviewing legislation and enhancing tools to choke off terrorist funding, among other aims—has been a major part of the international effort. These initiatives were vital for enabling countries to fulfill their obligations under Resolution 1373, though their actual effects on fighting terrorism is more difficult to determine.

However, very little attention has been paid to capacity building in other areas that carry major implications for counterterrorism. For example, the Policy Working Group on the United Nations and Terrorism, created by the Secretary-General in 2001 and tasked with formulating recommendations for the United Nations in light of the challenges posed by terrorism, emphasized in its report: "International law requires observance of basic human rights standards in the struggle against terrorism. . . . States should be made aware of the responsibilities placed upon them by the various human rights instruments and reminded that key provisions of the International Covenant on Civil and Political Rights cannot be derogated from."[76]

Capacity building in, or even awareness-raising of, international human rights obligations has been negligible. Indeed, considering the seriousness with which member states responded to the obligations of Resolution 1373, it is as if that resolution has superseded once and for all the human rights obligations laid out in subsequent Security Council resolutions, not to mention preexisting obligations as laid out in the UN Charter, the Universal Declaration of Human Rights, and subsequent international treaties. Tellingly, when the newly established CTED made its first in-country visit (to Morocco) in March 2005, it was accompanied by experts from Interpol, the World Customs Organization, the Financial Action Task Force, and the European Union.[77] It would seem useful and feasible to incorporate into such a team a representative of a human rights body.

To be fair, the CTC/CTED and the OHCHR do hold briefings in an effort to address concerns expressed within and beyond the United Nations regarding the human rights aspects of counterterrorism. However, it is unclear whether these consultations have led to any concrete results.[78] The OHCHR in fact concluded in a study on this issue that "the United Nations has been unable to address the compatibility of national counter-terrorism measures with international human rights obligations in a comprehensive and integrated way."[79]

Neither have systematic efforts been made to build states' capacities in more indirect counterterrorism approaches, such as launching public information campaigns at the local level in particularly vulnerable areas. Even bilateral assistance, the discussion of which is beyond the scope of this chapter, has focused predominantly on increasing military, police, border security, and intelligence capabilities. Many developing countries no doubt welcome technical assistance in such areas; however, if what is needed is an "indirect strategy" to engage in a "political and ideological war" to win the "hearts and minds" of Muslims, as Barry Desker and Kumar Ramakrishna argue in the case of Southeast Asia,[80] then a strategy focusing predominantly on technical legal and law enforcement assistance seems to miss the mark by a wide margin. Not only that, but it also evades the political and social dimensions of terrorism and counterterrorism altogether, once again overlooking the domestic quandaries that states confront, and giving exclusive focus to counterterrorism at the expense of other problems that may be fueling grievances and insecurity.

Coordination Among Actors

The importance of coordination among all of the actors involved in counterterrorism is a given. As we have seen, among the organizations actively engaged in international counterterrorism there is significant coordination and cooperation in the areas of provision of legislative assistance, curbing the financing of terrorism, and strengthening law enforcement. However, there is need for far more coordination within and among these organizations and beyond, and for such coordination to be made more systematic. The report of the Policy Working Group on the United Nations and Terrorism offers concrete recommendations in this area.[81]

For instance, organizations working on counterterrorism through capacity building in domestic legislation, law enforcement, border control, and banking regulations would benefit from increased dialogue with development and humanitarian organizations in order to ensure that counterterrorism efforts are not jeopardizing broader development or peacebuilding activities. Counterterrorism can have a negative impact on development, as when the US government froze the assets of Al-Barakaat, a Somali banking group, on suspicions of links to terrorism and thereby cut off the lifeline of many Somalis who had depended on remittances from the diaspora in the United States.[82] On the flip side, development efforts also pose the danger of exacerbating the terrorism problem if not implemented properly, as when development aid in the southern Philippines was targeted at only one segment of the population, thus increasing inequality, leaving expectations unfulfilled, and ultimately nurturing support for extremist groups.[83] On such fronts, however, discussion at the level of international organizations has been minimal.

No doubt, despite the all-too-familiar appeals, improved coordination is easier said than done; in practice, coordination means extra time and effort to deal with strange bedfellows whose work seems only remotely related to one's own. However, past experiences show that when deliberately planned, coordination and cooperation are achievable and instructive.[84]

To sum, the global counterterrorism strategy adopted by the United Nations has been valuable, but has not adequately addressed the domestic motivations for, as well as risks associated with, cooperating with the world's dominant powers. The international counterterrorism framework is useful as a guide for action, but there continues to be a sense that counterterrorism should be more localized in its planning and implementation, involve a wider set of actors, and should be more relevant to each country's context in order to be effective and minimize the impingement on other priorities.

Conclusion

The fight against terrorism will take years to produce results. So far, international approaches have predominantly relied on military, intelligence, and law enforcement strategies to hunt down terrorist suspects or freeze their funds and operations. While these strategies may be vital in reducing the immediate threat posed by terrorist groups, they are inadequate and can be detrimental in the long run if not complemented by efforts to understand and deal with the political, social, and economic dimensions of terrorism and counterterrorism.

In essence, what is needed to confront the threat of terrorism is not so much a "global war" against it as more localized attention where needed, in order to examine the factors that may be contributing to the threat or may be affected by efforts to reduce the threat. This may include, for instance, the need to examine with more rigor some of the political and socioeconomic sources of discontent and disaffection; perceived or actual domestic or international discrimination against certain ethnic or religious groups; and the causes and consequences of protracted conflict, which may be far more difficult to deal with than the delivery of "technical assistance." Such an approach requires more actors from more diverse institutions and communities—those in development and rule of law programming, for example. While this might appear to further complicate an already overwhelming effort, if the causes of terrorism are many, then proper responses can only be expected to be multifaceted as well. In terms of priorities, keeping this range of political, social, and economic issues in sight helps us to recognize, in the final analysis, that the problem of terrorism, as dominant as it has been in international politics since September 11, 2001, is not the greatest of concerns for many countries, and neither should it become one through external pressure.

The United Nations, as the most visible and universal international organization, is well placed to push for a more inclusive, sustainable, and broad-based approach to counterterrorism. Most promising in marking a departure from the status quo is the counterterrorism strategy proposed by Secretary-General Kofi Annan in Madrid in March 2005, comprising the above-mentioned "five Ds." The proposed strategy includes, but goes far beyond, the current focus on developing international norms and building state capacity. It also raises the need to pay more attention to victims of terrorism; mentions the critical roles of such organizations as the UN Development Programme (UNDP) in strengthening governance and of the UN Educational, Scientific, and Cultural Organization (UNESCO) in promoting "modern education"; and has led to the creation of a special rapporteur on protecting human rights while combating terrorism. Additionally, the Secretary-General announced that he would create an "implementation task force" to execute his strategy. Implementing the "five Ds" strategy will be difficult. Already, several countries have sought to weaken the mandate of the special rapporteur,[85] while others, especially members of the Organization of the Islamic Conference, have lamented the fact that the strategy evades addressing the politically sensitive issue of the "root causes" of terrorism. It will also involve a wide array of national and international actors and approaches not traditionally associated with counterterrorism. However, given the serious repercussions of the counterterrorism initiatives thus far, the Secretary-General's strategy, if successfully implemented, will be an important step in the right direction.

But a "global" strategy will have little impact or significance for the majority of the world's states if not implemented with a high level of context-specificity, and may even be detrimental to the overall effort to improve security, as examples in this chapter have shown. The onus therefore remains on individual states and regional organizations to identify their own priorities and localize their counterterrorism strategies *within* the international legal and normative counterterrorism framework and through the assistance of those states that are able to provide it. In turn, those working at the global level to enhance the collective effort against terrorism need to respect domestic priorities and constraints, ensuring that counterterrorism efforts do not contribute to the problem they are trying to solve.

Notes

I thank Agnès Hurwitz, Gordon Peake, Catherine Guicherd, and an anonymous reader for their helpful comments on an earlier draft of this chapter, and Francesco Mancini for pointing me to important sources.

1. See, for example, Michèle Griffin, "The Helmet and the Hoe: Linkages Between United Nations Development Assistance and Conflict Management," *Global Governance* 9 (April 2003): 199–217.

2. I employ a broad definition of "counterterrorism" to refer to the whole gamut of measures and efforts available to or used by state and international institutions to prevent and suppress terrorism. Thus the term is not restricted to tasks performed by security institutions, as the US government is wont to define it, for example; rather, it encompasses political, social, economic, diplomatic, legal, and psychological approaches as well. In this sense "counterterrorism" as used here should be interchangeable with "antiterrorism."

3. For example, a white paper of Australia's Department of Foreign Affairs and Trade states: "Continued weak governance among some regional countries impedes these nations from dealing forcefully with transnational threats, including terrorism." See Government of Australia, Department of Foreign Affairs and Trade, "Promoting Good Governance, Human Rights, and Development," in *White Paper on Foreign Affairs and Trade: Advancing the National Interest* (Commonwealth of Australia, 2003), http://www.dfat.gov.au/ani/chapter_10.html.

4. See, for example, Kate Martin, "Intelligence, Terrorism, and Civil Liberties," *Human Rights Magazine* (American Bar Association), Winter 2002, http://www.abanet.org/irr/hr/winter02/martin.html.

5. Human Rights First, "Assessing the New Normal: Liberty and Security for the Post–September 11 United States" (2003), http://www.humanrightsfirst.org/pubs/descriptions/assessing/assessingthenewnormal.pdf.

6. See United Nations, *International Covenant on Civil and Political Rights,* art. 4. The right to life; the ban on torture, slavery, imprisonment for debt, and ex post facto crimes; recognition as a person before the law; and freedom of thought, consciences, and religion are nonderogable rights under this provision.

7. See, for example, Tom Malinowski, "By Infringing Basic Liberties the U.S. Undermines Its Own Terrorism Prevention Strategy," in *Human Rights and Terrorism* (The Hague: Netherlands Helsinki Committee, 2004), pp. 81–85; Asma Jahangir and Fateh Azzam, "Human Rights," in *Toward a Democratic Response: The Club de Madrid Series on Democracy and Terrorism,* vol. 3 (Madrid: Club de Madrid, 2005), pp. 27–28.

8. For an overview of the history of terrorism and its evolution in the latter half of the twentieth century, see Walter Laqueur, *The New Terrorism: Fanaticism and the Arms of Mass Destruction* (Oxford: Oxford University Press, 1999); Walter Laqueur, *No End to War: Terrorism in the Twentieth Century* (New York: Continuum, 2003).

9. For an overview of UN Security Council responses to terrorism prior to September 11, 2001, see Edward C. Luck, "Tackling Terrorism," in *The UN Security Council: From the Cold War to the 21st Century,* edited by David M. Malone (Boulder: Lynne Rienner, 2004), pp. 85–100.

10. Quoted in Martha Crenshaw, *Terrorism and International Cooperation* (New York: Institute for East-West Security Studies, 1989), pp. 26–27. The League of Nations sought to introduce antiterrorism law under its Convention for the Prevention and Punishment of Terrorism in 1937. See Julian Elgaard Brett, *Far from Business as Usual: United Nations' Responses to International Terrorism* (Copenhagen: Danish Institute of International Affairs, 2002), p. 27.

11. UN Security Council Resolution 748 (1992). This resolution was a response to Libya's failure to prosecute perpetrators of the 1988 bombing of Pan Am Flight 103.

12. UN Security Council Resolution 1054 (1996).

13. UN Security Council Resolution 1267 (1999). Two more resolutions were subsequently passed, again both based on Chapter VII, to strengthen Resolution 1267: Resolution 1333 (2000) and Resolution 1363 (2001).

14. UN Security Council Resolution 1269 (1999).

15. Jeffrey L. Dunoff, Steven Ratner, and David Wippman, eds., *International Law: Norms, Actors, Processes* (New York: Aspen Law and Business, 2002), p. 921.

16. Nicholas Rostow, "Before and After: The Changed UN Response to Terrorism Since September 11th," *Cornell International Law Journal* 35, no. 3 (2002): 479.

17. Luck, "Tackling Terrorism."

18. For General Assembly resolutions on terrorism, see http://www.un.org/terrorism/instruments.html.

19. All twelve conventions can be accessed at http://www.unodc.org/unodc/terrorism_conventions.html.

20. UN General Assembly Resolution 51/210 (1996).

21. Hans Correll, "International Instruments Against Terrorism: The Record So Far and Strengthening the Existing Regime," in *Combating International Terrorism: The Contribution of the United Nations,* proceedings of a symposium held at Vienna International Center, June 3–4, 2002, p. 23.

22. UN General Assembly Resolution 27/3034 (1972).

23. Malvina Halberstam, "The Evolution of the United Nations Position on Terrorism: From Exempting National Liberation Movements to Criminalizing Terrorism Wherever and by Whomever Committed," *Columbia Journal of Transnational Law* 41, no. 3 (2003): 547.

24. Codification of principles related to acts of terrorism is part of a broader development of international human rights norms, which, according to John Clarke, can have

significant domestic and international impact and "play an increasingly important role in international relations." See John N. Clarke, "Dimensions and Processes of Global Governance," in *Global Governance in the Twenty-First Century,* edited by John N. Clarke and Geoffrey R. Edwards (New York: Palgrave Macmillan, 2004), pp. 271–272.

25. Organization of American States, *Convention to Prevent and Punish Acts of Terrorism Taking the Form of Crimes Against Persons and Related Extortion That Are of International Significance* (February 1971).

26. See Crenshaw, *Terrorism and International Cooperation,* pp. 27–28.

27. See Correll, "International Instruments Against Terrorism."

28. See Crenshaw, *Terrorism and International Cooperation,* p. 28.

29. Ibid., p. 27.

30. UN Security Council Resolution 1368 (2001).

31. UN Security Council Resolution 1373 (2001).

32. United Nations, *Report of the Policy Working Group on the United Nations and Terrorism,* UN Doc. A/57/273 (August 6, 2002).

33. Sir Jeremy Greenstock, "Work of the Counter-Terrorism Committee of the Security Council," in *Combating International Terrorism.*

34. Ibid.

35. David Cortright, Alistair Millar, Linda M. Gerber, and George A. Lopez, "An Action Agenda for Enhancing the United Nations Program on Counter-Terrorism," report by the Fourth Freedom Forum and the Joan B. Kroc Institute for International Peace Studies, Goshen and Notre Dame, IN, September 2004, p. 5.

36. Ibid. Member states' reports to the CTC are available at the CTC website: http://www.un.org/sc/ctc/countryreports.shtml.

37. See United Nations, *Security Council Presidential Statement Invites Counter-Terrorism Committee to Accelerate Work on Assessing Needs of Member States,* press release, UN Doc. SC/8152 (July 19, 2004).

38. See United Nations, *Report by the Chair of the Counter-Terrorism Committee on the Problems Encountered in the Implementation of Security Council Resolution 1373 (2001),* UN Doc. S/2004/70 (January 26, 2004).

39. UN Security Council Resolution 1535 (2004).

40. United Nations, *Country Visits Signal New Phase of Work for United Nations Counter-Terrorism Body,* press release, UN Doc. SC/8333 (March 14, 2005).

41. UN Security Council Resolution 1566 (2004).

42. United Nations, *A More Secure World: Our Shared Responsibility: Report of the Secretary General's High-level Panel on Threats, Challenges, and Change,* UN Doc. A/59/565 (December 1, 2004), p. 52.

43. United Nations, *In Larger Freedom: Towards Development, Security, and Human Rights for All—Report of the Secretary General,* UN Doc. A/59/2005 (March 21, 2005), p. 26.

44. United Nations, *International Convention for the Suppression of Acts of Nuclear Terrorism,* UN Doc. A/59/766 (April 4, 2005). The convention opened for signature September 14, 2005, and entered into force on July 7, 2007.

45. United Nations, *Ad Hoc Committee Nears Consensus on Draft Nuclear Terrorism Convention, Chairman Says,* press release, L/3084 (April 1, 2005). See also Club of Madrid and the Security and Peace Institute, "Democracies Confronting Terrorism: Panel I," conference transcript of conference (New York, May 18, 2005), http://www.securitypeace.org/content/download/120/422/file/dct%20panel1.pdf.

46. See United Nations, *Secretary-General Offers Global Strategy for Fighting Terrorism, in Address to Madrid Summit,* press release, UN Doc. SG/SM/9757 (March 10, 2005).

47. United Nations, *2005 World Summit Outcome,* UN Doc. A/60/L.1 (September 20, 2005), p. 23.

48. Ibid.

49. See the UNODC website on terrorism: http://www.unodc.org/unodc/terrorism .html.

50. See UNODC, "Global Programme Against Terrorism," Terrorism Prevention Branch (May 2004); United Nations, *Strengthening International Cooperation and Technical Assistance in Preventing and Combating Terrorism: Report of the Secretary-General,* UN Doc. E/CN.15/2004/8 (March 17, 2004).

51. See United Nations, "Head of UN Counter-Terrorism Body Visits Vienna to Coordinate UN Anti-Terrorism Efforts," UNIS/CP/503, October 20, 2004.

52. See the OHCHR website: http://www.ohchr.org/english/issues/terrorism/index .htm.

53. OHCHR, Human Rights Resolution 2005/80, "Protection of Human Rights and Fundamental Freedoms While Countering Terrorism," http://ap.ohchr.org/documents/ e/chr/resolutions/e-cn_4-res-2005-80.doc.

54. See the FATF website on terrorist financing: http://www.fatf-gafi.org.

55. ASEAN, "Joint Communique of the Special ASEAN Ministerial Meeting on Terrorism," Kuala Lumpur, May 20–21, 2002, www.aseansec.org/5618.htm.

56. Mohammed Javad Zarif, "The Contribution of the Organization of the Islamic Conference," in *Combating International Terrorism.*

57. OSCE, Office for Democratic Institutions and Human Rights, "Preventing and Combating Terrorism: The Human Dimension" (September 2003), p.2.

58. Ibid., p. 4.

59. Ibid., p. 2.

60. See Agnès Hurwitz and Kaysie Studdard, "Rule of Law Programs in Peace Operations" (New York: International Peace Academy, August 2005).

61. Human Rights Watch, "Hear No Evil, See No Evil: The UN Security Council's Approach to Human Rights Violations in the Global Counter-Terrorism Effort," briefing paper (New York: August 10, 2004), www.hrw.org/backgrounder/un/2004/ un0804.

62. Ibid.

63. International Crisis Group, *Counter-Terrorism in Somalia: Losing Hearts and Minds?* (Brussels, July 11, 2005).

64. Mirko Sossai, "The Internal Conflict in Colombia and the Fight Against Terrorism: UN Security Council Resolution 1465 (2003) and Further Developments," *Journal of International Criminal Justice* 3, no. 1 (2005): 259–261.

65. See, for example, Victoria Garcia, "U.S. Military Assistance to 1460 Report Countries: 1990–2005" (Washington, D.C.: Center for Defense Information, April 12, 2004).

66. White House, Presidential Determination no. 2001-28 (September 22, 2001), http://www.whitehouse.gov/news/releases/2001/09/2001092-4.html; Dianne Rennack, "India and Pakistan: Current U.S. Economic Sanctions," CRS Report for Congress (October 12, 2001), http://fpc.state.gov/documents/organization/6202.pdf.

67. Jane Perlez, "Indonesia Welcomes U.S. Plan to Resume Training Its Military," *New York Times,* March 1, 2005.

68. Amnesty International, "Yemen: The Rule of Law Sidelined in the Name of Security" (September 24, 2003), http://web.amnesty.org/library/Index/ENGMDE 310062003.

69. Laurent Bonnefoy and Renaud Detalle, "The Security Paradox and Development in Unified Yemen (1990–2005)," in *Security and Development: Searching for*

Critical Connections, edited by Neclâ Tschirgi, Michael Lund, and Francesco Mancini (Boulder: Lynne Rienner, forthcoming).

70. United Nations, *The Rule of Law and Transitional Justice in Conflict and Post-Conflict Societies: Report of the Secretary-General,* UN Doc. S/2004/616 (August 23, 2004), p. 5.

71. Mark Chingono and Guy Lamb, *The New Partnership for Africa's Security: The United Nations, Regional Organizations, and Future Security Threats in Africa,* seminar report (Centre for Conflict Resolution, University of Cape Town, Cape Town, South Africa, October 2004), p. 31.

72. Sian Powell, "Jakarta MPs Cool on Terror Law Offer," *The Australian,* October 14, 2005, p. 4.

73. Ibid.

74. Jose T. Almonte, "Enhancing State Capacity and Legitimacy in the Counter-Terror War," in *After Bali: The Threat of Terrorism in Southeast Asia,* edited by Kumar Ramakrishna and See Seng Tan (Singapore: Institute of Defense and Strategic Studies, 2003), pp. 228–229.

75. International Crisis Group, *Yemen: Coping with Terrorism and Violence in a Fragile State* (Brussels, January 8, 2003), pp. 27, i.

76. United Nations, *Report of the Policy Working Group on the United Nations and Terrorism.* para. 28.

77. UN News Center, "UN Counter-Terrorism Campaign Kicks Off New Phase: On-Site Country Visits" (March 14, 2005).

78. Cortright et al., *An Action Agenda for Enhancing the United Nations Program on Counter-Terrorism,* p. 24.

79. United Nations, *Protection of Human Rights and Fundamental Freedoms While Countering Terrorism: Study of the United Nations High Commissioner for Human Rights,* UN Doc. A/59/428 (October 8, 2004), p. 17.

80. Barry Desker and Kumar Ramakrishna, "Forging an Indirect Strategy in Southeast Asia," in *The Battle for Hearts and Minds: Using Soft Power to Undermine Terrorist Networks,* edited by Alexander T. J. Lennon (Cambridge: Massachusetts Institute of Technology Press, 2003), p. 46.

81. United Nations, *Report of the Policy Working Group on the United Nations and Terrorism,* pp. 10–11.

82. National Commission on Terrorist Attacks upon the United States, *Terrorist Financing Staff Monograph,* chap. 5: "Al-Barakaat Case Study," August 21, 2004, http://www.9-11commission.gov/staff_statements/911_terrfin_ch5.pdf.

83. See Kim Cragin and Peter Chalk, "Terrorism and Development: Using Social and Economic Development to Inhibit a Resurgence of Terrorism" (Santa Monica: RAND, 2003).

84. A number of possible models exist, including cross-sectoral mechanisms such as the Executive Committee on Peace and Security and the Executive Committee on Humanitarian Assistance, both of which bring together various UN agencies and departments, as well as interagency task forces such as the West Africa Task Force and the Rule of Law Task Force.

85. Amnesty International, "2005 UN Commission on Human Rights: Monitor Needed to Protect Rights in Counter-Terrorism" (April 15, 2005), http://web.amnesty.org/library/index/engior410382005.

PART 4

Conclusion

12

The Rule of Law and Peacebuilding Processes

Agnès Hurwitz

Focusing on themes of increasing significance to rule of law policymakers and practitioners, this volume has sought to assess the relevance and use of rule of law programs as a part of peacebuilding; highlight the underlying tensions of the all-embracing claims commonly made about the expected achievements of rule of law programs; and identify policy-relevant recommendations, as a way to either consolidate existing practice or highlight important policy gaps and tensions in rule of law strategies undertaken as a part of peacebuilding.

Security, Development, Human Rights:
International Discourses and Policies on the Rule of Law

The recent focus on the rule of law as a rallying cry of the diplomatic community is primarily analyzed by Balakrishnan Rajagopal, in Chapter 3, as the product of the expanding scopes of, and growing convergence between, the security, development, and human rights discourses. The rule of law is now considered to be a key tool for (re)building state institutions and for remedying state or governance failure, which constitute some of the major challenges faced by the world community. In assessing the significance of rule of law work for security, development and human rights, the following considerations came to the fore.

First, it is now widely accepted, as reflected in the chapters of this volume, that a fundamental relationship exists between the rule of law and security. As noted by Rama Mani in Chapter 2, "In states undergoing or emerging from conflict, or at risk of collapse, the rule of law is seen to provide a bulwark of governance, and a mechanism for the nonviolent settlement of disputes." In peacebuilding contexts, rule of law programs are essential for establishing and maintaining internal security. In order to fight crime, the reform of criminal justice institutions must be prioritized, the goal being to ensure that these institutions are both efficiently managed and comply with fair trial and due process standards. As William O'Neill shows in Chapter 5, the importance of criminal justice reform has been reflected in the efforts of the United Nations, as part of its multidimensional peacekeeping operations, to include rule of law components in the Security Council mandates of recent peacekeeping missions, such as in Sierra Leone, Liberia, Sudan, Haiti, and Côte d'Ivoire. Consequently, it is also in this area that the United Nations has the most extensive programmatic experience. Current approaches are consolidating and improving on past practice: while the reform of criminal justice institutions once tended to be fragmented, for example, there is now a realization that the various institutions that make up a criminal justice system (judiciary, prosecutor's office, police forces, correctional institutions, and bar associations) should be viewed as components of a whole system and be reformed accordingly. The elaboration of model transitional codes, on the other hand, is a recent endeavor that seeks to address one of the most common problems faced by war-torn societies: the inadequacy of existing legal frameworks to tackle common crime.

The second assertion made by international policymakers, that the rule of law is crucial for achieving economic and social development, deserves a more nuanced treatment. What is clear is that the rule of law is certainly not indispensable for economic growth. Many development actors nevertheless consider rule of law programs as key components of developmental policies based on the view that fair and predictable laws and legal institutions will attract foreign investors and contribute to economic development based on a free-market economy in the long term. As highlighted in Chapter 2, the proponents of a "maximalist" reading of the rule of law go further, arguing that the rule of law, which demands that all be equal before the law, means that people should be empowered as political and legal actors. Thus, Mani analyzes the second rationale behind developmental strategies to strengthen the rule of law as arising from the objective of good governance, and especially "democratic governance." Regardless of ongoing ideological debates on free markets and democracy, there is growing consensus, as shown by Chandra Sriram in Chapter 4, myself in Chapter 9, and by Madalene O'Donnell in Chapter 10, that judicial reform, alternative dispute settlement mechanisms, anticorruption programs, and programs to ensure greater access to justice and to administrative authorities do contribute to the social empowerment of the poor, demonstrating the undeniable relevance to long-term development of the principles of equality before the law and of efficient and impartial justice.

In the end, is it the human rights regime that might possibly be the most natural "fit" for the rule of law? As I note in Chapter 1, the existence of the rule of law presupposes compliance with a number of fundamental principles and procedural standards that are enshrined in international human rights instruments. The organic nature of this relationship is also apparent at the operational level, as explained in Chapter 5. Another facet of the inseparable nature of the rule of law and human rights in the UN context can be observed in the emphasis placed on the fight against impunity, which is implemented through transitional justice mechanisms. After elaborating and promoting strict standards prohibiting gross human rights and humanitarian law violations, the implementation of these standards and their enforcement against the individuals responsible for such abuses required the establishment of institutions that could prosecute perpetrators in full compliance with due process standards. To that extent, the origins of UN interest in rule of law reform stem from the realization that international work should go beyond the short-term punishment of human rights violators and seek to reform state institutions, so as to prevent further abuses in the long term. As Pablo de Greiff notes in Chapter 8, "reparative benefits in the absence of reforms that diminish the probability of the repetition of violence are nothing more than payments whose utility, and furthermore, legitimacy, are questionable." While this may all be true, it would be inaccurate to infer that the rule of law and human rights are tautological. One basic difference is that the rule of law can be easily conceived as a tool of governance, while human rights are most often regarded as a safeguard against state intervention and as tools of "social transformation" and "emancipation."

Another basic difference between the rule of law and human rights, and a conclusion that has been drawn in many studies (as discussed in Chapters 1 to 3), is that the rule of law is extremely malleable. It has a unique ability to espouse wide-ranging policy objectives, a characteristic that might be largely responsible for the sudden popularity of the concept among international policymakers. The importance of the rule of law as a "statebuilding tool" used by international actors may also explain why the degree of conflict between the disparate security, development, and human rights agendas that the rule of law is supposed to implement tends to be underestimated. As noted by Rajagopal, the current international discourse is "remarkably conflict-free," underpinned by a belief in a harmonious and mutually reinforcing relationship between security, development, and human rights, and between divergent understandings within each of these discourses.

What several chapters in this volume highlight, however, is that these multiple agendas necessarily generate tensions. At least two distinct examples can be drawn here. First, Reyko Huang, in Chapter 11, shows that programs aiming at strengthening the capacity of law enforcement actors to fight terrorism may have serious unintended consequences for civil liberties. In other words, short-term objectives will undermine longer-term goals such as the promotion of democratic practices and the respect for individual freedoms. While it is true that the tension between law enforcement and human rights is not new and certainly not limited to counterterrorism strategies, the "war on terror" has made it increasingly overt.

Second, while less often emphasized, tensions are also apparent between human rights and developmental objectives. This comes up prominently in Chapter 9, in which I address housing, land, and property issues. In this area, policymakers and practitioners face difficult choices, torn as they are between the need to address restitution claims by former occupiers who often have been suffering serious human rights abuses, and the need to pay due consideration to the livelihoods of good faith secondary occupants so as to avoid vicious cycles of property disputes in the long term. Similarly, the competing interests of the victims of human rights abuses, whose plight reparation programs seek to address (as analyzed by Pablo de Greiff in Chapter 8), and of conflict actors, such as former combatants, underscore the tensions between the short-term goals of peace implementation and the duty to fight impunity.

If highlighting these tensions is relatively straightforward, addressing them is undoubtedly much more daunting. There are no easy solutions proposed here, and certainly no one-size-fits-all approach is advocated. Rather, the objective is to highlight these discrepancies so as to enhance awareness among policymakers and practitioners about the various factors that will affect the outcomes of the programs they design and implement, and to provide guidance in adjusting their approaches as necessary. As noted in Chapter 3, the current confusion between international policy objectives makes it unclear "who stands to lose or win" from the implementation of rule of law programs. In this perspective, Rajagopal rightly notes that the artificial belief in the ultimate rationality and objectivity of the law cannot hide the fundamental ideological objectives that underpin these internationally supported initiatives, such as the type or size of state to be built or the type of legal system to be advocated.

The Rule of Law and Civil War

As noted by Mani, the rule of law "offers the option that grievances could be addressed within the ambit of the law and existing politically accepted avenues, rather than through the resort to force." Several chapters in this volume provide clear examples of the importance of the rule of law as part of international peacebuilding strategies. In Chapter 5, William O'Neill reflects on the progressive integration of rule of law components in multidimensional peace operations and on the lessons learned in the past decade of international operations. In Chapter 7, on the other hand, Simon Chesterman deals with one of the most challenging concepts of recent multilateral efforts to build peace: the need to ensure "local ownership" of reforms in settings where, for the most part, intervention was made necessary because of the very inability of existing authorities to adequately govern. Other chapters focus on more specific questions, albeit crucial ones in peacebuilding contexts, such as housing, land, and property issues, and corruption. For both of these concerns, the reciprocal causal link between the absence of rule of law and the presence of civil war is obvious; in fact, these two issues are among the most urgent in postconflict settings, and warrant early attention in the postconflict phase to avert the recurrence of war.

While rule of law programs have now become a common feature of peacebuilding strategies, it is less clear whether rule of law programs implemented as part of peacebuilding have properly integrated recent academic and policy findings on civil war. Chandra Sriram notes in Chapter 4 that while donor discourses have integrated the notion that the absence of the rule of law often contributes to the initiation of conflict, support for rule of law programs in countries that are only at risk of conflict has not been forcefully voiced. Sriram acknowledges, however, that one of the problems here may have more to do with the fact that conflict prevention continues to be a highly loaded concept, and that interference in countries at risk of conflict understandably remains much more delicate than in postconflict countries.

Despite the fact that rule of law programs are now increasingly associated with international peacebuilding, they too often fail to integrate conflict and contextual analysis in their design, which explains to some extent why so-called template strategies still rule the day. The most significant advances seem to have been chartered in the fields of criminal justice reform, where initiatives such as the model transitional codes have been based on broad consultations and seek to provide for the possibility of "adjustments" so as to best suit each specific context. In most cases, however, "conflict" and "context" are more often than not only superficially acknowledged in rule of law programmatic approaches. Rule of law programs, regardless of where and at which stage of the conflict they are implemented, seem remarkably similar. While obviously essential, the technical-legal expertise must also be fully integrated into the broader political context in which it operates; in other words it needs to be both "conflict"- and "context"-sensitive. Housing, land, and property issues provide a telling example of the necessity of conflict-sensitive approaches. I advocate in Chapter 9 that housing, land, and property policies, particularly property registration and efficient dispute settlement mechanisms, be developed at an early stage in the postconflict phase in order to avert conflict arising out of competing claims. Context-sensitiveness, or rather the lack thereof, is also a common problem throughout peacebuilding, as addressed in several chapters in this volume. In this respect, while the development of standard procedures and more rigorous methodology may in fact have led to greater reliance on "template" strategies, there is no doubt that context-sensitiveness and better knowledge of the local language and culture can go a long way toward ensuring the successful outcomes of rule of law programs. Achieving a better balance between "template" and "context" must therefore remain a key goal of policymakers working on the rule of law.

Identifying Solutions: Recommendations on Rule of Law Programmatic Approaches

The Role of the United Nations

While the UN's involvement in rule of law programs has been increasingly significant over the past decade, particularly in the fields of transitional justice and peacekeeping, the world organization remains a relatively marginal actor compared to development actors, such as USAID, the World Bank, and the DfID. This being said, and as in other areas of peacebuilding work, the United Nations enjoys unique advantages, such as universal reach, greater legitimacy and impartiality, and solid field expertise. O'Neill stresses nonetheless that international organizations must act complementarily and that regional organizations may sometimes be best suited to implement rule of law programs, such as the OSCE in the Balkans or the OAS in Haiti. Second, coordination of rule of law strategies between the diverse UN agencies and departments working on rule of law programs (DPKO, OHCHR, UNDP, UNODC, OCHA, UNHCR, DPA, UNIFEM, UNICEF, OLA) still leaves much to be desired.

The recent reforms that have affected the United Nations should hopefully contribute to greater effectiveness and coordination of international actors on rule of law reforms. Three important institutional developments could play a key role in this area. First, the Human Rights Council, established to replace the Commission on Human Rights, is specifically mandated to mainstream human rights into the UN system, work toward the prevention of human rights violations, and promote technical assistance and capacity building in consultation with, and with the consent of, the member states concerned.[1] Second, the Peacebuilding Commission may have important implications for rule of law programming in countries recovering from conflict, in particular through the adoption of integrated peacebuilding strategies, such as institution building, and the provision of recommendations and information on peacebuilding work based on a thorough understanding of existing resources.[2] However, some of the fundamental characteristics of the Peacebuilding Commission, namely its advisory and intergovernmental nature, may significantly affect its impact and influence over non-UN actors.

Finally, and perhaps most relevant for the present discussion, has been the announcement by the Secretary-General of a long-awaited initiative to establish a Rule of Law Coordination and Resource Group consisting of the key UN actors in the field, namely OLA, DPKO, OHCHR, UNODC, UNDP, UNIFEM, and UNHCR, which, according to the Secretary-General's report, will "act as Headquarters focal point for coordinating system-wide attention on the rule of law so as to ensure quality, policy coherence and coordination."[3] The main tasks of the group will be, inter alia, to share information on rule of law developments; to act as a resource for the Peacebuilding Commission and Peacebuilding Support Office; to ensure effective response of the United Nations to state requests; to provide policy direction, develop overall rule of law strategies, and mediate disputes among UN rule of law assistance providers; and to maintain a global roster of professionals in the rule of law field. One of the group's first tasks, however, will be to conduct a consultative process with member states and other partners to identify key gaps in UN capacity in the rule of law area; the group will also coordinate the preparation of an inventory of current activities of the United Nations devoted to the promotion of the rule of law at the national and international levels, as was requested in Resolution 61/39 of the General Assembly.[4] Finally, while the institutional location of the group has been left to the new Secretary-General, the report specifically indicates that "given the broad remit of the new entity, it would not be appropriate to place it within the Peacebuilding Support Office."[5] This new development will surely be welcomed by supporters of the rule of law who have, since the release of the Secretary-General's report on the rule of law and transitional justice in conflict and postconflict societies,[6] called for greater coherence and enhanced policy direction.

Outcomes vs. Objectives

One of the major challenges faced by policymakers and practitioners lies in the fundamental discrepancy that exists between the ambitious objectives assigned to programs supporting the rule of law and their actual implementation, which tends to focus on "minimalist" approaches and therefore achieves only technical outcomes. This fundamental contradiction is most clearly highlighted by Mani, who recommends identifying more clearly what the "ends" of programmatic approaches ought to be rather than focusing on institutional attributes—that is, what rule of law institutions should look like. From a criminal justice perspective, for instance, the objective to be monitored should be the provision of physical protection from crime for all citizens, rather than a technical assessment revolving around the implementation and enforcement of criminal legislation. More broadly, devising better tools to measure the outcomes of rule of law reform is widely accepted as essential to achieving real progress. Consultation and polling processes are now regarded as an increasingly common assessment tool, recommended as such in the Secretary-General's report on the rule of law and transitional justice,[7] and studies on popular perceptions and opinions based on quantitative research and polling methodology have recently flourished.[8] While this growing body of quantitative studies on popular opinions about rule of law reforms is certainly an encouraging development, what must be ascertained is their impact on the design of rule of law programs.

Ownership and Accountability

While "ownership" has been hailed as a key concept for enhancing the legitimacy of development and peacebuilding work, Simon Chesterman points out in Chapter 7 that this most popular buzzword is extraordinarily vague. As he suggests, from a practical standpoint, it would be more useful to "disaggregate" the concept into more manageable and measurable objectives. Six different understandings of ownership found in practice are identified: responsiveness, consultation, participation, accountability, control by local authorities under international supervision, and, the ultimate goal, sovereignty, including the power to demand the departure of international staff. Not only are these subgoals conceptually clearer, but they are also better adapted to programmatic design and methodologies, as they can be more easily translated into programmatic objectives. Chesterman also argues that while the end of peacebuilding operations should be to achieve national ownership, the means to get there necessarily entail international interference.

Another important point, which is echoed in several chapters in this volume, is that, in spite of its claimed importance, ownership is often sacrificed in favor of strategic or economic interests of international actors. Thus, counterterrorism strategies that consist for the most part of military, intelligence, and law enforcement programs are rarely subjected to domestic priorities or based on a sound understanding of domestic contexts. These strategies sometimes fail to differentiate terrorist activism with legitimate political opposition, undermining essential components in the building of democratic societies based on the rule of law, and antagonizing thereby the very "reform constituencies" that the United Nations and external actors involved in rule of law programming are supposed to embolden.

Finally, much more needs to be done to develop and strengthen accountability mechanisms applying to international actors. Significant forays into this highly sensitive question have been made, in particular with regard to the criminal accountability of peacekeepers,[9] but this is not sufficient; accountability must be a reality across the whole gamut of peacebuilding work and for all international actors involved in it. O'Donnell considers that monitoring efforts should be directed not only toward domestic actors, but also toward international aid agencies, and be carried out by national audit offices of donor countries. Yet she notes that this solution may be resisted by officials in donor countries, precisely because they cannot control their own auditing institutions. De Greiff notes in a similar vein that while reparation programs should in most cases be financed by the state in which mass abuses have occurred, and be devised in consultation with victim groups, international actors could consider financial support to reparation programs, especially if they have played an important role in the conflict, and they should provide technical assistance in the design and implementation of such programs.

Strategic Frameworks

Programmatic design also calls for attention to strategic frameworks, which were highlighted in the Secretary-General's report on the rule of law and transitional justice. Two key points should be made here. First, conflict analysis, carried out by political experts and advisers, should be the starting point in the design of rule of law programmatic strategies. Second, strategic frameworks entail some important policy choices between the various tools at the disposal of international practitioners and therefore require rigorous assessments of their long-term goals and impact.

Rausch and O'Connor offer insightful recommendations on the use of model codes as part of long-haul law reforms of the criminal justice system. The first phase of such a process would begin with the identification of the applicable law in the preplanning phase of a peace operation, while in the planning phase a premission assessment would be carried out to determine the state of the current justice system and to assess the criminal laws in force in the state, with a view to identifying the applicable law and whether it is compliant with international standards of due process and adequate to tackle the most prevalent crimes. In the short term, a body of applicable law may be designated and a rudimentary justice system may be established.

Another relevant illustration of these principles is found in housing, land, and property policies, as I address in Chapter 9. Strategic planning is critical to the success of rule of law policies on housing, land, and property because of their relevance throughout the postconflict phase. This means first that conflict-sensitive approaches to these rule of law policies must be mainstreamed into current UN programs. In postconflict contexts, the United Nations should adopt comprehensive approaches on housing, land, and property and agree on the adoption of a strategic policy framework that goes beyond narrowly framed restitution policies and also addresses the other two key objectives—access to housing, land, and property, and tenure security. Successful comprehensive approaches require rigorous planning, including thorough conflict analysis, methodologically sound needs assessment, and program design effectively based on these preparatory procedures. Rule of law policies related to housing, land, and property should also be more systematically integrated into the work of UN peace operations; they should be seen as a crucial component of DDR, repatriation, and reconciliation processes.

Finally, progress needs to be made toward greater exchange and interaction between the many fields of expertise that are relevant to peacebuilding work. While rule of law expertise requires specific technical skills, many challenges faced by rule of law experts are common to all peacebuilding practitioners. For instance, as noted by O'Donnell in Chapter 10 anticorruption and rule of law specialists have too often worked in isolation from one another, even though the objectives sought in both cases are clearly mutually reinforcing.

Identifying the Applicable Law
One of the foremost problems faced by practitioners sent to the field in the immediate aftermath of conflict is relatively obvious but particularly difficult to

address: identifying the applicable law and, as is often necessary, filling existing gaps in the law. Determining the applicable law has proved particularly crucial in the fields of criminal justice and of housing, land, and property disputes. With regard to the former, Rausch and O'Connor regard the process of identifying the applicable law through the compilation of legislative documents as a crucial component of the preplanning stage and in the determination of the gaps to be filled by transitional criminal codes. The identification of the applicable law can prove even trickier in the case of housing, land, and property disputes, where multiple layers of conflicting titles exist for the same piece of land or property. In these cases, new approaches such as conditional titling and comprehensive legal reform must not only devise effective yet fair dispute resolution mechanisms, but also seek to prevent the reproduction of similar disputes for the future.

* * *

Though the preceding points reflect the broadest conclusions of this volume, more specific recommendations are found in each chapter. As the rule of law gains increasing significance, further assessment of its relevance and use in peacebuilding processes—and further examination of the underlying tensions contained in many of the all-embracing claims commonly made on its behalf—are imperative. Rather than provide ready-made solutions, our primary goal has been to provoke further debate about the objectives and design of rule of law programs. Such debate is integral to the capacity of international programs to support the rule of law as an important component of peacebuilding strategies.

Notes

I thank Reyko Huang, Adam Lupel, and James Cockayne for their comments on earlier versions of this chapter. All errors are my sole responsibility. The views expressed herein are those of the author and do not necessarily represent the views of the United Nations or the International Criminal Tribunal for the former Yugoslavia.

1. UN General Assembly Resolution 60/251 (2006), on the Human Rights Council, paras. 3, 5(a), 5(e).

2. UN General Assembly Resolution 60/180 (2005), on the Peacebuilding Commission, para. 2.

3. United Nations, *Uniting Our Strengths: Enhancing United Nations Support for the Rule of Law,* UN Doc. A/61/636-S/2006/980 (December 14, 2006), para. 3.

4. United Nations, *The Rule of Law at the National and International Levels,* General Assembly Resolution 61/39 (December 4, 2006).

5. United Nations, *Uniting Our Strengths,* para. 49.

6. United Nations, *The Rule of Law and Transitional Justice in Conflict and Post-Conflict Societies: Report of the Secretary-General,* UN Doc. S/2004/616 (August 3, 2004).

7. Ibid., para. 17.

8. See, for example, Refugee Law Project, *Whose Justice? Perceptions of Uganda's Amnesty Act 2000: The Potential for Conflict Resolution and Long-Term Reconciliation,* Working Paper no. 15 (February 2005). Asia Foundation, *Survey Report on Citizens' Perceptions of the Indonesian Justice Sector: Preliminary Findings and Recommendations,* survey research from AC Nielson (2001); USAID and Asia Foundation, *Law and Justice in East Timor: A Survey of Citizen Awareness and Attitudes Regarding Law and Justice in East Timor* (2004). See also Foundation for Coexistence, *Ethnic Relations and Human Security in Eastern Sri Lanka: A Report Based on Individual Interviews* (2004).

9. United Nations, *A Comprehensive Strategy to Eliminate Future Sexual Exploitation and Abuse in UN Peacekeeping Operations,* UN Doc. A/59/710 (March 24, 2005).

Acronyms

AIDS	acquired immunodeficiency syndrome
ASEAN	Association of Southeast Asian Nations
CIDA	Canadian International Development Agency
CNRT	National Council of Timorese Resistance
CSCE	Conference on Security and Cooperation in Europe
CTC	Counter-Terrorism Committee (United Nations)
CTED	Counter-Terrorism Executive Directorate (United Nations)
DAC	Development and Assistance Committee (OECD)
DDR	disarmament, demobilization, and reintegration
DfID	Department for International Development (United Kingdom)
DPA	Department of Political Affairs (United Nations)
DPKO	Department of Peacekeeping Operations (United Nations)
DRC	Democratic Republic of Congo
ECPS	Executive Committee on Peace and Security (United Nations)
EU	European Union
FALINTIL	National Liberation of East Timor
FAO	Food and Agriculture Organization
FARC	Revolutionary Armed Forced of Colombia
FATF	Financial Action Task Force (OECD)
HIV	human immunodeficiency virus
HLP	housing, land, and property
HRFOR	Human Rights Field Operation (Rwanda)
ICJ	International Commission of Jurists
IDP	internally displaced person
IFI	international financial institution
INTERFET	International Force in East Timor

IPA	International Peace Academy
IRM	Innovative Resource Management
KFOR	Kosovo Force
LURD	Liberians United for Reconciliation and Democracy
MCC	Model Criminal Code (Model Codes Project)
MCCP	Model Code of Criminal Procedure (Model Codes Project)
MDA	Model Detention Act (Model Codes Project)
MICIVIH	International Civilian Mission in Haiti
MINOPUH	UN Civilian Police in Haiti
MINUGUA	UN Verification Mission in Guatemala
MINUSTAH	UN Stabilization Mission in Haiti
MLEPA	Model Law Enforcement Powers Act (Model Codes Project)
MONUC	UN Organization Mission in the Democratic Republic of Congo
NATO	North Atlantic Treaty Organization
NGO	nongovernmental organization
OAS	Organization of American States
OCHA	Office for the Coordination of Humanitarian Affairs (United Nations)
OECD	Organization for Economic Cooperation and Development
OHCHR	Office of the High Commissioner for Human Rights (United Nations)
OLA	Office of Legal Affairs (United Nations)
ONUB	UN Operation in Burundi
ONUSAL	UN Observer Mission in El Salvador
OSCE	Organization for Security and Cooperation in Europe
OSI	Open Society Institute
PCIJ	Permanent Court of International Justice
SDC	Swiss Development Cooperation
SRSG	Special Representative of the Secretary-General
TI	Transparency International
TRC	Truth and Reconciliation Commission (South Africa)
UK	United Kingdom
UN	United Nations
UNAMA	UN Assistance Mission in Afghanistan
UNDAF	UN Development Assistance Framework
UNDP	UN Development Programme
UNESCO	UN Educational, Scientific, and Cultural Organization
UNHCR	UN High Commissioner for Refugees
UNHRP	UN Housing Rights Programme
UNICEF	UN Children's Fund
UNIFEM	UN Development Fund for Women
UNMIB	UN Mission in Bosnia and Herzegovina

UNMIH	UN Mission in Haiti
UNMIK	UN Interim Administration Mission in Kosovo
UNMIL	UN Mission in Liberia
UNOCI	UN Operation in Côte d'Ivoire
UNODC	UN Office on Drugs and Crime
UNOMIL	UN Observer Mission in Liberia
UNOMSIL	UN Observer Mission in Sierra Leone
UNPROFOR	UN Protection Force
UNSMIH	UN Support Mission in Haiti
UNTAC	UN Transitional Authority in Cambodia
UNTAES	UN Transitional Administration for Eastern Slavonia, Baranja, and Western Sirmium
UNTAET	UN Transitional Administration in East Timor
UNTMIH	UN Transitional Mission in Haiti
US	United States
USAID	US Agency for International Development

Bibliography

Abu Toameh, Khaled, and Larry Derfner. "A State of Corruption: Palestinians Desire Nationhood, but Is This the Kind of Nation They Want?" *US News and World Report,* July 2002.

Ades, Alberto, and Rafael Di Tella. "Rents, Competition, and Corruption." *American Economic Review* 89, no. 4 (September 1999): 982–993.

Afghan Assistance Coordination Authority. "National Development Framework." Consultation draft. Kabul, April 2002.

African Union. *African Union Convention on Preventing and Combating Corruption.* Maputo, 2003.

Alden Wiley, Liz. "Formalizing the Informal: Is There a Way to Safely Secure Majority Rural Land Rights?" Paper presented to the EGDI-WIDER conference "Unlocking Human Potential: Linking the Informal and Formal Sectors." Helsinki, September 17–18, 2004.

———. "Land and the Constitution." Policy brief. Kabul: Afghanistan Research and Evaluation Unit, September 2003.

———. "Land Rights in Crisis: Restoring Tenure Security in Afghanistan." Issue Paper Series. Kabul: Afghanistan Research and Evaluation Unit, March 2003.

Almonte, Jose T. "Enhancing State Capacity and Legitimacy in the Counter-Terror War." In *After Bali: The Threat of Terrorism in Southeast Asia,* edited by Kumar Ramakrishna and See Seng Tan. Singapore: Institute of Defense and Strategic Studies, 2003.

Alvarez, Jose. "The Security Council's War on Terrorism: Problems and Policy Options." In *Judicial Review of the Security Council by Member States,* edited by Erika de Wet and André Nollkaemper. Amsterdam: Amsterdam Center of International Law, 2003.

Amnesty International. "2005 UN Commission on Human Rights: Monitor Needed to Protect Rights in Counter-Terrorism." Geneva, April 15, 2005.

———. "Yemen: The Rule of Law Sidelined in the Name of Security." September 24, 2003.

Andersen, R. "How Multilateral Development Assistance Triggered the Conflict in Rwanda." *Third World Quarterly* 21, no. 3 (2000): 441–456.

Anderson, Christopher J., and Yuliya V. Tverdova. "Corruption, Political Allegiances, and Attitudes Toward Government in Contemporary Democracies." *American Journal of Political Science* 47, no. 1 (January 2003): 91–109.

Aristotle. *The Nicomachean Ethics.* Translated by David Ross. Revised by J. L. Ackrill and J. O. Urmson. Oxford: Oxford University Press, 1998.

Azfar, Omar. "Corruption and the Delivery of Health and Education Services." In *Fighting Corruption in Developing Countries: Strategies and Analysis,* edited by Bertram I. Spector. Bloomington, Conn.: Kumarian, 2005.

Bailey, Bruce. "Synthesis of Lessons Learned of Donor Practices in Fighting Corruption." Paper prepared for the OECD Development Assistance Committee's Network on Governance. Paris, June 23, 2003.

Baillet, Cecilia. "Property Restitution in Guatemala: A Transnational Dilemma." In *Returning Home: Housing and Property Restitution Rights of Refugees and Displaced Persons,* edited by Scott Leckie. Ardsley, N.Y.: Transnational, 2003.

Ballentine, Karen, and Jake Sherman, eds. *The Political Economy of Armed Conflict: Beyond Greed and Grievance.* Boulder: Lynne Rienner, 2003.

Banfield, Edward. *The Moral Basis of a Backward Society.* Chicago: Free Press, 1958.

Bannon, Ian, and Paul Collier. *Natural Resources and Violent Conflict: Options and Actions.* Washington, D.C.: World Bank, 2003.

Barahona de Brito, Alexandra. *Human Rights and Democratization in Latin America: Uruguay and Chile.* Oxford: Oxford University Press, 1997.

Baranyi, Stephen, Carmen Diana Deere, and Manuel Morales. *Land and Policy Development in Latin America: Opening for Policy Research.* Ottawa: North-South Institute and International Development Research Centre, 2004.

Bassiouni, Cherif M., ed. *Post-Conflict Justice.* Ardsley, N.Y.: Transnational, 2002.

Beauvais, Joel C. "Benevolent Despotism: A Critique of UN State-Building in East Timor." *New York University Journal of International Law and Politics* 33 (2001): 1101–1178.

Bennouna, Mohamed. "Les sanctions economiques des Nations Unies." *Collected Courses* 300 (2002): 14–77.

Benomar, Jamal. "Rule of Law Technical Assistance in Haiti: Lessons Learned." In *Empowerment, Security, and Opportunity Through Law and Justice.* World Bank conference, St. Petersburg, Russia, July 8–12, 2001. http://haiticci.undg.org/uploads/lessons%20learned%20justice_2001.pdf.

Benton, Lauren. "Beyond Legal Pluralism: Towards a New Approach to Law in the Informal Sector." *Social and Legal Studies* 3, no. 2 (1994): 223–242.

Berdal, Mats, and David M. Malone, eds. *Greed and Grievance: Economic Agendas in Civil Wars.* Boulder: Lynne Rienner, 2000.

Biebesheimer, C., and J. Payne. "IDB Experience in Justice Reform: Lessons Learned and Elements for Policy Formulation." Technical Paper Series. Washington, D.C.: Inter-American Development Bank, 2001.

Bingham, Lord of Cornhill. "The Rule of Law." Sixth Sir David Williams Lecture, Cambridge, November 16, 2006. http://cpl.law.cam.ac.uk/media/the%20rule%20of%20law%202006.pdf.

Blair, Harry, and Gary Hansen. "Weighing In On the Scales of Justice: Strategic Approaches for Donor-Supported Rule of Law Programs." Assessment Report no. 7. Washington, D.C.: US Agency for International Development, 1994.

Boisson de Chazournes, Laurence. *Les contre-mesures dans les relations internationales economiques.* Paris: IUHEI/Pedone, 1992.

———. "Qu'est ce que la pratique en droit international?" In *La pratique et le droit international.* Colloque de Genève de la Société Française pour le Droit International. Paris: Pedone, 2004.

———. "The United Nations on Shifting Sands: About the Rebuilding of Iraq." *International Law Forum* 5, no. 4 (2003): 254–261.

Bonnefoy, Laurent, and Renaud Detalle. "The Security Paradox and Development in Unified Yemen (1990–2005)." In *Security and Development: Searching for Critical Connections,* edited by Neclâ Tschirgi, Michael Lund, and Francesco Mancini. Boulder: Lynne Rienner, forthcoming.

Bordea, Ruxandra. "La Mission Intérimaire d'Administration des Nations Unies au Kosovo." LLM thesis, University of Paris I, September 2000.

Bossuyt, Jean, and Geert Laporte. "Partnership in the 1990s: How to Make It Work Better." Policy Management Brief no. 3. Maastricht: European Center for Development Policy Management, 1994. http://www.srds.co.uk/partnerships/docs/bossuyt.rtf.

Bossuyt, Marc. *The Adverse Consequences of Economic Sanctions on the Enjoyment of Human Rights.* UN Subcommission on the Promotion and Protection of Human Rights. UN Doc. E/CN.4/Sub.2/2000/33, June 21, 2000.

Bossuyt, M., P. Lemmens, K. De Feyter, and S. Parmentier, eds. *Out of the Ashes: Reparation for Victims of Gross and Systematic Human Rights Violations.* Brussels: Intersentia, 2006.

Bratton, Michael. "Statebuilding and Democratization in Sub-Saharan Africa: Forwards, Backwards, or Together?" Working Paper no. 43. *Afrobarometer,* September 2004. http://www.afrobarometer.org/abseries.html.

Bratton, Michael, Robert Mattes, and E. Gyimah-Boadi. *Public Opinion, Democracy, and Market Reform in Africa.* Cambridge: Cambridge University Press, 2004.

Braun, Miguel, and Rafael Di Tella. "Inflation, Inflation Variability, and Corruption." *Economics and Politics* 16, no. 1 (March 2004): 77–100.

Brinkerhoff, Derek W., and Arthur A. Goldsmith. "Clientelism, Patrimonialism, and Democratic Governance: An Overview and Framework for Assessment and Programming." Paper prepared for the USAID Office of Democracy and Governance. Cambridge, Mass.: Abt Associates, December 2002. http://www.abtassociates .com/reports/2002601089183_30950.pdf.

Brown, Michael, Phillipe Ngwala, Albert Songo, and Leonard Wande. "Combating Low-level Corruption on Waterways in the Democratic Republic of Congo: Approaches from Bandundu and Equateur Provinces." Public Law Research Paper no. 116. Washington, D.C.: George Washington University Law School, October 1, 2004.

Brown, Stephen. "Quiet Diplomacy and Recurring 'Ethnic Clashes' in Kenya." In *From Promise to Practice: Strengthening UN Capacities for the Prevention of Violent Conflict,* edited by Chandra L. Sriram. Boulder: Lynne Rienner, 2003.

Bryden, Alan, and Heiner Hanggi, eds. *Reform and Reconstruction of the Security Sector.* Geneva: Geneva Centre for the Democratic Control of Armed Forces, 2004.

Buckles, Daniel. *Cultivating Peace: Conflict and Collaboration in Natural Resources Management.* Washington, D.C.: World Bank Institute, 1999.

Burg, Elliot M. "Law and Development: A Review of the Literature and a Critique of 'Scholars in Self-Estrangement.'" *American Journal of Comparative Law* 25 (1977): 492–530.

Burnside, Craig, and David Dollar. "Aid, Policies, and Growth." *American Economic Review* 90, no. 4 (September 2000): 847–868.

Call, Charles T., ed. *Constructing Justice and Security After War.* Washington, D.C.: US Institute of Peace, 2006.

———. "Democratization, War, and State-Building: Constructing the Rule of Law in El Salvador." *Journal of Latin American Studies* 35, no. 4 (2003): 827–862.

Calus, Andrzej. "Estimates: 2004–2005 Part III—Report on Plans and Priorities." Minister for International Cooperation, Ottawa. http://www.acdi-cida.gc.ca/inet/images .nsf/vluimages/publications2/$file/cida-rpp-2004-05.pdf.

————. "The Right of a State to International Intercourse." *Polish Yearbook of International Law* 7 (1975): 209–253.

Caplan, Richard. *International Governance of War-Torn Territories: Rule and Reconstruction.* Oxford: Oxford University Press, 2005.

Carment, David. "Creating Conditions for Peace: What Role for the UN and Regional Actors?" Meeting note. New York: International Peace Academy, 2002.

Carnegie Commission on Preventing Deadly Conflict. "Preventing Deadly Conflict: Final Report." New York, 1997.

Carothers, Thomas. "The Many Agendas of Rule of Law Reform in Latin America." In *Rule of Law in Latin America: The International Promotion of Judicial Reform,* edited by Pilar Domingo and Rachel Sieder. London: Institute of Latin American Studies, 2001.

————. "Promoting the Rule of Law Abroad: The Problem of Knowledge." Washington, D.C.: Carnegie Endowment for International Peace, January 2003.

————. "The Rule of Law Revival." *Foreign Affairs* 77, no. 2 (1998): 95–106.

Carothers, Thomas, ed. *Promoting the Rule of Law Abroad: In Search of Knowledge.* Washington, D.C.: Carnegie Endowment for International Peace, 2006.

Cartier-Bresson, Jean. "From the State of the Question to the Question of the State." Copenhagen: Copenhagen Consensus Opponent Notes on Poor Governance and Corruption, April 2004.

Carver, Jeremy P. "Making Financial Sanctions Work: Preconditions for Successful Implementation of Sanctions by the Implementing State." Report of the Expert Seminar on Targeting UN Financial Sanctions. Bern: Swiss Federal Office for Foreign Economic Affairs, 1998.

Cedergren, Jan. "What Do State Actors and Voluntary Organisations Expect from Each Other as Concrete Contributions?" In *Preventing Violent Conflict and Building Peace: On Interaction Between State Actors and Voluntary Organizations,* edited by Bernt Jonsson. Stockholm: European Centre for Conflict Prevention and Swedish Peace Team Forum, 2002.

Center for Global Development. *On the Brink: Weak States and US National Security.* Washington, D.C., 2004.

Centre for Humanitarian Dialogue. *Assistance to Justice and the Rule of Law in Afghanistan.* Geneva, February 2004.

Centre on Housing Rights and Evictions. *Protecting Housing Rights, Preventing Evictions: Activity Report 2000–2002.* Geneva, 2003.

Chandler, David. *Bosnia: Faking Democracy After Dayton.* London: Pluto, 1999.

Chang, Ha-Joon. *Kicking Away the Ladder: Development Strategy in Historical Perspective.* London: Anthem, 2002.

Chapman, David. "Corruption and the Education Sector." *Sectoral Perspectives on Corruption.* Study prepared by Management Systems International, Washington, D.C., November 2002.

Checkel, Jeffrey T. "Compliance and Conditionality." ARENA Working Paper no. 00/18. http://www.arena.uio.no/publications/wp00_18.htm.

Chesterman, Simon. *Just War or Just Peace? Humanitarian Intervention and International Law.* Oxford Monographs in International Law. Oxford: Oxford University Press, 2001.

————. "Occupation as Liberation: International Humanitarian Law and Regime Change." *Ethics and International Affairs* 18, no. 3 (2004): 51–64.

————. "The Use of Force in UN Peace Operations." External study. New York: UN Department of Peacekeeping Operations, Peacekeeping Best Practices Unit, August 31, 2004. http://pbpu.unlb.org/pbpu/library/chesterman%20(final%20final).pdf.

————. *You, the People: The United Nations, Transitional Administration, and State-Building.* Oxford: Oxford University Press, 2004.

Chesterman, Simon, Michael Ignatieff, and Ramesh Thakur, eds. *Making States Work: State Failure and the Crisis of Governance.* Tokyo: UN University Press, 2005.

Chingono, Mark, and Guy Lamb. "The New Partnership for Africa's Security: The United Nations, Regional Organizations and Future Security Threats in Africa." Seminar report. Cape Town, South Africa: Centre for Conflict Resolution, October 2004.

Chua, Amy. *World on Fire: How Exporting Free Market Democracy Breeds Ethnic Hatred and Global Instability.* New York: Doubleday, 2003.

Clagett, Brice M., and O. Thomas Johnson. "May Israel as a Belligerent Occupant Lawfully Exploit Previously Unexploited Oil Resources of the Gulf of Suez?" *American Journal of International Law* 72, no. 3 (July 1978): 558–585.

Clague, Christopher. *Institutions and Economic Development: Growth and Governance in Less Developed and Post-Socialist Countries.* Baltimore: Johns Hopkins University Press, 1997.

Clarke, John N. "Dimensions and Processes of Global Governance." In *Global Governance in the Twenty-First Century,* edited by John N. Clarke and Geoffrey R. Edwards. New York: Palgrave Macmillan, 2004.

Coetzee, Martin. "An Overview of the TRC Amnesty Process." In *The Provocations of Amnesty: Memory, Justice, and Impunity,* edited by Charles Villa-Vicencio. Trenton, N.J.: Africa World, 2003.

Colletta, Nat J., and Michelle L. Cullen. *Violent Conflict and the Transformation of Social Capital: Lessons from Cambodia, Rwanda, Guatemala, and Somalia.* Washington, D.C.: World Bank, 2000.

Collier, Paul, et al. *Breaking the Conflict Trap: Civil War and Development Policy.* New York: Oxford University Press, 2003.

Collier, Paul, Anke Hoeffler, and Mans Soderbom. "On the Duration of Civil Wars." *Journal of Peace Research* 41, no. 3 (May 2004): 253–273.

Conca, Ken, and Geoffrey D. Dabelko, eds. *Environmental Peacemaking.* Baltimore: Johns Hopkins University Press, 2002.

Corell, Hans. "A Challenge to the United Nations and the World: Developing the Rule of Law." *Temple International and Comparative Law Journal* 18, no. 2 (2004): 391–402.

Cortright, David, and George A. Lopez. "Reforming Sanctions." In *The UN Security Council: From the Cold War to the 21st Century,* edited by David M. Malone. Boulder: Lynne Rienner, 2004.

Cortright, David, Alistair Millar, Linda M. Gerber, and George A. Lopez. "An Action Agenda for Enhancing the United Nations Program on Counter-Terrorism." Report by the Fourth Freedom Forum and the Joan B. Kroc Institute for International Peace Studies, September 2004.

————. "Sanctions Against Iraq." In *The Sanctions Decade: Assessing UN Strategies in the 1990s,* edited by David Cortright and George A. Lopez. Boulder: Lynne Rienner, 2000.

Council of Europe. *The Convention for the Protection of Human Rights and Fundamental Freedoms.* Rome, November 4, 1950.

————. *Civil Law Convention on Corruption.* Strasbourg, November 4, 1999. http://conventions.coe.int/treaty/en/treaties/html/174.htm.

————. *Criminal Law Convention on Corruption.* Strasbourg, January 27, 1999. http://conventions.coe.int/treaty/en/treaties/html/173.htm.

Cousens, Elizabeth M., and Charles K. Cater. *Toward Peace in Bosnia: Implementing the Dayton Accords.* Boulder: Lynne Rienner, 2001.

Cox, Marcus, and Madeline Garlick. "Musical Chairs: Property Repossession and Return Strategies in Bosnia and Herzegovina." In *Returning Home: Housing and Property Restitution Rights of Refugees and Displaced Persons,* edited by Scott Leckie. Ardsley, N.Y.: Transnational, 2003.

Cragin, Kim, and Peter Chalk. "Terrorism and Development: Using Social and Economic Development to Inhibit a Resurgence of Terrorism." Santa Monica: RAND, 2003.

Crawford, Gordon. "Foreign Aid and Political Conditionality: Issues of Effectiveness and Consistency." *Democratization* 4, no. 3 (1997): 69–108.

Crenshaw, Martha. *Terrorism and International Cooperation.* New York: Institute for East-West Security Studies, 1989.

Crook, Richard. "Civil War in Côte d'Ivoire: Behind the Headlines." Sussex: Institute of Development Studies, University of Sussex, January 25, 2005. http://www.ids.ac.uk/ids/govern/pdfs/cdicivilwarlongv.pdf.

Crowley, Eve. "Women's Rights to Land and Natural Resources: Some Implications for a Rights-Based Approach." Rome: Food and Agricultural Organization, January 1999. http://www.fao.org/sd/ltdirect/ltan0025.htm.

Culolo, Astrigildo Joao Pedro. "Combating Organised Crime in Angola." In *Organised Crime in Southern Africa: Assessing Legislation,* edited by Charles Goredeman. Monograph no. 56. Cape Town, South Africa: Institute for Security Studies. http://www.iss.co.za/pubs/monographs/no56/chap9.html.

Dailler, P. "Article 42." In *La Charte des Nations Unies,* edited by Jean-Pierre Cot and Alain Pellet. Paris: Economica, 2005.

Daniel, Clifton, ed. *Chronicle of the 20th Century.* Mount Kisco, N.Y.: Chronicle, 1987.

Danish Ministry of Foreign Affairs. *DANIDA's Annual Report 2002.* Copenhagen, 2002.

———. *Vietnam: Strategy for Danish Bilateral Development Cooperation with Vietnam.* Copenhagen, February 2000.

———. *A World of Difference: The Government's Vision for New Priorities in Danish Development Assistance, 2004–2008.* Copenhagen, June 2003.

Dashti-Gibson, Jaleh, and Richard W. Conroy. "Taming Terrorism: Sanctions Against Libya, Sudan, and Afghanistan." In *The Sanctions Decade: Assessing UN Strategies in the 1990s,* edited by David Cortright and George A. Lopez. Boulder: Lynne Rienner, 2000.

Daudet, Yves. "L'action des Nations Unies en matiere d'administration territoriale." *Cursos Euromediterráneos Bancaja de Derecho Internacional* 6 (2002): 459–542.

David, Pedro. "Technical Cooperation in Strengthening the Rule of Law in Latin America: Applicability of United Nations Standards and Norms in Crime Prevention and Criminal Justice to Facilitate Access to Justice." In *The Application of United Nations Standards and Norms in Crime Prevention and Criminal Justice.* http://www.unodc.org/pdf/crime/publications/standards%20&%20norms.pdf.

de Greiff, Pablo, ed. *The Handbook of Reparations.* Oxford: Oxford University Press, 2006.

———. "Reparations Efforts in International Perspective: What Compensation Contributes to the Achievement of Imperfect Justice?" In *To Repair the Irreparable: Reparations and Reconstruction in South Africa,* edited by Erik Doxtader. Cape Town: David Phillips, 2004.

de Greiff, Pablo, and Marieke Wierda. "The Trust Fund for Victims of the International Criminal Court: Between Possibilities and Constraints." In *The Right to Reparation for Victims of Gross and Systematic Human Rights Violations,* edited by M. Bossuyt. Brussels: Intersentia, forthcoming.

De Soto, Hernando. *The Mystery of Capital: Why Capitalism Triumphs in the West and Fails Everywhere Else.* New York: Basic, 2000.

de Sousa Santos, Boaventura. "The Law of the Oppressed: The Construction and Reproduction of Legality in Pasagada." *Law and Society Review* 14, no. 3 (1977): 279–302.

de Soysa, Indra. "The Resource Curse: Are Civil Wars Driven by Rapacity or Paucity?" In *Greed and Grievance: Economic Agendas in Civil Wars,* edited by Mats Berdal and David M. Malone. Boulder: Lynne Rienner, 2000.

de Waal, Alex. "Counter-Insurgency on the Cheap." *London Review of Books* 26, no. 15 (August 2004).

Deininger, Klaus. *Land Policies for Growth and Poverty Reduction.* Washington, D.C.: World Bank and Oxford University Press, 2003.

Department for International Development. *Safety, Security, and Accessible Justice: Putting Policy Into Practice.* London: Department for International Development, July 2002.

Department for International Development, Foreign and Commonwealth Office, and Department for Treasury. "Partnerships for Poverty Reduction: Changing Aid 'Conditionality.'" Draft policy paper. London: Department for International Development, September 2004. http://www.dfid.gov.uk/pubs/files/conditionality change.pdf.

Department for International Development, Foreign and Commonwealth Office, and Ministry of Defence. *The Global Conflict Prevention Pool: A Joint UK Government Approach to Reducing Conflict.* London: Foreign and Commonwealth Office, 2003.

Department for International Development, Foreign and Commonwealth Office, Ministry of Defence, and Cabinet Office. *Evaluation of the Conflict Prevention Pools; UK Government Response.* London: Department for International Development, July 2004.

Desker, Barry, and Kumar Ramakrishna. "Forging an Indirect Strategy in Southeast Asia." In *The Battle for Hearts and Minds: Using Soft Power to Undermine Terrorist Networks,* edited by Alexander T. J. Lennon. Cambridge: Massachusetts Institute of Technology Press, 2003.

Dexter, Tracy, and Philippe Ntahombaye. *The Role of Informal Justice Systems in Fostering the Rule of Law in Post-Conflict Situations: The Case of Burundi.* Geneva: Centre for Humanitarian Dialogue, July 2005.

Dhundale, Lis, and Erik André Andersen, eds. *Revisiting the Role of Civil Society in the Promotion of Human Rights.* Copenhagen: Danish Institute for Human Rights, 2005.

Di Tella, Rafael, and Ernesto Schargrodsky. "The Role of Wages and Auditing During a Crackdown on Corruption in the City of Buenos Aires." *Journal of Law and Economics* 46 (April 2003): 269–292.

Dicey, Albert Venn. *An Introduction to the Study of the Law of the Constitution.* 8th ed. London: Macmillan, 1915, 1959.

Djankov, Simeon, Rafael La Porta, Florencio Lopez-De-Silanes, and Andrei Shleifer. "Courts." *Quarterly Journal of Economics* 11, no. 18 (May 2, 2003): 453–517.

Dodson, Alan, and Veijo Heiskanen. "Housing and Property Restitution in Kosovo." In *Returning Home: Housing and Property Restitution Rights of Refugees and Displaced Persons,* edited by Scott Leckie. Ardsley, N.Y.: Transnational, 2003.

Dollar, David, Raymond Fisman, and Roberta Gatti. "Are Women Really the 'Fairer' Sex? Corruption and Women in Government." Washington, D.C.: World Bank, 2001.

Doyle, Michael. "War-Making and Peace-Making: The United Nations' Post Cold War Record." In *Turbulent Peace: The Challenges of Managing International Conflict,* edited by Chester A. Crocker. Washington, D.C.: US Institute of Peace, 2001.

du Plessis, Jean. "Slow Start on a Long Journey: Land Restitution Issues in East Timor, 1999–2001." In *Returning Home: Housing and Property Restitution Rights of Refugees and Displaced Persons,* edited by Scott Leckie. Ardsley, N.Y.: Transnational, 2003.

Duffield, Mark. *Global Governance and the New Wars: The Merger of Development and Security.* London: Zed, 2001.

Dunoff, Jeffrey L., Steven Ratner, and David Wippman, eds. *International Law: Norms, Actors, Processes.* New York: Aspen Law and Business, 2002.

Durch, William, and Victoria Holt. *The Brahimi Report and the Future of UN Peace Operations.* Washington, D.C.: Henri Stimson Center, 2003. http://www.stimson .org/pub.cfm?id=90.

Dworkin, Ronald. *A Matter of Principle.* London: Harvard University Press, 1987.

———."'Natural' Law Revisited." In *The Nature and Process of Law,* edited by Patricia Smith. Oxford: Oxford University Press, 1993.

Easterly, William, Ross Levine, and David Roodman. "Aid, Policies, and Growth: Comment." *American Economic Review* 94 (June 2004): 774–780.

Eldon, Stewart. "East Timor." Statement to the UN Security Council. January 26, 2001.

Elgaard Brett, Julian. *Far from Business as Usual: United Nations' Responses to International Terrorism.* Copenhagen: Danish Institute of International Affairs, 2002.

Eliott, Kimberly Ann. "Analysing the Effects of Targeted Financial Sanctions." In *Report on the Second Interlaken Seminar on Targeting United Nations Financial Sanctions.* Geneva, March 29–31, 1999.

Ellis, Mark. "Strengthening Democracy: The Rule of Law and Institution Building." Paper presented at the conference "InterAction: Strengthening African Democracy." Abuja, Nigeria, November 22–25, 2004.

Enloe, Cynthia H. *Bananas, Beaches, and Bases: Making Feminist Sense of International Politics.* London: Pandora, 1989.

Escobar, Arturo. *Encountering Development: The Making and Unmaking of the Third World.* Princeton: Princeton University Press, 1994.

European Commission. *The European Union's Role in Promoting Human Rights and Democracy in Third Countries.* COM (2001) 252.

European Union. "Communication from the Commission on Conflict Prevention." 2001. http://www.europa.eu.int/comm/external_relations/cfsp/news/com2001_211 _en.pdf.

———. "EU Programme for the Prevention of Violent Conflicts." 2001. www.eu2001.se/static/eng/pdf/violent.pdf.

———. "European Commission Check-list for Root Causes of Conflict." http:// europa.eu.int/comm/external_relations/cpcm/cp/list.htm.

———. "One Year On: The Commission's Conflict Prevention Policy." March 2002. http://ec.europa.eu/external_relations/cfsp/cpcm/cp/rep.htm.

European Union Presidency. "Justice and the Rule of Law: The UN Role." Statement delivered to the UN Security Council. September 30, 2003. http://www.europa-eu -un.org/articles/de/article_2844_de.htm.

Evans, Gareth. *Cooperating for Peace: the Global Agenda for the 1990s and Beyond.* St. Leonards: Allen and Unwin, 1993.

Evans, Peter. *Embedded Autonomy: States and Industrial Transformation.* Princeton: Princeton University Press, 1995.

Fairlie, Megan A. "Affirming Brahimi: East Timor Makes the Case for a Model Criminal Code." *American University International Law Review* 18, no. 5 (2003): 1059–1102.

Faundez, Julio, ed. *Good Governance and Law: Legal and Institutional Reform in Developing Countries.* New York: St. Martin's, 1997.

Fawaz, Mona. "Strategizing for Housing: An Investigation of the Production and Regulation of Low-Income Housing in the Suburbs of Beirut." PhD diss., Cambridge, Massachusetts Institute of Technology, 2004.

Fernandes, Edesio, and Ann Varley, eds. *Illegal Cities: Law and Urban Change in Developing Countries.* New York: St. Martin's, 1998.

Fitzpatrick, Daniel. "Land Policy in Post-Conflict Circumstances: Some Lessons from East Timor." Working paper. UN High Commissioner for Refugees, February 2002.

Food and Agriculture Organization. "Land Tenure." http://www.fao.org/sd/in1_en.htm.

Fox, Gregory H. "The Right to Political Participation in International Law." *Yale Journal of International Law* 17 (1992): 539–607.

Fox, Gregory H., and Brad R. Roth, eds. *Democratic Governance and International Law.* Cambridge: Cambridge University Press, 2000.

Fox, Merritt B. "Imposing Liability for Losses from Aggressive War: An Economic Analysis of the UNCC." *European Journal of International Law* 13, no. 1 (2002): 201–222.

Fox, William F. *Understanding Administrative Law.* 4th ed. Newark: Matthew Bender, 2000.

Franck, Thomas. "The Emerging Right to Democratic Governance." *American Journal of International Law* 86 (1992): 46–91.

Friedman, Thomas. "The Arabs at the Crossroads." *New York Times,* July 3, 2002.

Fukuyama, Francis. *State-Building: Governance and World Order in the 21st Century.* Ithaca: Cornell University Press, 2004.

Fuller, Lon. *The Morality of Law.* London: Yale University Press, 1969.

Garcia, Victoria. "U.S. Military Assistance to 1460 Report Countries: 1990–2005." Washington, D.C.: Center for Defense Information, April 13, 2004. http://www.cdi.org/pdfs/1460.pdf.

Gardish, Hafizullah. "Chief Justice Under Scrutiny." Afghan Recovery Report no. 54. Washington, D.C.: Institute for War and Peace Reporting, April 1, 2003.

Garro, Alejandro, and Henry Dahl. "Legal Accountability for Human Rights in Argentina: One Step Forward and Two Steps Backward." *Human Rights Journal* 8 (1987): 283–344.

Gibbons, Elizabeth. *Sanctions in Haïti: Human Rights and Democracy Under Assault.* Westport: Praeger, 1999.

Golding, Martin. *The Philosophy of Law.* London: Prentice Hall, 1975.

Goldstone, Jack A., et al. *State Failure Task Force Report: Phase III Findings.* McLean, Va.: Science Applications International, September 30, 2000.

Golub, Stephan. "Beyond Rule of Law Orthodoxy: The Legal Empowerment Alternative." In *Promoting the Rule of Law Abroad: In Search of Knowledge,* edited by Thomas Carothers. Washington, D.C.: Carnegie Endowment for International Peace, 2006.

Goodhand, Jonathan. "Conflict Assessments: A Synthesis Report: Kyrgyzstan, Moldova, Nepal, and Sri Lanka." London: King's College Conflict, Security, and Development Group, 2001.

Gordon, Ruth. "Saving Failed States: Sometimes a Neocolonialist Notion." *American University Journal of International Law and Policy* 12, no. 6 (1997): 903–974.

Governance Access Learning Network. "Corruption in Post-War Reconstruction: Breaking the Vicious Cycle." Baabda, Lebanon: Lebanese Transparency Association, January 2005.

Government of Australia. Department of Foreign Affairs and Trade. "Promoting Good Governance, Human Rights, and Development." In *Advancing the National Interest: White Paper on Foreign Affairs and Trade.* Commonwealth of Australia, 2003. http://www.dfat.gov.au/ani/chapter_10.html.

Government of Cambodia. *Provisions Relating to the Judiciary and Criminal Law and Procedure Applicable in Cambodia During the Transitional Period.* Phnom Penh, September 10, 1992. http://www.icrc.org/ihl-nat.nsf/0/1eacfb8b87785c69c1256a3f0055cac3?opendocument.

Government of South Africa. *Promotion of National Unity and Reconciliation Act no. 34.* Cape Town, 1995.

Griffin, Michèle. "The Helmet and the Hoe: Linkages Between United Nations Development Assistance and Conflict Management." *Global Governance* 9 (2003): 199–217.

Grote, Rainer. "Rule of Law, Rechtstaat, and Etat de Droit." In *Constitutionalism, Universalism and Democracy: A Comparative Analysis,* edited by Christian Starck. Baden-Baden: Nomos, 1999.

Gupta, Sanjeev, Hamid Davoodi, and Rosa Alonso-Terme. "Does Corruption Affect Income Inequality and Poverty?" Working Paper no. 98/76. Washington, D.C.: International Monetary Fund, 1998.

Gutto, Shadrack B. O. *Property and Land Reform: Constitutional and Jurisprudential Perspectives.* Johannesburg: Butterworths, 1995.

Gwaltney, Captain Alton L., III. "Law and Order in Kosovo: A Look at Criminal Justice During the First Year of Operation Joint Guardian." In *Lessons from Kosovo: The KFOR Experience,* edited by Larry Wentz. Command and Control Research Program Publication Series. Washington, D.C.: Department of Defense, Command and Control Research Program, 2002.

Hager, Barry. "The Rule of Law: A Lexicon for Policy Makers." Washington, D.C.: Mansfield Center for Pacific Affairs, 1999.

Halberstam, Malvina. "The Evolution of the United Nations Position on Terrorism: From Exempting National Liberation Movements to Criminalizing Terrorism Wherever and by Whomever Committed." *Columbia Journal of Transnational Law* 41, no. 3 (2003): 547.

Hall, Ruth. "Redistributive Land Reforms in Southern Africa." Paper presented at the International Peace Academy workshop "Land, Property, and Conflict: Identifying Options for Rule of Law Programming. New York, December 2–3, 2004.

Hamber, Brandon, and K. Rasmussen. "Financing a Reparations Scheme for Victims of Political Violence." In *From Rhetoric to Responsibility: Making Reparations to the Survivors of Past Political Violence in South Africa,* edited by Brandon Hamber. Johannesburg: Center for the Study of Violence and Reconciliation, 2000.

Hammarberg, Thomas, and Patrick Gavigan. "Human Rights and Post-Conflict Institution Building." In *Honoring Human Rights: From Peace to Justice,* edited by Alice Henkin. Washington, D.C.: Aspen Institute, 1998.

Hammergren, Linn. "Do Judicial Councils Further Judicial Reform? Lessons from Latin America." Democracy and Rule of Law Project, Rule of Law Series no. 28. Washington, D.C.: Carnegie Endowment for International Peace, 2002.

Hampson, Fen Osler, Karin Wermester, and David M. Malone. "Introduction: Making Conflict Prevention a Priority." In *From Reaction to Conflict Prevention: Opportu-*

nities for the UN System, edited by Fen Osler Hampson. Boulder: Lynne Rienner, 2001.

Hand, Learned. *The Spirit of Liberty.* 3rd ed. Chicago: University of Chicago Press, 1960.

Hanggi, Heiner, and Theodor Winkler, eds. *Challenges of Security Sector Governance.* Geneva: Geneva Centre for the Democratic Control of Armed Forces, 2003.

Hart, H. L. A. *The Concept of Law.* Oxford: Clarendon, 1961.

Hayde, Wayne. "Ideals and Realities of the Rule of Law and Administration of Justice in Post-Conflict East Timor." *International Peacekeeping: The Yearbook of Peace Operations* 8 (2003): 73.

Hayner, Priscilla. *Unspeakable Truths.* London: Routledge, 2002.

Hegre, Havard, ed. "Special Issue on Duration and Termination of Civil War." *Journal of Peace Research* 41, no. 3 (2004).

Heller, Michael A. "Rule of Law Task Force Overview." New York: Initiative for Policy Dialogue, Columbia University, 2003. http://www0.gsb.columbia.edu/ipd/pub/ROLoverforweb.pdf.

———. "The Tragedy of the Anticommons: Property in the Transition from Marx to Markets." *Harvard Law Review* 111 (1998): 621–688.

Hellman, Joel, Geraint Jones, and Daniel Kaufmann. "Far from Home: Do Foreign Investors Import Higher Standards of Governance in Transition Economies?" Draft. August 2002.

———. "Seize the State, Seize the Day: State Capture, Corruption, and Influence in Transition." Policy Research Working Paper no. 2444. Washington, D.C.: World Bank, September 2000.

Heyman, Josiah, ed. *States and Illegal Practices.* New York: Berg, 1999.

Holbrooke, Richard. *To End a War.* New York: Random House, 1998.

Holm, Tor Tanke, and Espen Barth Eide, eds. *Peacebuilding and Police Reform.* Portland: Cass, 2000.

Holsti, Kalevi J. *The State, War, and the State of War.* Cambridge: Cambridge University Press, 1996.

Howard, Jessica, and Bruce Oswald, eds. *The Rule of Law on Peace Operations.* Melbourne: Asia Pacific Centre for Military Law, 2002.

Huang, Reyko. "Securing the Rule of Law: Assessing International Strategies for Post-Conflict Criminal Justice." New York: International Peace Academy, November 2005.

Hubbard, Michael. "Changing Customs: Lessons from Mozambique." Presentation to the Christian Michelsen Institute. Bergen, Norway, February 17, 2005.

Huber, Martina. "Monitoring the Rule of Law: Consolidated Framework and Report." Conflict Research Unit occasional paper. The Hague: Clingendael Institute, July 2002.

Human Rights First. *Assessing the New Normal: Liberty and Security for the Post–September 11 United States.* New York, 2003. http://www.humanrightsfirst.org/pubs/descriptions/assessing/assessingthenewnormal.pdf.

Human Rights Watch. "Hear No Evil, See No Evil: The UN Security Council's Approach to Human Rights Violations in the Global Counter-Terrorism Effort." August 10, 2004. http://www.hrw.org/backgrounder/un/2004/un0804/.

———. "UN: Sanctions Rules Must Protect Due Process." March 4, 2002. http://hrw.org/english/docs/2002/03/04/global5839.htm.

Huntington, Samuel S. *Political Order in Changing Societies.* New Haven: Yale University Press, 1968.

Hurwitz, Agnès, and Gordon Peake. "Strengthening the Security-Development Nexus: Assessing International Policy and Practice Since the 1990s." New York: International Peace Academy, April 2004.

Hurwitz, Agnès, and Kaysie Studdard. "Rule of Law Programs in Peace Operations." New York: International Peace Academy, August 2005.

Hurwitz, Agnès, Kaysie Studdard, and Rhodri Williams. "Housing, Land, Property, and Conflict Management: Identifying Policy Options for Rule of Law Programming." New York: International Peace Academy, October 2005.

Hutchinson, Allan, and Patrick Monahan, eds. *The Rule of Law: Ideal or Ideology?* Toronto: Carswell, 1987.

Huther, Jeff, and Anwar Shah. "Anti-Corruption Policies and Programs: A Framework for Evaluation." Working Paper no. 2501. Washington, D.C.: World Bank, 2000.

Ignatius, David. "Crusaders Against Corruption." *Washington Post,* March 4, 2001.

International Advisory and Monitoring Board for Iraq. *Report of the International Advisory and Monitoring Board of the Development Fund for Iraq.* December 2004. http://www.iamb.info/pdf/iambreport.pdf.

International Budget Project. "Development, Human Rights, and the Rule of Law." Conference report. The Hague, April 27–May 1, 1981. http://www.icj.org/article .php3?id_article=3092&id_rubrique=11.

———. *A Taste of Success: Examples of the Budget Work of NGOs.* Washington, D.C., October 2000. http://www.internationalbudget.org/resources/cide.pdf.

International Court of Justice. *Questions of Interpretation and Application of the 1971 Montreal Convention Arising from the Aerial Incident at Lockerbie (Libyan Arab Jamahiriya v. United Kingdom).* Provisional Measures. Order of April 14, 1992. ICJ Reports 1992.

International Crisis Group. *Bosnia: Reshaping the International Machinery.* Brussels: International Crisis Group, November 29, 2001.

———. *Bosnia's Brcko: Getting In, Getting On, and Getting Out.* Balkans Report no. 144. Sarajevo, June 2, 2003.

———. *Bosnia's November Elections: Dayton Stumbles.* Balkans Report no. 104. Sarajevo, December 18, 2000.

———. *The Congo's Transition Is Failing: Crisis in the Kivus.* Africa Report no. 91. Brussels, March 30, 2005.

———. *Côte d'Ivoire: No Peace in Sight.* Africa Report no. 82. Brussels, July 12, 2004.

———. *Counter-Terrorism in Somalia: Losing Hearts and Minds?* Brussels, July 11, 2005.

———. *Courting Disaster: The Misrule of Law in Bosnia and Herzegovina.* Balkans Report no. 127. Sarajevo, March 25, 2002.

———. *EU Crisis Response Capability: Institutions and Processes for Conflict Prevention and Management.* Brussels, June 26, 2001. http://www.crisisweb.org/ home/index.cfm?id=1830&l=1.

———. *Judicial Reform and Transitional Justice.* Brussels, January 2003.

———. *Liberia and Sierra Leone: Rebuilding Failed States.* Africa Report no. 87. Brussels, December 8, 2004.

———. *Why Will No One Invest in Bosnia and Herzegovina?* Europe Report no. 64. Brussels, April 21, 1999.

———. *Yemen: Coping with Terrorism and Violence in a Fragile State.* Brussels, January 8, 2003.

International Development Research Centre. *The Responsibility to Protect: Report of the International Commission on Intervention and State Sovereignty.* Ottawa, December 2001. http://www.iciss.gc.ca/report-en.asp.

International Institute for Democracy and Electoral Assistance. *Handbook on Funding of Political Parties and Electoral Campaigns.* Stockholm, 2003.

International Labor Organization. *Convention Concerning Indigenous and Tribal Peoples in Independent Countries.* Geneva, June 27, 1989.

International Peace Academy and War-torn Societies Project International. "Building Effective Partnerships: Improving the Relationship Between Internal and External Actors in Post-Conflict Countries." Peacebuilding Forum conference report. New York, October 7, 2004.

Jackson, John H. *The World Trading System: Law and Policy of International Economic Relations.* Cambridge: Massachusetts Institute of Technology Press, 1997.

Jackson, Stephen. "Land and Conflict in the Kivus, DR Congo." Paper presented at the International Peace Academy workshop "Land, Property, and Conflict Management: Identifying Policy Options for Rule of Law Programming." New York, December 2–3, 2004.

Jahangir, Asma, and Fateh Azzam. "Human Rights." In *Toward a Democratic Response: The Club de Madrid Series on Democracy and Terrorism,* vol. 3. Madrid: Club de Madrid, 2005.

Jensen, Erik, and Thomas C. Heller, eds. *Beyond Common Knowledge: Empirical Approaches to the Rule of Law.* Palo Alto: Stanford University Press, 2003.

Johnston, Michael. "Corruption and Democratic Consolidation." Paper presented at the conference "Democracy and Corruption." Princeton, Shelby Cullom Davis Center for Historical Studies, Princeton University, March 1999.

———. "The Political Consequences of Corruption: A Reassessment." *Comparative Politics* 18, no. 4 (1986): 459–477.

———. "Public Officials, Private Interests, and Sustainable Democracy: When Politics and Corruption Meet." In *Corruption and the Global Economy,* edited by Kimberly Ann Elliott. Washington, D.C.: International Institute for Economics, June 1997.

———. *Syndromes of Corruption: Wealth, Power, and Democracy.* New York: Cambridge University Press, 2005.

Kapur, Devesh, John P. Lewis, and Richard Webb. *The World Bank: Its First Half Century.* Washington, D.C.: Brookings Institution, 1997.

Kaspersen, Anja, Espen Barth Eide, and Annika Hansen. *International Policing and the Rule of Law in Transition from War to Peace.* Oslo: Norwegian Institute of International Affairs, October 2004.

Kaufmann, Daniel. "Corruption, Governance and Security: Challenges for the Rich Countries." In *Global Competitiveness Report 2004–2005.* Geneva: World Economic Forum, 2004.

———. "Governance Redux: The Empirical Challenge." In *Global Competitiveness Report 2003–2004.* Geneva: World Economic Forum, 2003.

———. "Rethinking Governance: Empirical Lessons Challenge Orthodoxy." March 11, 2003. http://ssrn.com/abstract=386904.

Kaufmann, Daniel, and Art Kraay. "Growth Without Governance." *Economia* 3, no. 1 (Fall 2002): 169–229.

Kaufmann, Daniel, Art Kraay, and Massimo Mastruzzi. "Governance Matters IV: Governance Indicators for 1996–2004." Policy Research Paper no. 3630. Washington, D.C.: World Bank, May 2005.

Kemp, Walter A., ed. *Quiet Diplomacy in Action: The OSCE High Commissioner on National Minorities.* The Hague: Kluwer Law International, 2001.

Kennedy, David. *The Dark Sides of Virtue: Reassessing International Humanitarianism.* Princeton: Princeton University Press, 2004.

Kennedy, Duncan. *A Critique of Adjudication* [fin de siècle]. Cambridge: Harvard University Press, 1997.

———. "Form and Substance in Private Law Adjudication." *Harvard Law Review* 89 (1976): 1685–1778.

Khouri-Padova, Lama. "Haiti: Lessons Learned." Discussion paper. Peacekeeping Best Practices Unit, March 2004. http://pbpu.unlb.org/pbpu/document.aspx?docid=249.

Kimberly Process. *Interlaken Declaration of 5 November 2002 on the Kimberley Process Certification Scheme for Rough Diamonds.* http://www.kimberleyprocess.com/ images/stories/docs/plenary_meetings9/interlaken_declaration.pdf.

Kleinfeld Belton, Rachel. "Competing Definitions of the Rule of Law: Implications for Practitioners." Democracy and Rule of Law Project, Rule of Law Series, No. 55, Carnegie Endowment for Intenational Peace, 2005, www.carnegieendowment .org/files/CP55.Belton.Final.pdf.

Klitgaard, Robert, *Controlling Corruption.* Berkeley: University of California Press, 1988.

Krasner, Stephen. "Shared Sovereignty." *Journal of Democracy* 16, no. 1 (2005): 69–83.

Krastev, Ivan. *Shifting Obsessions: Three Essays on the Politics of Anti-Corruption.* New York: Central European University Press, 2004.

Kritz, Neil, ed. *Transitional Justice: How Emerging Democracies Reckon with Former Regimes.* 3 vols. Washington, D.C.: US Institute of Peace, 1995.

LaFerrara, Eliana, and Robert H. Bates. "Political Competition in Weak States." *Economics and Politics* 13, no. 2 (July 2001): 159–184.

Lahoud, Nina. "Rule of Law Strategies for Peace Operations." In *The Rule of Law on Peace Operations: Papers from the "Challenges of Peace Operations" Project Conference,* edited by Jessica Howard and Bruce Oswald. New York: Kluwer Law International, 2002.

Lambsdorff, Johann Graf. "Corruption in Empirical Research: A Review." Working paper. Berlin: Transparency International, November 1999.

Landler, Mark. "Rare Bosnia Success Story, Thanks to US Viceroy." *New York Times,* June 17, 2003.

Langenkamp, R. Dobie, and Rex J. Zedalis. "What Happens to the Iraqi Oil? Thoughts on Some Significant, Unexamined International Legal Questions Regarding Occupation of Oil Fields." *European Journal of International Law* 14, no. 3 (2003): 417–435.

Lau, Martin. *Afghanistan's Legal System and Its Compatibility with International Human Rights Standards.* Geneva: International Commission of Jurists, 2003. http://www.icj.org/img/pdf/doc-46.pdf.

Le Billon, Philippe. "Buying Peace or Fueling War: The Role of Corruption in Armed Conflicts." *Journal of International Development* 15 (2003): 413–426.

Leckie, Scott. "New Directions in Housing and Property Restitution." In *Returning Home: Housing and Property Restitution Rights of Refugees and Displaced Persons,* edited by Scott Leckie. Ardsley, N.Y.: Transnational, 2003.

Le Sage, Andre. *Stateless Justice in Somalia: Formal and Informal Rule of Law Initiatives.* Geneva: Centre for Humanitarian Dialogue, July 2005.

"Li, Bo. "What Is Rule of Law?" *Perspectives* 1, no. 5 (2000). http://www.oycf.org/ perspectives/5_043000/what_is_rule_of_law.htm.

Lindholt, Lone, Paulo de Mesquita Neto, Danny Titus, and Etannibi E. Alemika, eds. *Human Rights and the Police in Transitional Countries.* The Hague: Kluwer Law International, 2003.

Lira, Elizabeth. "The Reparations Policy for Human Rights Violations in Chile." In *The Handbook of Reparations,* edited by Pablo de Greiff. Oxford: Oxford University Press, 2006.

Lister, Marjorie, ed. *European Union Development Policy.* London: Macmillan, 1998.

Lopes, Carlos, and Thomas Theisohn. *Ownership, Leadership, and Transformation: Can We Do Better for Capacity Development?* New York: UN Development Programme, 2003.

Lord, Christopher. "Advisory Note for Stimson Center/United Nations Panel on Peace Operations." Prague Project on Emergency Criminal Justice Principles. Prague: Institute of International Relations, June 27, 2000.

Lowenfeld, Andreas F. *International Economic Law.* Oxford: Oxford University Press, 2003.

Luck, Edward C. "Prevention: Theory and Practice." In *From Reaction to Conflict Prevention: Opportunities for the UN System,* edited by Fen Osler Hampson. Boulder: Lynne Rienner, 2001.

———. "Tackling Terrorism." In *The UN Security Council: From the Cold War to the 21st Century,* edited by David M. Malone. Boulder: Lynne Rienner, 2004.

Lund, Michael. *Preventing Violent Conflicts: A Strategy for Preventive Diplomacy.* Washington, D.C.: US Institute of Peace, 1996.

MacLean-Abaroa, Ronald, Robert Klitgaard, and H. Lindsey Parris. *Corrupt Cities: A Practical Guide to Cure and Prevention.* Oakland: Institute for Contemporary Studies, 2000.

Malinowski, Tom. "By Infringing Basic Liberties the U.S. Undermines Its Own Terrorism Prevention Strategy." In *Human Rights and Terrorism.* The Hague: Netherlands Helsinki Committee, 2004.

Malloch Brown, Mark. Foreword to Carlos Lopes and Thomas Theisohn, *Ownership, Leadership, and Transformation: Can We Do Better for Capacity Development?* New York: UN Development Programme, 2003.

Malone, David M., and Heiko Nitzschke. "Economic Agendas in Civil Wars: What We Know, What We Need to Know." Discussion Paper no. 2005/07. Helsinki: United Nations University World Institute for Development Economics Research, 2005.

Mamdani, Mahmood. "Reconciliation Without Justice." *Southern African Review of Books* 46 (November–December 1996): 3–5.

Mani, Rama. *Beyond Retribution: Seeking Justice in the Shadows of War.* Cambridge: Polity, 2002.

———. "Conflict Resolution, Justice, and the Law: Rebuilding the Rule of Law in the Aftermath of Complex Political Emergencies." *International Peacekeeping* 5, no. 3 (1998): 1–25.

———. "Contextualizing Police Reform: Security, the Rule of Law, and Post-Conflict Peacebuilding." In *Police Reform and Peacebuilding,* edited by Espen Eide and Tor Tanke Holm. London: Cass, 2000.

———. "Ending Impunity and Building Justice in Afghanistan." Kabul: Afghanistan Research and Evaluation Unit, December 2003.

Maravall, José María, and Adam Przeworski, eds. *Democracy and the Rule of Law.* Cambridge: Cambridge University Press, 2003.

Marks, Susan, and Andrew Clapham. *International Human Rights Lexicon.* Oxford: Oxford University Press, 2005.

Marshall, David, and Shelley Inglis. "The Disempowerment of Human Rights–Based Justice in the United Nations Mission in Kosovo." *Harvard Human Rights Journal* 16 (2003): 95–146.

Martin, Ian. "After Genocide: The UN Human Rights Field Operation in Rwanda." In *Honoring Human Rights: From Peace to Justice,* edited by Alice Henkin. Washington, D.C.: Aspen Institute, 1998.

Martin, Kate. "Intelligence, Terrorism, and Civil Liberties." *Human Rights Magazine* Winter 2002. http://www.abanet.org/irr/hr/winter02/martin.html.

Martinez-Vazquez, Jorge. "Corruption, Fiscal Policy, and Fiscal Management." Washington, D.C.: US Agency for International Development, 2004.

Mathieu, P., S. Mugangu Matabaro, and A. Mafikiri Tsongo. "Enjeux fonciers et violences and Afrique: la prévention des conflits en se servant du cas du Nord-Kivu (1940–1994)." Rome, September 1999. http://www.fao.org/sd/frdirect/ltan0034.htm.

Mauro, Paolo. "The Persistence of Corruption and Slow Economic Growth." *IMF Staff Papers* 51, no. 1 (2004): 1–18.

———. "Why Worry About Corruption?" IMF Economic Issues no. 6. Washington, D.C.: International Monetary Fund, February 1997.

Mazurana, Dyan E., and Susan R. McKay. *Women and Peacebuilding.* Montreal: International Centre for Human Rights and Democratic Development, 1999.

McAuslan, Patrick. "Law, Governance, and the Development of the Market: Practical Problems and Possible Solutions." In *Good Governance and Law: Legal and Institutional Reform in Developing Countries,* edited by Julio Faundez. New York: St. Martin's, 1997.

McNamara, Dennis. "UN Human Rights Activities in Cambodia: An Evaluation." In *Honoring Human Rights and Keeping the Peace: Lessons from El Salvador, Cambodia, and Haiti,* edited by Alice Henkin. Washington, D.C.: Aspen Institute, 1995.

Merry, Sally Engle. "Legal Pluralism." *Law and Society Review* 22, no. 5 (1988): 869–896.

Michelman, Frank. "Possession vs. Distribution in the Constitutional Idea of Property." *Iowa Law Review* 72, no. 5 (July 1987): 1319–1350.

Miller, Laurel, and Robert Perito. "Establishing the Rule of Law in Afghanistan." Special Report no. 117. Washington, D.C.: US Institute of Peace, March 2004.

Moreno Torres, Magüi, and Michael Anderson. "Fragile States: Defining Difficult Environments for Poverty Reduction." Poverty Reduction in Difficult Environments Team, Working Paper no. 1. London: Department for International Development, August 2004.

Morgenthau, Hans J. *Politics Among Nations: The Struggle for Power and Peace.* New York: Knopf, 1978.

Naarden, Gregory L., and Jeffrey B. Locke. "Peacekeeping and Prosecutorial Policy: Lessons from Kosovo." *American Journal of International Law* 98, no. 4 (2004): 727–743.

Naím, Moisés. "The Corruption Eruption." *Brown Journal of World Affairs* 2 (1995): 245–261.

Narayan, Deepa, with Raj Patel, Kai Schafft, Anne Rademacher, and Sarah Koch-Schulte. *Voices of the Poor: Can Anyone Hear Us?* New York: Oxford University Press, 2000.

Neier, Aryeh. "Rethinking Truth, Justice, and Guilt After Bosnia and Rwanda." In *Human Rights in Political Transitions: Gettysburg to Bosnia,* edited by Carla Hesse. London: Zone, 1999.

Ngugi, Joel. "Re-examining the Role of Private Property in Market Democracies: Problematic Ideological Issues Raised by Land Registration." *Michigan Journal of International Law* 25, no. 2 (2004): 467–527.

Nield, Rachel. "Can Haiti's Police Reforms Be Sustained?" Washington, D.C.: Washington Office of Latin America, 1998.

Nino, Carlos S. "The Duty to Punish Abuses of Human Rights Put Into Context: The Case of Argentina." *Yale Law Journal* 100 (1991): 2619–2640.

Noble, Ronald. "The Role of Police in Fostering Political Commitment." Tenth International Anti-Corruption Conference. Prague, October 8, 2001.

North, Douglas. *Institutions, Institutional Change, and Economic Performance.* New York: Cambridge University Press, 1990.

Norwegian Ministry of Foreign Affairs. *Peace Building: A Development Perspective.* Oslo, September 2004.

Nye, Joseph. "Corruption and Political Development: A Cost-Benefit Analysis." *American Political Science Review* 61 (June 1967): 417–427.

O'Connor, Vivienne, and Colette Rausch, eds. *Model Codes for Post-Conflict Criminal Justice: Volume I—Model Criminal Code.* Washington, D.C.: United States Institute of Peace Press, 2007.

Office of the High Representative in Bosnia and Herzegovina. "Communiqué by the PIC Steering Board." Sarajevo, April 1, 2004. http://www.ohr.int/pic/default.asp ?content_id=32163.

Ombudsperson Institution in Kosovo. "Second Annual Report: 2001–2002." Prishtina, 10 July 2002.

———. "Special Report no. 1 on the Compatibility with Recognized International Standards of UNMIK Regulation no. 2000/47 on the Status, Privileges, and Immunities of KFOR and UNMIK and Their Personnel in Kosovo (18 August 2000)." Prishtina, April 26, 2001.

O'Neill, William G. "Gaining Compliance Without Force: Human Rights Field Operations." In *Civilians in War,* edited by Simon Chesterman. Boulder: Lynne Rienner, 2001.

———. *Kosovo: An Unfinished Peace.* Boulder: Lynne Rienner, 2002.

———. "Postscript." In *Honoring Human Rights,* edited by Alice Henkin. Washington, D.C.: Aspen Institute, 2000.

———. "Rebuilding the Rule of Law in Iraq: Ten Tips from Recent Experience." Washington, D.C.: Henri Stimson Center, 2003.

Orford, Anne. "Locating the International: Military and Monetary Interventions After the Cold War." *Harvard International Law Journal* 38 (1997): 443–485.

Organization of American States (OAS). *American Convention on Human Rights,* OAS Treaty Series no. 36, 1144 UNTS 123. Reprinted in *Basic Documents Pertaining to Human Rights in the Inter-American System,* OEA/Ser.L.V/II.82 doc.6 rev.1 at 25 (1992).

———. Inter-American Commission on Human Rights. *The Kichwa People of the Sarayako Community and its members vs. Ecuador.* Report no. 64/04, Petition no. 167/03 (Admissibility). October 13, 2004. http://www.cidh.oas.org/annualrep/ 2004eng/"ecuador.167.03eng.htm.

Organization for Economic Cooperation and Development (OECD). "Aid Statistics: Preliminary Official Development Assistance (ODA) by Donor in 2004." Paris, April 11, 2005. http://www.oecd.org/document/7/0,2340,en_2649_34447_ 35397703_1_1_1_1,00.html.

———. *Convention on Combating Bribery of Foreign Public Officials in International Business Transactions.* Paris, April 8, 1998. http://www.olis.oecd.org/olis/1997 doc.nsf/linkto/daffe-ime-br(97)20.

———. Development Assistance Committee (DAC). "Development Partnerships in the New Global Context." Paris, May 1995. http://www.oecd.org/dataoecd/ 31/61/2755357.pdf.

———. "Shaping the 21st Century: The Contribution of Development Co-operation." Paris, May 1996. http://www.oecd.org/dataoecd/23/35/2508761.pdf.

Organization for Security and Cooperation in Europe (OSCE). *Best Practices in Combating Corruption.* Vienna: Office of the Co-ordinator for Economic and Environmental Activities, 2004.

——. "Observation and Recommendations of the OSCE Legal System Monitoring Section: Report 1—Material Needs of the Emergency Judicial System." OSCE Department of Rule of Law and Human Rights, 1999.

——. *OSCE Report of the Copenhagen Round Table on United Nations Sanctions in the Case of the Former Yugoslavia.* 1996.

——. *Annual Report on OSCE Activities.* 1996.

——. Mission to Bosnia and Herzegovina. "Conclusions of the Peace Implementation Conference." Bonn: Peace Implementation Council, December 9–10, 1997.

——. Office for Democratic Institutions and Human Rights. "Preventing and Combating Terrorism: The New Security Environment." Paper prepared for the second annual OSCE Security Review Conference. Vienna, June 23–24, 2004.

Oswald, Bruce M. "Model Codes for Criminal Justice and Peace Operations." *Journal of Conflict and Security Law* 9, no. 2 (2004): 253–275.

Ottaway, Marina. "The Post-War 'Democratic Reconstruction Model': Why It Can't Work." Paper presented to the US Institute of Peace. Washington, D.C., 2002.

Packer, John. "The Work of the OSCE High Commissioner on National Minorities as an Instrument of Conflict Prevention." In Chandra Lekha Sriram, Albrecht Schnabel, John Packer, and Augustine Touré, *Sharing Best Practices on Conflict Prevention: The UN, Regional and Subregional Organizations, National and Local Actors.* New York: International Peace Academy, 2002.

Paris, Roland. *At War's End: Building Peace After Civil Conflict.* Cambridge: Cambridge University Press, 2004.

Pauwelyn, Joost. "WTO Compassion or Superiority Complex? What to Make of the WTO Waiver for 'Conflict Diamonds.'" *Michigan Journal of International Law* 24 (2003): 1177–1207.

Peluso, Nancy Lee, and Michael Watts. *Violent Environments.* Ithaca: Cornell University Press, 2001.

Pepys, Mary Noel. "Corruption in the Justice System, Sectoral Perspectives on Corruption." In *Pervasive Corruption: Strategies for Prevention in Developing and Transitional Countries,* edited by Bertram Spector. Bloomfield, Conn.: Kumarian, 2004.

Perito, Robert. "Establishing the Rule of Law in Iraq." Special Report no. 104. Washington, D.C.: US Institute of Peace, April 2003.

Perito, Robert, Michael Dziedzic, and Beth C. DeGrasse. "Building Civilian Capacity for US Stability Operations: The Rule of Law Component." Special Report no. 118. Washington, D.C.: US Institute of Peace, April 2004.

Permanent Court of International Justice. *The Oscar Chinn Case.* PCIJ, Ser. A./B., no. 63 (1934).

Persson, Torsten, Guido Tabellini, and Francesco Trebbi. "Electoral Rules and Corruption." *Journal of the European Economic Association* 1, no. 4 (2003): 958–989.

Petersmann, Ernst-Ulrich. "How to Promote International Rule of Law." *Journal of International Economic Law* 1 (1998): 26.

Pfirter, Didier. "Property, Land, and Return in the Comprehensive Settlement Plan of the UN Secretary General for Cyprus (Annan Plan)." Paper presented at the International Peace Academy workshop "Land, Property, and Conflict Management: Identifying Policy Options for Rule of Law Programming." New York, December 2–3, 2004.

Philpott, Charles. "Though the Dog Is Dead, the Pig Must Be Killed: Finishing with Property Restitution in Bosnia-Herzegovina's IDPs and Refugees." *Journal of Refugee Studies* 18, no. 1 (2005): 1–24.

Pingree, Geoff. "To Right Past Wrongs, Spaniards Seek Present Change." *Christian Science Monitor,* February 2, 2005.

Plunkett, Mark. "Re-establishing Law and Order in Peace-Maintenance." *Global Governance* 4, no. 1 (1998): 61–80.

Pons-Vignon, Nicholas, and Henri-Bernard Solignac Lecomte. "Land, Violent Conflict, and Development." Working Paper no. 233. Paris: Organization for Economic Cooperation and Development, 2004.

Pope, Jeremy. *Confronting Corruption: The Elements of a National Integrity System.* Berlin: Transparency International, 2000.

Posner, Richard. "Creating a Legal Framework for Economic Development." *World Bank Research Observer* 13, no. 1 (1998): 1–11.

———. *The Problems of Jurisprudence.* Cambridge: Harvard University Press, 1990.

Post, Harry H. G. *International Economic Law and Armed Conflict.* Boston: Nijhoff, 1994.

Premdas, Ralph. "Fiji: Peacemaking in a Multi-Ethnic State." In *From Promise to Practice: Strengthening UN Capacities for the Prevention of Violent Conflict,* edited by Chandra L. Sriram. Boulder: Lynne Rienner, 2003.

Prempeh, H. Kwasi. "A New Jurisprudence for Africa." *Journal of Democracy* 10, no. 3 (1999): 135–149.

Public Affairs Centre. "Annual Report 2003–2004." Bangalore, 2004.

Rackley, Edward B. "Predatory Governance in the DRC: Civilian Impact and Humanitarian Response." London: Humanitarian Practice Network. http://www.odihpn .org/report.asp?id=2653.

Rajagopal, Balakrishnan. *International Law from Below: Development, Social Movements, and Third World Resistance.* New York: Cambridge University Press, 2003.

Rausch, Colette. "The Assumption of Authority in Kosovo and East Timor: Legal and Practical Implications." In *Executive Policing: Enforcing the Law in Peace Operations,* edited by Renata Dawn. SIPRI Research Report no. 16. Oxford: Oxford University Press, 2002.

———, ed. *Combating Serious Crimes in Post-Conflict Societies.* Washington, D.C.: US Institute of Peace, 2006.

———. "Justice and Police Reforms in Kosovo." In *Constructing Justice and Security After Wars,* edited by Chuck Call. Washington, D.C.: US Institute of Peace, 2007.

Rawls, John. *A Theory of Justice.* Oxford: Oxford University Press, 1971.

Rawski, Frederick. "Truth-Seeking and Local Histories in East Timor." *Asia-Pacific Journal on Human Rights and Law* 1 (2002): 77–96.

Raz, Joseph. *The Authority of Law: Essays on Law and Morality.* Oxford: Clarendon, 1979.

Razzaz, Omar. "Land Disputes in the Absence of Ownership Rights: Insights from Jordan." In *Illegal Cities: Law and Urban Change in Developing Countries,* edited by Edesio Fernandes. New York: St. Martin's, 1998.

Reinikka, Ritva, and Jakob Svensson. "Local Capture: Evidence from a Central Government Transfer Program in Uganda." *Quarterly Journal of Economics* 119, no. 2 (2004): 679–705.

Ricupero, Rubens. Preface to Carlos Lopes and Thomas Theisohn, *Ownership, Leadership, and Transformation: Can We Do Better for Capacity Development?* New York: UN Development Programme, 2003.

Rose, Carol M. "Crystals and Mud in Property Law." *Stanford Law Review* 40, no. 3 (1988): 577–610.

Rose-Ackerman, Susan. *Corruption: A Study in Political Economy.* New York: Academic Press, 1978.

———. *Corruption and Government: Causes, Consequences, and Reform.* Cambridge: Cambridge University Press, 1999.

————. "Trust, Honesty, and Corruption: Reflection on the State-Building Process." *Archives of European Sociology* 42, no. 3 (2001): 526–570.

Rostow, Nicholas. "Before and After: The Changed UN Response to Terrorism Since September 11th." *Cornell International Law Journal* 35, no. 3 (2002): 479.

Rubin, Barnett R. *Blood on the Doorstep: The Politics of Preventive Action.* New York: Century Foundation, 2002.

————. "Cases and Strategies for Preventive Action." Report of the 1996 Center for Preventive Action annual conference. New York: Century Foundation, 1998.

————. "Road to Ruin: Afghanistan's Booming Opium Industry." New York: Center for International Cooperation and the Center for American Progress, October 2004. http://www.cic.nyu.edu/archive/pdf/roadtoruin.pdf.

Sachs, Wolfgang, ed. *Development Dictionary: A Guide to Knowledge as Power.* Atlantic Highlands, N.J.: Zed, 1992.

Sands, Philippe. "L'exploitation des ressources naturelles en Irak." In *L'intervention en Irak et le droit international,* edited by K. Bannelier et al. Cahiers Internationaux no. 19. Paris: Editions A. Pedone, 2004.

Sano, Hans-Otto, and Lone Lindholt, *Human Rights Indicators, Country Data, and Methodology, 2000.* Copenhagen: Danish Institute for Human Rights, 2000.

Santiso, Carlos. "Governance Conditionality and the Reform of Multilateral Development Finance: The Role of the Group of Eight." *G8 Governance* no. 7 (March 2002). http://www.g7.utoronto.ca/governance/santiso2002-gov7.pdf.

Sassóli, Marco. "Legislation and Maintenance of Public Order and Civil Life by Occupying Powers." *European Journal of International Law* 16, no. 4 (2005): 661–694.

Saxby, John. "Local Ownership and Development Co-operation: The Role of Northern Civil Society." Ottawa: Canadian Council for International Cooperation, 2003. http://www.ccic.ca/e/docs/002_aid_the_role_of_northern_civil_society.pdf.

Schabas, William A. *Introduction to the International Criminal Court.* Cambridge: Cambridge University Press, 2001.

————. *The UN International Criminal Tribunals: The Former Yugoslavia, Rwanda, and Sierra Leone.* Cambridge: Cambridge University Press, 2006.

Schricke, Christian. "How the OECD Promotes the Rule of Law." Washington, D.C.: Center for International Private Enterprise, 1996.

Schrijver, Nico. "The Use of Economic Sanctions by the UN Security Council: An International Law Perspective." In *International Economic Law and Armed Conflict,* edited by Harry H. G. Post. Boston: Nijhoff, 1994.

Schwarzenberger, Georg. "Equality and Discrimination in International Economic Law." *Yearbook of World Affairs* 25 (1971): 163.

Scott, James C. "Corruption, Machine Politics, and Political Change." *American Political Science Review* 63, no. 4 (December 1969): 1142–1158.

Sedra, Mark. "Challenging the Warlord Culture: Security Sector Reform in Post-Taliban Afghanistan." Paper no. 25. Bonn: Bonn International Centre for Conversion, 2002.

Seligson, Mitchell. "The Impact of Corruption on Regime Legitimacy: A Comparative Study of Four Latin American Countries." *Journal of Politics* 64, no. 2 (2002): 408–433.

Sen, Amartya. *Development as Freedom.* New York: Knopf, 1999.

Shapiro, Ian, ed. *The Rule of Law: Nomos XXXVI.* New York: New York University Press, 1994.

Shapiro, Martin. "The Success of Judicial Review." In *Constitutional Dialogues in Comparative Perspective,* edited by Sally J. Kenney. New York: St. Martin's, 1999.

Shelton, Dinah. *Remedies in International Human Rights Law.* Oxford: Oxford University Press, 1999.

————. "The United Nations Draft Principles on Reparations for Human Rights Violations: Context and Contents." In *The Right to Reparation for Victims of Gross and Systematic Human Rights Violations,* edited by M. Bossuyt. Brussels: Intersentia, 2006.

Shklar, Judith. "Political Theory and the Rule of Law." In *The Rule of Law: Ideal or Ideology?* edited by Allan Hutchinson. Toronto: Carswell, 1987.

Sierra Leone Truth and Reconciliation Commission. *Final Report.* October 2004. http://trcsierraleone.org/drwebsite/publish/index.shtml.

Snyder, Jack. *From Voting to Violence: Democratization and Nationalist Conflict.* New York: Norton, 2000.

Sossai, Mirko. "The Internal Conflict in Colombia and the Fight Against Terrorism." *Journal of International Criminal Justice* 3 (2005): 259–261.

Speck, Paula. "The Trial of the Argentine Junta: Responsibilities and Realities." *University of Miami Inter-American Law Review* 18 (1987).

Spector, Bertram I., ed. *Fighting Corruption in Developing Countries: Strategies and Analysis.* Bloomington, Conn.: Kumarian, 2005.

Spector, Bertram I., Svetlana Winbourne, and Laurence D. Beck. "Corruption in Kosovo: Observations and Implications for USAID." Washington, D.C.: Management Systems International, July 2003.

Sriram, Chandra Lekha. *Confronting Past Human Rights Violations: Justice vs. Peace in Times of Transition.* London: Cass, 2004.

————. *Globalising Justice for Mass Atrocities: A Revolution in Accountability.* London: Taylor and Francis, 2005.

Sriram, Chandra Lekha, and Zoe Nielsen, eds. *Exploring Subregional Conflict: Opportunities for Conflict Prevention.* Boulder: Lynne Rienner, 2004.

Sriram, Chandra Lekha, Albrecht Schnabel, John Packer, and Augustine Touré. *Sharing Best Practices on Conflict Prevention: The UN, Regional and Subregional Organizations, National and Local Actors.* New York: International Peace Academy, 2002. http://www.ipacademy.org/pdfs/sharing_best_prac.pdf.

Sriram, Chandra Lekha, and Karin Wermester, eds. *From Promise to Practice: Strengthening UN Capacities for the Prevention of Violent Conflict.* Boulder: Lynne Rienner, 2003.

Stahn, Carsten. "NGOs and International Peacekeeping: Issues, Prospects, and Lessons Learned." *Zeitschrift für Ausländisches Öffentliches Recht und Völkerrecht* 61, nos. 2–3 (2001): 379–402.

Stanley, William. *The Protection Racket State: Elite Politics, Military Extortion, and Civil War in El Salvador.* Philadelphia: Temple University Press, 1996.

Stedman, Stephen John. "Spoiler Problems in Peace Processes." *International Security* 22, no. 2 (Fall 1997): 5–53.

Steinem, Gloria. Introduction to *North Carolina Journal of International Law and Commercial Regulation* 24, no. 2 (Winter 1999).

Stephenson, Matthew. "The Rule of Law as a Goal of Development Policy." Prepared for the World Bank, 2001. http://www1.worldbank.org/publicsector/legal/ruleoflaw2.htm.

Steves, Franklin, and Alan Rousso. "Anti-Corruption Programmes in Post-Communist Transition Countries and Changes in the Business Environment, 1999–2002." Working Paper no. 85. London: European Bank for Reconstruction and Development, December 2003.

Strohmeyer, Hansjörg. "Building a New Judiciary for East Timor: Challenges of a Fledgling Nation." *Criminal Law Forum* 11 (2000): 259–285.

————. "Collapse and Reconstruction of a Judicial System: The United Nations Missions in Kosovo and East Timor." *American Journal of International Law* 95, no. 1 (2001): 46–63.

———. "Making Multilateral Interventions Work: The U.N. and the Creation of Transitional Justice Systems in Kosovo and East Timor." *Fletcher Forum of World Affairs* 25, no. 2 (2001): 111–113.

Stromseth, Jane, David Wippman, and Rosa Brooks. *Can Might Make Rights? Building the Rule of Law After Military Interventions.* Cambridge: Cambridge University Press, 2006.

Swamy, Anand, Stephen Knack, Young Lee, and Omar Azfar. "Gender and Corruption." *Journal of Development Economics* 64 (2001): 25–55.

Swedish International Development Agency (SIDA). "Reflections on Development Co-operation and Violent Conflict." Stockholm, June 2003.

Swiss Development Cooperation (SDC). "SDC's Human Rights and Rule of Law Guidance Documents: Influence, Effectiveness, and Relevance Within SDC." Evaluation no. 2004/1. Berne, March 2004.

Tamanaha, Brian. *On the Rule of Law: History, Politics, Theory.* Cambridge: Cambridge University Press, 2004.

Tavits, Margit. "Causes of Corruption: Testing Competing Hypotheses." Working Paper in Politics no. 2005-W3. Nuffield College, Oxford University, March 23, 2005.

Teson, Fernando. *Humanitarian Intervention: An Inquiry into Law and Morality.* Irvington-on-Hudson, N.Y.: Transnational, 1997.

Thome, Joseph R. "Comment on McAuslan's 'Law, Governance, and the Development of the Market: Practical Problems and Possible Solutions.'" In *Good Governance and Law: Legal and Institutional Reform in Developing Countries,* edited by Julio Faundez. New York: St. Martin's, 1997.

Tisné, Martin, and Daniel Smilov. "From the Ground Up: Assessing the Record of Anticorruption Assistance in Southeastern Europe." CPS Policy Studies series. Budapest: Central European University, July 2004.

Tolbert, David, and Andrew Solomon. "United Nations Reform and Supporting the Rule of Law in Post-Conflict Societies." *Harvard Human Rights Journal* 19 (2006): 29–62.

Tonoyan, Vartuhi. "The Bright and Dark Sides of Trust: Corruption and Entrepreneurship." In *Trust and Entrepreneurship: A West-East Perspective,* edited by H. Hoehmann. Cheltenham: Elgar, 2003.

Torpey, John. "'Making Whole What Has Been Smashed': Reflections on Reparations." *Journal of Modern History* 73, no. 1 (2001): 333–358.

Transparency International. *Global Corruption Report 2004.* London: Pluto, 2004.

———. *Global Corruption Report 2005.* London: Pluto, 2005.

———. *The Integrity Pact: The Concept, the Model, and the Present Applications.* Berlin: Transparency International, December 2002.

Treisman, Daniel. "The Causes of Corruption: A Cross-National Study." *Journal of Public Economics* 76 (2000): 399–457.

Trubek, David. "Max Weber on Law and the Rise of Capitalism." *Wisconsin Law Review* 3 (1972): 720–753.

Trubek, David, and Marc Galanter. "Scholars in Self-Estrangement: Some Reflections on the Crisis in Law and Development." *Wisconsin Law Review* 4 (1974): 1062–1101.

Tschirgi, Neclâ. "Post-Conflict Peacebuilding Revisited: Achievements, Limitation, Challenges." Prepared for the WSP International and IPA "Peacebuliding Forum" conference. New York, October 7, 2004. http://www.ipacademy.org/pdfs/post_conflict_peacebuilding.pdf.

United Nations. *An Agenda for Development: Report of the Secretary-General.* UN Doc. A/48/935. May 6, 1994.

————. *An Agenda for Peace: Preventive Diplomacy, Peacemaking, and Peacekeeping: Report of the Secretary-General.* UN Doc. A/47/277-S/24111. June 17, 1992.

————. *Agreement on Provisional Arrangements in Afghanistan Pending the Re-establishment of Permanent Government Institutions.* Annex 2. December 2001. http://www.un.org/news/dh/latest/afghan/afghan-agree.htm.

————. *The Code of Justice and the Court System.* Reprinted in *Cambodian Humanitarian Assistance and the United Nations (1979–1991).* Office of the Special Representative of the Secretary-General of the United Nations for Coordination of Cambodian Humanitarian Assistance Programmes. 1992.

————. *Final Report of the Executive Committee on Peace and Security Task Force for Development of Comprehensive Rule of Law Strategies for Peace Operations.* August 15, 2002.

————. *Fourth Report of the Secretary-General to the Security Council on the United Nations Operation in Burundi.* UN Doc. S/2005/328. May 19, 2005.

————. *In Larger Freedom: Towards Development, Security, and Human Rights for All—Report of the Secretary General.* UN Doc. A/59/2005. March 21, 2005.

————. *A More Secure World: Our Shared Responsibility: Report of the Secretary General's High-Level Panel on Threats, Challenges, and Change.* UN Doc. A/59/565. December 1, 2004.

————. Preamble to *Universal Declaration of Human Rights.* UN Doc. A/810. December 10, 1948.

————. *Prevention of Armed Conflict: Report of the Secretary-General.* UN Doc. A/55-985-S/2001/574. June 7, 2001.

————. *Protection of Human Rights and Fundamental Freedoms While Countering Terrorism: Study of the United Nations High Commissioner for Human Rights.* UN Doc. A/59/428. October 8, 2004.

————. *Report by the Chair of the Counter-Terrorism Committee on the Problems Encountered in the Implementation of Security Council Resolution 1373 (2001).* UN Doc. S/2004/70. January 26, 2004.

————. *Report of the Panel on United Nations Peace Operations* (Brahimi Report). UN Doc. A/55/305-S/2000/809. August 21, 2000.

————. *Report of the Policy Working Group on the United Nations and Terrorism.* UN Doc. A/57/273-S/2002/875. August 6, 2002.

————. *Report of the Secretary-General on the Work of the Organization.* UN Doc. A/59/PV.3. September 21, 2004.

————. *Report of the Secretary-General to the General Assembly: Renewing the United Nations—A Programme for Reform.* UN Doc. A/51/950. July 14, 1997.

————. *The Rule of Law and Transitional Justice in Conflict and Post-Conflict Societies: Report of the Secretary-General.* UN Doc. S/2004/616. August 23, 2004.

————. *The Situation in Kosovo: Report to the Secretary-General of the United Nations.* UN Doc. S/2004/932. August 6, 2004.

————. *The Special Economic Problems of States as a Result of Sanctions Imposed Under Chapter VII of the Charter of the United Nations: Report of the Secretary General.* UN Doc. A/48/573–S/26705. November 8, 1993.

————. *Strengthening International Cooperation and Technical Assistance in Preventing and Combating Terrorism: Report of the Secretary-General.* UN Doc. E/CN.15/2004/8. March 17, 2004.

————. *Strengthening the Rule of Law: Report of the Secretary-General.* UN Doc. A/52/475. October 16, 1997.

————. *Strengthening the Rule of Law: Report of the Secretary-General.* UN Doc. A/55/177. July 20, 2000.

————. *Supplement to An Agenda for Peace: Position Paper of the Secretary-General on the Occasion of the Fiftieth Anniversary of the United Nations.* UN Doc. A/50/60-S/1995/1. January 3, 1995.

————. *Support by the United Nations System of the Efforts of Governments to Promote and Consolidate New or Restored Democracies: Report of the Secretary-General.* UN Doc. A/58/392. September 26, 2003.

————. *2005 World Summit Outcome Document.* UN Doc. A/RES/60/1. October 24 2005.

————. *Uniting Our Strengths: Enhancing United Nations Support for the Rule of Law.* UN Doc. A/61/636-S/2006/980. December 14, 2006.

————. *"We the Peoples": The Role of the United Nations in the 21st Century.* UN Doc. A/54/2000. http://www.un.org/millennium/sg/report.

United Nations Development Programme (UNDP). *Access to Justice: Practice Note.* New York: UNDP, September 2004.

————. *Arab Human Development Report 2002: Creating Opportunities for Future Generations.* New York: UNDP, 2002.

————. *Human Development Report 2000.* New York: Oxford University Press, 2000.

————. *Human Development Report 2002: Deepening Democracy in a Fragmented World.* New York: Oxford University Press, 2002.

————. *Human Development Report 2003.* New York: Oxford University Press, 2003.

————. *Human Development Report 2004: Cultural Liberty in Today's Diverse World.* New York: Oxford University Press, 2004.

————. *Integrating Human Rights with Sustainable Human Development: A UNDP Policy Document.* New York: UNDP, January 1998.

————. *Rule of Law.* UNDP Programme on Governance in the Arab Region. http://www.undp-pogar.org/themes/ruleoflaw.html.

United Nations High Commissioner for Refugees (UNHCR). *The Problem of Access to Land and Ownership in Repatriation Operations.* Inspection and Evaluation Service. UN Doc. EVAL/03/98. May 1998.

————. Executive Committee. "Legal Safety Issues in the Context of Voluntary Repatriation of Refugees." UN Doc. EC/54/SC/CRP.12. June 7, 2004.

United Nations Human Settlements Programme. *Vancouver Declaration on Human Settlement.* Final document of "Habitat: United Nations Conference on Human Settlements." Vancouver, May 31–June 11, 1976.

United Nations Millennium Project. *Investing in Development: Practical Plans to Achieve the Millennium Development Goals.* New York: Millennium Project Secretariat, 2005.

United Nations Office of the High Commissioner for Human Rights (OHCHR). *Global Review of the OHCHR Technical Cooperation Programme.* September 2003. http://www.ohchr.org/english/countries/coop/index.htm.

————. *Human Rights in Development: Mainstreaming Human Rights.* http://www.unhchr.ch/development/mainstreaming-01.html.

————. *Rule of Law Tools for Post-Conflict States: Mapping the Justice Sector.* Geneva, 2006.

————. *Rule of Law Tools for Post-Conflict States: Prosecution Initiatives.* Geneva, 2006.

————. *The OHCHR Plan of Action: Protection and Empowerment.* May 21, 2005.

————. *Report of the Special Rapporteur on Adequate Housing as a Component of the Right to an Adequate Standard of Living, and on the Right to Non-Discrimination.* UN Doc. E/CN.4/2003/5. March 3, 2003.

United Nations Office on Drugs and Crime (UNODC). *Combating International Terrorism: The Contribution of the United Nations.* Symposium proceedings. Vienna International Center, June 3–4, 2002.

United Nations. Peacekeeping Best Practices Unit, Department of Peacekeeping Operations. *Handbook on UN Multidimensional Peacekeeping Operations.* New York, September 2003.

United Nations. Strategic Planning Unit, Executive Office of the Secretary-General. "UN Sanctions: How Effective? How Necessary?" In *Report on the Second Interlaken Seminar on Targeting United Nations Financial Sanctions.* Geneva, March 29–31, 1999.

Upham, Frank. "Mythmaking in the Rule of Law Orthodoxy." Democracy and Rule of Law Project, Rule of Law Series no. 30. Washington, D.C.: Carnegie Endowment for International Peace, 2002. http://www.carnegieendowment.org/files/wp30.pdf.

US Agency for International Development (USAID). *Achievements in Building and Maintaining the Rule of Law.* Washington, D.C., 2002.

———. *Field Perspectives: A Report on the Field Mission Anti-Corruption Survey.* Washington, D.C., 2003.

———. *Land and Conflict: A Toolkit for Intervention.* Washington, D.C., 2004.

———. *Money in Politics Handbook: A Guide to Increasing Transparency in Emerging Democracies.* Washington, D.C., 2003.

US Army. *Field Manual on Peace Operations.* Washington, D.C., December 1994. http://www.dtic.mil/doctrine/jel/service_pubs/fm100_23.pdf.

US Department of State. *U.S. National Security Strategy.* Washington, D.C., September 2002. http://www.state.gov/r/pa/ei/wh/c7889.htm.

Uslaner, Eric. "Trust and Corruption." In *Transparency International, Global Corruption Report 2005.* London: Pluto, 2005.

van Boven, Theo (Special Rapporteur of the United Nations). *Study Concerning the Right to Restitution, Compensation, and Rehabilitation for Victims of Gross Violations of Human Rights and Fundamental Freedoms.* Final report. UN Doc. E/CN. 4/Sub.2/1993/8. July 2, 1993.

van Calster, Geert. "WTO Law and Contracts for Rebuilding Iraq." *International Law Forum* 5, no. 4 (2003): 270–275.

Villa-Vicencio, Charles, and Erik Doxtader, eds. *The Provocations of Amnesty: Memory, Justice, and Impunity.* Trenton, N.J.: Africa World, 2003.

von Benda-Beckmann, Franz. *Property in Social Continuity.* The Hague: Nijhoff, 1979.

———. "Relative Publics and Property Rights: A Cross-Cultural Perspective." In *Property and Values: Alternatives to Public and Private Ownership,* edited by Charles Geisler and Gail Daneker. Washington, D.C.: Island, 2000.

———. "Who Is Afraid of Legal Pluralism?" *Journal of Legal Pluralism* 47 (2002): 37–82.

von Carlowitz, Leopold. "Settling Property Issues in Complex Peace Operations: The CRPC in Bosnia and Herzegovina and the HPD/CC in Kosovo." *Leiden Journal of International Law* 17, no. 3 (2004): 599–614.

von Hayek, Friedrich. *Road to Serfdom.* London: Ark, 1968.

Wallensteen, Peter. *Preventing Violent Conflicts: Past Record and Future Challenges.* Uppsala: Uppsala University, Department of Peace and Conflict Research, 1998.

Walters, Barbara. "Does Conflict Beget Conflict? Explaining Recurring Civil Wars." *Journal of Peace Research* 41, no. 3 (May 2004): 371–389.

Weber, Max. *Economy and Society: An Outline of Interpretive Sociology.* New York: Bedminster, 1968.

Wedgwood, Ruth. "United Nations Peacekeeping Operations and the Use of Force." *Washington University Journal of Law and Policy* 5 (2001): 69–86.

Weiler, Todd. "NAFTA Article 1105 and the Principles of International Economic Law." *Columbia Journal of Transnational Law* 42, no. 1 (2003): 77–78.

Weschler, Lawrence. *A Miracle, A Universe: Settling Accounts with Torturers.* New York: Pantheon, 1990.

Weyland, Kurt. "The Politics of Corruption in Latin America." *Journal of Democracy* 9, no. 2 (1998): 108–121.

Whyatt, C. J., C. J. Mathew, and J. Whitton. "N. V. De Bataafsche Petroleum Maatschappli & Ors. v. The War Damage Commission." *Malayan Law Journal* 22, no. 155 (1956). Reprinted in Marco Sassóli and Antoine A. Bouvier, *How Does Law Protect in War? Cases and Teaching Materials on International Humanitarian Law in Contemporary Practice.* Geneva: International Committee of the Red Cross, 1999.

Wilde, Ralph. "From Danzig to East Timor and Beyond: The Role of International Territorial Administration." *American Journal of International Law* 95, no. 3 (2001): 583–606.

Wolfensohn, James. "A Proposal for a Comprehensive Development Framework." Washington, D.C.: World Bank, January 21, 1999. http://siteresources.worldbank.org/cdf/resources/cdf.pdf.

Woodward, Susan. *Balkan Tragedy: Chaos and Dissolution After the Cold War.* Washington, D.C.: Brookings Institution, 1995.

World Bank. *Anti-Corruption in Transition: A Contribution to the Policy Debate.* Washington, D.C.: World Bank, November 2000.

———. *Cambodia Governance and Corruption Diagnostic: Evidence from Citizen, Enterprise, and Public Official Surveys.* Washington, D.C.: World Bank, May 2000.

———. *Civil Service Reform: A Review of World Bank Assistance.* Report no. 19599. Washington, D.C.: World Bank, Operations Evaluation Department, 1999.

———. *Helping Countries Combat Corruption: The Role of the World Bank.* Washington, D.C.: World Bank, 1997.

———. Introduction to World Bank, *World Development Report: Building Institutions for Markets.* New York: Oxford University Press, 2002.

———. *Legal and Judicial Reform: Observations, Experiences, and Approach of the Legal Vice Presidency.* Washington, D.C.: World Bank, July 2002.

———. *Legal and Judicial Reform: Strategic Directions.* Washington, D.C.: World Bank, 2003.

———. "Legal Institutions and the Rule of Law." In World Bank, *World Development Report: From Plan to Market.* New York: Oxford University Press, 1996.

———. *Pakistan: A Framework for Civil Service Reform in Pakistan.* Washington, D.C.: World Bank, December 15, 1998.

———. *Post-Conflict Reconstruction: The Role of the World Bank.* Washington, D.C.: World Bank, 1998.

———. *Reforming Public Institutions and Strengthening Governance: A World Bank Strategy—Implementation Update.* Washington, D.C.: World Bank, April 2002.

———. "The Role of the World Bank in Conflict and Development: An Evolving Agenda." Washington, D.C.: World Bank. http://lnweb18.worldbank.org/essd/sdvext.nsf/67bydocname/theroleoftheworldbankinconflictanddevelopmentanevolvingagenda1/$file/conflictagenda2004.pdf.

————. *World Development Report: Building Institutions for Markets.* New York: Oxford University Press, 2002.World Commission on Dams. *Dams and Development: A New Framework for Decision-Making.* Sterling, Va.: Earthscan, 2000.

World Trade Organization. *Guide to GATT Law and Practice: Analytical Index.* Geneva: World Trade Organization and Bernan Press, 1995.

————. "United States: Trade Measures Affecting Nicaragua." GATT Panel report. GATT Doc. L/6053. October 13, 1986.

Yoshikawa, Motohide. "Implementation of Sanctions Imposed by the United Nations Security Council: Japan's Experience." In *Report of the Expert Seminar on Targeting UN Financial Sanctions.* Bern: Swiss Federal Office for Foreign Economic Affairs, 1998.

Zartman, I. William. "Early and 'Early Late' Prevention." In *Making States Work: State Failure and the Crisis of Governance,* edited by Simon Chesterman. Tokyo: UN University Press, 2005.

Ziegler, Melissa, and Rachel Nield. "From Peace and Governance: Police International Community." Washington, D.C.: Washington Office of Latin America, 2002.

Zisk, Kimberly Marten. *Enforcing the Peace: Learning From the Imperial Past.* New York: Columbia University Press, 2004.

The Contributors

Simon Chesterman is global professor and director of the New York University School of Law Singapore Program and associate professor of law at the National University of Singapore Faculty of Law. His books include *From Mercenaries to Market: The Rise and Regulation of Private Military Companies* (edited with Chia Lehnardt); *You, the People: The United Nations, Transitional Administration, and State-Building.*

Pablo de Greiff is director of the Research Unit at the International Center for Transitional Justice, prior to which he was an associate professor of philosophy at the State University of New York at Buffalo. He recently edited the *Handbook of Reparations,* and is currently completing a book titled *Redeeming the Claims of Justice in Transitions to Democracy.*

Reyko Huang is a doctoral candidate in political science at Columbia University. She is a former program officer at the International Peace Academy and former research analyst at the Center for Defense Information.

Agnès Hurwitz is deputy chef de cabinet in the Office of the President of the International Criminal Tribunal for the former Yugoslavia, prior to which she headed the Rule of Law Project at the International Peace Academy. She has published and edited several policy reports on rule of law programs (available at www.ipacademy.org).

Rama Mani is the executive director of the International Centre for Ethnic Studies–Colombo in Sri Lanka and former director of the New Issues in Security Course at the Geneva Centre for Security Policy. She is the author of *Beyond Retribution: Seeking Justice in the Shadows of War.*

Vivienne O'Connor is a rule of law program officer at the US Institute of Peace, prior to which she was the Rule of Law Project officer at the Irish Centre for Human Rights. She is the codirector of the Model Codes for Post-Conflict Criminal Justice Project and recently edited *Model Codes for Post-Conflict Criminal Justice, Volume I: Model Criminal Code.*

Madalene O'Donnell is a staff member of the UN Department of Peace-keeping Operations, prior to which she coordinated a program on postwar statebuilding at New York University's Center on International Cooperation. She is coeditor (with James K. Boyce) of *Peace and the Public Purse: Economic Policies for Postwar Statebuilding.*

William G. O'Neill is a lawyer specializing in humanitarian, refugee, and international human rights law. He chaired a UN Task Force on the Rule of Law in Peacekeeping Operations, led the UN Human Rights Field Operation in Rwanda, and is the author of *Kosovo: An Unfinished Peace.*

Balakrishnan Rajagopal is Ford international associate professor of law and development and director of the Center for International Studies' Program on Human Rights and Justice at the Massachusetts Institute of Technology. His books include *International Law from Below: Development, Social Movements, and Third World Resistance* and *Reshaping Justice: International Law and the Third World* (edited with Richard Falk and Jacqueline Stevens).

Colette Rausch is deputy director of the Rule of Law Program at the US Institute of Peace and codirector of the Model Codes for Post-Conflict Criminal Justice Project. She edited *Combating Serious Crimes in Post-Conflict Societies: A Handbook for Practitioners* and *Policymakers and Model Codes for Post-Conflict Criminal Justice, Volume I: Model Criminal Code*

Chandra Lekha Sriram is professor of human rights at the University of East London School of Law and director of the Center on Human Rights in Conflict. Her books include *Globalizing Justice for Mass Atrocities: A Revolution in Accountability* and *Confronting Past Human Rights Violations: Justice vs. Peace in Times of Transition.*

Index

Accountability: conflict prevention and rule of law, 91, 111(n1); defining rule of law, 3–4, 74–75; governance issues influencing development policy, 51; monitoring anticorruption, 249–250; ownership and, 153; policy recommendations for increasing, 293–294; in public administration, 106–107; transitional justice mechanisms, 8

Ad Hoc Committee on Terrorism, 265, 269

Adjudication. *See* Judicial mechanisms and administration

Administrative reforms to prevent corruption, 237–241

Afghan Assistance Coordination Authority, 150

Afghanistan: anticorruption, 247; corruption, tolerance of, 230; corruption measures, 233(table); customary law and ethnic violence, 198; interim law reform, 121; law reform utilizing previous law, 125; leadership and corruption, 245; limited progress of rule of law programs, 34–35; rule of law programs in peacekeeping missions, 99; transitional administration, 141, 150; UN peacekeeping operations, 96; UN rule of law programs through peacekeeping missions, 98; UN sanctions, 264; UN-Habitat HLP programs, 205; UN role in justice and rule of law in peacekeeping operations, 117

Africa: ownership of peacekeeping operations, 141; security and counterterrorism, 275. *See also specific countries*

African Union, 109, 236

Agenda for Development, 7

An Agenda for Peace (Boutros-Ghali), 5, 72–74, 140–141

Agreement on Identity and Rights of Indigenous Peoples, 210

Agreement on Resettlement of the Population Groups Uprooted by the Armed Conflict, 210

Agreement on Socioeconomic Aspects and the Agrarian Situation, 210

Agriculture, HLP issues and, 195, 197, 200–201

Aid: administrative reforms to prevent corruption, 237–241; conditionality, 82–84, 144, 242; development policies influencing rule of law aid, 10–12; donor dilemma, 80, 87(n43); leadership and corruption, 245; long-term investment incentives for Afghanistan, 35; post-WWII rule of law reform, 36; World Bank and EU strategies, 79

Albania: economic consequences of anticorruption, 231

American Convention on Human Rights, 166–167

Amnesty, 164–165, 174–175, 185(n4)

Amnesty International, 274

Angola: corruption measures, 233(table); land-related programs, 204; monitoring UN peacekeeping operations, 95

Annan, Kofi, 146, 275, 279. *See also Rule of Law and Transitional Justice in Conflict and Postconflict Societies* (Annan)

Annan Plan, 212

333

About the Book

How do rule of law programs contribute to conflict management? What strategies best address the challenges to securing the rule of law in fragile countries? What place do rule of law policies have in efforts to achieve stable and equitable development?

The authors of *Civil War and the Rule of Law* address these fundamental questions, analyzing rule of law programs in the context of conflict prevention, peacekeeping, and peacebuilding activities. Throughout the book, they emphasize the critical relationship linking the rule of law, security, development, and human rights.

Agnès Hurwitz is deputy chef de cabinet in the Office of the President of the International Criminal Tribunal for the Former Yugoslavia, prior to which she headed the Rule of Law Project at the International Peace Academy. **Reyko Huang**, formerly a program officer at the International Peace Academy, is a doctoral candidate in political science at Columbia University.